Anekdoten aus allen fünf Weltteilen

19. 9. 1985

Beatha agus sláinte!

Andrea Mhic Fhionnbhairr

European University Studies

Europäische Hochschulschriften
Publications Universitaires Européennes

Series I
German Language and Literature

Reihe I Série I
Deutsche Sprache und Literatur
Langue et littérature allemandes

Vol. / Band 864

PETER LANG
Berne · Frankfurt am Main · New York

Andrea MhicFhionnbhairr

Anekdoten aus allen fünf Weltteilen

The Anecdote in Fontane's Fiction and Autobiography

PETER LANG
Berne · Frankfurt am Main · New York

CIP-Kurztitelaufnahme der Deutschen Bibliothek

MhicFhionnbhairr, Andrea:
Anekdoten aus allen fünf Weltteilen: The Anecdote in Fontane's Fiction and Autobiography / Andrea MhicFhionnbhairr. – Berne; Frankfurt am Main; New York: Lang, 1985.
(European University Studies: Ser. 1, German Language and Literature; Vol. 864)
ISBN 3-261-04081-5

NE: Europäische Hochschulschriften / 01

Printed by Lang Druck, Inc., Liebefeld/Berne (Switzerland)

Table of Contents

“Es zieht sich ein gewisses ‘Davidtum, das den Goliath schlug’, durch die ganze Weltgeschichte”

Introduction

While the charm and interest of the anecdotes which Fontane interpolates into his works are apparent to every reader, their significance is often elusive. Although some brief attention has been paid to a small number of anecdotes in Fontane's works,[1] the function of anecdotes within the framework of longer works has to a large extent been ignored, not merely in connection with Fontane, but altogether.[2] On the whole, critics and commentators on German literature have shied away from dealing with the anecdote, even as an independent genre, so that more than sixty years after the first work on the genre, a great deal of ground still remains to be covered. In part, this situation may be due to the historical development of Germany in the twentieth century. The first two dissertations in German which appeared on the anecdote were rather restricted in scope, the one by its choice of the periods dealt with, the other by its ideological slant. Max Dalitzsch presents in "Studien zur Geschichte der deutschen Anekdote"[3] a broad historical outline of the anecdote stretching from examples in ancient times through the Middle Ages to the Renaissance and Reformation. The trend which characterizes

1 See Brenda Doust: "An examination of Theodor Fontane's autobiographical writings and their relation to his prose fiction with special reference to 'Meine Kinderjahre'." M. Phil. Thesis, London 1970, p. 158-179, Cornelie Ueding: 'Utopie auf Umwegen. Zwei Szenen in Fontane's Roman "Cécile".' in Gerd Ueding (ed.): "Literatur ist Utopie", Frankfurt am Main 1978, p.220-250 and S. Hajek in "Jahrbuch der Raabe-Gesellschaft 1979, p.72-93.

2 Symptomatic of this situation is the fact that Heinz Grothe's monograph on the anecdote: "Anekdote" (Stuttgart 1971) does not allude at all to the presence of anecdotes within the framework of larger literary genres. Thus he recognises the importance of the anecdotes in Fontane's autobiographical writing, travel works and correspondence, while ignoring those in the literary works (See Grothe: ibid. p.63).

3 Freiburg im Breisgau 1922

a considerable amount of critical literature on the anecdote, namely the attempt to establish lines of demarcation between it and other short forms, is initiated in Dalitzsch's thesis in his observations on the joke, the 'Schwank' and the 'Novelle' in connection with the anecdote. The second dissertation on the anecdote, "Typen deutscher Anekdotenerzählung",[1] by Hans Lorenzen is vitiated by its 'völkisch' approach. Kleist's anecdotes are seen e.g. as representing "die männliche Härte der norddeutschen Linie", while Hebel's are said to typify "die süddeutsch-liebenswürdige Linie".[2] Wilhelm Schäfer's stories are treated by Lorenzen as anecdotes and in them he sees a "völkische Erneuerung"[3] on the part of the anecdote in German. This ideological slant is already faintly foreshadowed in the late twenties in an article by Lorenzen's teacher, Robert Petsch, "Von der Kunst des Anekdotenerzählens".[4] This trend, which is only slightly hinted at in Petsch's article, is very strongly reflected in further work on the anecdote in the nineteen-thirties. Rudolf Hoffmann points out e.g. in a teachers' journal some aspects of the anecdote which he considers to be of contemporary relevance: e.g. the portrayal in anecdotes of heroism unto death as well as the ability of the 'best' anecdotes to manifest "die zwingende Gewalt des Führers".[5] Christian Jennsen concludes his article, 'Die deutsche Novelle und Anekdote von Kleist bis Wilhelm Schäfer'[6] with a laudation on the virtues of the German people which he claims to see reflected in the works of Schäfer.[7] The anecdote's popularity

1 Hamburg 1935
2 Ibid. p.24. Lorenzen is actually quoting here without page references from Hans Franck: "Anekdoten von Johann Peter Hebel" Reichenberg n.d.
3 Lorenzen: op. cit., p.24
4 "Schünemanns Monatshefte" 2, 1928, p. 1055-1061. About W. Schäfer's work Petsch writes: "Immer regt sich da etwas von deutscher Treuherzigkeit und Urwüchsigkeit" (p.1061).
5 'Die Anekdote in ihrer national-politischen Bedeutung' in "Zeitschrift für deutsche Bildung" 10, 1934, p.432.
6 In "Hochschule und Ausland" 14, 1936, p.625-631.
7 See ibid. p.631

during the National Socialist regime – "die Blütezeit der Anekdote im Deutschunterricht"[1] – was due to a recognition of the anecdote's ability to present in a concise and memorable way incidents and human characteristics which were at the time considered useful for the national self-image and self-confidence. For this purpose the eighteenth-century Prussian anecdotal tradition was especially abused. Hitler's interest in the Frederick the Second image is well known.

The first critical work to appear on the anecdote after the Second World War (and also the first without an ideological slant for a number of years), Gerhard Kopp's dissertation "Geschichte der deutschen Anekdote in der Neuzeit"[2] repeatedly points out the chauvinistic excesses of many anecdote anthologies and collections, whereby several of the Bismarck collections of the Wilhelmine Era remind him of the Frederick anecdotes of the eighteenth century because of their bombastic panegyrical outbursts, cheap patriotic sentimentality and lack of any critical sense of history.[3] It must be emphasized, however, that critical and conservative anecdotes have always existed side by side. While some anecdotes were minted in an obvious attempt to glorify the exploits and dicta of a powerful personality and to support a particular regime, there have always been other anecdotes which gave an anonymous person an opportunity to voice an honest and dissenting critical opinion (sometimes face to face with a powerful ruler) and to express a view of historical events which runs counter to the regime-boosting intention of the conservative anecdotes.

1 Walter Ernst Schäfer: 'Die Anekdote im Literaturunterricht der Bundesrepublik und der DDR' in WW 23, 1973, p.254.

2 Tübingen 1949. Kopp studies many different anecdote collections from the sixteenth century onwards and includes sub-sections on collections about famous personalities including Frederick the Second and Napoleon. Kopp emphasizes the oral origins of the anecdote, feeling that both the oral form and its written equivalent have been neglected from the critical point of view, in favour of highly artistic literary anecdotes, such as those of Kleist.

3 For Gerhard Kopp's observations on the Bismarck anecdote collections of the Wilhelmine Era, see op. cit., p.147

One of Fontane's anecdotes shows how he adapted a traditional anecdote to give it a slightly more critical ending. From a passage in Kaltenborn's "Briefe eines alten preußischen Offiziers"[1] describing the soldiers' vituperations against Frederick II at the Battle of Kolin, he formed the ending to the following anecdote: Frederick confronts grenadiers leaving the scene of battle during the fighting and shouts at them in indignation: "Rackers, wollt ihr denn ewig leben?" To which they reply: "Für fünfzehn Pfennig ist's heute genug".[2] The anecdote is variously associated with the Battles of Kolin (1757), Kunersdorf (1759) and Torgau (1760). In its truncated form the anecdote is often quoted ending with Frederick's question, and in this form is a plain, traditional anecdote demonstrating Frederick's own sangfroid and verbal brilliance. In Fontane's extended version the anecdote reveals the disproportion between the regal expectation that every soldier will die on the spot for his country against the overwhelming might of the enemy and the meagre wage offered to these anonymous soldiers, who continually stake their lives in battle.[3]

The 'occasio' here is the Battle of Kolin (1757) which signals to the reader without further detail a Prussian defeat in a long line of battles during the Seven Years' War (1756-1763). Frederick's angry words to the soldiers provides a challenge, but only apparently an unanswerable 'provocatio' for the grenadiers are not at all intimidated by the regal reproach and counter it with their 'dictum',

1 Rudolf Wilhelm von Kaltenborn: "Briefe eines alten preußischen Offiziers". Hohenzollern 1790. See Hermann Kügler on Fontane's adaptation of the prose description into a dramatic scene between monarch and men in the anecdote: H. Kügler: 'Quellen zu Theodor Fontane' in "Wilibald-Alexis-Bund", 2. Jahresbericht, 1927, p.28 and also NyA XX, 748 where the passage from Kaltenborn is quoted.

2 The anecdote is narrated in the form of a poem "Bei Torgau", NyA XX, 217

3 Although this anecdote strikes a criticla note, it does not of course question the waging of war as such, a theme which is found in some anecdotes from Grimmelshausen down to Brecht and other left-wing writers of the twentieth century.

which patently wins the battle of words.[1] This anecdote clearly manifests the tripartite structure of all anecdotes.

The traditional bias of literary science towards 'serious' literature is clear even within the sphere of anecdote research in its over-emphasis on the anecdotes of Kleist and its neglect of 'ordinary' anecdotes in their written, but not necessarily highly literary form.[2] Anecdote research has not been helped either by the fact that literary scholars are reluctant to deal with a form which has essentially oral roots.[3] The components of the anecdote have been the subject of disagreement among critics in the discussion which has taken place, and a satisfactory definition of the genre has not been provided.[4] The most useful brief description of the genre available

1 The terms 'occasio' and 'provocatio' have been brought into anecdote research by Rudolf Schäfer, who borrowed them from Hannjost Lixfeld's investigation on jokes in "Arbeitstexte für den Unterricht: Witz". Stuttgart 1978. See Rudolf Schäfer: "Die Anekdote. Theorie – Analyse – Didaktik. München 1982, p. 29-36. The term 'occasio' corresponds to 'introduction' or setting of a story in time, place and situation, 'provocatio' to the intermediary section between the beginning and the 'Pointe' in which the conflict between central character and milieu becomes clear, perhaps through misinterpretation, or a discrepancy of some kind. The discrepancy or inappropriateness contained in the 'provocatio' is immediately corrected, contradicted or rendered absurd in the statement ('dictum') or action, behaviour, event, fact ('factum'), which rounds off the anecdote at the end. (See R. Schäfer: op. cit., ibidem and p. 56-57)

2 Cf. the epilogue to Jürgen Hein's collection of typical German anecdotes: "Deutsche Anekdoten". Stuttgart 1976, p. 353-354.

3 See ibidem.

4 The earliest attempt at a definition is in Max Dalitzsch's abovementioned thesis: "Anekdote is die einen Einzelmenschen behandelnde kurze Geschichte ohne Nebenhandlung, in der durch individuelle Züge des Handelns und Sprechens die Charakteristik einer Persönlichkeit oder Kennzeichnung einer gemeinsamen womöglich allgemein-menschlichen Eigenschaft einer Gruppe von Menschen gegeben wird. Dabei ist wesentlich, daß diese Geschichte entweder tatsächlich auf eine historische Begebenheit zurückgeht, oder wenigstens den Anspruch erhebt, für historisch genommen zu werden in Bezug auf das zu charakterisierende Individuum". (Max Dalitzsch: op. cit., p.4) In the mid nineteen-twenties H. Beyer gives the following description of the genre: "Die Anekdote sucht im Spiegel

to date is that given by Walter Ernst Schäfer in his book which examines the process of the change in the anecdote into new short prose forms in the critical tradition of Brecht, Frisch and Wondratschek.[1] For his description, Schäfer bases himself on Klaus Doderer's[2] definition of the anecdote as a short narrative which refers to historical persons and facts without necessarily being authentic, and continues to give the following lengthier and more

eines, ohne jedes schmückende (und verhüllende) Beiwerk erzählten bezeichnenden Vorfalles das möglichst deutliche Bild einer Persönlichkeit, einer Zeit, einer geistigen Strömung zu geben, somit im einzelnen das Ganze aufzunehmen". ("Reallexikon der deutschen Literaturgeschichte". Ed. by Paul Merker and Wolfgang Stammler. Berlin 1925-26, vol. 1 p. 44) This description contains an advance over that of Dalitzsch in stressing that all extraneous matters are excluded from the true anecdote, whereas Dalitzsch only excluded a sub-plot. Heinz Grothe defines the anecdote as follows: "Die Anekdote ist eine knappe, auf eine Pointe zugeführte Erzählung, die in eigenwilliger, meist geschliffener Form eine bemerkenswerte, unbekannte Begebenheit in erstaunlicher Zuspitzung erzählt, die für einen Menschen, fur eine Persönlichkeit, für einen Stand, eine Gesellschaft, für eine Überzeugung, für eine Idee, für einen Zeitzustand eine blitzartige Erhellung gibt." Heinz Grothe: "Das neue Narrenschiff". Stuttgart 1968, p.335 and Heinz Grothe: "Anekdote" Stuttgart 1971, p.8. The latter is the first monograph on the anecdote and is undoubtedly at a disadvantage due to the lack of critical work on the anecdote to date. For a review of this book, see Hans Peter Neureuter: 'Zur Theorie der Anekdote.' In JbFDH 1973, p.472-473, W. E. Schäfer: 'Die Anekdote im Literaturunterricht der Bundesrepublik und der DDR', p. 254, Jan Knopf: 'Der klassische Bauer' in "Projekt Deutschunterricht 9: Literatur der Klassik – Lyrik – Epik – Ästhetik." Ed. by Bodo Lecke. Stuttgart 1975, p.95 and Rudolf Schäfer: op. cit., p.53-54.

1 W.E. Schäfer: "Anekdote – Antianekdote. Zum Wandel einer literarischen Form in der Gegenwart." Stuttgart 1977.

2 See Klaus Doderer: "Die Kurzgeschichte in Deutschland." Wiesbaden 1953. Reprint Darmstadt 1969, p.22. On this question of authenticity most scholars, like Doderer, believe it is sufficient if the principles of probability in the use of historical material are adhered to. For Max Dalitzsch on this point, see his definition of the anecdote quoted above p.9. See also C.F.W. Behl: 'Über das Anekdotische' in "Die Literatur" 38, 1935, p.11; Ernst Bender: 'Schwank und Anekdote' in DU 9, 1957, p.57;

comprehensive description of the genre, which makes further use of some of Doderer's terminology:

> Im Zentrum dieser Erzählung steht eine Figur, auf deren Reaktion in einer dargestellten Situation sich das Interesse richtet. Um diesen Zweck zu erreichen, muß die Situation so beschaffen sein, daß sie den Helden herausfordert, das heißt, 'Held' und 'Umwelt' (Doderer), Zentralfigur und provozierende Figur(en) stehen im Verhältnis eines Konflikts, eines Interessengegensatzes oder doch zumindest einer verschiedenen Ausgangslage in der Situation. Nur dadurch ist die Situation geeignet, den latenten Charakter der Zentralfigur in die Aktualität zu treiben. Um dieses Programm zu bewältigen, ist die Anekdote an ein bestimmtes Kompositionsprinzip gebunden: Sie umreißt auf möglichst knappem Raum zunächst die Ausgangslage, Ort und Zeit des Ereignisses, führt die Figuren ein. Sie berichtet sodann das Ereignis, in dessen Verlauf der Charakter sich enthüllt. Sie schließt mit der durch die Situation provozierten Geste oder dem Dictum des Helden. Insofern als diese Enthüllung unvermittelt eintritt, bringt sie ein Moment der Überraschung beim Leser hervor, das heißt, eine Pointe schließt die Anekdote ab.[1]

The above-mentioned aspect of brevity is perhaps the most striking feature of the anecdote, and all critics are agreed that it is an essential component of the form. The importance of brevity can

W. Grenzmann op. cit., p.64; Alfred Behrmann: "Einführung in die Analyse von Prosatexten." Stuttgart 1967, p.71; Jan Knopf: op. cit., p.95; Jürgen Hein: 'Die Anekdote' in "Formen der Literatur". Ed. by Otto Knörrich. Stuttgart 1981, p.18. A surprizing exception to the general concensus on authenticity is Hans Peter Neureuter's claim that genuineness is an essential feature of the genre. He admits that such a requirement rules out the majority of anecdotes. (See Neureuter: op. cit., p.463-467.)

1 W. E. Schäfer: op. cit., p.13. Critical opinion is divided on the question of the 'Pointe'. Gerhard Kopp: op. cit., p.222 and H. Grothe: "Anekdote", p.8 both see the 'Pointe' as an inherent part of an anecdote, but not all commentators agree that this is an essential feature. Helene Auzinger believes in "Die Pointe bei Tschechow" (Kempten 1956, p.40-47) that while humorous anecdotes almost always have a 'Pointe' serious ones do not. For Ernst Bender (op. cit., p.64) the 'Pointe' is not absolutely necessary. Cf. also Jürgen Hein: "Während Witz und Schwank weitgehend durch Komik und Pointe strukturiert sind, muß die Anekdote durchaus nicht immer witzig oder komisch sein, und sie kann auch auf die Pointe

hardly be stressed enough, because disregard for it among many would-be writers of anecdotes leads their stories into other genres and the specific quality of the typical tension built up in the anecdote proper is destroyed. This is often the case with the stories of the writer, Wilhelm Schäfer. It is rather ironical that his stories should have received considerable attention from critics examining the anecdote. It is now on the whole recognised that his short prose works are not anecdotes, the error having arisen in the first place through his own conscious misuse of the term 'Anekdote' in connection with his stories.[1] Clearly, brevity alone does not make any short prose form an anecdote. Hans Peter Neureuter enumerates in his morphological study of the genre three further features as being essential to it, facticity, representativeness ("Spiegelung eines

völlig verzichten. Wichtig ist allein die charakterisierende, wesenserhellende Darbietung des Stoffes, dessen Bedeutung allerdings vielfach durch komische Sprach-, Figuren-, und Situationsgestaltung akzentuiert wird." (J. Hein (Ed.): "Deutsche Anekdoten, p.364). Cf. also Jürgen Hein: 'Die literarische Anekdote, ihre Entwicklung und ihre Stellung in der Literatur' in "Universitas" 37, 1982, p.640. Hans Lorenzen (op. cit., p.9) and Klaus Doderer distinguish between a verbal 'Pointe' and one which is embedded in the incident or action, while Helene Auzinger (op. cit., p.44) prefers to speak of a 'Stilpointe' and a 'Strukturpointe'. Hans Peter Neureuter implicitly makes the same distinction in connection with the anecdote about the murder of Lorenzo and Giuliano de Medici during the consecration of the mass by two hired priests. Here, the 'Pointe' does not reside in anything verbal, but rather in the paradoxical coincidence that it is priests, and not the mercenary originally hired, who are impervious to the sanctity of the occasion. (See Neureuter: op.cit., p.466) Neureuter also draws attention to the fact that Ottilie's anecdote about Charles I of England in Goethe's "Wahlverwandtschaften" has no 'Pointe'. (ibid p.474.)

1 See K. Doderer: op. cit., p.27, Ludwig Rohner: "Theorie der Kurzgeschichte". Frankfurt am Main 1973, p.110, and H. P. Neureuter: op. cit., p.476. As examples of critics who regard Schäfer as a writer of anecdotes the following can be cited: Robert Petsch: op. cit., p.1062, Günter K. Eter: "Wilhelm Schäfer: Stil und Weltbild siner Anekdoten". Diss. Marburg 1938, W. Grenzmann: op. cit., p.64-65, Herman Pongs: "Romanschaffen im Umbruch der Zeit: eine Chronik von 1942 bis 1962." 4. Auflage, Tübingen 1963, p. 212 and Heinz Grothe: "Anekdote", p.65-69.

Großen im Kleinen"[1]) and the quality of 'Nachdenklichkeit',[2] the anecdote's effect of making both teller and listener reflect further. With regard to the feature of facticity Neureuter is, among commentators on the anecdote, in a minority in his insistence that an anecdote must be authentic or true in order for it to qualify for the designation 'anecdote'.[3] In recent years the feature of 'Nachdenklichkeit, the reflectiveness produced by the anecdote on the listener/reader has in consequence of Neureuter's emphasis on it, received slightly more attention in critical literature. As the analyses of Fontane's anecdotes will show, reflectiveness is a significant feature, because the reader is very much involved in the process of arriving at conclusions which, due to the allusive nature of Fontane's art are at best only hinted at on the surface.

With the quality of or representativeness, according to Neureuter, the anecdote reaches out beyond itself, indicating something more important and supertemporal. Representativeness in anecdotes lies for him in the 'existential attitude' which tells something about human nature above and beyond the tiny historical incidents which are recorded in them.[4] Our interest in historical anecdotes is therefore, in Neureuter's view, not an interest in history as such, (although it presupposes for Neureuter the facticity of anecdotes) but is rather an interest "am übergeschichtlichen Belang menschlichen Verhaltens in der Geschichte".[5] This 'existential attitude' means "daß wir vergangenes Menschleben als mitbürgerliche Existenz messen, im Gedanken an die eigene".[6] Neureuter' point about representativeness is accepted by two further commentators, Jürgen

1 Neureuter: op. cit., p.463.
2 Ibid p.477-480.
3 See ibid p. 463-467. See also Winfried Freund and Walburga Freund-Spork: 'Weltgeschichte aus der Froschperspektive – Ein Versuch über die Anekdote in Theorie und Praxis' in LfL 1979, p.117. For the general concensus, apart from these two exceptions, that facticity is not an essential feature of the anecdote, see above p.14.
4 See Neureuter: op. cit., p.467.
5 Ibid. p.468
6 Ibid. p.471.

Hein and Rudolf Schäfer,[1] but rejected by Walter E. Schäfer, who draws attention to the fact that the term 'representativeness' already exists in anecdote research since Klaus Doderer used it with a totally different meaning. Doderer employed it to denote a feature of the type of anecdote about 'unimportant' people insofar as they are representative of a social stratum, a racial or national community. For Schäfer, like Doderer, anecdotes concerning ordinary people can claim to have the quality of representativeness, while the traditional anecdote, that concerning a little-known fact about a well-known personality, does not. [2] This view does not give due recognition however to the fact that critical and conservative anecdotes have always existed side by side.[3]

Anecdote lies at the core of Fontane's work. It is remarkable feature of Fontane, both as a man and a writer, and is intimately related to several other aspects of his outlook and approach. Repeatedly in his work and correspondence he expresses the view

1 Cf. Jürgen Hein: "Dort wo die Nachdenklichkeit ausbleibt, verschwindet das besondere Ereignis hinter seiner Repräsentanz, das Menschlich-Bedeutsame tritt zurück und wird allenfalls durch den breiter ausholenden Erzähler 'künstlich' erzeugt. In diesen Fällen haben wir es meist ebensowenig mit der Anekdote zu tun wie dort, wo das reine Faktum berichtet wird. Auch hier stellt sich keine Nachdenklichkeit ein. Die 'echte' Anekdote will also nicht informieren, belehren, exemplifizieren, moralisieren usw., sondern 'nur' nachdenklich machen, zu einem Nachdenken anregen, welches das Überindividuell-Existentielle im besonderen Ereignis finden läßt. (J. Hein: "Deutsche Anekdoten", p.373). See also by the same author: 'Die literarische Anekdote', p.641. See Rudolf Schäfer: op. cit., p.37-45.

2 See W. E. Schäfer: "Anekdote – Antianekdote, p.16. In an age which is in many ways turning away from fiction, the value of the anecdote as a fragment of reality makes it attractive. Future researches on it will need a broader base than has hitherto been the case. Attention has been drawn to the necessity of an interdisciplinary approach to anecdote research, an approach which would combine the knowledge and methods of folklore studies, historiography, journalism and 'Germanistik', while not even the bibliographical basis for such a study exists at present. (See W. E. Schäfer: op. cit., p.7.) Linguistic research could also have a role to play in such an interdisciplinary study of the anecdote.

3 See above p.11. Cf. also Winfried Freund and Walburga Freund-Spork: op. cit., p.116-118 and p.125.

that he is attracted by that which is small[1] and which may seem to be of secondary or marginal significance, as opposed to that which is 'large' and important. A few examples of such statements from different decades of his writing career may suffice here. In a letter of 1881 he claims that true knowledge of the Frederician era and its people would be more accessible in half a dozen anecdotes than in the state papers of the age.[2] The 'large', impersonal events of history are not what interest him, and in his search for material on which to work for "Wanderungen durch die Mark Brandenburg", he is most interested in the memoirs and reports of little-known people such as pastors and local officials. He claims that only the personal is of enduring interest: "Nur das Persönliche ist das Siegreiche".[3] In the view (generally accepted as akin to Fontane's own) of the fictional character, Professor Wilibald Schmidt, in "Frau Jenny Treibel" (1892), a couple of Frederician anecdotes

1 Cf. the link here with Otto Ludwig, Auerbach, Stifter and Gottfried Keller. See Heinz Eugen Greter: "Fontanes Poetik", Bern, Frankfurt am Main 1973, p.67-69.

2 In a letter of 2.6.1881 to Hermann Wichmann. See Wichmann's memoirs: "Frohes und Ernstes aus meinem Leben". Berlin 1898, p.18 and Gotthard Erler: "Fontanes Briefe in Zwei Bänden". Berlin und Weimar 1968, vol. 2 p.35. It is not without significance that he distances himself in this context from Leopold von Ranke and ridicules condescension towards everything that is not to be found in files and state papers.

3 This observation summarizes Fontane's finding that the enmity between two officers gave rise to a household word in the Barnim-Lebus region which lived on long after their brilliance in battle was forgotten. (See "Das Oderland" NyA X, 316.) Compare Nietzsche's statement in a foreword to the fragment "Philosophie im tragischen Zeitalter der Griechen": "... An Systemen, die widerlegt sind, kann uns eben nur noch das Persönliche interessieren, denn dies ist das ewig Unwiderlegbare. Aus drei Anekdoten ist es möglich, das Bild eines Menschen zu geben; ich versuche es, aus jedem System drei Anekdoten herauszuheben, und gebe das Übrige preis." (Nietzsche: "Werke. Kritische Gesamtausgabe". Ed. by Giorgio Colli and Mazzino Montinari. Berlin, New York 1973. Third section. Vol. 2, p.297. On Nietzsche and the anecdote see Ernst Bertram: 'Anekdote' in "Nietzsche: Versuch einer Mythologie. Berlin 1929. Reprint Bonn 1965. (With an epilogue by Hartmut Buchner) p.249-259.

are of more value than an important Prussian military victory.[1] There is no doubt that Fontane's penchant for the anecdote is an expression of his abiding interest in human nature and of his conviction that it was possible to a large extent to present areas of interest and to present period through anecdotes in a way which might not at first view appear possible. The biographical basis of his love of the anecdote is well-known and is beautifully portrayed in his autobiographical rendering of his father's use of the anecdote in history lessons which were as fascinating for the young Theodor Fontane as they were pedagogically unorthodox.[2] Even in his last letters Fontane refers to his last 'historical' project, a history of the Bredow family, which uses anecdotes as part of its stock-in-trade, showing therefore that he never had reason to doubt the validity and efficacy of his anecdotal method.

Fontane was not particular with regard to the authenticity of the stories which he used and enjoyed. He did not require an anecdote to be authentic, as long as the essential revealing nature of the story did not do injustice to the person involved. In the course of his work he remarks several times that he considers the genuineness of anecdotes to be immaterial as long as their

1 See NyA VII, 62.

2 His comments on the effect on him of his father's anecdotes show their importance in his life and writings as opposed to the minimal effects of his formal education: "Nicht bloß gesellschaftlich sind mir in meinem langen Leben diese Geschichten hundertfach zu gute gekommen, auch bei meinen Schreibereien waren sie immer wie ein Schatzkästlein zur Hand und wenn ich gefragt würde, welchem Lehrer ich mich so recht eigentlich zu Dank verpflichtet fühle, so würde ich antworten müssen: meinem Vater, meinem Vater, der so zu sagen gar nichts wußte, mich aber mit dem aus Zeitungen und Journalen aufgepickten und über alle möglichen Themata sich verbreitenden Anekdotenreichtum unendlich viel mehr unterstützt hat, als alle meine Gymnasial- und Realschullehrer zusammengenommen. Was die mir geboten, auch wenn es gut war, ist so ziemlich wieder von mir abgefallen, die Geschichten von Ney und Rapp aber sind mir bis diese Stunde geblieben." (Theodor Fontane: "Autobiographische Schriften" Bd. 1. "Meine Kinderjahre". Berlin, Weimar 1982, p.126-127. Hereafter this edition will be referred to as Aufbau.)

significance is representative.[1] In his view, for example, the false anecdotes about Frederick the Second are better than the genuine ones, insofar as they tell us something essential about his character or about the Frederician Era. Fontane is always attracted to the historical anecdote: "historischen Anekdoten habe ich nie widerstehen können, bin auch jetzt noch" i.e. 1898, the year of his death "der Meinung, daß sie das Beste aller Historie sind."[2] Fontane's roots in connection with the anecdote lie undoubtedly in the anecdotal tradition in Prussian history (particularly that of the eighteenth century), which overemphasized the role of the personality and illustrated the achievements and personalities of leaders in anecdotes. He was a professed admirer, for example, of Wrangeliana, and anecdotes about Frederick the Second are scattered throughout his works. Walter Müller-Seidel has pointed out that Fontane's penchant for the anecdote even in his early period when he was still under the influence of historicism already shows signs of estrangement from the thinking of official German historiography.[3] The anecdote's preference for that which is 'small', marginal or secondary as opposed to the large and 'important' does not make it amenable to the monumentalist approach to history.[4] In fact Fontane uses the anecdote in a way which is very forward-looking, and at its best, his anecdotal art connects the past with the present and points towards the future.

Anecdotes appeal to Fontane's "Sinn för Thatsächlichkeiten"[5], his feel for the real and the concrete. Anecdotes are, or claim to be, part of reality in that they tell a story which is supposed to be real and, whether genuine or not, they are not fictional in the sense of being composed by a writer. In this connection one can see the

1 See NyA XV, 251.

2 Ibid. 252.

3 See Walter Müller-Seidel: "Theodor Fontane: Soziale Romankunst in Deutschland". München 1975, p.71.

4 Ibidem.

5 Fontane ascribes to himself this factual sense in a letter. See "Theodor Fontane: Briefe an Georg Friedlaender". Edited by Kurt Schreinert. Heidelberg 1954, p.235.

Realist Fontane at work, culling from a wide variety of sources – newspapers, memoirs, reports, histories, letters and oral communications – unusual and noteworthy stories and anecdotes. In many cases such a source became the basis of a literary work. There is an element of industriousness which makes the genius,[1] to use one of his own favourite Schiller quotations, in his seeking out suitable anecdotes and relating them, especially in the fictional and autobiographical contexts, to important complexes of ideas of his own. In reviewing "Wilhelm Meisters Lehrjahre", an important feature of Fontane's appreciation of Goethe's achievement was his recognition of Goethe's "Kunst des Anknüpfens, des Inbeziehungbringens, des Brückenschlagens"[2] In fact, making associations and building bridges between the literary/fictional context and the essentially alien anecdote in his writings is the kernel of Fontane's own work as far as the anecdote is concerned.

Not only the realiy value of the anecdote appealed to Fontane, but presumably also its surprise element. The anecdote's penchant for the unusual, the strange, the wonderful, can sometimes lead to the opposite of what might have been expected from its beginning. This presumably tickled Fontane's fancy for the paradoxical, a noted feature of his art in general. Here there may be a psychological link between Fontane, the aphorist, and Fontane, the narrator of anecdotes.[3] Both of these aspects of

1 Attributed only to Fontane himself in Büchmann: "Geflügelte Worte". München, Zürich 1959, p.209.

2 NyA XXII, ii, 109. Cf. Donald C. Riechel: 'Fontane and Goethe' in "Formen Realistischer Erzählkunst. Festschrift for Charlotte Jolles". Nottingham 1979, p.421-422. Compare the observation of an eighteenth-century English critic about anecdotes, albeit not on their function within the framework of larger genres: "A man of penetration sees relations in anecdotes, which are not immediately perceived by others; in his hands anecdotes (even should they be familiar to us) are made susceptible of a thousand novel turns." (Isaac D'Israeli: "A Dissertation on Anecdotes". London 1793. Facsimile reprint New York 1972, p.74.)

3 Wilhelm Grenzmann makes the connection between the anecdote narrator in general and the aphorist with regard to this feature of the anecdote: "Das stilistische Mittel der Anekdote is meist der Witz; es ist die Gabe nicht

his work tend to nudge the reader into active participation.[1] This active follow-up on the reader's part is an important aspect of the anecdote and is especially clear in the case of the anecdotes in Fontane's fiction. The author can condense meaning into an inserted anecdote and make it demonstrate in a brief and memorable way large areas of concern in the work as a whole. Little stories are not inserted into Fontane's fiction because he was a master of the art of conversation, and because the use of anecdotes offered more scope to demonstrate this area of perfection. This is in any case so, but Fontane succeeded in the majority of

nur Weitauseinanderliegendes miteinander zu verknüpfen, sondern an Stelle des erwarteten Endes mit einem einzigen Satz zu dem gerade entgegengesetzten Resultat zu führen. Dadurch ist die Haltung des Anekdotenerzählers dem des Aphoristikers verwandt." (W. Grenzmann: op. cit., p.65) Ernst Bertram makes a similar connection between the anecdotal and the aphoristic elements in Nietzsche. (See E. Bertram: op. cit., p.249.) Gerhard Neumann alludes in his book on the aphorism to a relationship between the aphorism and the anecdote, and examines some of Goethe's anecdotes in this connection. Neumann calls the anecdotal "jene Grenzform des Aphoristischen, wo Geschichte und Individuum (im Sinne des prägnanten Faktums) einerseits, künstlerische Gestaltungskraft (als produktive Aneignung) andererseits zusammenwirken. (G.Neumann: "Ideenparadiese: Aphoristik bei Lichtenberg, Novalis, Friedrich Schlegel und Goethe. München 1976, p.639.) Neumann comments in detail on two of Goethe's anecdotes, that of Madame Roland before her execution and Charles I of England at his trial in order to show "daß der anekdotische Anstoß bei Goethe nicht zufällig einen besonderen Höhepunkt seiner Maximenkunst hervorbringt". (Ibidem.)

1 Cf. Novalis' statement about the effect of the anecdote: "Sie" the anecdote "erhält die Einbildungskraft im Schweben oder im Wechsel, sezt sie in einen künstlich febrilischen Zustand." (Novalis: 'Anekdoten' in "Schriften". Vol. 2. Edited by Richard Samuel. Stuttgart 1965, p.569.) Hans-Peter Neureuter uses the term 'Nachdenklichkeit (Neureuter: op. cit., p.477-479) to describe this phenomenon. Cf. also Karlheinz Gärtner's observation in his study on Fontane: "Ihr" the anecdote's "Denkanstoß resultiert aus der von ihr beschriebenen individuellen – man kann auch sagen originellen – Reaktion auf einen zumeist bekannten allgemeinen Tatbestand. Das bloße Aufzeigen abstrakter Zusammenhänge löst beim Leser oder Hörer eine passive Rezeptionshaltung aus, die Anekdote reizt zur Auseinandersetzung." (K. Gärtner: "Theodor Fontane: Literatur als Provokation". Bonn 1978 p.149)

cases in making precise and significant links between the individual anecdotes and the whole framework of the larger literary genre. The clear establishment of such links proves that, for the most part, the charge of discursiveness in connection with the anecdote which was levelled at Fontane by various critics is unjustified.[1]

Detailed study of Fontane's use of the genre clarifies the interaction of interpolated anecdotes with the principal preoccupations of the larger literary works to which they belong. Helpful to Fontane in this connection was the fact that in the anecdote the psychological element is not important.[2] There is no delving into a character's heart in the anecdote. The character expresses himself directly in word or action or a combination of both. Human nature expresses itself in the anecdote in the most economical way possible. This brevity is one of the most remarkable and gratifying features of Fontane's use of the anecdote. His anecdotes are not strung out by a self-indulgent narrator; rather they restrict themselves austerely to the bare essentials. A great deal of the effect in Kleist's anecdotes is due to the author's uncompromising economy. Fontane shares with Kleist this quality of economy with regard to the anecdote and the result in both cases bears the unmistakeable hallmark of the writer's art.

How doe Fontane's anecdotes compare with their sources? What specifically interests Fontane in a given story? What material does he exclude? What, if anything, does he add to the story? In short how does he adapt the original material to make it more suitable for his purposes? Detailed analyses of specific anecdotes which are compared with the sources used by Fontane, help to answer these questions. The independent anecdote is of necessity restricted to

1 Paul Heyse's criticism in the year 1878 of "Vor dem Sturm" tended in this direction. See Aufbau I, 367-368. Even as recently as 1976, this charge has been made by Alan Robinson in his book "Theodor Fontane: An Introduction to the Man and his Work". Cardiff 1979, p.192.

2 Cf. Wilhelm Grenzmann on this aspect of the anecdote: "Das psychologische Element tritt weit zurück; die Hauptsache ist das Geschehen selbst und die Art, wie sich der Mensch darin enthüllt, bewahrt oder entlarvt." (W. Grenzmann: op. cit., p.64)

those elements within itself, for example, personality, incident, historical period, conflict between central character and milieu, between central character and other characters. The very same anecdote taken over by a creative writer and used in a larger context, for example, in the essay or the novel, retains the qualities which adhered to it in its independent form, but its potential uses in the new context are as profound, broad or varied as the writer's imagination and power of association can make them. In Goethe's "Wahlverwandtschaften" Ottilie tells how Charles I of England lost at his trial the golden knob of his cane and how nobody picked it up for him. Gerhard Neumann has shown how this anecdote reaches far beyond the individual scene in which it is an agent in the characterization of its narrator to encompass a complex of ideas which is central to the whole of Goethe's novel.[1] In Fontane's case, even as a novice preparing his first novel between the mid eighteen-sixties and the late eighteen-seventies, there is a similar conscious intention of linking the interpolated anecdotes with the novel's dominant themes. The anecdote which seems in the conversations that make up such an important part of Fontane's fiction to be at its most specific is often pointing outside of itself to matters of much greater importance than the individual context. It is exchanged in the give-and-take of conversation by characters who are often self-professed lovers of anecdote. The anecdote is part of the social exchange and brings people together in a shared narrative situation. The anecdote is clearly eminently appropriate to inclusion in the conversation of urbane and polished characters. It presupposes a certain standard of education and breadth of interests. Teller, listener and reader share the common ground of historical and cultural tradition. The listener and reader must be able to supply certain facts which enable him to understand the actual relevance of the anecdote. This is not simply a matter of knowledge, but also of openness to other times and other cultures. Openess to other cultures in fact is not merely an aspect of anecdote reception, but also a theme running through Fontane's works, one which finds its clearest and

1 See G. Neumann: op. cit., p.713-718.

most impressive expression in "Der Stechlin", the novel in which the anecdote celebrates its greatest triumph in Fontane's fiction. A parallel can be seen between the effect on the reader of inserted anecdotes in larger fictional forms and the effect of literary quotations and musical allusions. Herman Mayer has shown how quotations are fully integrated into the structure of Fontane's works as a whole, using the examples of "L'Adultera" and "Der Stechlin".[1] Between these quotations and the anecdotes used by Fontane there is a parallel, both in connection with the artistry of the author and in connection with the reader's enjoyment of the anecdotes. One can speak with some exceptions of full integration of the anecdotes into the novels as a whole, and the more well-versed the reader, the fuller the enjoyment. Understanding of the context often requires prior knowledge of the references.[2] In the case of the historical anecdote, the narrator can rely on prior knowledge of his listener/reader and is spared cumbersome introductions to the historical character and period. He can simply jump into his story 'in media res' with the mention of place and time or simply of a well-known personage. The anecdote's economy and brevity are linked with this assumption of prior knowledge. Fontane's versions of anecdotes are appreciably shorter, simpler, more dramatic and more trenchant that the originals, as textual comparisons demonstrate. The dramatic element in the little inserted anecdotes enlivens the prose of the fiction or autobiography.

Fontane's preference for the small and the marginal has wide-reaching effects on his art, not least on his tendency to avoid portraying the human being at the height of his passions. In several letters he expressly draws attention to this feature of his approach. He states for example in a letter of 30 January 1890:

1 See Herman Meyer: "Das Zitat in der Erzählkunst. Zur Geschichte und Poetik des europäischen Romans". Stuttgart 1961, p.155-185.

2 See Rudolf Schäfer on the assumption contained in most anecdote narration not only of general knowledge, but also of specialized knowledge on the reader's part. (R. Schäfer: op. cit., p.31) Of the effect on the reader of his effort Schäfer writes: "Das Verstehen von Anekdoten gewährt intellektuelles Vergnügen nach intellektueller Anstrengung." (Ibid. p.32)

"Ich bin nirgends auf das Große aus (das findet doch seine Darsteller), sondern auf das Mittlere, selbst auf das Kleine ..."[1] The extraordinary reticence of his characters as well as of his narrators leaves great scope for the use of anecdotes which have the appearance of being objective stories exchanged by characters. The character need not feel that he is laying bare his soul by telling a story about someone else, particularly if that person is not at all similar to himself, is someone from a far-off era or from thousands of miles away. Barbara Hardy mentions the preservation of privacy as a motive for story-telling in her book "Tellers and Listeners",[2] but of course this is only one intention behind the narration of anecdotes in a literary work, and there are many more narrative situations and nuances in the fictional use of anecdotes than this. A character may perceive a parallel with his own situation, or with that of his country, or if he does not perceive it, the story may emerge from the myriad strands of the novel to give the reader a pointer in such a direction. Anecdotes can act as emotional escape valves for the characters. Fontane's predilection is for portraying characters in the main through conversation and action rather than for telling the reader what the characters are feeling and thinking. This predilection makes the anecdote a most useful form of communication. The anecdote is therefore part of what has been called the 'outer skin' which has to contain almost all the information in Fontane's fiction.[3] An extraordinary amount of dexterity and ingenuity was required to pack this skin with the necessary information. His art avoids plumbing the depths of feelings through

1 To Heinrich Jacobi. "Briefe". Edited by Gotthard Erler, vol.2, p.262.

2 London 1974. Hardy writes (p.140) that Fontane like several major English authors, "knows stories are sometimes our only way of telling people our secrets while preserving secrecy or privacy."

3 See Horst Glaser: 'Theodor Fontane: "Effi Briest" (1894). Im Hinblick auf "Emma Bovary" und andere' in "Romane und Erzählungen des Bürgerlichen Realismus. Neue Interpretationen". Edited by Horst Denkler. Stuttgart 1980. p.362-377.

the ruthless laying bare of the innermost feelings by the characters themselves or by the narrator. Some commentators have referred to the detective-like qualities needed in the reader to discern what is really going on in a Fontane novel behind the layer of external plot and social conversations.[1]

Those fictional works which are relevant to the present study are "Vor dem Sturm", 'L'Adultera", "Schach von Wuthenow", "Graf Petöfy", "Unterm Birnbaum", "Cécile", "Unwiederbringlich", "Frau Jenny Treibel", "Effi Briest" and "Der Stechlin". Fontane's work from his first appearance as a novelist in 1878 until his death in 1898 demonstrates therefore a development in his use of the anecdote. It is not, however, a matter of a gradual, linear progression. "Schach von Wuthenow" (1882), a work in which all the inserted anecdotes fit comfortably into their new context, is followed by "Graf Petöfy (1884) in which this is not the case. The following works are not relevant for a study of the anecdote: "Grete Minde" (1880), "Ellernklipp" (1881), 'Irrungen, Wirrungen" (1888), "Stine" and "Quitt" (1890), "Die Poggenpuhls" (1896) and "Mathilde Möhring" (published posthumously in 1906). These works mentioned here have one thing in common: the central characters are all isolated from society. In "Grete Minde", "Ellernklipp" and "Quitt", the isolated characters must face an ineluctable fate, and in the stories of personal relationships, "Irrungen, Wirrungen" and "Stine", the lovers are cut off from society. It would seem, therefore, that the existence of a cohesive social circle among the fictional characters was an important factor in Fontane's decisions whether or not to include an anecdotal element.

Since the anecdote as an interpolated form is at home in biography and autobiography, it is to be expected that it would play an important role in Fontane's autobiographical writings.[2] Both of the

1 See e.g. Magdalene Heuser: 'Fontanes "Cécile". Zum Problem des ausgesparten Anfangs' in ZsfdPh 92, 1983, p.36-59 (especially p.55 ff.) for an interesting indication of a relationship between "Cécile" and the detective story. See also H. A. Glaser: op. cit., p.373.

2 His autobiography has indeed been criticised on this account. See Roy Pascal: "Die Autobiographie: Gehalt und Gestalt". Stuttgart 1965, p.116.

early eighteen-seventies and of the nineties. He was aware even before starting to write about his childhood in November 1892 that his anecdotal approach would assert itself and even to am extent determine the scope of the work.[1] Fontane's strongly autobiographical account of his experiences in German-occupied France, "Aus den Tagen der Okkupation (1871), which makes extensive use of anecdote, receives attention in Chapter Four before the discussion of "Meine Kinderjahre (1894) and "Von Zwanzig bis Dreißig" (1898).

1 See NyA XIV, 7.

I. "An einem Strohhalm sieht man am besten, woher der Wind weht"

Anecdote and the Heart

1. "L'Adultera" (1880)

Unlike his usual procedure of first presenting the surroundings or house of the main characters, Fontane gives at the beginning of this 'Novelle' a character description of the van der Straaten couple. Ostensibly, the narrator is building up an impression of a happy marriage of ten years duration, while in fact he subtly undermines this impression with slight hints and indications that on the contrary all is not well. The ominous note struck here is further emphasized in the second chapter, entitled 'L'Adultera', where the undercurrents in the apparently happy marriage become clearer in the breakfast-time conversation of the couple. The initially light-hearted chat becomes a discussion of the husband's fears about adultery, a discussion which several times threatens to become a serious conversation. Yet by virtue of the lack of real communication between the partners, the conversation never quite leaves the realm of the jocose long enough for a full exchange of thoughts on the subject of adultery.

Melanie's yearning at the sight of the dancing snowflakes outside and her sudden seriousness during her husband's interpretation of the Tintoretto copy (even before a connection is made between herself and the picture) point out a basic lack in her existence as well as a certain premonition. The premonition is strengthened by van der Straaten's conviction that the picture of the adulterous woman will be to him what coffins are to Capuchin monks. His very choice of words is significant for the rest of the plot: "Und alles wie vorherbestimmt"[1].

1 NyA IV, 13.

In reply to his smiling silence at her objection to having the picture hung in the drawing-room, where it would be a cause of insinuations on the part of guests, Melanie then relates a rather gruesome anecdote to characterize her husband. She tells the anecdote as a direct reaction to his smiles, as part of an objection to his tendency to laugh too much in general. This is one of the main bones of contention between the couple in later chapters – Melanie is constantly offended by her husband's lack of taste and his penchant for amusing himself at the expense of the sensibilities of others. This very coarseness brings about her initial attraction to Rubehn in Chapter 10 after her intense irritation and disgust at her husband in the preceding chapter.

Melanie's indictment of her husband in the anecdote in Chapter 2 sharpens the reader's attention to the still obscure inner rift between them.

> Ich weiß recht gut, du bist nicht so harmlos, wie du dich stellst. Und ich weiß auch, daß es wunderliche Gemütlichkeiten gibt. Ich habe mal von einem russischen Fürsten gelesen, ich glaube Suboff war sein Name. Eigentlich waren es zwei, zwei Brüder. Die spielten Karten, und dann ermordeten sie den Kaiser Paul, und dann spielten sie weiter Karten. Ich glaube beinah, du könntest auch so was! [1]

The very lack of a serious reaction on van der Straaten's part to his wife's serious condemnation of him with this anecdote proves the correctness of her assessment. The anecdote is obviously not meant to prove that van der Staaten is capable of cold-blooded murder, but to show his wife's grave doubts about his sensitivity and her fear that his jocose manner hides a sinister coldness. Instead of being perturbed at this analogy with the Suboff brothers, van der Staaten laughingly refers to a joke from their courtship days, which gives Melanie an opportunity to contrast her knowledge of his character in those days and now: "Und ich kannte dich damals noch nicht. Jetzt aber kenn ich dich und weiß nur nicht, ob es etwas sehr Gutes oder etwas sehr Schlimmes ist, was in dir steckt ... "[2]

1 NyA IV, 13.
2 Ibidem.

This statement takes away from the certitude with which Melanie compared her husband to the Suboff brothers, the anecdote being a rather intuitive outburst, whereas the second statement appears to echo Melanie's frequent ponderings on the subject of her husband's character. When the conversation resumes, it is on the basis of the narrator's remark that in spite of lots of friendship, van der Staaten really has no friend or confidant. For this reason, he is driven to confide in his wife that he is constantly plagued by fear in connection with adultery. Therefore he has brought the copy of Tintoretto's "Woman Taken in Adultery" (1546) in order to ward off the evil, "denn es ist erblich in unserm Haus".[1] The straight character sketch which the narrator provided in Chapter 1 laid most emphasis on his "Vorliebe für drastische Sprichwörter und heimische 'geflügelte Worte von der derberen Observanz'."[2] This trait, though still subdued in Chapter 2, is insufficiently apparent to justify Melanie's condemnation of her husband's 'Gemütlichkeit'.[3] The repressed nature of the couple's differences is admirably portrayed once again at the close of Chapter 2 where Melanie quits the room in order to prepare for an outing to purchase a gown which she "needs much more urgently" than he his Tintoretto. With this return of good humour, the narrator shows with great delicacy the fluctuations of the relationship between husband and wife. In under two pages, the reader has been brought from the obscure and threatening associations of the Suboff anecdote to the frivolous topic of the urgently-needed new gown. A better example of the problem behind the couple's marriage could hardly be had: van der Straaten's insensitivity was during their courtship more than adquately compensated for by the amount of his wealth. At that stage, in any case Melanie was still "ein halbes Kind"[4] as she claims directly after her narration of the anecdote.

The Suboff anecdote should not be taken as straight characterization of van der Straaten. Fontane's characters sometimes

1 NyA IV, 14.
2 Ibid. 7.
3 Ibid. 13.
4 Ibidem.

inadvertently reveal more about themselves than about the others they think they are describing. The anecdote here is an expression of van der Straaten's effect on Melanie: his 'Gemütlichkeit' is not at all to her taste, and her revulsion is expressed through telling him of a similar revolting 'Gemütlichkeit' on the part of the Suboff brothers. This anecdote shows how much her husband's personality grates on Melanie, long before this becomes apparent in group scenes in the 'Novelle'. Thus the anecdote has an anticipatory function as well as being of value for informing the reader of Melanie's view on her husband.

Melanie does not date the assassination of Tsar Paul I (1754-1801), and she is also slightly vague about the characters in the anecdote: "Ich habe mal von einem russischen Fürsten gelesen, ich glaube Suboff war sein Name. Eigentlich waren es zwei, zwei Brüder." In reality the brothers were counts, Nicholas and Valerian Suboff. The 'prince' element in Melanie's story has its counterpart in history in Prince Plato Suboff, who had been the lover of Catherine II, (1729-1796), Paul's mother. All three Suboffs, Nicholas, Valerian and Plato were party to a conspiracy among the military to assassinate the Tsar. Paul's shifting foreign policy and tyrannical behaviour made him unpopular with the military and his unpopularity was exacerbated by the harsh discipline which he imposed on the army. The situation culminated in the conspiracy between Counts von der Pahlen and von Bennigsen and the Suboffs to strangle Paul in his bedroom on 23 March 1801.

Immediately after Melanie's narration of the anecdote and the couple's remarks on their own relationship, the discussion of adultery begins. Thus, the reader is given a hint already in Chapter 2 of the 'Novelle' as to reasons for Melanie's later adultery and departure from home.

"L'Adultera", Fontane's first work on Berlin society, shows an extremely sparing use of the anecdote in comparison with the preceding work, his first novel, "Vor dem Sturm". This is to be expected, since both the size and the content of this historical novel allow greater scope for the use of anecdote. Other very economical works of Fontane which, like "L'Adultera", concentrate on the relationship between a man and a woman, "Stine",

"Irrungen, Wirrungen" and "Mathilde Möhring", do not use the anecdote at all. The Suboff anecdote in 'L'Adultera" is used for the purposes of character motivation, anticipation of plot development and revelation of the as yet hidden discord between the marriage partners. Because the reader is not yet fully conscious of the great divide between them, the radical nature of Melanie's comparison of her husband to a pair of cold-blooded assassins seems at first sight rather uncalled for. Through the inclusion of Melanie's vagueness with regard to the exact date of the historical incident, however, the author avoids the impression that he is imposing his own wide knowledge of history on the character. This is a frequent feature of Fontane's later employment of the anecdote in his fiction. The fictional characters often indicate that they are not sure about the more technical aspects of historical incidents, such as dates and proper names. This feature makes the inclusion of anecdotes in conversations seem natural, psychologically convincing and also protects the writer from complaints about historical inaccuracy. The Suboff anecdote in "L'Adultera" stands out as the only example in Fontane's fiction in which a character consciously characterizes another fictional figure to his face by relating an anecdote. Perhaps Fontane decided that this device was not realistic and shelved it along with some other instances of lack of sophistication found in this work. The next work in which he concentrates on the relationship between a man and a woman, "Graf Petöfy", shows greater sureness of touch and sensitivity in its employment of anecdote than is the case in "L'Adultera".

2. "Graf Petöfy" (1884)

Story-telling plays a large part in "Graf Petöfy", which was the sixth of Fontane's longer fictional works to be published. It shows him moving steadily in the direction of the social novels which achieved him lasting fame. Yet this novel remains one of his less appreciated works. Three of the four central characters in "Graf Petöfy" are presented as lovers of conversation and anecdote:

Franziska Franz, Graf Adam Petöfy and his sister, Judith. On one occasion, Franziska ironically describes herself as a 'Plaudertasche'.[1] She wins through her charming manner and story-telling talents the hearts of both the Redemptorist, Pater Fessler, and the pious and originally disapproving Judith. Both Adam and Judith refer to themselves as lovers of anecdote.[2] Only Graf Egon Asperg is not specifically alluded to by the narrator in connection with Franziska's narrative talent, but, as we shall later see, it is on the occasion of Franziska's narration of an anecdote that Egon first displays a more personal interest in her.

Franziska therefore, unlike other female characters in Fontane's works who are shown as fascinating conversationalists (such as Corinna in "Frau Jenny Treibel" and Melusine in "Der Stechlin") is specifically cast in the role of story-teller and narrator of anecdotes.[3] The fact that she is an actress, i.e. an entertainer, is stressed in this connection. Indeed Graf Adam, the passionate lover of theatre, cites Franziska's narrative powers as an extremely important point in favour of his marrying her. In spite of his sister's doubts about the wisdom of such an alliance, he disregards the dangers inherent in the age discrepancy between him and Franziska. In general, Adam appears to regard the proposed marriage with the complacency of an old man, who looks forward to the solace of entertaining companionship. In his view, Franziska "übt die Kunst der Erzählung und Causerie wie keine Zweite",[4] and, after years of bachelorhood, this alone seems to be a good enough reason to marry her, in spite of the odds against the success of such a union. Adam's use of the image of the good fairy during the conversation in which he breaks the news of his plan to Judith is itself symptomatic of his lack of realism: Franziska will be the good fairy, who will scare away the wicked fairy of his restlessness.[5] Each time

1 NyA II, 62.
2 Cf. NyA II, 149-150.
3 NyA II, 64-65 and 69-70.
4 NyA II, 65.
5 Ibidem.

doubts are expressed by other parties, Adam quickly overrules them. Judith doubts his motives,[1] and Franziska herself claims when he proposes that he is looking for a 'Redefrau' and a teller of fairy-tales.[2] In spite of the overall sympathetic portrayal of Adam in "Graf Petöfy", all the emphasis in both these scenes with Judith and Franziska in Chapters 10 and 11 is placed on what Adam wants from the proposed relationship.

Adam rejects his sister's doubts about Franziska's happiness in such a marriage basing his argument, not on anything he knows of Franziska's character, but on his own alleged tolerance of the possible attentiveness of other, younger men to Franziska. His only condition is the preservation of due decorum.[3] In a letter to Emilie of 15 June 1883, Fontane comments on the problem of Adam's character and of his decision to marry Franziska:

> Und was den alten Grafen angeht, so will er nichts als unter 'Beobachtung aller Dehors' eine geistreiche pikante Person um sich haben. Er berechnet nicht klug genug, daß dies seinem im Ehrenpunkte schließlich doch sehr diffizilen Charakter gegenüber, auf die Dauer nicht geht und an diesem Rechenfehler geht er zu Grunde. Einen Tugendspiegel heiraten zu wollen, davon ist er weit ab.[4]

It is clear therefore that Fontane's own view concurs with the initially expressed doubts of Judith and Franziska. Adam realizes the nature of his mistake in the chapters preceding his suicide. During the proposal scene, Franziska protests that a woman wants to be courted for herself and not for any talent she may have. To this Adam protests that he by no means wants a mere narrator of anecdotes.[5] Yet the daily programme which he draws up six chapters later for their life in Arpa Castle lays heavy emphasis on Franziska's

1 NyA II, 65.
2 Cf. ibid. 69.
3 Cf. ibid. 66.
4 Th. Fontane: "Briefe". Ed. K. Schreinert and C. Jolles, Berlin 1968, vol. 1, p.201.
5 Cf. NyA II, 69.

powers of entertainment.[1] It is therefore ironic that Chapter 17 should end with h e r statement that such a life is like something out of a fairy-tale. Franziska objected in Chapter 11 to Adam's looking for a fairy-tale narrator. It is also ironic that Adam should express in Chapter 17 his foreboding that real people were lacking in fairy-tales and that Franziska will miss people at Arpa.[2] This fairy-tale motif, sounded in Chapter 11 and taken up again in Chapter 17, makes an appearance also in Chapter 34 after Adam's discovery of a bond between Franziska and Egon. Here at this late stage, he blames himself for having let Franziska believe their life had a fairy-tale quality, while he remembers that he had at the same time warned her against that.[3] Such a return to an earlier apparently random observation is typical of Fontane's careful art of association and pre-figuration.[4]

Basically, Graf Adam tries to transpose the world of the theatre in which he has such an avid interest into the world of everyday reality. He attempts this in marriage to an actress much younger than himself, hoping thereby to brighten his old age. He expressly seeks the daily enjoyment of her narrative talent. To Judith in Chapter 10 Adam mentions three 'pagan goddesses' who are of importance in his life, "die Göttin der Zerstreuung, dann die der Beschwichtigung und Einlullung und endlich die der Plauderei".[5] The very

1 NyA II, 98-99.
2 Ibid. 99.
3 Ibid. 161.
4 Like Franziska in Chapter 17 of "Graf Petöfy", Effi in "Effi Briest" makes several enthusiastic and erroneous assumptions about her future existence at Kessin. She sees an exotic element in that future, e.g. her notion about having a red bedroom lamp and Japanese bed-screen, about Innstetten's being like an Oriental prince etc. This exotic element is completely at variance with the reality of life in Kessin and already in Chapter4, Effi's mother had warned her against such imaginings, using the fairy-tale image- "Es kommt dir vor wie ein Märchen ... " (NyA VII, 191). The fairy-tale motif in "Graf Petöfy" indicates the irreality of the marriage relationship based mainly on Franziska's ability to converse engagingly. The dearth of 'real people' which Adam fears in this existence is filled by the relationship with Egon.
5 NyA II, 65.

choice of substantives here makes the reader suspicious that impossible demands will be made on Franziska. The 'marriage pact',[1] based on the principles of entertainment, freedom and the preservation of decorum, shatters in the face of the demands made on Franziska by nature. That Fontane intended this is clear from warning statements such as Judith's in Chapter 10 that 'young blood wants young blood'[2] and from Fontane's above-mentioned letter to his wife in which he states (in answer to his wife's comment on improbability in the plot) that Franziska is in love with Egon from the very beginning.[3]

It would be expected that the anecdotes in "Graf Petöfy" would mirror the major preoccupations of the novel. To a certain extent, this is so, or at least the reader can see that Fontane had this as his aim, even if it is not properly realized. Two of them are taken from theatrical or literary sources, which is appropriate for the background of Franziska and her friend, Phemi. While Franziska is depicted as a brilliant conversationalist, Phemi wields language in a rather mannered, stagey way. Her speech is full of theatrical and literary allusions. In Chapter 5 at the spa, she relates to Egon and Franziska an anecdote based on the historically inaccurate plot of the drama, "Un verre d'eau" (1840) by the French writer, Eugène Scribe. In the play, Queen Anne of England is in love with the officer, Masham. The anecdote concerns her confusion of the amount of the state debt with the number of losses sustained at the Battle of Malplaquet (1709). The queen's mistake arises out of her relief that Masham is not among the dead. Phemi's point is that the great are not concerned with matters of great importance, as here with the soldiers who have given their lives, but with personal matters. The anecdote is related after Franziska's reproach that Phemi speaks like a stage character, even in normal life. This context gives the story some significance for the novel as a whole. The marriage (which has not even been planned at this stage) is an attempt on Adam's part to transpose theatre life into real life.

1 Adam's term. NyA II, 66.
2 Ibid. 65.
3 See Fontane: "Briefe". Ed. Schreinert/Jolles, vol. 1, p. 201.

Franziska's role in this plan has already been commented on. Her admonishment to Phemi in Chapter 5 is therefore ironic. Although she recognises theatricality in her friend's mode of speech and condemns it, she is not able to follow her initial instincts which forbid role-playing in real life, i.e. becoming Adam's 'Redefrau'. When Adam later asks Franziska to invite Phemi to the castle so that she may entertain them with her conversation, Franziska refuses almost entertain them with her conversation, Franziska refuses almost abruptly. The arrival of Phemi, who represents almost a caricature of the theatrical element, would make Franziska's own existence as a chatterbox only too apparent. The unnaturalness of the relationship between Adam and Franziska cannot be hidden by their game of meeting at set times for the specific purpose of entertaining each other. As in the case of Queen Anne and her love affair in the anecdote, reality makes itself apparent and exposes the game as a sham. When Franziska decides not to bring up the subject of the Barcsai ballad at afternoon tea with Adam, the discrepancy between reality and illusion is plain. Material dealing with real life, in this case, adultery and punishment, would contrast too much with the Petöfys' game and show the dangers which overshadow their false way of life. The marriage of convenience is not working out, and no amount of story-telling will gloss over that fact, because the story-telling reflects realities which the marriage tries to ignore. Even the story-telling has to stop when it touches issues which indicate the reality behind the game. Recent commentary has dwelt in particular on the aspect of social criticism in the novel. From this point of view, the life of the Petöfys in its isolation and sterility becomes an example of a whole class which is threatened by social change. The Queen Anne anecdote also supports this interpretation, for here an aristocratic person shows isolation from and contempt for the lives of ordinary people, so peroccupied is she with her own private emotions.

In Chapter 6, the love relationship between Franziska and Egon is brought a step further. The fact that this relationship is portrayed in such a restrained manner in the novel led Emilie Fontane to complain to her husband that the couple's intimacy was not prepared for in the narrative. The anecdote about the poet, Nikolaus Lenau

(1802-1850), is one of the indirect means by which the narrator anticipates the bond between these two characters, just as Franziska's "pointerte, halb leidenschaftliche Sprechweise"[1] in Egon's presence betrays to the attentive reader her love for him.

Lenau's poetry was the subject of part of the conversation in Chapter 4, when Franziska won the hearts of the company in Judith's drawing-room with her stories of her North German home and her attraction to the south. When Franziska claims in Chapter 6 not to remember having already shown enthusiasm for Lenau, this is merely the dissimulation of a woman in love. The fact that Fontane uses this anecdote once more in "Von Zwanzig bis Dreißig" indicates that he found it particularly attractive. Franziska narrates the anecdote to Egon because she feels too keenly the similarity between her own profession and that of the fun fair performers whom they pass during their outing. A comparison of Franziska's Lenau anecdote with the source version in Karl Mayer's biography of Lenau[2] shows the changes which Fontane made on the material in order to fit it in more closely with the requirements of the fictional context.

Karl Mayer's biography version (1853)	Fontane's fictional version (1884)
Niembsch hatte in seinem Zimmer Handschriftliches, die Briefe von mir und andern Freunden frei herumliegen und ein Stubenmädchen des Gasthofes machte sich diese ihr offenstehende mannigfaltige Leserei zu Nutz. Gerade als ich bei dem Freunde übernachtete, war durch diese sich selbst verschaffte Kenntnis das Vertrauen des Mädchens zu ihm so hoch gestiegen, daß sie eine	In irgendeinem Wiener Restaurant, in dem Lenau verkehrte, befand sich eine junge Person, die nicht bloß die Gäste bediente, sondern auch Verse machte. Diese Verse nun wurden bei bestimmter Gelegenheit an Lenau gegeben, der sie las und sofort in eine befangene Stellung zu der neuentdeckten Dichterin geriet. Alles was sie geschrieben hatte, war unter mittelmäßig, aber sich auch

1 Fontane used this argument to counter his wife's criticism that the love between Egon and Franziska was not sufficiently anticipated in the novel. See Theodor Fontane: "Briefe". Ed. Schreinert/Jolles, vol. 1, p. 201.

2 Karl Mayer: "Lenau". Stuttgart 1853.

Sammlung eigener handschriftlicher Gedichte brachte, welche von Niembsch mit seiner gewohnten Gutmütigkeit aufgenommen wurde und uns durch ihren empfindsamen Schwung, wie die Person selbst Stoff zur Heiterkeit gab. Es war komisch anzusehen, wie Niembsch, der Dichter, das Mädchen gleich einer Schwester in Apollo behandelte und diese eine solche Anerkennung als etwas sich von selbst Verstehendes aufnahm.[1]

fernerhin von ihr bedienen zu lassen, erschien ihm nichtsdestoweniger unmöglich oder doch im höchsten Grade peinlich. Er sah in ihr die Kollegin, die Mitschwester und wußte sich schließlich nicht anders zu helfen als daß er fortblieb.[2]

Like Melanie, Effi and others, Franziska claims in her preface to the Lenau anecdote not to remember the exact details of reality: "Ich habe die Namen und näheren Umstände vergessen, aber gleichviel"[3] This gives a psychologically convincing touch of realism and also saves Fontane from complaints about inaccuracies. Therefore the setting of the Lenau anecdote can be switched from the Stuttgart of reality to Vienna in the novel, which fits in with the novel's own setting. Appropriately for Franziska's profession, she claims to have heard it from Bauernfeld, the director of the Vienna Burgtheater. The Viennese café setting makes it more likely as a story being circulated by Bauernfeld. Fontane's version shortens and simplifies the language of the original and makes it more colloquial. This is a feature which makes the foreign material more suitable and natural for the dialogue. It is a consistent feature of his art that becomes evident each time his anecdotes are compared with the original. The rather stiff participial adjectival clauses, "diese ihr offenstehende mannigfaltige Leserei ... diese sich selbst verschaffte Kenntnis ... etwas sich von selbst Verstehendes", which characterize

1 Karl Mayer: op. cit., p.70-71. The room referred to is Lenau's room in Stuttgart in the Gasthof zum König von England. See ibid, p. 69 and Anton X. Schurz: "Lenaus Leben". Stuttgart, Augsburg 1855, p. 174

2 NyA II, 44.

3 Ibidem.

Mayer's version, are omitted. The rather highflown phrase of the original, "Niembsch behandelte sie gleich einer Schwester in Apollo', becomes in Fontane's version the more sober: " Er sah in ihr die Kollegin, die Mitschwester." In "Graf Petöfy" the original chambermaid's nosiness in reading Lenau's manuscripts and correspondence is omitted, whereby the poetaster becomes more enobled. Fontane's version stresses delicacy of feeling, and for this purpose it is appropriate that he cuts out the emphasis placed in the original on the sentimentaliy of the girl's poetry and the comicality of her demeanour. In the original, she appears as a figure of fun and the new relationship between her and the famous poet is also seen from the point of view of the amusing contrast between the sublime and the ridiculous. The attitude is natural enough in the real situation, where a divide is evident in the original between the poet and poetaster on the one hand and his scoffing friends on the other. Fontane's version keeps the feelings of the timid poetess and the generous and noble-hearted poet in the forefront of the narration. The story of Lenau's gentle and noble treatment of a waitress, who was a mediocre poetess, shows refinement of feeling and natural nobility of soul, qualities which Fontane always found compelling and which are the subject of several anecdotes in his works. The largest factual difference between the two versions of the anecdote is the addition in Fontane's version of Lenau's staying away from the establishment in order not to allow himself be served by a colleague.

Franziska clearly makes the parallel between herself, the actress, and the fun fair performers, and Lenau, the poet, and the poetaster waitress. She claims that she does not want to attribute to herself by telling the anecdote Lenau's qualities of amiability and refinement. This immediately leads Graf Egon to do precisely this, while taking her hand. The conversation continues on the impression made on Egon during their first meeting when Franziska sang Lenau's poem "Nach Süden". Franziska's apparent forgetfullness of that evening is merely a feint to hide how important it was to her, because she had that time fallen in love with Egon. His revocation of the evening from memory presumably gives her reason to believe that the evening was important for him too. All the narrator lets us know however is that Franziska is surprised and manages to hide her embarrassment.

In this scene the anecdote serves to draw them together by referring to their first experience together, spent in enjoyment of the southern poet, Lenau. In their appreciation of Lenau's nobility and refinement of feeling, the two characters reach an intimacy unwarranted by their social relationship, an intimacy which finally expresses itself in their sexual union. In the context of the conversation of Chapter 6, the anecdote about Lenau is made to connect with the notion of a 'performer' within the Petöfys' marriage, before the marriage has even been mooted. Franziska's misfortune is that she becomes, not the wife of the young count who listens with interest to her story of the refined Lenau, but rather the 'Redefrau', anecdote narrator and entertaining companion of old Graf Adam, the life-long enthusiast for the theatre.

In Chapter 31 after Egon and Franziska have become lovers, an anecdote plays an important role in the external development of the plot. Franziska's involvement with Egon becomes clear, firstly to the reader, through her reaction to Judith's reading out of the newspaper the story about the madman in Charenton, who believed himself to be made of glass. Adam makes the connection between this allusion and a man's virtuous life. This anecdote provides a further variation of the theme of reality and illusion in the novel. Because of the narrator's reticence it is only with Franziska's reaction to this anecdote that the reader can be sure she has compromised herself: "War dies alles Zufall, oder war es mehr?"[1] The inner confusion of Franziska since the shipwreck scene and the fact that she and Egon are avoiding each other are now clearly linked with the guilt which is proven in her reaction to the anecdote. In the conversation following the sudden disappearance of Egon and Franziska after the "homme de verre" anecdote, Judith by implication reveals their guilt to Adam.

Each of the anecdotes in "Graf Petöfy" supports the theme of reality and illusion. Graf Adam's illusion that he can detract from the solitude and boredom of old age by simply marrying an actress with prodigious narrative powers can clearly never become reality. The inserted anecdotes being out the theme of role-playing and

1 NyA II, 150.

point forward to the inevitable crumbling of the theatrical facade. Other references in the novel, such as the Lenau quotations, the Barcsai ballad and Zola's novel "La faute de l'Abbé Mouret"[1] indicate the factors which will bring about the downfall of that facade, namely human longing and passion. Because of the reticence of the narration, the anecdotes are useful indications of matters which are not explicitly stated. Although the anecdotes in "Graf Petöfy" link up with each other and with the main theme, they do not give the impression of being naturally embedded in the larger framework of the novel. The Queen Anne story retains its independence as a separate narrative form and appears to be superimposed on the fictional text instead of fully merging with it. The connection between the Lenau anecdote and the subtleties it is intended to point out remains slightly obscure, and in spite of its elegance this story does not reach the level of the most successful anecdotes in Fontane's fiction.

3. "Cécile" (1887)

In a letter to Mathilde von Rohr of 19 April 1887, Fontane calls his novel, "Cécile", a moral story, because it preaches the sentence: "Sitzt man erst mal drin, gleichviel ob durch eigne Schuld oder unglückliche Constellation, so kommt man nicht mehr heraus. Es wird nichts vergessen."[2] Society indeed forgotten neither Cécile's past as the mistress of a prince, nor the duel in which her husband killed an officer who suggested Cécile was an unsuitable match. Because of the past, the couple are in spite of their respectable marriage ostracized from the circles to which they would otherwise belong.

1 Paris 1875. It is the subject of conversation between Graf Adam, Franziska and Phemi in Chapter 7 (NyA II, 51-53) Fontane lists this novel by Zola in his answer to the 1889 questionaire "Die besten Bücher". See NyA XXI, i, 499.

2 Fontane: "Briefe" (ed. Schreinert/Jolles) vol. 3, p. 225.

The novel does not therefore depict a really cohesive social circle. The dinner scene at their house adequately portrays a circle of misfits, who because of some disappointment no longer move in the best society in Berlin. The circle around the St. Arnauds in the Harz region is merely a pot-pourri of characters from the hotel or met during outings into the surrounding countryside. Only one of these, Leslie-Gordon, makes it his business to unravel the mystery of the oddly-matched St. Arnauds. The secret is not revealed to him however until the arrival of his sister's letter (Chapter 21) by which stage his emotional involvement with Cécile is already advanced. A combination of this and his impetuosity and headstrong nature brings about the dénouement, which is his own and Cécile's death.

The large element of retardation in the novel, the mystery being cleared only in the twenty-first of twenty-nine chapters, creates many questions in the reader's mind as to the relationship between the St. Arnauds and the character of Cécile and her past. Gordon is portrayed as a knowledgeable and entertaining conversationalist. For this reason alone the St. Arnauds would be pleased with his company on excursions from Thale, but he is also a member of that society which has repudiated them. Therefore his company offers them an element which they normally lack in Berlin, where their history is known. Gordon's cosmopolitanism is apparent from the range of his interests in geography, history, saga and legend.

The conversation in Chapter 7 during the excursion by train to Quedlinburg proves the specific interest taken by the narrator in Gordon as opposed to the other main participants, Rosa Hexel and Pierre St. Arnaud. As in the case of Professor Wilibald Schmidt in Chapter 7 of "Frau Jenny Treibel", Fontane appears to put into the mouth of a character one of his own ideas with regard to stories and story-telling, when Gordon remarks on his experience as a widely-travelled person:

> Überhaupt sind die besten Geschichten uralt und überall zu Haus, also Welteigentum, und ich habe manche, von denen wir glaubten, daß sie zwischen Havel und Spree das Licht der Welt erblickten oder ohne die Gebrüder Grimm gar nicht existieren würden, in Tibet oder am Himalaja wiedergefunden.[1]

1 NyA IV, 157.

This generalization is evoked by Gordon's comment that the fortunes of wealthy families in at least six cities where he has lived were said to have been built on a pin, as is the case with the Nathusius family of Neinstadt. This quotation expresses in a different way one of the central themes of Fontane's work, namely, that 'Heimat', i.e. in his case, Berlin and the March Brandenburg, can be representative of the larger world. This theme is most clearly articulated in "Der Stechlin", where the backwardness of the rural place does not necessarily mean a narrow outlook on the part of the characters. Gordon's comment on the universality of stories indicates the sameness of human experience the world over. The narrator is interested only in Gordon's part of the conversation here, for he forecloses it by reporting to us that Rosa disagrees completely with this theory and that she continues to do so until the train halts at Quedlinburg. Thus, Rosa's disagreement is used merely as a transition to another scene.

A similar lack of interest is shown by the narrator in St. Arnaud's reaction to Gordon's anecdote about the imprisonment of the highway-man, Graf Albrecht von Regenstein. This anecdote serves on the one hand to indicate Cécile's lack of cultural interests – as the narrator remarks, she is more interested in the story of the count's imprisonment than in Klopstock. The ramifications of the anecdote are wider than this however. The only fact emerging from Gordon's narration is that the count was imprisoned outside the town hall in Quedlinburg for some twenty months. Gordon and Cécile make surmises regarding ill-treatment of him by the Quedlinburgers, which leads to a blanket condemnation of the middle class for their treatment of criminals. Gordon blames liberal historians for their tendency towards championing the bourgeois and attributing guilt to the aristocracy. St. Arnaud's obvious interest in this topic and his wholehearted agreement with Gordon's view are merely commented on by the narrator, who 'interrupts' St. Arnaud's intended observations by having the train halt. These two instances of a deliberate dropping of the conversation once Gordon has had his say proves the narrator's overriding interest in him and Cécile, to the exclusion of the other two. Cécile is the main object of the narrator's interest, but a great deal of the novel must be presented from

Gordon's point of view, for otherwise Cécile's secret would have to be divulged sooner. Gordon's character is not however dwelt on for its own sake, but as a foil for Cécile, and since he is mostly preoccupied with Cécile, ultimately the narrator is dealing with her. Only when the action starts to take place, i.e. after the revelation of Chapter 21, does the psychological make-up of Gordon become of greater importance, since it is he and not the passive Cécile who precipitates events. Even when Gordon relates an anecdote, it is chosen not so much for the light which the choice throws on Gordon, as for its function in the overall interest of the book, Cécile and her fate. The anecdote in Chapter 7 does throw light on Gordon's outlook in fact, on his anti-middle class attitude. A similar note of contempt for the bourgeois is sounded in Chapter 8, where the warden at Quedlinburg Castle informs the group that King Frederick William IV stopped coming to Quedlinburg once the citizens had in 1848 refused to allow him freedom to hunt there. Gordon agrees with the monarch's displeasure and comments: "Bourgeoismanieren."[1] However, besides indirectly revealing Cécile's lack of culture and Gordon's aristocratic disdain for the bourgeois, the Regenstein anecdote also operates on a more general level. This is true of most of Fontane's anecdotes in the fictional works. They have both an immediate situational interest as well as a function in the overall interpretation of the story.

Frequently, the narrator indicates that Cécile pays little attention to subjects which do not touch her personally. This is so in the case of discussions on art and history between Gordon, Rosa and Pierre. Besides being indicated indirectly, this lack of interest is also stated explicitly by the narrator on occasion, e.g. we are told directly before the narration of the anecdote in Chapter 7 that she has no appreciation of little temples and cast-iron monuments. Yet even the languid Cécile pays great attention to the anecdote of the imprisoned count, and she actually makes a contribution to the imaginative picture which Gordon draws of the man's existence in a cage outside the town-hall. Her contribution is significant because it indicates a parallel to her own position. She sees as particularly

1 NyA IV, 163.

noteworthy the reaction of the respectable female citizens whom she imagines pricking the disgraced thief with their parasols. By virtue of her past, she knows the treatment meted out by society to those who do not conform to its norms. Like Albrecht von Regenstein, she too has been isolated from society. She has been subjected to its 'grinning' and is ostracized by her peers. How deeply she suffers from this ostracism is revealed in Chapters 23 and 27 during the conversations in which Gordon oversteps the line of respectability which Cécile has drawn for herself as St. Arnaud's wife. This respectability is the outward expression of her vow over the body of Dzialinski to live for her duty and never again be the cause of a man's death. In Chapter 23 she speaks of society's mockery. Her heartfelt tones here remind the reader of the earlier Regenstein anecdote which arouses such interest and fellow-feeling in Cécile.

In an obvious reminiscence from Fontane's visit to Quedlinburg in June 1884, the narrator in Chapter 8 dwells with amusement on the castle warden's embarrassment. This is due to the lack of anything worth seeing in the castle. The missing objects are therefore conjured up by means of anecdote. The most interesting object which originally belonged to the castle, the visiting group learns, was the rock crystal mirror owned by Princess Josephine Albertine, niece of Frederick the Second. On King Jerome's installation, Josephine Albertine had to abandon the mirror, but repossessed it for an enormous sum when Jerome was obliged, because of his extravagance, to auction the contents of Quedlinburg Castle. This anecdote gains the appreciation of everyone but Cécile. While her husband is better pleased with the story than with the actual article, the narrator informs us that Cécile would have liked to have seen her reflection in the mirror. She looks out the window during the second half of the story which was too dragged out for her taste. Here again, her lack of interest in anything which does not concern herself is indicated by the narrator, but he also gives a clue to her psychological make-up which is still very much a mystery to Gordon as well as to the reader in Chapter 8. The mirror obviously points to vanity. Cécile is interested – to a degree – only in the first half of the story. The princess's story might have shown some parallel to her own as a prince's mistress. When it is merely a story about the recovery of a mirror, involving as it does, some knowledge of history,[1] Cécile loses interest and looks out the window. Her vanity and desire for attention help to explain her involvement with Gordon in spite of her vow. Pierre does not suffer as she does from social ostracism but neither does he provide her with the male attentiveness which she requires.

In Chapter 11, Fontane forms one of his personal experiences from the summer of 1884 into an anecdote which shows up vanity and arrogance on the part of the characters in the main plot and also prefigures Cécile's later return to Catholicism.[2] The anecdote concerns the preceptor of Altenbrak, Rodenstein, who voluntarily resigned his post after he had appropriated to himself the function of preacher. This anecdote forms the main part of the lunch-time conversation in the hotel in Chapter 11, and on the plot level, it directly leads to the party's decision to visit Altenbrak. This visit is described in Chapters 13 and 14 and is one of the highlights of the St. Arnauds' holiday in the Harz mountains. Cécile's interest in the anecdote about Rodenstein stems from her general enthusiasm for religious sects. However, the story of a man who has to change his whole life's pattern also mirrors her own fate. Because of the strong retardation element in this work, the narrator again takes the opportunity of Cécile's reaction to the promise of the anecdote in order to reveal more about her. "Ein in ihrer Natur liegender mystisch-religiöser Zug"[3] is mentioned by the narrator

1 The following episodes (inspection of the Baroque princess's obelisk to her faithful dog and of the portrait of Aurora von Königsmarck) show Cécile's intense interest in even historical itemsin cases where she sees a parallel with her own fate

2 This function is also fulfilled by Court Preacher Dörffel's anecdote about Pope Gregory XVI's coldness in rejecting a woman's almost hysterical request that he should give her absolution during a journey by boat to Terracina. Dörffel wants to warn Cécile with the anecdote against exuberant emotions which now express themselves in her request for prayers, so that her burden of dread may be removed. Ironically, her forebodings here later prove to be right, and Dörffel's common sense does not prevail. (NyA IV, 235)

3 NyA IV, 180.

as the reason for her sudden change, on hearing of the preceptor, from indifference and boredom to lively interest.

The appropriation by Rodenstein of a vicar's duty in preaching was initially due to his failing sight at seventy years of age, which rendered impossible his duty as reader in church. The analogy with Cécile is clear: she also at a particular stage in life repented of a wrong done, and the remainder of her life is spent in trying to forget or atone for it. Her desire for an idyllic existence of peace and quiet contains a longing for a return to innocence. Later in Chapter 23 she tells Gordon that she has seen enough guilt.[1] Her lively enthusiasm for the preceptor anecdote is denoted also in the unusual vivacity of her reaction to Gordon's suggestion that they should visit Altenbrak. The interpretation given by the old scholar when he tells the anecdote in Chapter 11 is however turned on its head by the preceptor himself in Chapter 14, when he reveals to St. Arnaud that conscience played the lesser part in his resignation than arrogance. This arrogance expressed itself in his desire to avoid the presentation from the community of a little volume, which he regarded as less than his due on the occasion of his jubilee. His resignation was therefore a refusal to be treated according to the usual pattern for a poor village schoolmaster. The fact that Rodenstein is a humorous character seems to have distracted the attention of commentators from his own claim to arrogance. Besides his humour however Rodenstein's only claim to superiority over the other figures would be his recognition of the fault which they also share. The very fault therefore, which was being expiated in the anecdote as told by the old scholar in Chapter 11, namely arrogance, is in fact the motivation for the teacher's resignation, not the humility which comes from pangs of conscience. In both the scholar's anecdote and the true account of the story given by the teacher himself in Chapter 14, the word 'Dünkel'[2] is used. Instead of resigning on recognizing his arrogance, he resigned f r o m arrogance. Gerhard Friedrich sees the teacher's story as another example of things' not being what they should be or what they appear to be in the novel,

1 NyA IV, 262.
2 Ibid. IV, 181 and 206.

as in the empty castle at Quedlinburg, a shell containing no realities or Gordon, the moralist, who quickly adopts society's condemnation of Cécile once he discovers the truth about her, but who does not abjure her company because it may profit him, and the so-called honour of St. Arnaud which requires a duel to appease his vanity and possessiveness.[1]

Like Cécile and St. Arnaud, the village teacher is a prey to vanity. His resignation was prompted by a mixture of arrogance and wounded vanity. In Chapter 23 Cécile also admits to her vanity, which had been the cause of her involvement with Gordon, but he has already forgiven her for it on grounds of her superficial upbringing as a being destined to please.[2] St. Arnaud fails to see through his own over-sensitivity in matters of honour as a form of vanity. His last letter to Cécile shows how little he has learnt from the death of Gordon. This second duel merely repeats the pattern of the first with Dzialinski, with the variation that Gordon loves Cécile. In his letter St. Arnaud admits that Cécile was emotionally attached to Gordon, but the measure of his own coolness and detachment is shown when he draws the curtain on this intimate sphere with the words: "Aber nimm das Ganze nicht tragischer, als nötig: die Welt ist kein Treibhaus für überzarte Gefühle."[3] The hothouse metaphor, meant by Pierre as encouragement and consolation, could only be an insult to a woman as sensitive as Cécile, and is a last indication of the width of the abyss between her and her husband. After this, Cécile's suicide comes as no surprise to the reader.

In this novel anecdotes play an important role in the gradual revelation of the character of Cécile. As already indicated, the narrator's task in the first twenty chapters is to conceal her secret, while at the same time revealing as much as possible about Cécile's character. The fact that Gordon and the reader are both intrigued by her character and past means that each indication about these is carefully registered. However, it is not until Chapter 21 with the

1 See G. Friedrich: 'Die Schuldfrage in Fontanes "Cécile"' in JDSG 14, 1970, p. 541-542 and 544.

2 NyA IV, 255 (Chapter 22).

3 Ibid. 282.

revelation of Cécile's secret that the pieces of the jigsaw-puzzle fall into place. The important role of the anecdotes in the chapters preceding the revelation resides therefore in their relationship with that revelation. The anecdotes indirectly hint in advance at the secret which the narrator cannot divulge.[1] Since the narrator only rarely reveals the thoughts of Cécile, the anecdotes provide an externalization of certain facets of her psychological make-up. As we have seen, they also provide parallel indications to the main plot, e.g. the isolation of Pierre, and more especially of Cécile, from society is reflected in the Regenstein and Rodenstein anecdotes.[2] Society's retaliation on those who do not accept its norms is indicated in these stories also. It is the hidden parallel provided by these tales which rouses Cécile each time from her own preoccupation with herself to show an interest in something else. However, the only reason for this interest is precisely because of the parallels indicated. The Rodenstein anecdote and the mirror anecdote both help to illustrate the theme of vanity. Vanity is the main motive force of the characters, even though they do not all realize it. Cécile at least admits this fault, but not very long before the dénouement. The mirror anecdote makes the point not just about vanity, but also about Cécile's imprisonment within her own circumstances. Thus this story is a reflection within the narrative of Fontane's above-quoted

1 Cf. in this connection Magdalene Heuser: op. cit., p. 55-56 on the relationship between "Cécile" and the 'Kriminalgeschichte'. The analysis of the anecdotes used in "Unterm Birnbaum" (see below Chapter 2) clearly shows that Fontane had no difficulty in using little inserted stories to maximum effect in the context of the 'Kriminalgeschichte'.

2 Although the St. Arnauds are divorced from society in the ordinary sense, a temporary cohesion is built up in the Harz region between them, the hotel guests, Rosa and Gordon, so that the requisite social atmosphere is created in which anecdotes can thrive. When they return to Berlin the narration of anecdotes abruptly breaks off – with the exception of Dörffel's tale about Pope Gregory XVI. This narrative item alone indicates Cécile's social dilemmna. The exception of Dörffel proves the rule: he is the only one of Cécile's Berlin acquaintances who sincerely cares for her – even Gordon's motives turn out to be ulterior. Gerhard Friedrich's view of Dörffel is excessively negative. See G. Friedrich: op. cit., p.545.

statement to Mathilde von Rohr about guilt.[1] The change in Gordon's treatment of Cécile after the revelation about her past is due both to his appropriation of society's disapproval and to a mixture of arrogance and vanity. Frequently in Fontane's fiction a character who is himself far from perfect correctly points out the inadequacies in someone else. In this case, St. Arnaud's letter after the duel characterizes Gordon in one short sentence: "Im Grunde seines Herzens was er hochmütig und eingebildet."[2]

The anecdotes in "Cécile" are employed in order to give indirect characterization, to provide parallels to the characters' situation, to provide anticipation of future plot development and to hint at the important motive force which brings about the denouement, namely the characteristic of vanity.[3]

4. "Frau Jenny Treibel" (1892)

"Frau Jenny Treibel" is extremely economical with regard to narration, the complete work comprising only seventeen chapters. Similarly there is economy in the use of anecdotes in this novel. This economy is allied with a highly artistic use of anecdotes, anecdote reflections and reflections on the anecdote. Subtle parallels are created between the novel as a whole and the foreign material from which it borrows. The anecdotes occur in "Frau Jenny Treibel" in the chapters about the dinner-party given by Professor Wilibald Schmidt for his colleagues, the school-teachers who call their group: "Die sieben Waisen Griechenlands".[4] The significance of this name

1 See above p. 45.
2 NyA IV, 283.
3 Only in one other work did Fontane use the same anecdote more than once, in "Vor dem Sturm". For a discussion of this device, see Chapter Two below. The repetition of the key-anecdote about Rodenstein in "Cécile" is very effective, because the second narration in Chapter 14 totally changes the interpretation offered in Chapter 11. Thereby the reader's attention is drawn to the anecdote's great significance for the novel as a whole.
4 NyA VII, 51.

has not yet been fully commented on in critical literature. A group of seven was a favourite notion of Fontane, but in practice in this novel only four of them are presented to the reader in person, Schmidt, who is a major character in any case, Distelkamp and Friedeberg who play a certain role in Chapters 6 and 7, and Charles Etienne, who is very much a sound-box for Schmidt. The remaining three, Hannibal Kuh, Professor Rindfleisch and Immanuel Schultze, are mentioned on only a few pages of the novel and remain very much within the sphere of narrator comment. Not only does Schmidt aim at self-irony, "den denkbar höchsten Standpunkt",[1] by styling the group The Seven Sages of Greece, but also the reader's attention is drawn immediately to the many anecdotes associated with the Seven Sages and to their aphoristic wisdom, much of which can be related to themes in "Frau Jenny Treibel". Constancy and fidelity, a subject of discussion in the Sages' aphorisms, is a major theme of the novel, especially in Chapters 5 and 6. Frivolity, extravagance and avarice are condemned by the Sages; for a time, these tendencies hold sway over Corinna, when she tries to follow the lure of wealth and luxury. An amusing parallel between the aphorisms and the novel is the warning of Cleobulus that one should only marry someone of similar rank, so that one avoids getting masters instead of relations.[2] Similarly, Pittacus on the question of choosing a marriage-partner advises: "Keep to your own sphere!"[3] The major theme of the Seven Sages is also implicit in the novel, that of the necessity of moderation. The motto of Cleobulus was: "Moderation is best," and throughout the aphorisms of the Seven Sages great emphasis is placed on the middle road as opposed to extremes. Another theme of the Seven Sages, self-knowledge,[4] is reflected in the novel as a whole and is implicit in the Barfus anecdote narrated in Chapter 6.

1 NyA VII, 51.

2 See Diogenes Laertius: "Lives of Eminent Philosophers". With an English translation by Robert Drew Hicks, London, New York 1925, vol. 1, p.95.

3 Ibid. p. 83.

4 A quotation from Pindar: "Werde, der du bist," used by Schmidt in Chapter 16 before Corinna's reconciliation with Marcell, points in the same direction. See NyA VII, 159.

The narrator of the Barfus anecdote is Distelkamp, whose views on education differ from those of Professor Schmidt. The former prefers a more traditional and stricter approach to disciplining school-boys. This difference of views about their profession and Distelkamp's narration of the Barfus anecdote (both of which can ultimately be related to each other, as an analysis of that anecdote will show) appear to be the only reasons for his inclusion in the novel. His toast is mentioned in Chapter 16 as being the best at Corinna's wedding, but his role in that chapter is reflected only in comments of the narrator. The Barfus anecdote was a favourite of Fontane, and his artistic achievement in employing it in "Frau Jenny Treibel" lies in the manner in which it is naturally introduced into the conversation and ultimately becomes an important link for an interpretation of the entire novel. This story appears also in the "Oderland" volume of Fontane's "Wanderungen durch die Mark Brandenburg" and he also refers to it in correspondence. This military anecdote fits in admirably with the novel as a whole which makes mock-heroic use of military images and metaphors. Its narrator, the former history teacher, Distelkamp, was obliged as a young teacher, who was only one step ahead of his pupils, to read up historical memoirs at night in order to have enough material for class next day. The immediate cause for the narration of this anecdote is the deliberate absence from the dinner-party of another colleague, who has made a blunder in class that day and has gone to the theatre in order to recover some of his standing. Thus, the anecdote from the military sphere is made to relate directly to the situation in hand, the absence of a particular guest, which provides a realistic and convincing opening for the evening's conversation between teachers. It is interesting from the point of view of Fontane's art as a novelist to observe the changes made by him for "Frau Jenny Treibel", both on the original anecdote[1] and on his own earlier version in "Das Oderland".

1 His source for the anecdote was Franz Wilhelm von Barfus-Falkenberg's book: "Hans Albrecht von Barfus. Königlich-Preußischer Generalfeldmarschall. Ein Beitrag zur Kriegsgeschichte unter den Kurfürsten Friedrich Wilhelm und Friedrich III von Brandenburg". Berlin 1854. See Aufbau VI

Barfus-Falkenberg's version (1854)	Fontane's novel version (1892)
	... da las ich – denn wir waren gerade beim ersten König – allerhand Biographisches und darunter auch was vom alten General Barfus, der, wie die meisten damaligen, das Pulver nicht erfunden hatte, sonst aber ein kreuzbraver Mann war. Und dieser Barfus präsidierte, während der Belagerung von Bonn, einem Kriegsgericht, drin über einem jungen Offizier abgeurteilt werden sollte. ...
Ich beklagte mich über die Feigheit des Offiziers bei dem General von Barfus. Hören Sie, Graf, man muß Mitleid mit seinem Nächsten haben und ihm nich alles Ueble anthun, was man mit Gerechtigkeit würde anthun können. Es gibt schlechte Viertelstunden im Leben, vielleicht wird dieser Offizier ein andermal sich besser zeigen. Ich werde mit ihm allein reden. – Er sprach wirklich mit ihm allein und dieser Offizier, indem er zu einem andern Angriffe kommandirt wurde, setzte sich, um seinen Fehler wieder gut zu machen, so sehr aus, daß er getödtet wurde.[1]	Der Abzuurteilende hatte sich, das mindeste zu sagen, etwas unheldisch benommen, und alle waren für Schuldig und Totschießen. Nur der alte Barfus wollte nichts davon wissen und sagte: "Drücken wir ein Auge zu, meine Herren. Ich habe dreißig Rencontres mitgemacht, und ich muß Ihnen sagen, ein Tag ist nicht wie der andere, und der Mensch ist ungleich und das Herz auch und der Mut erst recht. Ich habe mich manches Mal auch feige gefühlt. Solange es geht, muß man Milde walten lassen, denn jeder kann sie brauchen.[2]

The version of this story which Fontane included in "Das Oderland" (1863) is included here, as the differences between it and the version in "Frau Jenny Treibel" are also significant. It runs as follows:

541. The anecdote is also contained in the memoirs of another character from the historical story, Christoph Graf Dohna. See "Die Denkwürdigkeiten des Burggrafen und Grafen Christoph zu Dohna (1665-1733)". Eingeleitet, erläutert und deutsch herausgegeben von Rudolf Frieser, Göttingen 1974, p. 55.

1 Barfus-Falkenberg: op. cit., p. 37.

2 NyA VII, 53.

> Tapfer, wie Hans Albrecht war, besaß er auch in hohem Maße jenen liebenswürdigen, am häufigsten bei bewährten alten Soldaten vorkommenden Zug, schwache Momente nachsichtig zu beurteilen. Nur die Leute hinterm warmen Ofen dringen auf beständiges Heldentum. Einmal beklagte sich der Graf Christoph Dohna über die Feigheit eines Offiziers, der ihn während des Gefechts kläglich im Stich gelassen habe. Barfus trat an Dohna heran und sagte: "Hören Sie, Graf, man muß Mitleid mit seinem Nächsten haben und ihm nicht alles Üble antun, was man ihm mit Gerechtigkeit antun könnte. Es gibt schlechte Viertelstunden im Leben. Vielleicht wird dieser Offizier ein andermal sich besser zeigen. Ich werde mit ihm allein reden." Barfus tat es, und wenige Tage später fiel der Offizier an der Spitze der Angriffskolonne.[1]

Count Christoph Dohna narrates the story in the Barfus book, is retained as a character in the "Oderland" version of the story, and he also plays a role in the rest of the chapter on the historical Barfus there, but Dohna is excluded from the novel: an extra character would only unnecessarily confuse the narration in the novel situation. Dohna's concern about the cowardice of the officer, which is recorded in the source material and retained in "Das Oderland", is altered in "Frau Jenny Treibel" into a military tribunal, the members of which, except Barfus, are all for the condemnation of the offending officer. The altered situation in the novel version as opposed to the earlier versions makes the anecdote much more dramatic: Barfus confronts with his own opposing view this united group, which has the power of an immediate decision affecting the life or death of the officer. It is no longer simply a matter of a difference of approach between two senior officers, as is the case in the earlier versions.

The narrator in "Das Oderland" introduces the story with some generalizations on the topic of attitudes towards heroism, a favourite topic of Fontane which comes in for treatment again in his last novel in the form of an anecdote. The "Wanderungen" version of the story about Barfus is related in order to characterize what kind of soldier he was, the portrayal of Barfus being divided into two sections dealing with Barfus the soldier and Barfus the

1 NyA X, 377-378.

soldier and Barfus the courtier. The death of the officer, a fact of the source material, is omitted in the novel. This death is – at least for the non-military reader – a rather gruesome proof of the correctness of Barfus' prognostication.

While the message of the speech by Barfus is the same in all three versions, his language is more clipped and soldierly in Barfus-Falkenberg's version and in "Das Oderland" than in "Frau Jenny Treibel". In the novel he expresses himself more like one of Fontane's fictional characters. The conversational style in the novel version is simpler and lays more emphasis on the personal element. Barfus' statement lays heavy emphasis on the first person. The first person plural appears once, followed by three sentences beginning with the first person singular in a style that is marked by the use of the conjunction 'and': "Drücken w i r ein Auge zu, meine Herren. I c h habe dreißig Rencontres mitgemacht, u n d i c h muß Ihnen sagen, ein Tag is nicht wie der andere, u n d der Mensch ist ungleich u n d das Herz auch u n d der Mut erst recht. I c h habe mich manches Mal auch feige gefühlt." The only time in the earlier versions that Barfus uses the first person singular is in his statement that he will speak to the offending officer, which he does not do in the novel version. In the fictional version it is not merely a matter of letting mercy go before justice as in the earlier ones, but of admitting one's own weakness. In stressing that all human hearts are inconstant, that we all i.e. even the bravest and most experienced, have moments of weakness, the fictional Barfus makes a broader statement about human nature than that contained in the rather terse original: "Es gibt schlechte Viertelstunden im Leben." The death of the reformed officer in the original is replaced in the fictional context by an admittance that human weakness is universal and that one must exercise mildness because one may need it one day oneself. Thus the stylistic emphasis on the first person in the fictional version of the anecdote has its counterpart in the new message. In none of the earlier versions, Dohna's memoirs, Barfus-Falkenberg's monograph and "Das Oderland" does Barfus admit to having himself been cowardly on occasion. He does so in "Frau Jenny Treibel" in order to excuse the officer and to support his general point that the individual behaves differently in similar situations at different moments during his lifetime. This point is particularly well brought out in the novel version with its stress – appropriate for a Fontane character! – on terms like human being, heart and courage. The statement by Barfus about the human being's differing reactions at different moments is proven in a concrete way by the subsequent death of the officer in the earlier versions. A neat concurrence exists between Barfus' statement and the end of the anecdote in these earlier versions. This neat proof is dispensed with in the novel in favour of a more open ending which lays emphasis on the general statement that leniency should be exercised because all men may at some stage need it. An understanding of the significance of the Barfus anecdote as used in "Frau Jenny Treibel" requires familiarity not merely with its context in Chapter 6, but also with the surrounding chapters and with the plot of the novel as a whole. Inconstancy of the heart, hinted at in the anecdote, has already been brought up in the narrower sense of disloyalty to a beloved in Chapter 5, when Marcell reproaches Corinna for trying to dazzle Leopold Treibel during Jenny's dinner-party. The external cause of the reproach is their hearing the clock chime the tune: "Üb' immer Treu' und Redlichkeit".[1] This theme of 'Treue' receives further emphasis – a f t e r the narration of the Barfus anecdote – during the teachers' conversation at the end of Chapter 6, when Schmidt praises the loyalty of Friedeberg's dog and indirectly chastizes Friedeberg himself for his lack of loyalty to his wife: "Denn die Treue, von der heutzutage jeder red't, wird in Wahrheit immer rarer."[2] Marcell complains to Schmidt at the end of Chapter 7 after the teachers disperse, that although Schmidt appreciates his daughter's good points, he is unaware of the extent to which she has become affected by the negative,superficial aspects of the era. A little later Marcell summarizes on the painful revelations of his conversation with Corinna in Chapter 5: "Ich sah zu meinem Schmerz, wie veräußerlicht sie ist, und wie die verdammte neue Zeit sie ganz in Banden hält."[3] Corinna's surrender to the lure of luxury

1 NyA VII, 46.
2 Ibid. 59.
3 Ibid. 69.

offered by Leopold's attraction to her is interpreted by her lover as a surrender to the materialism of the Wilhelmine Era.[1] It is a betrayal of the values of the educated class to which she, as Professor Schmidt's daughter and a person of obvious intelligence, rightly belongs. Corinna realizes that the monied bourgeois manufacturing class to which the Treibels belong does not offer her everything she appreciates. This does not, however, prevent her from going ahead with plans to marry Leopold in spite of opposition from both social poles in the novel, represented by Marcell and Jenny.

Marcell's recognition of Corinna's error and his impatience with Schmidt's lack of interference in Corinna's plan is paralleled in the Barfus anecdote by the military tribunal, which wants immediate action taken against the offending officer. Schmidt, however, who enjoys the anecdote so much and promises to remember it, favours a Barfusian approach. He knows, like Barfus, that a person reacts differently at different moments in life, and it is essentially this message which Schmidt conveys to Marcell in Chapter 7, although he expresses it in different words. A similar sentiment is expressed in Melusine's wise words about humility to Lorenzen in "Der Stechlin": "Wer demütig ist, der ist duldsam, weil er weiß, wie sehr er selbst der Duldsamkeit bedarf; wer demütig ist, der sieht die Scheidewände fallen und den Menschen im Menschen."[2]

Fontane's use of the Barfus anecdote in the novel version shifts the focus of attention, as has already been indicated, from the actual events of the source to the personal element. The language used in the novel version is more expressive and the subjective element comes more to the fore with the stress on the 'I' of Barfus and on words like 'heart'. The fact that the fictional Barfus confesses his own lack of courage at times is endearing and adds moral authority to his judgement. The story's being told, not in a military situation as in the original, but in a social situation –teachers talking about education – prepares the reader for a wider application of the

1 This tallies with Corinna's own statement about sharing the modern desire for wealth: "Ein Hang nach Wohlleben, der jetzt alle Welt beherrscht, hat mich auch in der Gewalt, ganz so wie alle anderen." (NyA VII, 49).

2 NyA VIII, 250.

anecdote. Professor Schmidt's reception of it indicates that it well expresses his own feeling for life. In his lack of reaction to Corinna's temporary 'Treibelei',[1] her 'Schritt vom Wege',[2] i.e. her abandonment of the principles of her educated background in the attempt to surround herself with an atmosphere of luxury and wealth, Professor Schmidt puts into practice the message of the Barfus anecdote. Leniency must be exercised at all times towards the faults of others. They may act differently on another occasion and one may oneself at times be in need of leniency.

To interpret Schmidt's lack of action here exclusively as demonstrating the passivity of the German educated bourgeoisie of the later nineteenth century, as Dieter Kafitz does, ignores both the important pointer of the Barfus anecdote in the crucial setting in Chapter 6 and the overall sympathetic portrayal of Schmidt.[3] Schmidt's faults, such as they are, do not essentially endanger his daughter's fate. His lack of action cannot be interpreted as a thoroughly culpable passivity, whether personal or standing for a whole class. The novel never leaves the level of comedy, because Corinna's basic good sense and intelligence assure her ultimate safety. Her illusion of self-determination is not shattered from the beginning by the machinations of an interfering parent. In Chapter 7, Schmidt defines for Marcell the 'Schmidt element',[4]

1 NyA VII, 81.
2 Ibid. 159.
3 Dieter Kafitz: 'Die Kritik am Bildungsbürgertum in Fontanes Roman "Frau Jenny Treibel" ' in ZfdPh. 92, 1973, SH, p.74-101.
4 On the portrayal of the educated class as opposed to the monied class, see Walter Müller-Seidel: "Theodor Fontane. Soziale Romankunst in Deutschland", p. 285-319, Walter Horace Bruford: 'Frau Jenny Treibel (1892)' in W. H. Bruford: "The German Tradition in Self-Cultivation. 'Bildung' from Humboldt to Thomas Mann". Cambridge 1975, p. 299-320, Gerhard Wedereit: 'Leitmotivische Wiederholung: Beobachtungen zu Tecknik und Ethos in Fontanes "Frau Jenny Treibel" ' in "Acta Germanica" 7, 1972, p. 117-125, and Hartmut Reinhardt: 'Die Wahrheit des Sentimentalen: Bemerkungen zu zwei Romanschlüssen bei Theodor Fontane: "Frau Jenny Treibel" und "Effi Briest" ' in WW 5, 1979, p. 318-326.

'das Schmidtsche', in terms which reflect the moral message of the Barfus anecdote. His confidence is based on the knowledge that Corinna's apparent waywardness and attraction to the materialism of the age are simply due to a passing fancy and to her verbal brilliance:

> ... Und wenn sie sich darin gefallen hat, dir von Modernität zu sprechen, und dir vielleicht eine Pariser Hutnadel oder eine Sommerjacke, dran alles chic und wieder chic ist, zu beschreiben und so zu tun, als ob es in der ganzen Welt nichts gäbe, was an Wert und Schönheit damit verglichen werden könnte, so ist das alles bloß Feuerwerk, Phantasietätigkeit, jeu d'esprit, und wenn es ihr morgen paßt dir einen Pfarramtskandidaten in der Jasminlaube zu beschreiben, der selig in Lottchens Armen ruht, so leistet sie das mit demselben Aplomb und mit derselben Virtuosität.[1]

The juxtaposition of differing ideals is jocosely made here by Schmidt with the symbol of the Paris hatpin and the idyllic image of Lottchen and the poor clergyman. These indicate the poles of wealth and elegance (and implicitly, emotional sterility) versus true love and financial insecurity. These are in fact the poles between which Corinna swings in the story until the happy denouement. To abandon the hope of an alliance with Leopold and accept Marcell's proposal requires courage on Corinna's part. She has to admit her own blindness in giving way to social ambitions instead of following more closely her natural instincts. The courage element here is a further link between the main plot and the inserted Barfus anecdote. Some criticism of the educated class is undoubtedly contained in the novel. Fontane is never so one-sided as to show only faults in any section of society. Corinna's attempt to marry into the monied class parallels Jenny's own striving, but on Corinna's part this is a definite "Schritt vom Wege", whereas on Jenny's it is a life-long role. Corinna is never blind to the fact that her action represents a betrayal of the values of her class. Finally she admits defeat and a willingness to return to the fold.

1 NyA VII, 69

The gastronomical conversation of Chapter 7 incorporates another of Fontane's favourite anecdotes. Friedeberg by virtue of his place of origin relates the tale of the time it rained crabs in the eighteenth century in Kustrin. This is a perfectly natural subject of conversation for a dinner-party starting with a crab dish,[1] and the conversation may jump smartly from the personal qualities and lacks of Schmidt's housekeeper, Frau Schmolke, via George Sand's relations with Alfred Musset to Schmidt's favourite topic, namely that what is normally taken as the important material of history is in fact far less interesting than the human element.

Schmidt supports his argument with the concrete example that a few Frederician anecdotes mean more to him than important Prussian battles like Hohenfriedberg, Leuthen or Torgau. Thus the landmarks of the Seven Years' War are relegated to a position of less importance than stories which reveal a personal characteristic of Frederick the Second. In the anecdotes from the military sphere, a more military type of heroism is evident. The anecdotes referred to by Schmidt in connection with Frederick demonstrate the monarch's pessimism and contempt for human nature, his desire for fairness and fear of corruption in high places, his power of witty formulation and his expectation that his soldiers are always ready to die in battle. Schmidt's favourite stories are standard Frederician anecdotes: the one about wanting to be buried with his dogs, because mankind is a 'mechante Rasse';[2] his reprimand to Kupferberg, president of the tribunal which decided against the Miller Arnold in the Miller Arnold law case; his witty reproach to retreating soldiers in battle: "Rackers, wollt ihr denn ewig leben?"[3]

1 D. Kafitz however sees this conversation as showing a "Verlust an Inhalt" and finds that the teachers' humanist education is merely "unengagiertes Epigonentum". (Kafitz: op. cit., p.82) Alan Bance contrasts on the other hand Jenny's warning to Leo not to rob himself through an engagement to Corinna of the foundations on which life rests (i.e. money) with Schmidt's "hymn to life in the form of a paean to the humble crab". (A. Bance: "Theodor Fontane: The Major Novels". Cambridge 1982, p.151)

2 NyA VII, 62.

3 Ibidem. This is a truncated version of the anecdote which Fontane renders

Schmidt's defence of his position against Distelkamps's dismissive rejoinder that only 'das Große'[1] is for him of interest in history, has often been noted as an expression of Fontane's own outlook:

> Das Nebensächliche, so viel ist richtig, gilt nichts, wenn es bloß nebensächlich ist, wenn nichts drin steckt. Steckt aber was drin, dann ist es die Hauptsache, denn es gibt einem dann immer das eigentlich Menschliche.[2]

The large historical events only are of interest to Distelkamp. To Schmidt, like Fontane, the smaller ones are of great interest. The anecdote, which draws its interest from small things, shows also 'das Menschliche', the human element. Schmidt's observation quoted above amounts to a defence of the place of anecdote in history and an immediate connection is made with literature, for Schmidt immediately goes on to a hobby-horse of his, as the narrator lets us know, by saying: "Das Poetische wächst über das Historische hinaus."[3] In mid-sentence, this discussion is interrupted by the return of Marcell and Corinna from the Treibels' dinner-party. But the interruption is neatly arranged a f t e r the important points have been made. It is not simply fortuitous either that the two should enter precisely at this point. The narrator wishes to make a link

in full in his poem "Bei Torgau", (included in his "Gedichte" since 1889), where the grenadiers give Frederick a saucy reply (NyA XX, 217):

> Auch die Grenadiere wollen nicht mehr.
> Wie ein Rasender jagt der König daher
> und hebt den Stock und ruft unter Beben:
> "Racker, wollt ihr denn ewig leben?
> Bedrüger ..."
> "Fritze, nichts von Bedrug;
> Für fünfzehn Pfennig ist's heute genug.

1 NyA VII, 62. Compare similar sentiments in the characters' discussion of the anecdote about Christian IV of Denmark in "Unwiederbringlich". (NyA V, 149-150)

2 NyA VII, 62

3 Ibidem. As so often in this novel, Schmidt makes a pronouncement which could equally well have been made by Fontane himself.

between the Corinna-Marcell plot and the foregoing conversation.

Retrospectively, Schmidt's reflections on the anecdote in Chapter 7 give the reader the clue to an understanding of why he was so enthusiastic about the Barfus anecdote in Chapter 6. The 'officially' important siege is merely alluded to in the anecdote, which concerns a humane and wise approach to a human problem. In the light of the history of the times, it may seem a minor detail, a secondary item, but to Schmidt, as in the case of the Frederician anecdotes, the anecdote contains that element which is eminently worthwhile: the human element. By the clever tacit linking of Schmidt's reflections on the anecdote as such in Chapter 7 with the practical example of the Barfus anecdote in Chapter 6 and the coupling of this with the entry of Corinna, the narrator is able to establish a further implicit relation between Corinna and the Barfus anecdote.

In a follow-up conversation between Schmidt and Marcell in Chapter 15, the latter is confirmed in his resolve to propose to Corinna again. This conversation again contains allusions which underline the relevance of the Barfus anecdote, e.g. the term "brief aberration"[1] is used to describe Corinna's action, while Marcell expresses himself as being glad that he does not belong to "den Feierlichen".[2] Marcell also makes a passing reference to the old Jewish law according to which it is wrong to shame a fellow human being in public.[3] This is another reflection which offers a parallel to the message of the Barfus story.

The motif of the heart, which is heralded in the sub-title, "Wie sich Herz zum Herzen findet", recurs throughout the novel and is also given an important place in the Barfus anecdote.[4] Fontane must have deliberately chosen to make a further connection between the Barfus story and the rest of the novel by including a heart reference in Distelkamp's narrative. There is no reference whatsoever to the

1 NyA VII, 155.

2 Ibid. 157.

3 Ibidem. See TB Baba Mezia 59A: "Man should rather have himself thrown into a furnace than put his neighbour to shame." Cf. Misnah Aboth 3: 11.

4 See the list of heart references in "Frau Jenny Treibel" noted in A. Bance: op. cit., p. 155-156.

heart either in the source material or in Fontane's own 1863 version of the incident. In Chapter 5 Marcell describes his new rival, Leopold, as an insignificant person who has however "ein gutes, weiches Herz, nichts von dem Kiesel, den die Geldleute sonst hier links haben".[1] Jenny's favourite song, her 'Herzenslied'[2] with its key-line: "Was soll Gold",[3] draws attention through its direct contradiction in the plot itself to the lack of heart in Jenny's machinations. To use Marcell's metaphor, she has a 'pebblestone on the left-hand side" in spite of her show of fine feeling and values of the heart. Only through being true to her own heart (described as healthy, honest and sincere by Schmidt in Chapter 15) and through renunciation of 'gold' can Corinna turn the tragicomedy into a story with the happy ending which is hinted at in the sub-title. One cannot speak of course of an absolutely happy ending. This is shown both in Corinna's observations on happiness: "Aber wer ist glücklich? Kennst du wen? Ich nicht,"[4] and also in the fact that the close of the novel

1 NyA VII, 48. Not only are references made to the hearts of main characters, but even the deceased Herr Schmolke, who lives on only in his wife's stories, had "ein Herz im Leibe". (NyA VII, 120) This was his comforting phrase to assuage his wife's jealousy when he had to deal with prostitutes in the line of duty. It was precisely such a scene in which Frau Schmolke would talk of her deceased husband and then comment on the following day's menu, which Corinna paints in Chapter 5 to Marcell in order to describe her distaste for the limitations of her present life and to show how, in the light of such a scene, Leopold appears as the 'Rettungsanker' (ibid. 49) of her life. This scene with Marcell is certainly a conscious prefiguration of the scene in Chapter 10 after the engagement. Corinna has just been ensnaring the biddable Leopold and laying her plans for rise into higher spheres. Immediately afterwards, she is confronted with Frau Schmolke's simple story of the love of two people for each other and the anguish that jealousy can cause' "Aber Eifersucht ist sehr stark, viel stärker als Liebe;" (ibid. 119) While the Barfus anecdote is addressed to Schmidt (and more widely to the reader), and helps to explain his non-interference in Corinna's life, Frau Schmolke's story is addressed to Corinna, and helps her (unknown to the teller) to understand what she is doing to Marcell, although it takes longer for her to come to terms with the problem.

2 Ibid. 165.

3 Ibid. 43 and 166.

4 Ibid. 160.

alludes to a synthesis of the poetic and the historical, the natural and the moral, a synthesis which remains unrealized, indeed unrealizable.[1]

A comparison of Fontane's use of the same Barfus story in the context of the travel literature of the early eighteen-sixties and the fictional context of the early eighteen-nineties with the source material allows some observations on his different approach as a novelist to the same material. Through his subtle alterations in the second version of the tale, it receives at the same time a more personal imprint a n d a wider application than was the case in his original use of the anecdote. Repetition of the Barfus anecdote does not at all suggest a falling-off in Fontane's originality or powers of composition – the anecdote in its later setting of the nineties is changed considerably and intimately worked into the structure of the literary work. It is made a significant part of the new context. It provides a good example of Fontane's productive appropriation of foreign material as well as of his own development as a writer between the eighteen-sixties and the nineties. Fontane's fiction of the nineties shows a sharpened sensitivity to the possibilities of the use of anecdote, a sensitivity which may have already been present in the writer of "Vor dem Sturm", but which was not always successfully realized there or in the following work, "L'Adultera". It becomes increasingly apparent however (with the exception of "Graf Petöfy") in the works of the eighteen-eighties following "Schach von Wuthenow". After the appearance of "Frau Jenny Treibel", two further creations of the eighteen-nineties demonstrate Fontane's greater assurance in the employment of anecdote. These are "Effi Briest" (1894) and "Der Stechlin" (1898).

1 Cf. W. Müller-Seidel: op. cit., p. 318-319. Note Fontane's incorrect reference to Friedrich Schlegel's dictum: "Der Historiker ist ein rückwärts gekehrter Prophet" in his review of Josef Viktor von Scheffel's novel "Ekkehard" (1855): 'Wenn mit Recht gesagt worden ist, der große Historiker müsse immer auch Poet sein, so ist es ebenso wahr, daß jeder echte Poet ein Verständnis für das Historische mitbringt." (NyA XXI, i,251)

5. "Effi Briest" (1892)

In one sense, "Effi Briest" is the novel which of all Fontane's works offers the bleakest picture of life. Even an initially apparently charmed life like Effi's becomes fraught with anxiety and loneliness. The only refuge is resignation. The anecdotes support this underlying message. Marianne Devine rightly emphasizes that the novel with its broad net of chiffres and motif repetitions is not simply making a point about conflict between individual and society, but is indirectly questioning whether it is possible at all to form a true relationship.[1] Human frailty is clear in the story: Effi is unfaithful to Instetten, Crampas often deceives his wife, and on the level of minor characters, Briest's gardener's wife has an affair, and Roswitha has in the past been abandoned by the father of her illegitimate child. In Chapter 15, Effi's father discusses with her the loyalty of dogs and claims that animals are superior to humans. Innstetten's dog protects Effi from the 'ghost' and grieves for days without eating on her grave at the end of the novel. The only lasting testimonies of loyalty in the story are those of the simple maid, Roswitha, and of the dog, Rollo.

Just as Crampas uses literature, Heine's poems, to impress Effi in their first scene alone together in Chapter 17, Effi's anecdotes in the novel are of literary origin. In Chapter 18 Effi avoids Crampas during the party at Uvagla, just as she had avoided him all during the winter rehearsals of Ernst Wichert's play "Ein Schritt vom Wege". The scene takes place just before the crucial situation in the sleigh on the way back to Kessin, in which Effi succumbs for the first to Crampas's advances. Her anecdote at the party is based on

1 M. Devine: 'Erzähldistanz in Fontanes Effi Briest'. In "Formen Realistischer Erzählkunst".Festschrift for Charlotte Jolles. Ed. by Jörg Thuneke in conjunction with Eda Sagarra. Nottingham 1979, p. 548: "In der Ehe erfährt der Mensch die Fragwürdigkeit und Vergeblichkeit echter Bindungen; aber erst im Ausbruch aus der Ehe, im Ehebruch, erschließt sich ihm die ganze Einsicht in die eigene Isolierung und Entfremdung, die einen Anderen nicht erreichen kann".

Brentano's ballad "Gottesmauer" and it appropriately expresses her conscious wish to avoid danger and surrender:

> Da war irgendwo Krieg, ein Winterfeldzug, und eine alte Witwe, die sich vor dem Feinde mächtig fürchtete, betete zu Gott, er möge doch 'eine Mauer um sie bauen', um sie vor dem Landesfeinde zu schützen. Und da ließ Gott das Haus einschneien, und der Feind zog daran vorüber.[1]

The circumstances in which Effi tells Crampas this little story make her narration of it convincing. The possibility of their being snowed up in Uvagla makes the association with the snowfall in the anecdote seem natural and unforced. But this circumstantial reference to her notion of "Schutz und Beistand"[2] is of course a reference to her moral situation. Her references back to the Heine poems, "Seegespenst" and "Vitzliputzli", which were the subject of their first intimate conversation, as well as Crampas's visible embarrassment and changing of the subject, show this. This use of the anecdote to externalize a basic fear or emotion on the character's part is a good example of the restrained nature of Fontane's art – the fictional characters refer to their innermost feelings indirectly, with a minimum of pathos and without sentimentality.

The extent of Effi's feeling of endangerment through the advances of Crampas is well brought out through her return to this Romantic ballad. Significantly, the childhood setting in which she learned the poem also is the only happy setting she had known.[3] The home in Hohen-Cremmen exists as a constant yardstick by which Effi can measure the sterility of the present. Only there does she also reach peace again before her death. The reference to childhood in

1 NyA VII, 299.

2 Ibid. 298.

3 According to Cordula Kahrmann, the indirect associations with death of the apparent idyllic setting of Hohen-Cremmen ultimately make of the idyll a "Signal der tatsächlichen Glücklosigkeit". (C. Kahrmann: "Idyll im Roman: Theodor Fontane". München 1973, p. 180) For the problem of death in "Effi Briest" see Jürgen Kolbe: "Goethes 'Wahlverwandschaften' und der Roman des neunzehnten Jahrhunderts". Stuttgart 1968, p. 187-189.

connection with Brentano's poem also underlines Effi's extreme youth which is mentioned in her parents' final conversation as perhaps the factor responsible for her fate. Significantly, the religious feeling expressed in the ballad and in the anecdote is that of a childlike fervour: the old widow believes against all rational objections that God will protect her home. Effi's own religious feeling is summed up towards the end of her life in her childlike hope of going to heaven, when she talks to Niemeyer of her joy on the swing.[1]

In Chapter 19, Effi tries to emulate the 'Mütterchen' in the poem by praying to God for a protecting wall during her sleigh-ride with Crampas.[2] These repeated attempts at prayer fail, and she does not have the will to break out of the spell. The use of this anecdote is convincing. Though ill-educated, Effi easily remembers stories which catch her imagination, e.g. the fate of unfaithful wives in Turkey (Chapter 2). Also appropriate is the fact that Effi does not mention the poet's name, nor can she give the dating of the incident: "irgendwo Krieg, ein Winterfeldzug". The erotic connotation suggested in the image of the protective wall is even more clearly brought out in "Effi Briest" through the story of the Chinese.

References to the Chinese are particularly prominent in those chapters of the novel immediately after the couple's return from their honeymoon. In this way the narrator appears to be indicating that all is not well in the intimate sphere of their marriage. The nearest the narrator comes to explicit reference to the erotic sphere is in a passage in Chapter 13. He describes the usual evening routine which culminates in Innstetten's well-meant but tired caresses after a night's paper-work, which evoke only half-hearted responses from Effi.[3] Already in Chapter 9, which gives an outline of the boring

1 Chapter 34. (NyA VII, 414)

2 See Peter-Klaus Schuster: "Effi Briest. Ein Leben nach christlichen Bildern". Tübingen 1978, p.2. He draws attention to the significance of the wall protecting a woman's modesty in classical literature. Fontane frequently uses this image particularly with reference to the legend of the "eingemauerte Nonne" of Stendhal.

3 The factor of repressed sexuality has been frequently commented on in

social visits which Effi is obliged to make during the first few weeks of her married life in Kessin, the reader learns that Innstetten is in Effi's view, as frosty as a snowman on the way home[1] In the same chapter, the Chinese 'appears' to Effi during Innstetten's absence at Bismarck's house and in the following chapter, their quarrel about the ghost takes place.

Innstetten's admonishment to Effi not to find things charming because they are 'different' seems overly didactic; he talks down to his wife as so often in the novel, not to her as an equal. The conversation ends with a further piece of irony: Effi's assurance that what she really longs for is peace and quiet falls on incredulous ears, and Innstetten dismisses this as mere caprice.[2] That he is wrong is shown through the use of peace motifs in the novel, which are all concerned with Effi's longing. This is especially true at the end and is mirrored in her final anecdote about the banquet.

The conversation in Chapter 10 built around the Chinese is of great significance for the characterization of both husband and wife and as a harbinger of the final outcome of the novel. Far from

recent criticism. Cf. Fritz Martini: "Deutsche Literatur im bürgerlichen Realismus 1848-1898". Second Edition. Stuttgart 1974, p. 791; George C. Avery: 'The Chinese Wall: Fontane's Psychograph of "Effi Briest" ' in "Views and Reviews of Modern German Literature. Festschrift for Adolf Klarmann". München 1974, p. 18-38; Diethelm Brüggemann: 'Fontanes Allegorien' in NR 82, Heft 2, 1971, p. 300; Margret Rothe-Buddeberg: "Spuk im Bürgerhaus: Der Dachboden in der deutschen Prosaliteratur als Negation der gesellschaftlichen Realität". Berlin 1972, p. 149 ff.; Carin Liesenhoff: "Fontane und das literarische Leben seiner Zeit: Eine literatursoziologische Studie". Bonn 1976, p. 106; and Ulrike Rainer: ' "Effi Briest" und das Motiv des Chinesen' in ZsfdPh 101, 1982, p. 557. Peter-Klaus Schuster in commenting on the Chinese makes the interesting connection between the Fall of Man and Effi's transgression, whereby Innstetten's Chinese ghost corresponds to the tree of knowledge, pointed out as a warning to Adam and Eve by God the Father. See P.-K. Schuster: op. cit., p. 97. See also Dirk Mende: 'Frauenleben. Bemerkungen zu Fontanes "L'Adultera" nebst Exkursen zu "Cécile" und "Effi Briest" ' in "Fontane aus heutiger Sicht". Ed by Hugo Aust. München 1980, p. 183-213.

1 NyA VII, 224.

2 Ibid. 242.

being dispelled, Effi's fear of the ghost grows and is augmented by a suspicion of her husband's real motives in this regard, once Crampas has drawn her attention to Innstetten's pedagogical stance. The notion of his using the ghost as an "Angstapparat aus Kalkül"[1] is the factor which really estranges her from Innstetten, because of the coldness and ultimate lack of love that it entails. To this lovelessness in her husband Effi returns in conversation with her mother on her death-bed: Innstetten was "ohne rechte Liebe", [2] she claims, without blaming him for what has happened.

With great economy the last three chapters of "Effi Briest" draw together the strands of the plot. Effi's breakdown through her daughter's rejection of her, Innstetten's change of outlook since the duel, Effi's resignation, death and her parent's attitude to her whole story – all of this is packed into three short chapters. In this economical space two anecdotes are given the function of depicting very important changes in the attitudes of both Effi and Innstetten.

In the early parts of the novel, the reader was rarely allowed to know the workings of Innstetten's mind, since the narrator was mainly interested in Effi as the central character. Since the duel in Chapter 28, the reader was not allowed any insight into Innstetten's psychological make-up, and only in Chapter 35 does the narrator return to Innstetten, but not for the purposes of condemning him as a stickler for principles, as might be expected. Instead, the reader finds a more mature man, who how measures everything with a different yardstick. It is a "half-forgotten ministerial anecdote"[3] which is given the function of describing this change in Innstetten. His present joyless life is indicated with great economy through his reaction to the story. The fact that he is now capable of appreciating the sentiment in the Ladenberg anecdote is proof of his ultimate realization of the emptiness of all he had striven for while he still had the chance of domestic happines.. The response of Minister Ladenberg to reception of the Hohenzollern Red Eagle

1 NyA VII, 283.
2 Ibid. 425.
3 Ibid. 417

decoration: "Da liege, bist du s c h w a r z wirst"[1] is endorsed by Innstetten's reaction, that, had Ladenberg got the Black Eagle decoration later, it would in any case have been far too late and he would have had no satisfaction from it. The return to the topic of public honours, which already found a place in "Schach von Wuthenow" and which was slightly touched upon in Chapter 14 of "Cécile",[2] indicates Fontane's strong personal interest in the subject.[3] The social and professional striving which characterized Innstetten in the early part of the novel and which in no small way brought about the estrangement of his wife, has given way to the insight that advancement is not a guarantee of happiness. Formerly, Innstetten was willing to sacrifice something as important as Effi's peace of mind by not selling his 'haunted hause' for fear of seeming ridiculous to others. Nor would he excuse himself to Bismarck on grounds that his wife was afraid to be alone at night. It is even hinted by Crampas that Innstetten believed his interest in the supernatural would recommend him as having a certain cachet to those in authority.

Innstetten's change is therefore visible in his different conceptions of happiness in the novel – early on he was willing to make any sacrifices for the advancement of his career. Since the death of

1 NyA VII, 418. Innstetten's promotion, the notice of which has prompted him to recall the Ladenberg anecdote, comes too late. He has lost Effi and by that experience come to see the worthlessness of his ambitions.

2 NyA IV, 207: "Sich ein Genüge tun, ist die beste Dekoration."

3 Fontane's scepticism about public honours is well known. It is reflected in his letters with reference to the reception of his work as well as to the 'official' response to his books on the Prussian wars. The few marks of public respect which he did receive came too late – as Innstetten supposes about Ladenberg – to afford Fontane much satisfaction. He did not however despise them as is clear from a letter to Friedlaender of 7.1.1889: "Wäre ich ein gesellschaftlich angesehener Mann, ein Gegenstand von Huldigungen oder auch nur Achtung,"..."so bedeutete mir solche Auszeichnung so gut wie nichts. Angesichts der Tatsache aber, daß man in Deutschland und speziell in Preußen nur dann etwas gilt, wenn man 'staatlich approbiert' ist, hat solch Orden wirklich einen praktischen Wert: man wird respektvoller angekuckt und besser behandelt." (Theodor Fontane: "Briefe an Georg Friedlaender." Ed. by Kurt Schreinert, Heidelberg 1954, p.103)

Crampas and the loss of Effi however, his outlook on happiness is much different. It no longer resides for him in the honours received within the framework of society. He even toys with the idea of turning his back on society and emigrating to Africa. His new conception of happiness is very modest: "Wenn einem die siebenhundertzwanzig Minuten eines zwölfstündigen Tages ohne besonderen Ärger vergehen, so läßt sich von einem glücklichen Tag sprechen."[1] The change in both Effi and Innstetten in the novel is brought about by resignation with regard to those things that once meant most to them. For Innstetten career came first. Throughout the novel until Effi's period of resignation she was characterized as loving change, entertainment, excitement and even danger. This latter element seemed to bring her a feeling of intensified living, and goes some way to explain her involvement in an affair with a man she did not love.

Effi' deathbed conversation with her mother is important for the light it throws on her final outlook, both with regard to early death and to Innstetten's role in her fate. This is the first time that Effi mentions his name to her mother since her return home, and significantly it is in the context of his pedagogical attitude: he did not like the fact that Effi was not well-read. In response to Frau von Briest's doubts that Effi is really resigned to early death, she then tells the anecdote from "one of Innstetten's good books":

> Es sei wer von einer fröhlichen Tafel abgerufen worden, und am anderen Tage habe der Abgerufene gefragt, wie's denn nachher gewesen sie. Da habe man ihm geantwortet: 'Ach, es war noch allerlei; aber eigentlich haben Sie nichts versäumt'.[2]

Although this mood of resignation may appear to contradict the life-loving Effi of earlier times, this stage of her development has in fact been anticipated very early in the novel. Her longing at times for peace and quiet is indicated already at the end of Chapter 10. Here Innstetten dismisses it as a fantasy on her part, thus showing his

1 NyA VII, 418.
2 Ibid. 425.

superior attitude towards her. Ironically, he does so directly after the narration of the story about the Chinese, whose 'ghost' becomes a factor of such importance in their relationship. The death of Effi is also anticipated in several other ways in the novel, e.g. when she muses before the birth of her baby on where she would like to be buried. Also in saying farewell to Gieshübler in Kessin, she says: "Auch Junge können sterben."[1]

Effi's attempts to atone for her affair by living completely for her duties as wife and mother and attempting to suppress the past come to nought when Innstetten accepts the norms of society, kills Crampas in the duel and rejects her forever. Yet the deathbed scene which is introduced with an anecdote from Henry Fielding's "Tom Jones" (1749)[2] shows Effi's acceptance of both her early death and the limbo to which Innstetten's action subjected her. Her only negative observation about his character is expressed completely without bitterness: "Denn er hatte viel Gutes in seiner Natur und

1 Ibid. 332. The ubiquitousness of the notion of death sets the tone for the whole development of Effi. The relationship between the venue for the adulterous occasions and death references has been commented on by Charles Nelson Hayes in "Symbol and Correlative in Theodor Fontane's Fiction" (Ph. D. Brown University, Providence 1967, p. 100) and by M. Devine: op. cit., p. 546-548. The parallels which exist between the graves of Effi and the Chinese ensure that the associations between repressed sexuality, anxiety, adultery and death are continued until the very end.

2 The style of Fontane's English source for this anecdote provides an interesting contrast to the economical and restrained style of the deathbed scene in "Effi Briest". In the English novel Mr. Allworthy consoles those at his death-bed: "If the wisest of men hath compared life to a span, surely we may be allowed to consider it as a day. It is my fate to leave it in the evening but those who are taken away earlier have only lost a few hours, at the best little worth lamenting, and much oftener hours of labour and fatigue, of pain and sorrow. One of the Roman poets, I remember, likens our leaving life to our departure from a feast – a thought which hath often occurred to me when I have seen men struggling to protract an entertainment, and to enjoy the company of friends a few moments longer. Alas! how short is the most protracted of such enjoyments! how immaterial the differences between him who retires the soonest, and him who stays the latest." (H. Fielding: "The History of Tom Jones." London 1909, p. 179)

war so edel, wie jemand sein kann, der ohne rechte Liebe ist."[1]

Anecdotes are employed in "Effi Briest" with great artistry and figure in a broad canvas of references, many of them from other literary sources, which provides parallels to the plot and illuminations of the themes. In Effi's case, this use of literaty sources remains convincing, because, although she cannot remember details like authors' names, she has an ability to apply little stories read in the past to her own case. Like the other parallels such as the stories from Heine's "Spanische Atriden" and the story of the Chinese, Effi's 'Gottesmauer" and "Tom Jones" anecdotes become clear through comparison with the main plot of the novel. An element of mystery and contradiction adheres to all these references, and the reader is thus prompted to further questioning in his own mind. On the motif of the Chinese in "Effi Briest" Peter Demetz makes a comment which is relevant to the effect of the anecdote in Fontane's fiction: it spurs the reader on to ever new decodings of the text.[2] Demetz' thesis that "Effi Briest" represents on Fontane's part a triumphant exhaltation above the level of 'Belletristik' still apparent in "L'Adultera" is supported by the examination of the anecdotes in "Effi Briest". It is clear that such a story is in danger of falling into the sentimental, yet whenever the anecdote is used in this novel it prevents this from happening. Through telling each other stories (or even repeating one inwardly, as in the case of Innstetten's Ladenberg anecdote), Fontane's characters avoid sentimental scenes which would dwell more on direct exposure of subjective emotions. This factor is particularly appropriate where scenes are in danger of reminding the reader of similar scenes of the traditional 'tearjerker' variety in trivial literature.

By using objective stories the characters may externalize their own problems and even demonstrate a psychological development which is at first sight surprising. Instead of employing long conversations which would demonstrate the changed attitudes of the two

1 NyA VII, 425

2 This dissatisfied re-reading, which continues to look for new answers demonstrates perhaps, according to Demetz, the presence of literary qualities in a text. See P. Demetz: "Kitsch, Belletristik, Kunst: Theodor Fontane." Berlin 1970, p. 21.

major characters, Effi and Innstetten, Fontane has each of them characterize themselves towards the end through the narration of a short anecdote. This is achieved with plausibility and in each case the situation underlines the speaker's isolation and loneliness. Innstetten only t h i n k s of the anecdote (the narrator tells us) which reveals his new outlook on life. This is an extreme case of isolation. The eminently social form of the anecdote thus becomes internalized in the character's mind in a way which emphasizes the loneliness of this man whose whole striving was determined by social factors. Effi has only her mother at her death-bed – the fact that she is the more critical of the parents is significant, because thereby a further de-sentimentalizing factor is introduced into the scene. Through the use of a story from a book to describe Effi's attitude to death, the danger of sentimentaliy in the death-bed scene, which was so much indulged by some other nineteenth-century novelists, such as Dickens, is avoided by Fontane. The element of distance is retained.

It is interesting to speculate on why Fontane chose to have Effi narrate only anecdotes from literary sources, especially since she is not well-read. Brentano's "Gottesmauer" is based on an allegedly historical incident, which was reported in the newspapers in 1812, but Effi's source is the ballad which she had learned at school. The literary provenance of the anecdotes in "Effi Briest" make the novel stand out in this respect from the rest of Fontane's fiction. Fontane is possibly hereby indicating that, in spite of the strong element of the child of nature in her, Effi is living at a second remove from real life.[1] The fact that Crampas's stories in Chapter 17 all have literary

1 Cf. Hans Otto Horch: ' "Das Schlechte ... mit demselben Vergnügen wie das Gute". Über Theodor Fontanes Beziehungen zu Heinrich Heine'. In "Heine-Jahrbuch" 18, 1979, p. 168: "Crampas und Innstetten agieren teils bewußt, teils unbewußt nach literarisch bzw. gesellschaftlich präformierter Topik: Crampas nach dem Muster eines – von Heine selbst schon als Rolle konzipierten – Don Juan, Innstetten nach dem Muster Wagners, Bismarcks und der 'preußischen Idee'. Effi reagiert scheinbar 'natürlicher', unmittelbarer; aber auch ihre Unmittelbarkeit wird vom Erzähler als gebrochen, literarisch präformiert vorgeführt. Kreatürlichkeit als wahre Unmittelbarkeit ist allein dem Tier vorbehalten: Gegenbild einer 'nature naturelle', die der Mensch im Prozeß der Institutionalisierung schon längst verloren hat und auf die

sources seems to point also to the artificiality of the intimate relationship between him and Effi, which is no more based on love or compatibility than is the relationship between Innstetten and Effi. The fact that Crampas relates stories from literature relieves him of a likely alternative, telling them from his life. As he is already married with a family and is a known womanizer, this subject could be dangerous and would lead away from rather than towards the flirtation which he seeks.

The successful employment of anecdotes in this 'Einheitsroman' shows that the firm line of the story did not militate against the use of inserted stories. Plot, theme and characterization are supported through the employment of anecdotes. In the works of fiction discussed here under the heading "Anecdote and the Heart", "L'Adultera", "Graf Petöfy", "Cécile", "Frau Jenny Treibel", and "Effi Briest", there is a marked improvement in Fontane's use of anecdote from "Cécile"(1887) onwards. The art of the anecdote is much subtler and more elegant in the last three works than in the first two, in which inserted anecdotes tend to retain their independence and fail on the whole to merge completely into the body of the fictional works. In summary, the following specific functions can be attributed to the anecdote as used in these five works: Firstly, it can mark a turning point in the plot, frequently underlining the personal crisis of a character (Melanie and the Suboff anecdote, Effi and the "Gottesmauer" anecdote). Secondly, it can bring a truth out into the open confirming something which the narrator otherwise only partially reveals (the Lenau and the "homme de verre" anecdotes in "Graf Petöfy"). Thirdly, it can provide parallels to the actions of the main characters and help explain their motivation (the Rodenstein and Rodenberg anecdotes in "Cécile"). Fourthly, it can signal to the reader a state of mind which has already been shared by characters for some time, but which because of 'Zeitraffung' or narrator reticence has not otherwise been made apparent (Innstetten's Ladenberg anecdote, Effi's "Tom Jones"

angesichts der im 19. Jahrhundert pervertierten viktorianischen 'nature artificielle' als auf einen gleichsam paradiesischen Zustand verwiesen wird."

anecdote). In the case of these last two examples from "Effi Briest" the characters summarize their whole philosophy of life after that life has been ruined, and do so in the most unsentimental terms possible by relating a funny or curious story they have heard somewhere. By analogy they communicate feelings which they will not openly lay bare. Fifthly, an anecdote like the Barfus story in "Frau Jenny Treibel" can offer an example of true humanity, which by its refinement of feeling, delicacy of treatment and wide-reaching implications earns itself a place in the front rank of Fontane's anecdotes.

II. "Historischen Anekdoten habe ich nie widerstehen können":

Anecdote and Period

1. "Vor dcm Sturm" (1878)

On 27 November 1878 shortly after the appearance of Fontane's first novel, Paul Heyse, wrote to the publisher, Wilhelm Hertz, criticizing among other things an excess of the historical and anecdotal element in "Vor dem Sturm".[1] In his monograph of 1919, which was to have a large influence on subsequent Fontane scholarship, Conrad Wandrey put forward the view that "Vor dem Sturm" was marred by a general lack of attention to form and by the tendency to digress, which had been a feature of Fontane's "Wanderungen durch die Mark Brandenburg". On the anecdotal element in particular Wandrey observed: "Macht Fontanes Neigung zur Unterbrechung, zur Einlage, zum Detail sich durch das ganze Gewebe des Werkes hin fühlbar, so wird endlich diese Tendenz noch unterstrichen durch das Anekdotische, eine Vorliebe, die die Personen des Romans mit ihrem Schöpfer gemein haben, den Hang, ein Großes durch ein charakteristisch Kleines, ein umfangreich Wirkliches durchs Gleichnis auszudrücken."[2] Wandrey believed that both Fontane's art of conversation and his art of anecdote narration were still at the formative stage in this first novel. Peter Demetz' positive evaluation of "Vor dem Sturm" as an historical novel which tended towards being a social novel gave new impetus to critical assessment of it.[3] This had previously been rather negative. One of the errors of Wandrey's approach was that he regarded all interpolated stories as anecdotes, e.g. the accounts of the battles of

1 See Aufbau I, 367-368.
2 Conrad Wandrey: "Theodor Fontane." München 1919, p. 115
3 P. Demetz: "Formen des Realismus: Theodor Fontane. Kritische Untersuchungen." München 1964, p. 51-76.

Plaa and Borodino as well as Tante Schorlemmer's story about Karjarnak, the Greenlander.[1] Fontane inserted these accounts written by others into his own text and allowed them to take up considerable space. Wandrey failed to see any relevance for the interpolations beyond, in the case of the chapters on Plaa and Borodino, the loose connection of creating atmosphere for the war against Napoleon.

In proportion to its large size, the amount of true anecdotes in "Vor dem Sturm" is not excessive, although criticism may be levelled at some of them on other grounds. The first part of the novel, Chapters 1 to 36 (in which the reader is introduced to the settings of Hohen-Vietz and Guse, as well as Kirch-Göritz) contains over twice as many anecdotes as the latter two parts of the novel, Chapters 37 to 59 and 60 to 82. In the first part, which is mainly descriptive, Fontane gives free rein to his penchant for the anecdote, thereby reminding the reader of his procedure in "Wanderungen durch die Mark Brandenburg". The second and third parts contain the action element in the novel: the attack on Frankfurt on the Oder, Lewin's imprisonment, Kathinka's elopement, Lewin's illness, Tubal's death, the marriage of Lewin and Marie, and Renate's retreat to a convent. The retardations through interpolated stories here generally take the form of legendary references e.g. the Bredow ring stories and legends connected with Kloster Lehnin. The military stories occur here also. The fact that "Vor dem Sturm" contains characters who are extremely conscious of tradition, history and the past, as well as being conscious of the present political situation, undoubtedly favours the use of anecdote. The groups which meet in Hohenvietz, Guse and Berlin are well versed, not just in Prussian history, but also in the history of France. Lewin's hobby is legend and local history.

A detailed analysis of the use of anecdote in "Vor dem Sturm" shows that Fontane was at pains to provide common ground for many of the anecdotes which he draws on. In other words they are

1 See C. Wandrey: op. cit., p. 113. These reports and stories are far too extensive to qualify as anecdotes.

not all freely drawn on merely because of a love of digression on the author's part. Six chapters of the first part of the novel are concerned with Gräfin Amelie Pudaglia, her home, Schloß Guse, and the political disagreement between her and her brother, Berndt von Vitzewitz. The last of these six chapters describes the after-dinner conversation in Schloß Guse at Christmas 1812. In the course of the conversation, Amelie and Berndt recount stories about Henry Henry IV of Navarre (1553-1610) which bring out his inherent goodness, naturalness, humanity, refinement of feeling and humour. The anecdotes about "le bon roi" are sandwiched between disagreements about the contemporary political situation, i.e. the tension between Napoleonic France and Prussia. They thus provide comic relief, but that is not their only function.

These French anecdotes also help to build up the characterization of Amelie as an aristocrat, who is typical of eighteenth-century court life: she is a lover of witty and intelligent conversation, has the gift of repartee and can call at will on many anecdotes. She does this in the conversation in question in order both to entertain her guests and to give them an insight into the character and times of Henry IV, her favourite among historical monarchs. Amelie's politics reflect the respect felt in eighteenth-century Germany for French culture, as does her choice of language with its liberal use of French phrases and quotations. The narration of anecdotes from France allows her to switch with ease and without affectation to her second language, as the original is always more effective for the point of an anecdote. Her choice of story supports her definition of what constitutes the essence of being French: "Scherz, Laune, Leichtigkeit".[1]

Four well-known anecdotes concerning Henry are used in this conversation. Berndt relates one of them in order to cast aspersions on Henry: the king was caught by the Spanish ambassador while playing on the ground with the dauphin, an incident which gave rise to Mme de Simier's remark that she had seen the king, but not His Majesty.[2] For Berndt, this anecdote proves that Henry's deportment was too free and easy for his station, while for Amelie it proves his

1 NyA I, 156.

2 Ibid., 157. Fontane was probably familiar with a pictorial representation

freedom from rigidity. Her insight into Henry's character lies in her appreciation of his generosity of soul and his readiness to admit his faults. His Gascon roguishness led him to admit about his habit of taking things which belonged to others: he admitted that if he had not been king, he would have been hanged.[1] Amelie's important sentence with regard to her favourite monarch is: "Er verschwieg nichts und persiflierte sich selbst in dem heiteren Darüberstehen eines Grandseigneurs."[2] The affection of the French for Henry is illustrated in Amelie's anecdote about the reaction of the people of Pau (Henry's place of birth) to a gesture of Louis XIV, Henry's grandson. When Louis sent his own statue to be put on a proposed monument to Henry IV, the townspeople of Pau retaliated by inscribing it with the words: "Celui-ci est le petit-fils de notre bon Henri."[3] It is with this anecdote that the conversation returns to its base in contemporary politics: the disagreement had started with Medewitz' and Berndt's diverging opinions on Hardenberg's policies vis-a-vis Napoleon. By ending this part of the conversation (the anecdotes about Henry) with an anecdote which combines the figures of Henry and Louis XIV (the Pau story), the narrator neatly brings it back to the present with the contrast of French and German. Louis' alleged failings as a military strategist bring the conversation back once more to the delicate subject of Prussia with the final disagreement between Amelie and Berndt about the merits of Frederick the Second and Prince Henry. Berndt appears to win the argument, for his moving description of the Prussian people's love and respect for Frederick on the occasion of his return from his last army review ends the chapter. Berndt's point that the people will always choose the better man as the object of their affection (i.e. Frederick rather than Henry, whom Amelies loves) actually has already been proven in a concrete way by Amelie's Pau anecdote.

of such an anecdote about Henry IV on all fours by Ingres in his picture "Henry IV Playing with his Children While the Spanish Ambassador is Being admitted".

1 NyA I, 157.

2 Ibidem.

3 Ibid., 158.

Berndt, Bamme, Drosselstein and Krach share the anti-Hardenberg position in contemporary politics, which Medewitz opposes with his "ministeriellen Rechtgläubigkeit".[1] In drawing the conversation away from the acrimonious level of contemporary politics, Amelie had as a good hostess relaxed the atmosphere at her social gathering. The stories about Henry IV provide comic relief, but their significance goes further than that. The discussion on Henry IV (including all the accompanying anecdotes about Napoleon's entourage) is clearly intended to show the clash of the two traditions: the earlier Francophile tradition and the nationalistic feeling of the 1812-1813 period. The passage on Henry is appropriate as a way of showing the diametrically opposed approaches of brother and sister. In view however of the plethora of anecdotes between Chapters 22 and 24, the reader must ask himself if Fontane's enthusiasm for "le bon roi" is not the real basis for this passage. If this is the case, then the Henry passage is simply an unnecessary digression, however entertaining. The full significance of the passage cannot emerge until the anecdotes connected with the loyalty theme have been examined.

Many of the inserted stories in "Vor dem Sturm" concern unhappy love or touch on the theme of loyalty. Such stories and references include the fate of Johanna Susmihl,[2] Struensee and the Queen of Denmark,[3] the ring stories,[4] the story of the first Abbot of Kloster Lehnin,[5] the story of the lady who loved a monk from Kloster Lehnin,[6] and the 'White Lady' stories. All of these stories, ghost stories and family legends, are connected in the narrative with Lewin, and many of them are narrated in the presence of Kathinka, who does not love him. After initial enthusiasm for his narrative powers, she takes on a negative attitude towards his tales, presumably because she realizes that their constant theme is that of

1 NyA I, 155.
2 Ibid. 315
3 Ibid. 368
4 Ibid. 400-405.
5 Ibid. 413.
6 Ibid. 415-417

unhappiness in love. This change in her reception of his stories parallels the movement in their relationship as a whole. Her initial attraction was to Lewin as a poetic nature. Rejection of Lewin brings with it a rejection of her father's adoptive country, Prussia, and a return to roots in her love for Graf Bninski and in her support for the Polish cause and reconversion to Catholicism.

The earliest piece of external description in the novel of the Vitzewitz brother and sister brings out the quality of loyalty. This dominant characteristic is then demonstrated on the level of the private plot (love story) through their disappointed love for the Ladalinski brother and sister. In the many chapters that intervene between the first intimations of this love and its final outcome, the inserted stories, anecdotes and legends concerning unhappy love and loyalty or lack of loyalty serve as a certain unifying factor.

The loyalty theme works itself out on the political level in the conflict between Napoleonic imperialism and the Prussians' wish for independence from France. Fontane's intention in writing the novel was to capture, as he himself claimed, "das große Fühlen"[1] of 1812-1813 in Prussia. The fact that the independence movement came primarily from below, not from the authorities, gives Fontane an added dimension for the loyalty theme – it is a loyalty in apparent disloyalty. Several of the stories related in the novel have this as their raison d'être. Thus, in Chapter 30 Othegraven tells Kniehase the story of Andreas Hofer (1767-1810), the innkeeper from the Tyrol, who lead the Tyrolean revolt against Bavarian and French occupation in 1809 and continued to fight even after the Peace of Schönbrunn was concluded between the Austrians and the French. Hofer "war schuldig bei Freund und Feind"[2] and was executed by the French in 1810. However, as Othegraven emphasizes to Kniehase, Kaiser Franz would not dream of connecting the name

1 In his letter to Wilhelm Hertz of 17.6.1866. In "Theodor Fontane. Der Dichter über sein Werk." Edited by Richard Brinkmann in conjunction with Waltraud Wiethölter. München 1977, vol. 2, p. 189.

2 NyA I, 195. This anecdote with its touch of dialect: "Der Franzl hat's gemußt, ich muß es n i c h t" (ibidem) contains a humorous element which contrasts with the seriousness of Berndt's anecdote.

of Hofer with disloyalty. The analogy with the present Prussian situation in the novel is clear. Earlier in this conversation, Berndt relates a gruesome anecdote about the execution by the French of Karl Friedrich Schulz in 1807. Kniehase is already familiar with the story, but Berndt tells it again in the hope of gaining his support for the cause of independent action:

> Es war um dieselbe Zeit, Sie entsinnen sich Kniehase daß sie den Kyritzer Kämmerer, der so unschuldig war wie Sie und ich, vor eins ihrer feigen und feilen Kriegsgerichte stellten und ihn aburteilten und niederschossen. Was sage ich: "niederschossen"? Hinwürgen war es. Denn so schlecht wie das Urteil, so schlecht war seine Vollstreckung. Er lag am Boden, der unglückliche tapfere Mann, und konnte nicht sterben. Da sprang ein mitleidiger Westfale vor und schoß ihm ins Herz: "Aus Liebe zu dir, du unschuldig Blut, will ich dir zum Tode helfen."[1]

Berndt's motto in the present political situation is "mit dem König, solang es geht; o h n e ihn, wenn es sein muß".[2] With the help of the examples given in anecdotal form, both of the death of Karl Friedrich Schulz in Kyritz in 1807 and of the veneration in which the name of Andreas Hofer is held, Berndt and Othegraven are able to convince the hesitant Kniehase that support of the militia against the French does not mean disloyalty to the king's express wishes, but in fact true loyalty to Prussia in the face of the threat from Napoleon.

Two Frederician anecdotes in "Vor dem Sturm" underline the theme of loyalty and self-sacrifice. The question allegedly posed by Frederick II during the Prussian defeat at the Battle of Kunersdorf: "Will denn keine verdammte Kugel mich treffen?"[3] is quoted by Lewin to Tubal as part of his revelations on local history. Many of the references to loyalty are connected with Tubal in anticipation

1 NyA I, 193. Fontane took the anecdote almost word for word from H. Bauer's "Denkschrift über die Hinrichtung des Kämmerers Karl Friedrich Schulz und des Kaufmanns Karl Friedrich Kersten durch die Franzosen in Kyritz am 8. April 1807". Kyritz 1845. See Aufbau I, 339.

2 NyA I, 193.

3 Ibid. 173.

of his own lack of that quality. For the petit-bourgeois circle depicted in the novel, Frederick is important as an incorporation of Prussian courage. Rabe reports Klemm's claim to have been favoured in conversation by the king at the Battle of Torgau for his bravery. However, this claim is discounted by Stappenbeck behind Klemm's back with the anecdote of Frederick's sharp reprimand to scattering grenadiers at Torgau: "Rackers, wollt Ihr denn ewig leben?"[1] Stappenbeck reckons Klemm to have been one of these grenadiers In order to encourage the local militia from Lebus-Barnim, Bamme quotes Frederick in his pep-talk before the attack on Frankfurt.[2]

Besides references to Frederick himself and anecdotes about him, the Frederician era is very much present in the novel through Fontane's use of an anecdote from the period as a 'Leitmotiv' throughout the broad sweep of the novel. The incident of the death of an officer, who let himself bleed to death by tearing off his bandages after the defeat of Prussia by Austria and Russia at the Battle of Kunersdorf (1759) during the Seven Years' War is recounted three times. This is a narrative device in connection with anecdote which is unique in Fontane's writings.[3] Two characters and the narrator share the narration of this anecdote. In each case a different flavour and atmosphere is accorded to the story, ranging from the emotion of the narrator's version in Chapter 5 through the overly-patriotic, didactic version of Berndt in Chapter 49 to the restrained narration of the sexton, Kubalke, in Chapter 79. In all three cases, subtle differences are made in the tone of the anecdote,[4] so that the daring use of the same story three times in the one novel does not seem excessive, but adds layers of meaning to the same

1 NyA I, 284. The incident is again referred to in Chapter 40.

2 See ibid. 560.

3 He had used the same story twice in "Cécile", but with the intention of overturning the interpretation offered on the first narration. See above p. 50-52.

4 On these differences, see Siegfried Hajek: 'Anekdoten in Theodor Fontanes Roman "Vor dem Sturm".' In "Jahrbuch der Raabe-Gesellschaft" 1979, p. 72-93. Only a few anecdotes from Fontane's novel are commented on in this article.

incident in different contexts. The basic facts in each case remain the same: a wounded officer is carried by grenadiers of the Itzenplitz Regiment to the church at Hohen-Vietz after the disastrous defeat of the Prussians. He tears off his bandages in the pew and cries: "Kinder, ich will sterben."[1] The bloodstains remain indelibly on the seat and nobody will use it. The motif of the indelible bloodstain, familiar from legends and ghost-stories, is used here in the immediately recognisable 'occasio' of Frederick's and Prussia's loss in 1759. The most obvious purpose of this anecdote in the novel is to underline the theme of loyalty unto death.[2] This loyalty is manifested in the form of love of the fatherland in the story of the Kunersdorf officer, and on the plot level it is eventually made manifest in the death of the initially unfaithful Tubal. Berndt tells the anecdote in order to persuade the still hesitant Lewin (who is of course already fully conversant with it as part of the history of his locality) to join the cause of combat against the French. When Ladalinski visits the church at Hohen-Vietz in order to see his son's corpse there, the 'action' of the novel in the form of the attack on Frankfort is over. No mention is made at first of the purpose of his visit and a simple conversation on mundane matters takes place between him and Kubalke. Kubalke then tells the story of the dying officer without any comment of an historical, didactic or patriotic character. He adds only a tiny detail to the sum of knowledge presented in the first two tellings by the narrator and Berndt. This detail is a testimony to the truth of his memory: the incident happened on 12 August, the day before his birthday in 1759.[3] The birthday, and not his knowledge of Prussian history, makes the sexton remember the date! This in itself apparently insignificant fact is a hint to the reader that in this telling of the same story for the last time the emphasis has been quite different from the first two narrations. The historical dimension is not stressed here, but the personal. And so it is the phenonemon of death itself which

1 NyA I, 33, 398 and 620.

2 The inscription "Sei getreu bis in den Tod" features on one of the rings talked about at the ball in Chapter 50. See ibid. 401.

3 See NyA I, 620

interests both the heartbroken father and, presumably, the ageing sexton. Ladalinski feels the positive side of death having heard the tale and feels justified in his resignation: death is not terrible, but freedom and release. Effi Briest expresses similar sentiments, again supported by an anecdote, on her deathbed in the novel of the nineties. In the third repetition of the Kunersdorf anecdote, history imperceptibly merges with the present.[1] This transition from past to present is a basic and very important feature of Fontane's use of the anecdote in general and ensures that the historical anecdote does not become a fossilized artefact, rigid and unchanging in its outlines. The very words with which the narrator shows Kubalke drawing Ladalinski away from that side of the church where the 'Major' died are a (perhaps even unwitting) signal to the reader that here not an incident of Prussia's defeat or glory is remembered, but the universal human confrontation with death: "Bei diesen Worten hatte der alte Kubalke den Geheimrat nach der anderen Seite hinübergezogen"[2] to a place where the "two old men" have a coffin right beside them, "not three paces away". The physical constellation of the scene underlines no doubt its resignation and lack of high emotion.

Anecdotes about Napoleon in "Vor dem Sturm" are related only by the anti-French characters. For Berndt he is "der B ö s e s t e auf Erden",[3] and the anecdotes are told in order to bring out alleged negative sides of Napoleon's character and attitudes. Berndt tells his children, in order to warn them against admiration for the French ruler, the anecdote about Napoleon saying to Queen Luise: "Wie können Sie es nur wagen, mit mir zu kämpfen?"[4] The theme of Napoleon's effrontery is brought up also by Berndt in the Guse circle with the anecdote of Napoleon's regret at having left Prussia intact, and his asking the Austrian ambassador the rhetorical question in this regard: "Was ist ein Thron? Ein Holzgerüst mit Samt beschlagen."[5] In two further anecdotes, Napoleon or a member of

1 See Siegfried Hajek: op. cit., p. 91.

2 NyA I, 620.

3 Ibid. 26.

4 Ibid. 156.

5 Ibidem.

his regime shows up badly, as far as the Prussian characters are concerned. One concerns Napoleon's superstitiousness about the White Lady ghost at Bayreuth,[1] and the other shows Murat being frightened by a musical cupboard playing the Hohenfriedberg March.[2] Several anecdotes in Chapter 22 told in the aristocratic Guse circle throw a dubious light on members of Napoleon's regime, like Sieyes and Narbonne. Narbonne's role in both the ancien regime and under Napoleon links up with the loyalty theme of the novel. The prejudices of these Prussians against Napoleon's marshals[3] is based not simply on political antagonism, but on class distinction as well. Krach refers to them in a derogatory fashion as sons of coopers and publicans, and even the otherwise tolerant Drosselstein, while appreciating them as soldiers, is conscious of their humble origins.[4] This factor of aristocratic disdain contrasts with the aspect which emerges from several of the loyalty anecdotes: namely, that it comes from the people. This was precisely the point which Berndt wished to make in persuading Kniehase to join the patriotic cause. On one level in the novel, the Prussian anecdotes support the loyalty theme, while those on Napoleon and his associates concern disloyalty (changing sides from ancien to new regime, lack of respect for throne and state, and personal weakness: Murat, Bayreuth, Narbonne's telegramme). Amelie contests Berndt's condemnation of Napoleon in Chapter 22 with the statement that at least he opposes "our" prejudices.[5]

The discussion of Henry IV which leads on from this statement centres essentially around Henry's qualities of humour, self-persiflage and undogmatic flexibility. These are qualities not shown by Berndt in the early part of the novel. Later, he must see the need for them both on the private level (the marriage of his son with the daughter

1 NyA I, 522.
2 Ibid. 146-147.
3 Fontane's own interest in the marshals stemmed from his father's love of anecdotes about them and use of them in his instruction of the young Theodor. (See "Meine Kinderjahre", Chapters 13 and 16.)
4 He refers to their "Korporalslitzen". (NyA I, 146)
5 NyA I, 156.

of a circus performer) and on the public level (the revaluation of his motivation in involving the others in the attack on Frankfort). Lewin's own sympathy for the members of the French regiments[1] in their dishevelled state on the return from the Russian campaign (Chapter 48) shows that Berndt's Francophobe-style patriotism is neither the only nor the best expression of Prussian sentiments. The portrait of Henry shows that true nobility lies in the heart: even though he was king, he could by virtue of his inner strength and true greatness afford to be natural, unassuming and admit his faults with good humour.[2]

In playing host to Tubal on the road to Kirch-Göritz, Lewin entertains him with anecdotes from local religious history. The first again incorporates the loyalty unto death motif, illustrated by the last words of a nun before being beheaded by a Polish attacker: "In manus tuas, Domine, commendo spiritum meum."[3] Lewin's second anecdote in this context concerns the iconoclastic attack on the miraculous statue of the Virgin at Kirch-Göritz during the Reformation. The relevance of this incident to the novel's theme is brought out by Lewin's observation that the iconoclasts were the same people who only a few weeks earlier had prayed and offered their pennies there.[4]

To the first of these stories Tubal reacts negatively because of its Polish association: it throws a bad light on the country of his origin. He disagrees with Lewin's interpretation of the second story's demonstrating how little faith really existed in the so-called religious times and how much savagery went under the guise of

1 The true humanity which is a theme in the novel is also clear in this encounter. Lewin cannot see these French soldiers as his enemies, because he sees them in their suffering first and foremost as humans.

2 Katherina Mommsen sees the portrait of Henry as an incorporation of the quality of "heiteres Darüberstehen" which Amelie claims for him (NyA I, 157). Cf. K. Mommsen: "Gesellschaftskritik bei Fontane und Thomas Mann". Heidelberg 1973, p. 46-56. Hans-Heinrich Reuter sees the portrait of the French monarch as a "verschleiertes Selbstbildnis" of Fontane. (H.-H. Reuter: "Fontane." Berlin 1968, vol. 1, p. 109)

3 NyA I, 174.

4 Ibid. 175.

faith.[1] This difference of opinion is interrupted before Tubal has a chance to explain his view of the story, and the matter is dropped in the novel as far as discussion is concerned. However, it is not coincidental that these two stories should be associated with Tubal as the listener, since it is he whose fate most reflects loss of loyalty and its subsequent recovery in death. For the same reason, the recurrent anecdote of the Kunersdorf officer's death is finally associated with Tubal when his father hears the story at his bier. The use of the Catholic association in these two anecdotes about Kirch-Göritz also possibly indicates the turning away from their traditional belief on the part of the Ladalinskis and their final return to it. This is another reflection on the loyalty-disloyalty theme.

Pehaps the most interesting anecdote connected with loyalty is that about the green coffins which is related by Frau Hulen at her dinner-party. Her tale contrasts on the one hand with Ziebold's account of the return to Berlin of the 'Löffelgarde' after the Battle of Jena, and on the other with the quarrel between Klemm and Schimmelpennig about Klemm's role in the Battle of Torgau. The source Fontane used for his version of the green coffins anecdote was the memoirs of Cavan George.[2] A comparison of the original with Fontane's version helps to demonstrate his skill in adapting an historical, but little-known, incident to suit his own purposes in the fictional context.[3] It will be seen from the comparison that, already here in his first novel, Fontane took great care to ensure that the tale from real life was modified so as to make it appropriate for the fictional character who narrates it, as well as for the principal theme of the book.

1 NyA I, 175.

2 C. George: "Erinnerungen eines Preußen aus der Napoleonischen Zeit". Grimma 1840.

3 Hermann Kügler in his article: 'Die grünen Särge. Eine Quelle zu Fontanes "Vor dem Sturm"' in "Zeitschrift des Vereins für die Geschichte Berlins" 1934, Heft 3, p. 57-59 quotes Fontane's letter to F. W. Holtze in connection with George's book which he had borrowed: "George, der mir sehr wertvoll ist, darf ich noch ein paar Monate behalten." (See H. Kügler: op. cit., p. 59 and also Brinkmann/Wiethölter: op. cit., vol. 2, p. 199.)

George's version
(1840)

Zwei alte Eheleute, die gleichzeitig gestorben waren, verordneten, daß sie in grünen Särgen begraben würden, und sollte es öffentlich mitgeteilt werden, wie sie diese Farbe noch sterbend gewählt, um damit ihre süße Hoffnung von der baldigen Rückkehr ihres geliebten Königs kundzugeben. Dieser Verordnung wurde nachgekommen, und es gab ein wahres Volksfest, als das Begräbnis stattfand. Das Rondeel am Halleschen Tore war gedrängt voll Menschen, die des Schauspiels warteten, und als der Leichwagen erschien, musste dem Drängen der Menschen gewillfahrt und die Umhüllung gelüftet werden, damit die grünen Särge sichtbar würden, die jeder mit Entzücken betrachtete. Der Kirchhof konnte gar die Schar der Schaulustigen nicht fassen, und ernsthaftes Einschreiten der Polizei und Bürgergarde vermochte nur die Tore desselben zu schließen; sonst möchte manches Grab und Denkmal vernichtet worden sein.

Fontane's version
(1878)

Die beiden alten Sängebuschens, die hier gleich um die Ecke wohnten, zwei Häuser von der Waisenkirche, die waren es also. Er war Registrator, aber früher war er Soldat gewesen und hatte unter vier Königen gedient, und als das Rheinsberger Denkmal fertig war und Prinz Heinrich alle alten Soldaten einlud, da lud er auch den alten Sängebusch ein, daß er mit dabei sein sollte. Ich habe den Brief selbst gesehen, alles deutsch geschrieben, aber Henri war französisch. Und als er nun starb, ich meine den alten Sängebusch, da fanden sie einen Zettel, darauf geschrieben stand, daß er in einem grünen Sarg begraben werden wolle, bloß um seinen Glauben und seine Zuversicht zu zeigen, daß sein liebes Vaterland Preußen wieder aufkommen würde...Und nun starb ja die Frau, die auch alt und krank war, denselben Tag, und so kam es, daß z w e i grüne Särge bestellt wurden. Der alte Prediger Buntebart aber, als sie begraben werden sollten, ließ eine schwarze Bahrdecke darüber decken, weil er ängstlich war und keinen Lärm und keinen Aufstand haben wollte. Aber da kennt er die Berliner schlecht, und als der Zug sich in Bewegung setzte, rissen sie die Bahrdecke herunter, daß die grünen Särge wieder sichtbar wurden, und so trugen sie sie zwischen vielen Tausend Menschen hin, und alles nahm den Hut ab und dachte bei sich: "Ob wohl der alte Sängebusch recht behalten wird?"

Part of Frau Hulen's conversational lead-up to the story is included here before her narration of the anecdote proper, because this lead-up to the story gives important variations against the original text. In Fontane's version, many aspects of the text are made more personal and more intimate. The modifications in this direction include the naming of the characters. The historical character involved was a master-tailor called Friedrich Wilhelm Meinerd. Neither his name nor the date of the incident are given in the source used by Fontane at the time of composition, the memoirs of Cavan George, but they had appeared more than twenty years previously in the "Neues Berlinisches Historienbuch" by Fontane's friend and "Kreuzzeitung" colleague, George Hesekiel,[1] who had also used

1 Berlin 1851. See the chapter entitled "Die grünen Särge und die Louisen-insel", p. 388-389. Here the date of the death is given as 1808, while Hesekiel's pedestrian patriotic poem is entitled "Ein grüner Sarg 1807". The second last stanza runs as follows:

> Und also ist's geschehen
> Einst in der Stadt Berlin,
> Man hat das Paar begraben
> Im Sarge, der war grün.

(G. Hesekiel: "Preußenlieder." Magdeburg 1848, p. 25). Frau Hulen dates it as 1807. Through its verbosity and tendency to pad out the incident, Hesekiel's fictional use of the anecdote in Chapter 12 of his novel "Graf d'Anethan d'Entragues" makes an interesting contrast to Fontane's tauter version:

> Es waren zwei Särge, die man da hertrug neben einander. Die Särge waren ganz schlicht, aber sie waren mit grüner Farbe angestrichen; das schon fiel dem Grafen auf, aber noch mehr der unendlich lange Zug von Leidtragenden, der paarweise, an ihm vorüberwallte und sich noch vergrößerte durch Männer, die hier und da einzeln aus den Häusern oder gruppenweise aus den nächsten Straßen hervortraten und sich anschlossen. Die Leidtragenden gehörten sichtlich zum größten Theil dem Handwerkerstand an, aber man sah auch alte Herren darunter, deren Haltung den Soldaten verrathen haben würde, auch ohne das "pour le mérite-" oder Johanniterkreuz am Halse und die Ordensbänder im Knopfloch. Der Graf ließ den langen Zug an sich vorübergehen und

the anecdote in two literary works of his own. Fontane was familiar with Hesekiel's works, as we know from "Von Zwanzig bis Dreißig" and his reviews of Hesekiel's productions. The names invented by Fontane for the "Vor dem Sturm" version are ones which strike the ear as well as the eye, Sängebusch and Buntebart. These names have a slightly comic element, which fits in with the general treatment of the petit-bourgeois circle in the novel. The minister, Buntebart, appears to have been totally invented by Fontane, since he does not appear in any of the other versions. This is a significant addition, because it lends the incident a figure in authority, and one who is anxious not to have a political demonstration which might be displeasing to the French authorities.

The action concerning the unveiling of the coffins is described in the original with the aid of impersonal verbs in the passive voice: "wurde nachgekommen"; "musste gewillfahrt"; "gelüftet werden"; "sichtbar wurden". The difference of opinion between the ordinary people and Buntebart makes the novel version more dramatic and interesting than the impersonal expression of the incident in George's version. In the latter the covering is removed, while in the novel the Berliners tear it off the coffins. Frau Hulen lapses into the present tense when commenting on Buntebart's lack of understanding of the

erschöpfte sich in Vermuthungen. Die Haltung des Leichengefolges, die ernst war, aber auch hier und da eine Art von Trotz verrieth, imponierte ihm. Er sich um nach Jemanden, der ihm das Rätsel löse..... "Es ist das eine unschädliche Demonstration," erklärte der Gefällige, "es ist ein alter Schneidermeister, den sie dort begraben; er ist an einem Tage mit seiner Frau gestorben und hat letztwillig verfügt, daß man ihm (sic) und seine Frau in grünen Särgen beerdigen möge, weil grün die Farbe der Hoffnung sei und er sowohl als sein Weib in der festen Hoffnung sterbe, daß der König und die Königin bald wieder siegreich zurückkommen würden nach Berlin. Sie wissen nun, meine Herren, daß alle Verständigen nicht mehr an die Rückkehr des Königs glauben, da Seine Majestät der Kaiser unüberwindlich ist, aber das Volk sieht das nicht ein in seiner Beschränktheit, es denkt wie der alte bornirte Schneidermeister, und zum Zeichen, daß es an die siegreiche Rückkehr des Königs glaubt, zieht es hinter den grünen Särgen her. (G. Hesekiel: "Graf d'Anethan d'Entragues." Berlin 1856, p. 197-198)

Berliners in having the coffins draped in black: "Da kennt er die Berliner schlecht." While the original stresses the fact that this funeral is a spectacle: "Menschen, die des Schauspiels warteten" and "Särge, die jeder mit Entzücken betrachtete" and finally "die Schar der Schaulustigen", the novel version omits all references to a theatrical quality in the scene. This feature is appropriate for the depth of feeling which is expressed in Frau Hulen's version, and which is completely lacking in the original. George relates the anecdote as an onlooker, while Frau Hulen brings out the emotions of the people concerned. For this reason her tale ends with the statement that everyone removing his hat for the cortege wondered if Sängebusch would be right (in his hopes for the ultimate victory of Prussia). Not only does the novel version give the dead couple a name, but also an address, which again makes the anecdote seem close to those of whom it is being related: Herr Sängebusch lived "just around the corner, four doors from the orphanage".

The treatment of Sängebusch's will is another factor which distinguishes the two versions. George mentions the "directive" of the poor couple, which was to be "publicly communicated" (another theatrical element), while the fictional Sängebusch merely leaves a note behind. In George's version the old couple die at the same time, whereas the fictional version mentions first the death of Sängebusch, then the death of his wife, who was also sick and old, thus again emphasizing the individual element. Frau Sängebusch is also buried in a green coffin, although there is no evidence in the novel that she and her husband had agreed on this. His note tell of h i s wish to be buried in such a coffin, so the reader supplies that the community, or like-minded friends, decided to order two green coffins. The wording of the note or directive varies significantly in both versions: George's couple wanted a public announcement of their wish for green coffins in order to demonstrate their "süße Hoffnung von der baldigen Rückkehr ihres geliebten Königs". The rather sentimental language in this phrase is modified into Sängebusch's "dear fatherland, Prussia" in Frau Hulen's version.

The alteration of the motif of loyalty to the king to loyalty to the fatherland is the most significant change of content in the novel version. It is precisely because it is not loyalty to the king that this anecdote is relevant to the main plot and theme of the novel. The longing for freedom of the people in 1813 is the factor which really brings about liberation, and this is so in spite of the authorities' initial distaste for fighting. This aspect is mirrored again in the reaction of the authority figure, the vicar, Buntebart, in Frau Hulen's words. The conclusion in both versions again underlines their differences: Georges's version is concerned with police activity and the fear of damage to graves and monuments. Frau Hulen's story is concerned only with the hopes of the people paying their last respects to Sängebusch. The 'Fronde' element[1] which is hinted at in the references to Prince Henry's monument in the conversational lead-up to Frau Hulen's anecdote throws further illumination on Sängebusch's politics. Although he served as a soldier under four kings, Fontane's Sängebusch was probably not uncritical of the monarchy. The fact that he was invited by Prince Henry to Rheinsberg seems to suggest this. Fontane's deliberate alteration of the wording on the old man's note removes the emphasis on loyalty to Frederick William III, who is a mere individual. The fact that all the people are concerned for the country makes the story appropriate for 1813.

It is clear that for one half-page of this novel's text, Fontane did a great deal of work in modifying the original and adapting it down to the last detail to suit his own work. He produces in the end a story which seems similar to the original, but which on analysis can be seen to be full of new associations and nuances that considerably alter the impact of the facts. His story is at once much more personal (thereby suiting the petit-bourgeois Frau Hulen, who thinks in restricted terms) a n d more political. The modifications of this story of an incident which took place after the Battle of Jena and defeat of Prussia make it relevant to the 1813 situation. It is such little features which show Fontane to be capable of masterful adaptation of anecdotes for his fiction already in 1878. Frau Hulen's story carries more significance for the contemporary political

1 It also links up with the historical fact that the starting-point of the liberation was the act of the 'frondeur', Yorck von Wartenburg.

situation than she is herself aware of. Her limited vision is brought before the reader immediately after her narration of the anecdote, when she claims that Sängebusch w a s right, because her baker has said: "Preußen kommt wieder auf."[1] This final feature emphasises once again the striking characteristic of the green coffins anecdote: that loyalty is coming directly from the people. The green coffins story, coming immediately after the extemely well-known and in no way novel Frederician anecdotes provides a fresh contrast to the canon drawn on by Klemm and Schimmelpenning in their bickering, and constitutes the most original contribution of Fontane to the anecdotes supporting the theme of loyalty unto death in "Vor dem Sturm".

In general, the figures in "Vor dem Sturm" are introduced by means of 'en bloc' characterizations by the narrator. This technique, which features also in "L'Adultera",[2] is used very little by Fontane in the Berlin novels but reappears strikingly in "Der Stechlin". In those works in which 'en bloc' characterizations are rare, the characters show their nature almost totally through their actions and conversations. They are also analysed in the conversations of others.

The figure of Bamme is remarkable in "Vor dem Sturm" on several counts.[3] He is not a major figure, yet he is one of the most memorable of Fontane's less important characters. As well as giving an 'en bloc' characterization of Bamme, the narrator leans heavily on the use of the anecdote in order to draw a picture of this character. Possibly in order to prepare us for the string of anecdotes which almost completely make up the characterization of Bamme,

1 NyA I, 309. See W. Wagner: "Die Technik der Vorausdeutung in Fontanes 'Vor dem Sturm' und ihre Bedeutung im Zusammenhang des Werkes." Marburg 1966, p. 117 on Frau Hulen's story as "Vorausdeutung zum Zeitgeschehen".

2 First published in the journal "Nord und Süd" in 1880, approximately two years after "Vor dem Sturm".

3 It is interesting to note that even in his first novel, Fontane chooses someone to carry a 'message', who is an outsider. Bamme, although a nobleman, is not conventional, and is the first of the aristocratic figures in "Vor dem Sturm" to formulate the point (supported by the plot) about the equality of human beings.

the narrator informs us about one of his attributes: "Dazu kam, daß er sich gab, wie er war, und sein eigenes Leben rückhaltlos in den pikantesten Anekdoten aufdeckte."[1]

The narrator does not however allow Bamme to tell all of his own anecdotes, or another character to relate them about him, but tells two of them himself as an introduction to the figure of Bamme in Chapter 20, 'Allerlei Freunde'. In the context of the information that the house of Bamme will die out with his demise (which, the narrator confides to the reader, will be no great loss!), an anecdote is related from Bamme's dissipated youth. This concerns a former girlfriend, who, now mad, shouts as the coffin of Bamme's father is being lowered into the crypt at Rathenow: "Seht, nun fährt er in die Hölle."[2] Bamme's presence of mind comes out in this as well as in the story about his insult to a neighbour whose barn has burned.[3]

In Chapter 22, during Tante Amelie's dinner, Bamme shocks the the more sensitive guests with his scurrilous and blasphemous anecdotes. His account of settling a score with the local pastor depends for its wit on the coincidence between his own name and that of Lot's grandson in the Old Testament.[4] With this anecdote Bamme claims a victory over the pastor's disapproval of his necrophiliac tendencies. Fontane borrowed this necrophiliac feature for the characterization of Bamme from Prince Henry of Prussia, and it adds to the general air of scurrility and inscrutability which surrounds Bamme in the novel. About Bamme at the side of his beloved beautified corpses, the narrator comments: "Was dabei durch seine Seele ging, wußte niemand."[5] Bamme's disregard for the

1 NyA I, 133.
2 Ibid. 132.
3 Ibid. 133.
4 Ibid. 148.
5 Ibid. 133. The same observation is made in Chapter 13 of "Der Stechlin", where Woldemar chides Armgard for assuming that "etwas Infernales" (NyA VIII, 123) was taking place in the prince's mind on such occasions. This again provides an example of tolerance and the ability to recognise that appearances are deceptive, or that one should be sceptical of rigid interpretations. See Heiko Strech: "Die Synthese von Alt und Neu." Berlin 1970, p. 44 for an analogy with Montaigne's tolerance.

conventions of polite society in the matter of subjects of conversation leads him to tell the story of the traveller who, observing flirting couples through a great portal, is suddenly flung out into their midst "als handele es sich um den Einzug eines Triumphators".[1] This provides the signal for Amelie to break up the group around the dinner-table out of consideration for her niece, Renate. Bamme is contrasted with characters who represent opposite poles, e.g. the pietistic Tante Schorlemmer, or Renate who leads a sheltered life, and especially Marie Kniehase, to whose charm and innocence he immediately succumbs.

It is interesting that Fontane picks precisely this strange character to demonstrate the old truth that appearances are deceptive. The character of Bamme stands out among the minor characters of "Vor dem Sturm" precisely because of its scurrility. In any case, Bamme is not merely included in the novel in order to augment the number of finely-drawn figures of the Prussian aristocracy. In many ways he is shown to be typical of the March Brandenburg aristocracy, but he show a healthy disregard for snobbery and prejudice. Although a product of two famous families, Bamme blames intermarriage for his own physical degeneration. His expression of views on the relation of the Junkers to the throne is also unusually forthright: "Legitimität, Loyalität! Bah! Alles ist Akkord und Pakt und gegenseitiger Vorteil."[2] In order to illustrate his point here, he first relates the early sixteenth-century anecdote about Junker Otterstedt writing "Jochimke, Jochimke, höde di"[3] on the door of Joachim I Nestor, Elector of Brandenburg.

Bamme's unorthodoxy again comes out in his espousal of the idea of equality among all men with express reference to the three ideals of the French revolution, whereby he does not see much future for the first two. According to Bamme, equality merely means "Mensch ist Mensch".[4] This statement of equality has been

1 NyA I, 150.
2 Ibid. 498.
3 Ibid. 297. Fontane also relates the story in "Wanderungen durch die Mark Brandenburg" (NyA XII, 87) where the Junker's rebellious warning is quoted in full: "Jochimke, Jochimke höde Dy,/ Wo wi di krigen do hängen wi Dy."
4 Ibid. 633.

proven beyond doubt on the plot level, through the brave deaths of Othegraven and Hansen-Grell and through the marriage of Lewin and Marie Kniehase, which transcends class boundaries. Bamme's final message to Berndt is the lesson that noble lineage does not necessarily mean nobility of soul, and his testament quotation of a phrase of Marie Kniehase: "Ich hab es früh erfahren, wie wenig der Schein bedeutet"[1] alludes once more to that lesson. Bamme's scurrility, which is a feature of his anecdotes and conversations, subsides in the novel in the presence of Marie, which shows his sensitivity to the goodness of this very idealized figure. Thus, a link is formed between two characters of very different background, Bamme of a lineage which can boast of a Zieten in every generation, and Marie whose origins are completely obscure. Both are outsiders, and both demonstrate the point about true nobility: Bamme, through his convictions which are unorthodox for his class, and Marie, through her natural nobility.

The portrait of Henry IV of France shows a figure who combines both kinds of nobility, the hereditary and the natural, while the characterization of Bamme and Marie as well as the external line of the plot bear out this early message in the novel.

Certain artistic flaws can be noted in Fontane's first novel in the employment of anecdote. Firstly, it has a tendency to quote sources for anecdotes, which appears rather naive in the fictional context. Bamme does this in the argument about the White Lady stories in Chapter 66. The element of competition between Bamme and Drosselstein here and Amelie and Drosselstein with regard to anecdotal 'knowledge' in Chapter 36 is hardly convincing. Amelie actually quotes her source for anecdotes about Henry IV as Tallemant des Réaux, and Drosselstein refers in Chapter 36 for his Lemierre anecdotes to a collection called "Anecdotes dramatiques".[2]

1 NyA I, 638.

2 Ibid. 157. Fontane must have read "Les Historiettes" of Tallemant des Réaux (1619-1692) in the original. The first six-volume edition appeared in Paris in 1834-1835, but the first German translation by Otto Flake did not appear until 1913. The characteristics which play an important role in "Vor dem Sturm" are also among those admired by Tallemant, loyalty and magnanimity.

In later fictional works Fontane does not repeat the device of having his characters refer in such a precise way to sources for their stories In a much more natural and convincing way, Effi Briest, for example, cannot even remember the author of the poem about the 1812 incident which she sees as a parallel to her own situation. Secondly, Chapters 22, 24 and 36 of "Vor dem Sturm" give the impression that the characters are vying with each other to produce better and more amusing anecdotes, and that the narrator through hinting at this element of competitiveness is trying to render the conversations more dramatic. The element of the dramatic tension already exists in the Guse chapters with the political antagonism of Berndt and Amelie, but since this topic cannot monopolize all the Guse chapters, other elements are introduced such as the outrageousness of Bamme's character and conversation. None of Fontane's later works suffer from overuse of the anecdote, such as is the case in Chapters 22 and 24 of "Vor dem Sturm", which between them contain ten anecdotes. These two chapters have something of the air of an anecdote anthology.[1] Thirdly, the device of having the narrator tell anecdotes does not always appear successful in the novel.[2] While the narrator's telling the Kunersdorf officer's death fits comfortably into the description of the locality in Chapter 5, and as we saw, plays its role in the threefold artistic presentation of that anecdote in "Vor dem Sturm", his use of anecdotes to present the characterization of Bamme appears a trifle unsophisticated. Again this device is dropped by Fontane in later works. Henceforth, only characters tell anecdotes. Fourthly, the author's inexperience is visible in the fact that a character may tell another a full account of an anecdote with which the listener is already perfectly familiar.[3] Fifthly, a feature of artistic excellence in the employment of anecdote in "Vor dem Sturm" sometimes may not be sufficiently

1 S. Hajek considers Chapter 24 enchanting (op. cit. p.83). On the contrary, the balance of the conversations in Chapters 22 and 24 is upset by the inclusion of so many anecdotes. In refraining from this procedure in later works, Fontane possibly came to hold this opinion himself.

2 For examples of this see NyA I, 115, 132 and 133.

3 See NyA I, 93 and 398 for instances of this.

clear to the reader and some of its efficacy is thereby lost. As we have seen, the anecdotes in Chapters 22 and 24 serve a useful function for characterization, for underlining political tension and adding a note of humour, as well as for linking up through Henry IV with the theme of true nobility. This last however is the most important of their functions, and is also probably the least apparent. This would account for their being sometimes dismissed in critical literature as digressive.This may be partly due to the comprehensiveness of the novel. On the other hand, "Der Stechlin" is also a very large novel, but the significance of its anecdotes within the whole context becomes clear in a way which is not true of all the stories in "Vor dem Sturm".

The most frequent criticism levelled at Fontane's first novel is that contained in the above-mentioned letter of Paul Heyse to Wilhelm Hertz, namely, that the work digresses, and therefore lacks unity. Fontane's own defence of his novel as a 'Vielheitsroman' which has a period of time rather than a single hero as its focal point, deserves to be quoted here in the context of his intention with regard to the use of anecdote:

> Das größere dramatische Interesse, soviel räum ich ein, wird freilich immer den Erzählungen "mit e i n e m Helden" verbleiben, aber auch der Vielheitsroman, mit all seinen Breiten und Hindernissen, mit seinen Porträtmassen und Episoden, wird sich dem Einheitsroman ebenbürtig – nicht an Wirkung, aber an Kunst – an die Seite stellen können, wenn er nur nicht willkürlich verfährt, vielmehr immer nur solche Retardierungen bringt, die, während sie momentan das Gesamtwerk zu vergessen scheinen, diesem recht eigentlich dienen.[1]

It would be difficult to gainsay this eloquent defence, which indeed demonstrates the virtue of the alleged fault. Not for nothing has "Vor dem Sturm" been called one of the best historical novels in German.[2] If we apply Heyse's criticism of digressiveness to the problem of the anecdote in "Vor dem Sturm" and ask whether the anecdotes are digressive, the answer must be that in the stricts this

1 "Briefe". Ed. by Erler, vol. 1, p. 463.
2 See Walter Müller-Seidel: op. cit., p. 132.

is untrue, allowing for two exceptions.[1] It is clear that the author wanted to link all the stories and anecdotes to matters of thematic importance in the novel. That this is not totally successful can be attributed to Fontane's lack of experience as a writer of fiction in 1878. Already in a review on Julius Rodenberg's book "Studienreisen in England", he had shown in the early eighteen-seventies that he was aware of the dangers of arbitrariness in the use of the anecdote – even in a non-fictional context like Rodenberg's book.[2]

Among the original plans for the novel,[3] there is evidence that Fontane intended yet another social circle or at least a further dimension to the Ladalinski Berlin circle. This group, outlined in the plans, was to have frequented the house of Consistory Councillor Chrysander's widow,[4] and it would have provided representatives of the Saxon aristocratic and educated classes. Such notable figures of the arts and the intelligentsia as Rahel Lewin, Schadow,[5] Schinkel, Schleiermacher and Fichte were to have been included, as well as various diplomats, civil servants and army officers.[6] Had Fontane adhered to this original plan, there is no doubt, given the composition of this group that the strong anecdotal element in "Vor dem Sturm" would have been even more reinforced. The decision to drop this plan was a wise one, and even in later works Fontane avoids introducing such well-known members of the

1 These are Drosselstein's story about an incident during a performance of Lemierre's "Guillaume Tell" in Chapter 36 (NyA \ ,1263) and the narration of the big boot story in Chapter 46 (ibid. 365-366). The latter is discussed below.

2 See NyA XVIII, 557.

3 See Aufbau I, 341 and 346-347.

4 She was to be characterized as a "feine adlige Dame aus Dresden" and would have possibly been a relation of the Ladalinski or the Vitzewitz family. See Aufbau I, 346.

5 Fontane's anecdotes about Schadow are among his best-known. See "Spreeland" (NyA XIII, 299-312). These are seen as sufficiently typical of his work to represent his art of the anecdote in Jürgen Hein's anecdote anthology: "Deutsche Anekdoten." (See p. 112-119.)

6 See Aufbau I, 347.

intelligentsia, whose ideas and personalities are familiar to the reader from their own works, correspondence and other sources.

The longer of the two anecdotes which we have designated as digressive is that concerning an outsize boot acquired through a bet by Jürgaß during his days as a young officer in the Regiment Gendarmes. In itself, this is an excellent story. It is also a useful anecdote to indicate the frivolous behaviour of Prussia's crack regiment of the pre-1806 period, the Regiment Gendarmes. This point is made by the narrator, but since no further links are made with the period just before Prussia's defeat at Jena, the anecdote exists in a void. If it had not already been employed in "Vor dem Sturm" it might have been a useful element in the pre-Jena atmosphere of "Schach von Wuthenow" (1882). The narrator almost draws attention to the fact that the boot anecdote has no further function in "Vor dem Sturm" than to depict a daring practical joke played by Jürgaß as a youth. The passage in question ends with the sentence:

> Er machte übrigens nicht mehr und nicht weniger von der Sache, als sie wert war, und wenn er, die Geschichte vom "großen Stiefel" erzählend, einerseits viel zu viel Urteil hatte, um einen Fähnrichsstreich als Heldentat zu behandeln, so war er doch auch keck und unbefangen genug, sich des Übermuts seiner jungen Jahre nicht weiter zu schämen.

Thus, this anecdote remains on the level of simple characterization, a function which it performs well. The character is however a very minor one, and the reader asks if it were worth devoting over a full page to such a function. The only other function the story could have would be to create a parallel between the officers' defiance of the order from the Minister of Defence and the independence of authority shown in the main plot of the novel. However, this might be stretching interpretation a little too far. If such an interpretation were true, it would mean that the anecdote was n o t digressive, but the practical joke remains too frivolous a venture to stand as a parallel to the main plot.

Jürgaß is characterized by one anecdote from his past, and equally Bamme, as we have seen, is characterized by several from his life, which serve to make the point of his being an outsider and eccentric. The picture of Amelie as a rather eighteenth-century style lady, a lover of wit and French culture, is admirably brought out in the Guse conversations through the use of anecdote. However, as has been shown, these stories have a further function in regard to the themes of the novel. The anecdote is used in the Guse setting for the purposes of constructing conversation: the to and fro of argument is supported by the pro-French and the pro-Prussian faction by the use of anecdote. A reflection of this is visible in the conversations of the petit-bourgeois circle.[1] The anecdote performs a useful function therefore in indicating political antagonism and this is a function which recurs in "Schach von Wuthenow".

In summary, it may be said that the anecdote in "Vor dem Sturm" shows certain weaknesses in the author's art, corresponding to his relative inexperience in the sixties and seventies in the field of fiction-writing. However, the study of the anecdote shows that it is not as responsible for digression as critical literature has implied. The fact that Fontane, for example after the fashion of his "Wanderungen durch die Mark Brandenburg", includes anecdotes on local history in Chapter 27, is not proof that such anecdotes are digressive, since as we have seen, they directly relate to the theme disloyalty and also have an anticipatory function. If, however, one adds all the anecdotes to all the other forms of inserted stories (legends, ghost stories, military reports), clearly a very large inner framework of stories within stories exists in "Vor dem Sturm". To claim that these are all digressive is however false since the author uses them for various legitimate functions. They are of course r e t a r d a t i o n elements, and it is obviously a novel which is based very much on the retardation principle, which Fontane saw as serving the overall purpose of the novel, n o t as hindering it.

1 Cf. Brigitte Hauschild: "Geselligkeitsformen und Erzählstruktur. Die Darstellung von Geselligkeit und Naturbegegnung bei Gottfried Keller und Theodor Fontane." Frankfurt am Main, Bern 1981, p. 149-150 on parallels between conversations in aristocratic and 'lower' class circles in Fontane's works.

2. "Schach von Wuthenow" (1882)

Because of the multiple perspectives employed in Fontane's "Schach von Wuthenow" the reader is offered conflicting views of the novel's problematical main character and also of the problematical historical period in which it is set, i.e. Prussia just before her defeat at the battles of Jena and Auerstedt in 1806. Positive and negative opinions are voiced concerning Schach von Wuthenow by various characters in the novel, both colleagues and social acquaintances, such as Nostitz, Alvensleben, Frau von Carayon, her daughter, Victoire, Bülow and Sander. The narrator does not take sides, although the reader senses a certain sympathy on his part for Schach. This is implicitly clear throughout the story, and explicitly so when the narrator breaks his usual stance of apparent objectivity to exclaim in Chapter 13: "Armer Schach! Es war anders in den Sternen geschrieben."[1] The tension between this sympathy and the implied parallel between Schach's case and the downfall of Prussia is probably the factor which makes this novel peculiarly compelling.

Opinions are presented about Schach either directly in the form of discussion of his qualities and faults or through the use of scenes such as that in Tempelhof in Chapter 4, or indirectly through the use of anecdote. The salient features of the apparently contradictory opinions held about Schach can be summarized as follows: he is one of the best in the crack Gendarmes Regiment; he is one of the really chivalrous army officers; he is pompous and over-aware of his handsome appearance and his importance; he is not made for marriage; he is painfully aware of the opinions of others; he greatly fears ridicule and loss of social prestige; he lacks moral courage; he clings to traditional beliefs, for example, to the notion that the Frederician army is the great buttress of the state and that Prussia is invincible. Finally, his fate is seen by at least one character as merely a symptom of the general downfall of Prussia in 1806.

Early on in the novel, Schach is characterized from a critical point of view with the help of an unusual and amusing anecdote. This is related in Chapter 3 by the publisher, Sander, following a

1 NyA II, 345.

disagreement between Bülow and Schach about the political situation in Chapter 2. The introductory conversations served to supply the political setting of the novel and also to indicate the divergence of reaction to Schach: he is personally and socially attractive to the Carayons, but politically anathema to Bülow, who disapproves of Schach's reliance on the mottoes of the Frederician era. In the relaxed atmosphere of the restaurant, Bülow can be more trenchant in his criticism of Schach and his outlook than in the social setting in the Carayon salon. Schach's positive features are indicated in Chapter 3 by his army colleagues, Nostitz and Alvensleben.

This summary takes the form of an anecdote about the posthumous appointment of Saint Anthony to officer rank in the Brasilian army. Anthony (1195-1231), theologian and Franciscan preacher, called Saint Anthony of Padua after the place of his death, is the patron saint of his native country, Portugal. He had a curious posthumous role, when he was given the rank of captain in the army in 1683 and in 1814 was made lieutenant-colonel by King John VI. The presence of a statue of the saint in the ranks of battle was thought to have a good effect on the morale of the troops. The salary which the saint earned posthumously was paid to the Franciscan order.[1]

In the novel, Sander follows his anecdote about Saint Anthony with a toast to Schach which shows by implication the anecdote's relevance to the subject on hand:

> Es sind keine drei Tage,"..."daß ich in der Haude und Spenerschen gelesen, der Kaiser von Brasilien habe den heiligen Antonius zum Oberstleutnant befördert und seinen Kriegsminister angewiesen, besagtem Heiligen die Löhnung bis auf weiteres gutzuschreiben. Welche Gutschreibung mir einen noch größeren Eindruck gemacht hat, als die Beförderung. Aber gleichviel. In Tagen derartiger Ernennungen und Beförderungen wird es nicht auffallen, wenn ich die Gefühle dieser Stunde, zugleich aber den von mir geforderten Entscheid und Richterspruch, in die Worte zusammenfasse: Seine Majestät der Rittmeister von Schach, er lebe hoch![2]

1 See article 'Santo Antonio' in "Grande Enciclopedia Portugesa e Brasileira". Lisbon 1935-1960, vol. 2, p. 844-846.

2 NyA II, 289.

Sander's claim to have read the incident in the "Haude und Spener'sche Zeitung"(in 1805) amounts to a deliberate anachronism on Fontane's part, since the saint's promotion to lieutenant-colonel took place in 1814.[1] In reality, Saint Anthony was not made lieutenant-colonel by the Emperor of Brazil. Brazil did not become an empire until 1822, and in 1814, Dom John's title was Prince Regent, becoming King John VI of Portugal and Brazil only after the death of his mother, Maria I, in 1816. It is unlikely that Fontane was unfamiliar with the development of Portuguese/Brazilian history in the early nineteenth century, and probable that he deliberately chose to insert the anachronistic title of 'Emperor' (which John never held in any case), in order to strengthen the links in the novel between Schach's name and the notion of 'emperor'. The fact that Fontane took liberties with regard to dates and facts probably indicates his interest in using the anecdote to characterize Schach and throw light on the Prussian stiuation of 1805-1806. Out of a politically harmless report, of the kind which was common in Prussian newspapers under Frederick William III,[2] Fontane fashions a story which has very political undertones. Not merely the character of Schach himself, which is the subject of interest to the characters in this conversation, but the whole state of a country, which depends for its political and military strength on outmoded mottoes and beliefs, is reflected in the insertion of the anecdote about the promotion of Saint Anthony. This aspect shows Fontane's careful tying-in of anecdote with both the level of personal characterization and that of indirect political comment. A picture of the times is transmitted here through the use of a story which itself had nothing at all to do with Prussia, but which is used by Fontane as an indirect parallel. For Bülow, Schach's most severe critic in the novel, this anecdote perfectly catches the whole ludicrousness of the man's character: "Der kleine Mann in den großen Stiefeln".[3] Later in the

1 Pierre-Paul Sagave draws attention to this discrepancy in his annotated edition of the novel: "Theodor Fontane: Schach von Wuthenow." München 1966, p. 105.

2 On the frequency of such politically harmless reports during this era see Sagave: op. cit., p.103.

3 NyA II, 289.

novel this aspect of Schach's character is again exposed in a cruel and public way through the use of caricature to satirize his relations with the Carayon women. In this case, the imperial majesty referred to is the Shah of Persia, particularly suitable as an analogy because of the associations of splendour, a harem and the coincidence of Schach's name. This public satire brings about Schach's downfall insofar as he is unable to withstand it, to continue with the plans made in Chapter 13 to marry Victoire and make the best of the situation. The association of Schach with the Brazilian emperor is particularly apt from the viewpoint of a critic like Bülow, who considers Schach's political stance as outmoded and inappropriate, if not downright dangerous in the present political climate. The element of illusion in Schach's outlook is also subtly indicated through his being characterized by this anecdote. Those in the company who are aware of Schach's good qualities. Nostitz and Alvensleben, do not object to the anecdote's being connected with him, so the reader must assume that it is apt.

Significantly, in this historical novel all the anecdotes employed are concerned with either military or political affairs or personalities. This uniform tenor of the anecdotes does not make for monotony however due to the ingenuity with which Fontane exercises his anecdotal art in "Schach von Wuthenow". Within the relatively short space of twenty-one chapters, a dozen anecdotes are related and two others are referred to through the use of pictorial representation.

Already in this novel, that feature which has won Fontane most praise, namely, conversation, is used with more artistry than in the four previously published works "Vor dem Sturm", "Grete Minde", "L'Adultera" and "Ellernklipp". "Schach von Wuthenow" has been called both an historical and a social novel.[1] The subject of conversation which is of most interest to the novel's characters is naturally the clash between Napoleonic imperialism and the Prussian wish to determine its own future. This theme-complex is supported by the anecdotes which concern two great figures from

1 Sagave:: op. cit., p. 119

the French and Prussian cultures, Napoleon and Frederick the Second. The latter's death took place about twenty years before the time depicted in the novel, while the former was still at the height of his fame. A person's reaction to or interpretation of an anecdote about either of these rulers is shown by Fontane as an indication of his political outlook.

The anecdotes about Napoleon are all related in the circle around Prince Louis Ferdinand in Chapter 6, where military and political affairs are discussed. The tension of the discussion lies in the divergence of the beliefs of the participants: on the one hand, there is the member of the Prussian royal family, who is extremely critical of the French ruler's character and his utterances; on the other hand there is Bülow, personally an admirer of Napoleon and a critic of Prussia's present military and political standpoints. Yet Bülow is concerned for Prussia's welfare. Between these two poles there are the other officers, who can admire Napoleon's military strategy while deploring his politics.

The topical theme which is the starting-point of the discussion is Minister Haugwitz' negotiations for peace with France. Prince Louis Ferdinand relates the anecdote of Napoleon's scornful reaction to the 1805 dispostion of Prussia's troops: "Ah, ces Prussiens"..... "ils sont encore plus stupides que les Autrichiens."[1] Louis Ferdinand argues that if this anecdote, which he finds annoying, is genuine, the Prussians will have to be satisfied with Haugwitz' peace. To encompass a fairly complicated military situation here and to tie it up with the political events, Fontane employs a lively anecdote which appears to be of his own fabrication. Pierre-Paul Sagave's detailed study of the sources for "Schach von Wuthenow" has shown that whereas this anecdote is not to be found elsewhere, the gist of the idea in the anecdote is to be found in Karl von Nostitz' memoirs: "Leben und Briefwechsel"[2] in the passages dealing with the disposition of Prussian troops in 1806.[3] Fontane therefore shifts the

1 NyA I, 308.
2 Dresden 1848.
3 See Sagave: op. cit., p. 105.

date as given in his source back one year to suit the setting of his novel, and creates out of an attitude shown by Napoleon an anecdote with an amusing point, which is stylistically in keeping with hundreds of other anecdotal utterances of Napoleon.

Bülow's argument in this scene that the Prussian army has lost the capacity to march, because of its constant preoccupation with parading, reflects a general theme in the novel: that of the concern for appearances and lack of concern for essentials, which is a problem for Schach as well as for the army of which he is an officer. Bülow's conviction is that all modern battles have been won "mit den Beinen".[1] Prince Louis Ferdinand counters this however with the claim that Napoleon stoops to bribery in order to win battles. To prove this, he relates the anecdote of Napoleon's guessing from the very formation of the Austrian army at the Battle of Austerlitz their proposed military strategy. What seems to the Prince proof of ignoble baseness is understood by Bülow, and also by the army officers present, as another proof of Napoleon's military genius. To buttress his opinion Bülow relates the anecdote about Napoleon's order to his soldiers to annihilate four escaping Russian battalions at Austerlitz, by simply shooting not at the men but at the ice beneath their feet:

> Als das Zentrum schon durchbrochen war, hatte sich ein Teil der russischen Garde, vier Bataillone, nach ebensoviel gefrorenen Teichen hin zurückgezogen, und eine französische Batterie fuhr auf, um mit Kartätschen in die Bataillone hineinzufeuern. In diesem Augenblick erschien der Empereur. Er überblickte sofort das Besondere der Lage. "Wozu hier ein Sichabmühen en détail?" Und er befahl, mit Vollkugeln auf das E i s zu schießen. Eine Minute später, und das Eis barst und brach, und alle vier Bataillone gingen en carre in die morastige Tiefe.[2]

In Bülow's view Napoleon is a military genius, who has to deal with only mediocre strategists in his European opponents. A genius, who would think up the strategy of shooting at ice in Austerlitz, did

1 NyA II, 310.
2 NyA II, 311. Compare the fictional Bülow's version with the historical Bülow's version of the same incident:

not need to stoop to the baseness of bribery in order to win battles. Schach's contribution to the Chapter 6 conversation is in keeping with his character and political opinions as revealed so far in the novel. He firmly believes that God is on the side of Napoleon's opponents and praises Tsar Alexander I's bravery at Austerlitz. The chapter may thus end with Bülow's reaction to this, which consists of scathing remarks about the Tsar's categorization of types of female beauty, made a few days after his solemn entry into the crypt of Frederick the Second to mark friendship between Russia and Prussia in the face of French aggression. This personal anecdote is meant to denigrate the Tsar as frivolous in view of the political situation, but also allows the reintroduction of the theme of beauty which had already been anticipated in the exchange between Schach and Victoire on Philippe le Bel in Chapter 4. The theme of beauty is further discussed in Chapter 7, thus preparing the way for the conversation which ends in the sexual union of Schach and Victoire in Chapter 8.

The use of anecdotes in Chapter 6 serves repeatedly to make points in a political-military argument which is based on a fundamental issue of contemporary Prussian politics – the making and holding of a peace with France. According to Bülow, this peace is essential for the Prussians because of their weak position, and for this reason he supports Haugwitz' policy of appeasement of the French. Bülow's arguments here are, as hitherto in the novel, suspect to Schach as being unpatriotic. Bülow's anecdotes and his reception of anecdotes here are based on his admiration of Napoleon coupled with a critical appraisal of the present Prussian situation.

Die Seen waren mit flüchtenden Russen, die auf dem Eise sich davon machen wollten, übersäet. Die Französischen (sic) Artilleristen, welche gern nichts unvollendet lassen, schießen nach den Moskowitern. Napoleon kommt und ruft: nicht nach den Leuten schießen, sondern werft Granaten auf das Eis, damit es berste und zersprenge. Sogleich werden zwanzigtausend Mann verschlungen. Sie fallen ins Wasser durch die Wirkung des Feuers. (Dietrich Heinrich von Bülow: "Der Feldzug von 1805, militärisch und politisch behandelt." Berlin 1806, p. 44-45.) Cf. C. von Massenach: "Historische Denkwürdigkeiten zur Geschichte des Verfalls des Preußischen Staates seit dem Jahre 1794." Amsterdam 1809, p. 79.

Prince Louis Ferdinand and Schach show their patriotism in their anti-Napoleonic and pro-Alexandrian stance. A lesser political figure, Lombard, is dismissed by the Prince with an anecdote about Lombard's sense of humour. It concerns his unillustrious background as son of a hairdresser and son-in-law of a barber. A comparison of Fontane's version of the anecdote with the original, which is to be found in Clausewitz' "Nachrichten über Preußen in seiner großen Katastrope",[1] shows the extent to which Fontane simplifies and otherwise alters the original.

Clausewitz' version (1838)	Fontane's version (1882)
Er war von der französischen Kolonie und von geringer Geburt. Sein Vater war Perruquier; er heiratete in der Folge die Tochter eines Regimentschirurgus, die bekanntlich in der preußischen Armee ihre Laufbahn als Kompaniechirurgus mit Rasieren anzufangen pflegten. Dies gab ihm Veranlassung, seine Frau, die auf dem Punkt der Abstammung etwas empfindlicher war als er, damit zu necken, indem er frug: "Quel vers préférez-vous, ma chere? L'hirondelle d'une aile rapide frise la surface des eaux; oder rase la surface des eaux; le premier me rappelle mon père, le second le tien."	Sie wissen doch, sein Vater war Friseur und seiner Frau Vater ein Barbier. Und nun kommt ebendiese Frau, die nicht nur eitel ist bis zum Närrischwerden, sondern auch noch schlechte französische Verse macht, und fragt ihn, was schöner sei: "L'hirondelle frise la surface des eaux" oder "l'hirondelle rase la surface des eaux". Und was antwortet er? "Ich sehe keinen Unterschied, meine Teure; L'hirondelle frise huldigt meinem Vater und l'hirondelle rase dem deinigen."[2]

Prince Louis Ferdinand telling the story in Fontane's version has a more natural and conversational manner than the tone in Clausewitz' passage. The Prince shows his good breeding by not mentioning the

1 Berlin 1838, p. 450.

2 NyA II, 309. In a contemporary review, Eduard Engel, editor of "Das Magazin für die Literatur des In- und Auslandes", singled out this anecdote to indicate Fontane's assiduousness and care in the reproduction of the

low birth of Lombard in so many words, while it is expressly mentioned in the original. The mention of the occupation of Lombard's father suffices to set the picture. In Fontane's version the regimental surgeon remains a simple barber and does not promote to surgeon status, and thus the lowliness of Lombard's background is more dramatized. That barbers advanced to surgeons was in any case a well-known fact, which in this context adds nothing to the anecdote. Thus Fontane, ever-wary of extra loading in an anecdote, jettisons this detail given by Clausewitz. Not only does Lombard's wife become a poetaster in Fontane's version, but she is also given a significant new characteristic: vanity. She is a person consumed by vanity. From the technical point of view this change emphasizes the difference between the married partners (vanity on the wife's part and a good-humoured facing of facts on the husband's) and also enables the more dramatic give-and-take of conversation in Fontane's version rather than the more one-sided teasing of his wife which occurs in Clausewitz' version. This allows the 'turn-taking' in conversation which characterizes the dialogic nature of anecdotes. Only through the inclusion of Frau Lombard's question is the anecdote lent a 'provocatio': in Clausewitz' version there is none. The embarrassment of Frau Lombard at her humble origins in Clausewitz' version becomes a pretentious vanity in Fontane's version. Thus in Fontane's version the story becomes livelier and more conversational. In the fiction version, the question "Quel vers préférez vous, ma chère?" is rendered "und fragte ihn, was schöner sei?" thus making the passage more accesible to the German reader.

The most significant change made in Fontane's version, as far as content is concerned, is the addition of the characteristic of vanity,

atmosphere of pre-Jena Prussia. Before quoting the anecdote in full, Engel writes: "Daß Fontane ..... zu seinem altberlinischen Roman die fleißigsten Quellenstudien in Memoirenwerken, Briefsammlungen und sonstigem Gerümpel gemacht hat, versteht sich bei ihm von selbst: er ist ja so zu sagen der novellistische Archivdirektor der Mark Brandenburg. Solche intime Anekdoten, wie die folgende, sehr echt klingende vom Minister Lombard, findet man nicht auf der Straße." ("Das Magazin für die Literatur des In- und Auslandes", 52, 1882, p. 720.)

an addition which provides yet another reference in the novel to the theme of appearances and reality. This theme is not simply restricted to the personal vanity of the main character. Things are not what they seem to be. Clinging to Frederician modes of thinking and operating has already become outdated and unreal in the Prussia of 1805-1806. Prince Louis Ferdinand is not aware that his story has a part in indirectly describing the perilous state of his country. With the story he merely intends to characterize Lombard himself, to show the minister's gift for self-persiflage. However, even the prince thinks that the minister is 'not a character, but a buffoon', and thus an apt comment is made on a politician to whom much blame attached a f t e r the Battle of Jena.

The Lombard anecdote which lives in Fontane's version on the tension between the wife's vanity and self-delusion on the one hand and the husband's honesty, humour and self-persiflage on the other has its counterpart in the Frederician anecdote told shortly afterwards by Bülow:

> Erinnern Sich Königliche Hoheit der Worte des Großen Königs, als General Lehwald ihm seine dreimal geschlagenen Regimenter in Parade vorführte? "Propre Leute", hieß es. "Da seh Er meine Sehen aus wie die Grasdeibel, a b e r b e i ß e n."[1]

With this anecdote from the Seven Years' War Bülow illustrates the overemphasis of Prussia on appearances before the Battle of Jena. By allowing Bülow to relate this story, Fontane shows that he is not mere negative critic of his country. He is appealing to the example of a figure admired even by his political opponents in order to win his argument that the present Prussian army is too interested in outward show and too little aware of its deficiencies in war-time. For the present trend towards "Dressur und Spielerei"[2] in 1805 Bülow finds an eighteenth-century parallel in the impressive-looking but ineffective regiments of General Lehwald. Bülow's arguments concerning the present Franco-Prussian conflict are based on the belief that it is a case of genius versus mediocrity. Significantly, the

1 NyA II 310.
2 Ibidem.

conflict between Schach, the upholder of traditional Prussian values,[1] and Bülow, the 'Zeitkritiker', is also portrayed as a tension between the mediocre and outstanding. Even Victoire, who loves Schach, has to admit that socially and intellectually he is no match for Bülow.

Fontane avoids a possible longueur in an extension of the Chapter 6 discussion. Having broken off the conversation at the point where the political element meets the beauty theme, which is of importance for the love plot, he allows the entry of the composer and pianist, Dussek, to interrupt this topic, to which the characters only return at a later stage of the evening in Chapter 7. The theme of appearances receives an extra dimension in Chapter 7 through the discussion on the topic of official decorations. The news conveyed to the group around Louis Ferdinand by Dussek of Iffland's having being refused a decoration through court intrigue sparks off an argument, which is less heated than that about Napoleon and the present state of Prussia. In this second argument, which gives scope for humour and more narration of anecdotes, Schach himself plays no part, but it is none the less relevant to his characterization and, like the discussion on Napoleon and Prussia, to the future state of his country. Bülow shows aristocratic disdain for the bourgeois love of old-fashioned advancements like decorations. Sander, the only bourgeois[2] present besides Dussek (who only appears in order to bring the news of Iffland and thus change the topic and tone of the conversation), takes his revenge by telling an anecdote about Generalfeldmarschall Kalckreuth. He was not liked by Frederick the Second and, on receiving the Red Eagle decoration, the second highest order of the Prussian monarchy (the highest being the Black Eagle), threw it down in

1 Schach's resolution of his dilemma shows that this aspect of his character involves more a rigorous adherence to the letter rather than the spirit of Prussian values, hence the importance of the theme of appearances in the novel, a theme which refers both to the main character and to the country itself, and which is supported by anecdotes.

2 In Chapter 4, Schach had spoken with aristocratic disdain of Sander, calling him "diesen aufgedunsenen Roturier" (NyA II, 297)

anger, saying "Da liege, bis du schwarz wirst".[1] relates two anecdotes on the subject of public honours and decorations, and in doing so shows that he is capable of seeing both sides of the problem. His first anecdote concerns a general who would have given back the Black Eagle decoration, had he been able to get rid of the red one again!

The second anecdote shows that Bülow can appreciate the worth of honours where they reward a great achievement. Interestingly, although the name of Napoleon is not mentioned, Bülow's second anecdote concerns the defence of Acre by Admiral Sidney Smith in 1799 against Napoleon's siege. Bülow can claim that although Sidney Smith normally had contempt for decorations, he accepted as a recompense for his services to the city the medallion of Richard the Lion-Hearted from the Bishop of Acre. This anecdote earns Bülow the Prince's praise: "ein neuer Beweis, daß der Teufel nicht halb so schwarz ist, als er gemalt wird."[2] By having Bülow relate two anecdotes on the same subject which demonstrate that he can see both the pros and the cons, and also by his choice of an anecdote from the anti-Napoleonic side, Fontane implicitly shows that Bülow an admirer of Napoleon, is a person of balanced views who can be listened to by people of the opposite political persuasion. In a similar way to the employment of the Frederician-Lehwald anecdote, this anecdotal discussion proves that Bülow's approach is balanced and not one-sided. Therefore, while Schach, the main character of the novel is of the opinion that Bülow is an unpatriotic critic of his native country, the narrator subtly suggests through the use of anecdote already in the early part of the novel that Bülow, though

1 NyA II, 316. In "Effi Briest" this anecdote plays an important role in throwing light on Innstetten's development. Innstetten attributes the anecdote to Ladenberg, who was minister from 1837 until 1842. Edgar Groß attributes the anecdote to neither Kalckreuth nor Ladenberg, but to the Berlin inn-keeper, Louis Drucker, who was well-known at a wit in the 1840's (See NyA VII, 469.) The Aufbau editors concur with P.-P. Sagave in noting Fontane's source for the anecdote about Kalckreuth as being Dietrich Heinrich von Bülow's book "Der Feldzug von 1805", vol. 2, p. xxviii. Cf. Aufbau III, 639 and P.-P. Sagave: op. cit., p.107.

2 NyA II, 317.

critical of the system, is by no means unpatriotic or lacking in respect for tradition. Fontane stresses hereby the quality of Bülow's judgement and hence his ability to judge Schach.

The theme of the genuineness of Old Prussia runs through "Schach von Wuthenow", in particular the genuineness of the Frederician Era as opposed to the instability of the present. This is clear from references in conversation, and also in situations such as the review in Chapter 8, when an old officer exclaims to Frau von Carayon and her daughter: "Es ist die Abschiedsrevue der friedericianischen Armee",[1] a statement that is proven true by history itself. The Frederician anecdotes support the theme of the genuineness of Old Prussia which shows up the present of 1805-1806. Bülow bases his criticism of Frederick's achievement on the notion that a great power was called into being which did not have enough territorial backing and which therefore had to utterly rely on military prowess against its opponents. Yet Bülow is not characterized as being totally critical of Frederick, as his use of the Lehwald anecdote as a warning to the outlook of the contemporary Prussian army indicates. Bülow's regret is merely that present-day Prussia shows too much of the Lehwaldian approach in emphasizing the outward splendour of troops which were militarily weak. The parallel with the Prussia of the pre-1806 period and with the army as portrayed in the novel is clear.

In Chapter 14, the emphasis of the narrative shifts from analysis of the political situation or of the ambivalent character of Schach through reflection in conversation towards a different kind of revelation of the hero's situation and outlook. This shift and the resulting significance attached to inanimate objects in Schach's surroundings at Schloß Wuthenow provide an unusual caesura in the novel, during which the reader is for the first and last time introduced in a sustained way to the inner working of Schach's mind. Until this point in the novel, the reader has been dependent for his notion of Schach's character on the views of other characters (as exemplified in one case by the Saint Anthony anecdote), on the sparing use of his encounters with individuals outside of the group

1 NyA II, 323.

conversation situations (e.g. with Frau von Carayon and Victoire) and on the very limited amount of hints from the narrator.

In the caretaker's drawing-room in Chapter 14, the objects and furnishings described in a seemingly neutral fashion, can be related on closer analysis to Schach's own situation.[1] Even the very pictures in this drawing-room are of significance. They are illustrations of alleged incidents from the life of Frederick the Second which have gone into anecdote tradition and which demonstrate his cleverness in dangerous and difficult situations. In the first instance, he intimidates a threatening Pandour at the Battle of Soor in 1745 during the Second Silesian War by simply brandishing his sword and shouting: "Du, Du!"[2] In a patriotic poem written for the occasion of the unveiling of Rauch's monument to Frederick in 1851, Fontane had referred to this incident, invoking a similar reaction from a statue to Prussia's present foes.[3] The second illustration in the caretaker's drawing-room depicts Frederick calmly greeting a group of Austrian officers after the Battle of Leuthen in 1757 in Leuthen Castle, which is still being occupied by them, with the words: "Bon soir, Messieurs."[4] These two Frederician anecdotes, as

1 Of the whole of Chapter 14 H. Rudolf Vaget claims in his article ' "Schach von Wuthenow": 'Psychographie' und 'Spiegelung' im 14. Kapitel von Fontanes "Schach von Wuthenow" ' in "Monatshefte", 61, 1969, p. 7: "Alle Motive, die später zu Schachs Selbstmord führen, sind schon an dieser Stelle versammelt, sie bildet den Angelpunkt des Romans."

2 NyA II, 356. The Pandour anecdote is recounted in Friedrich Nicolai: "Anekdoten und Karakterzüge aus dem Leben Friedrichs des Zweiten." Third edition, Berlin 1787, p. 23-24.

3 The reference to the Pandour anecdote in the poem "Der alte Fritz" runs as follows (NyA XX, 260):

> Blitz' nur herab von deiner Wacht,
> Solch Wächter mag uns taugen:
> Wir brauchen wieder, Tag und Nacht,
> Die Alten-Fritzen-Augen;
> Blitz' nur herab! und wenn im Nu
> Die Schleicher du erraten,
> Dann heb den Stock und droh: "Du, Du!"
> Wie weiland dem Kroaten.

4 In commenting on the Leuthen anecdote here, Edgar Groß (NyA II, 413)

they appear in "Schach von Wuthenow", are not prominently presented and their significance might easily be missed. The narrator is satisfied with the merest references to Frederick's words on both occasions. This disregard for the setting and exact dating of the battles in question is a realistic recognition of the fact that Schach merely observes the presence of these pictures in the caretaker's drawing-room and that in any case as a good Prussian and military man Schach is presumably perfectly familiar with these incidents from Prussian history. The anecdotes recall Prussia's military past, as well as Frederick's 'sangfroid' and bravery in remaining master of potentially dangerous situations. Schach, the ardent admirer of Frederick and officer in one of Prussia's crack regiments in 1805, cannot come to terms with the social disgrace within his own circle of marrying a less than beautiful woman. His almost dishonourable flight from Berlin in order to avoid the Carayons shows his inability to cope with a threatening situation. The element of Frederick's supreme disdain for the reactions of other people, shown in the anecdotes contrasts with Schach's fatal dependence on the opinions of others. This aspect creates a link between the calendar anecdotes in Chapter 14 and the Lehwald anecdote in Chapter 6, which shows Frederick's disdain for appearaneces.

The wreaths of everlastings which adorn these pictures provide an anticipatory reference to the death of Schach,[1] but more likely Fontane was not content here with a reference to the plot of the novel only. For the wreaths are tied with black and white bows. This use of the Prussian colours in connection with the contrasting past (Frederick) and in connection with the forward reference to

suggests poetic licence on Fontane's part, and draws attention to the well-known picture of the incident made by Arthur Kampf in 1889. The illustration in Chapter 14 of "Schach von Wuthenow" is however most certainly that of Adolph Menzel, which appeared both as an illustration of the Leuthen incident in Franz Kugler's book "Geschichte Friedrichs des Großen" (Berlin 1840-1842, p. 366) and as a large picture.

1 Cf. H. R. Vaget: op. cit., p. 6. Fontane's use of everlastings as a death motif in other novels permits this interpretation. See e.g. "Irrungen, Wirrungen", Chapters 21 and 22, and "Effi Briest", Chapter 28.

future doom can be taken as a pointer to the fate of Prussia itself in 1806. The case of Schach is representative of Prussia, not just in the overall interpretation of events given in the penultimate chapter by Schach's critic, Bülow, but even in such a tiny detail as this forward reference to the hero's death. In Chapter 20 Bülow's critical pen presents Schach's case as indicative of a Prussian situation which has been brewing since the time of Frederick the Second. A debased concept of honour in the army, which Bülow sees as having merely arrogance in place of real honour, is fundamentally the cause of both Schach's problem and the present Prussian dilemma. Nature is sacrificed to the prejudices of society. To illustrate his thesis that the cult of false honour is merely vanity and perverseness, Bülow relates a seventeenth-century anecdote from China concerning the fall of the Ming Dynasty:

> Als es mit der Mingdynastie zur Neige ging und die siegreichen Mandschuheere schon in die Palastgärten in Peking eingedrungen waren, erschienen immer noch Boten und Abgesandte, die dem Kaiser von Siegen und wieder Siegen meldeten, weil es gegen 'den Ton' der guten Gesellschaft und des Hofes war, von Niederlagen zu sprechen. Oh, dieser gute Ton! Ein Stunde später war ein Reich zerstrümmert und ein Thron gestürzt.[1]

Bülow interprets the reason for this: "Weil alles Geschraube zur Lüge führt und alle Lüge zum Tod."[2] In this letter, written a month before the defeat of Jena, Bülow sees Schach's fate as symptomatic of the whole situation in Prussia, and the use of an anecdote concerning a dynasty[3] is an obvious indication of his fears for the downfall of his own country through the war with the French: Prussia will suffer for its addiction to appearances, just as Schach himself does. When Fontane offered his novel to Julius Grosser on 31 January

1 NyA II, 384.
2 Ibidem.
3 Schach's death by his own hand is paralleled in the Chinese anecdote by the suicide of the last Ming Emperor, and care has been taken already in the work to associate him with the notion of an emperor, both in connection with the Saint Anthony anecdote in Chapter 3 and in the caricatures showing him as Shah of Persia with the Carayons in Chapter 13.

1882, he gave a similar, though very short, explanation of Schach's fate: because he cannot bear the laughter of his regiment colleagues, Schach shoots himelf after the wedding. Fontane ends his observations in this letter on a more general level: "Alles ein Produkt der Zeit, ihrer Anschauungen, Eitelkeiten und Vorurteile."[1]

In the letter to Sander, Bülow's reference back to his warning: "Hannibal ante portas"[2] is appropriate again in the context of the Ming Dynasty anecdote. During the time-gap between Chapters 20 and 21, Prussia's fate, about which Bülow has been issuing warnings since the beginning ot the novel, has been sealed at the Battle of Jena. By juxtaposing the political and personal interpretations of Schach's fate in Chapters 20 and 21, the narrator ensures an open ending. To claim that Victoire's version comes last in the novel and is therefore more valid than Bülow's creates the notion that the reader must choose between the two. One interpretation must precede the other, and it is much more in Fontane's style to give the final word, even if this is not a definitive one, to the personal voice rather than to the more abstract intellectualizing of Bülow's argument. The very presence of two apparently opposing interpretations indicates the probability of both being at least partly correct. The anecdotes in the novel certainly point to the general correctness of Bülow's assumptions, while there is nothing to suggest that Victoire is wrong in her personal assessment of Schach. The mystery of Schach's character and fate is preserved, however, from an over-rigid and exclusive explanation of any kind by her statement: "Ein Rest von Dunklem und Unaufgeklärtem bleibt, und in die letzten und geheimsten Triebfedern andrer oder auch nur unsrer eignen Handlungsweise hineinzublicken, ist uns versagt."[3] The main character is not portrayed in this novel as being endowed with intellectual or conversational brilliance, and indeed he does not relate any anecdotes, though this is quite normal for a central character in Fontane's works. His critic and opponent, Bülow, tells four, i.e. the lion's share of the anecdotes in the novel. These, even

1 Erler: "Briefe", vol. 2, p. 56.
2 NyA II, 281 and 384.
3 Ibid. 385.

where amusing in themselves, are not on frivolous or merely entertaining topics. They all relate seriously to the situation of a country in jeopardy. Even the Sidney Smith anecdote has its link with politics for two reasons. Firstly, opposition to Napoleon is the background to the siege of Acre and to the perilous political situation in Prussia. Secondly, Bülow's interpretation of the anecdote that decoration for a worthy deed is worth receiving reflects the important theme in the novel of reality versus appearances, a theme which in the context of the Prussia of pre-1806 is extremely political. Because Bülow is an admirer of Napoleon, the picture of the French emperor which emerges from the anecdotes about him in this novel is more consistent with historical reality than that provided in "Vor dem Sturm". Fontane called the latter "meinen vaterländlischen Roman"[1] and on the whole, the Napoleonic anecdotes in it are restricted to anti-Napoleonic circles, those around Berndt von Vitzewitz and Count Drosselstein. Therefore, these anecdotes stressed Napoleon's weaknesses rather than his good qualities. History – in particular the pre-1806 period in Prussia and the background of the Frederician era – is presented in "Schach von Wuthenow" in a most palatable way, created by the use of intelligent and witty conversation, which has the added attraction of being shared by upholders of differing political views. In the presentation of conversation, Fontane here reaches a degree of excellence which was promised, but not altogether attained in the four preceding works "Vor dem Sturm", "Grete Minde", "L'Adultera", and "Ellernklipp". The style and situation of both "Grete Minde" and "Ellernklipp" make them unsuitable for such conversation, and no anecdotes occur in them. In looking at Fontane's development therefore up until 1882, "Vor dem Sturm" and "L'Adultera" can be seen as the real forerunners of "Schach von Wuthenow",[2] as far as the employment of anecdotes is concerned. In proportion to its overall length, the "Schach" novel

1 To Friedrich Paulsen (29.11.1897) in "Briefe an die Freunde". Edited by Friedrich Fontane and Hermann Fricke. Berlin 1943, vol. 2, p. 612.

2 "Vor dem Sturm" is a closer forerunner than "L'Adultera", by virtue of its sharing with "Schach von Wuthenow" the historical aspect.

makes very extensive use of the anecdote. Including the references to the two Frederician anecdotes brought in by way of pictorial representation, a dozen anecdotes appear within the space of twenty-one short chapters.

The historical setting was obviously favourable in Fontane's view to the use of anecdote in the work. In the use of a string of anecdotes within one chapter, "Schach von Wuthenow" still partly shares the anecdotal tendency which Fontane did not altogether control in "Vor dem Sturm". But the impression in Chapters 22 and 24 of "Vor dem Sturm" that the reader is temporarily reading an anecdote anthology is not reproduced in "Schach von Wuthenow". Where several appear, as for example during Prince Louis Ferdinand's evening entertainment in Chapters 6 and 7, they are plausibly introduced in view of the company present, as well as integrally related to the themes under discussion. A slight tendency exists here to let the narration of anecdotes almost carry the whole conversation, as is the case in the disucssion of public honours and decorations, while the discussion of the Prussian political and military situation and the figure of Napoleon also relies heavily on the use of anecdote. This is perhaps due to the very economy of the novel, which was, however, not the case in "Vor dem Sturm", where the tendency is also apparent.

The analysis of the use of anecdote in "Schach von Wuthenow" shows that it predominantly serves to delineate the political, military and social situation in Prussia during the pre-1806 period. Even where used for the purposes of characterization, i.e. Sander's anecdote about Saint Anthony, the story indirectly shares in the general picture provided of Prussia, because of the links established between the main character and the country itself. Bülow's critical theme that Prussia has not moved with the times and still holds to outdated concepts of itself is opposed by Schach in conversation, namely by someone who himself shares these concepts. The use of the Saint Anthony anecdote, which relies for its humour on the discrepancy between concept and reality, is therefore particularly apt as a method of characterization.

As befits a novel in which Fontane gives a vivid picture of a circumscribed and critical period of history, the majority of anecdotes used is contemporary to the action: the Saint Anthony anecdote, the stories about Napoleon, Lombard and Admiral Sidney Smith. Four anecdotes take their origin in the eighteenth century from the time of Frederick the Second and are employed either as a solemn warning to the present by contrasting reality and appearances (Lehwald), or to comment on human weakness with regard to decorations (Kalckreuth), another variation on the theme of appearances, or as an indirect contrast to the indecisive weakness of the main character (Frederick).

The final anecdote in the novel is also the one which is the most removed in time and space from the contemporary setting. In employing this story from the fall of the Ming Dynasty in 1644, Fontane shows his penchant for associating seemingly unrelated factors. A close connection is actually established between the Ming story and Prussia's story of 1806: Peking court protocoll prevented the narration of defeats, a refusal to face reality up until the last moment; the cult of false honour and reliance on appearances prevents Prussia from facing reality. Like the Ming dynasty and like Schach himself, it was to meet with a sudden downfall.

The anecdote is of great importance in "Schach von Wuthenow" because here Fontane uses it consistently as a pointer towards factors which underlie a general analysis of Prussia's situation in a difficult period, while at the same time linking it with the individual fate of the hero. Because of the sympathy with which Schach is portrayed, the reader is pulled between compassion for the main character and a growing realization that he unfortunately mirrors the problems of his country. The anecdote is used mostly to comment on the present situation in Prussia, and where it refers directly to the hero, it is also an indirect comment on the general situation. Fontane uses the anecdote in "Schach von Wuthenow" in three ways: firstly, to build up the social atmosphere: the anecdote is an integral part of the urbane, polished conversation of the Berlin salon, secondly, (and arising directly out of the choice of anecdotal theme) to convey the sense of a weakness at the core of army and state and also of the hero and thirdly, arising from these factors, the sense of threat and inevitable doom.

3. "Unterm Birnbaum" (1885)

Already in the year of its appearance a reviewer noted the importance of anecdotal elements for the purposes of characterization in "Unterm Birnbaum".[1] In 1904, Josef Ettlinger connected the genesis of the 'Novelle' with Fontane's preference for "interessante Fälle", which he saw as typical of Fontane's matter-of-fact nature and of his penchant for ballad and anecdote.[2]

Unlike other works of Fontane in which one of the protagonists has committed or is destined to commit a crime, "Grete Minde" and "Ellernklipp", the criminal in "Unterm Birnbaum" does not become divorced from society. A social circle exists in Tschechin with which Hradscheck is associated by virtue of his position as publican in the rural community. Thus, although he may not be particularly liked, as far as character goes, by the peasants, the criminal is nevertheless a constant participant in their social gatherings, because these take place in his own premises. In this 'Novelle' interest in the crime is minimal.[3] Fontane's overriding preoccupation is the psychological aspect. The deliberate exclusion of a description of the crime itself, of a statement that the murder of Szulski was committed by Hradscheck or even that a murder had taken place, constitutes one of the most admirable aspects of the 'Novelle', leaving Fontane free to dwell on perspectives other than Hradscheck's, such as the accounts of Mutter Jeschke and Jakob of events at the inn on the night of Szulski's disappearance.

Besides being a story of an individual's involvement in crime, the

1 Possibly Karl Frenzel. See Aufbau IV, 552.

2 Josef Ettlinger: "Theodor Fontane." Berlin 1904, p. 30.

3 Although frequently used for pedagogical purposes, "Unterm Birnbaum" has not yet received extensive critical attention. Fontane's use of the anecdote in it demonstrates the great attention which he paid to detail as well as the way in which such detail contributes to the overall complex of the work. Hugo Aust rightly draws attention to the subtlety of one of its aspects, namely the narrator's use of substitutes or paraphrases for balder terminology which he might have used for Hradscheck's deed. See H. Aust: 'Die Bedeutung der Substitute für die Interpretation. Zu Theodor Fontanes "Unterm Birnbaum" ' in DU 29, Heft 6, p. 44-51.

'Novelle' presents a picture of the period around 1830, an era which because of its political upheavals had been a subject of great interest to the young Fontane. The figure of Szulski is given life through his characterization as a would-be Pole. In the context of his romantic and affected embracing of the Polish cause the first anecdote of the 'Novelle' is related. The Polish question is the main topic of conversation in Hradscheck's inn for one of the twenty chapters.

Through antedating the actual murder which was committed in 1836 and discovered in 1842,[1] Fontane was able to introduce into "Unterm Birnbaum" the added interest of the post-1830 period. This allows him to make the Polish revolution of November 1830 the main subject of conversation in Chapter 5, so that Szulski is given a position of importance which he otherwise could not plausibly have held as a mere travelling salesman. During the convivial evening with the locals in Hradscheck's inn, Szulski plays an 'eye-witness' of events in Warsaw, thus bringing the otherwise politically isolated peasants into contact with the world outside. The antedating to the period between 1831 and 1833 also enables Fontane to make allusions to Louis Philippe and the Paris Revolution of 1830. This happens in Chapter 13 and serves as a basis for depicting Hradscheck's ambivalent political stance.[2]

Chapters 5 and 13 form a larger political backdrop for the normally quiet Oder village. In Chapter 5, the political situation in

1 See H. Spremberg: 'Fontane's "Unterm Birnbaum" ' in "Brandburgische Zeitschrift für Heimatkunde", 1928, Heft 2, p. 26 ff. Spremberg gives an account of the murderer, Fitting, in the village of Letschin, where the Fontanes lived from 1838 until 1850. Lionel Thomas draws attention to a case which was similar, that of the English couple called Manning, who murdered a wealthy bachelor in 1849. (L.T.C. Thomas: 'Fontane's "Unterm Birnbaum" ' in GLL 1970, p. 199)

2 The narrator remarks after the French officers' conservative rejection of a constitution and of the 'bourgeois monarchy' of Louis Philippe: "Wenn so das Gespräch ging, ging unserm Hradscheck das Herz auf, trotzdem er eigentlich für Freiheit und Revolution war. Wenn es aber Revolution nicht sein konnte, so war er auch für Tyrannei. Bloß gepfeffert mußte sie sein. Aufregung, Blut, Totschießen, – wer ihm das leistete war sein Freund, und so kam es, daß er über Louis Philipp mit zu Gericht saß, als ob er die hyperloyale Gesinnung seiner Gäste geteilt hätte." (NyA III, 375)

Poland is sketched, albeit with a bias, by the employment of Szulski as a kind of messenger from abroad. The full impact of the tragic nature of the Polish insurrection is not transmitted by this sort of messenger, since his identity as a Pole is suspect. Furthermore, his narrations turn out to be rather inconsequential anecdotes, so that the revolution simply becomes 'Stammtischdecor' in Hradscheck's inn.[1] The narrator regards Szulski, who was formerly merely Schulze from Upper Silesia, with some irony. Even the question of Szulski's participation or non-participation in armed combat in Warsaw is ironically pointed out by the narrator: "Er ließ dies vorsichtig im Dunkel."[2] His anecdote about the storming of a house in Warsaw is, like the teller himself, tinged with ambiguity. It descends to the melodramatic with the story of the beautiful woman who threw herself with her children into the Vistula in order to escape the advancing Russians. Szulski's ambiguous remark "ich hätte ihr was Bessres gewünscht"[3] is made to back up his assertions of the truth of the anecdote in the face of Kunicke's doubts about its veracity, and is also the kind of double entendre which particularly appeals to the peasants. Szulski repeatedly makes assertions about the truth of his account, using his alleged nationality as a guarantee of its truthfulness. Such assertions make the reader all the more suspicious of his sincerity. But any possible lack of sincerity is counterbalanced by his qualities as a narrator of anecdotes, a fact which is pointed out twice by the narrator of the 'Novelle' and which is the raison d'etre of the social gathering in Chapter 5.[4]

On the heels of the personal anecdote about the Dlugastraße incident, Szulski gives a revolutionary explanation of Poland's ills,

1 Irene Ruttmann's term in her epilogue to the Reclam edition of "Unterm Birnbaum". Stuttgart 1971, p. 131.

2 NyA III, 338.

3 Ibid. 339.

4 In a generalization typical of Fontane we are told that Szulski "als guter Weinreisender natürlich auch ein guter Erzähler war" (Ibid. 338) and also later "auch darin durchaus Anekdoten- und Geschichtenerzähler von Fach war, daß er sich nicht gern unterbrechen ließ". (Ibid. 340-341)

namely that it was betrayed only by the money-loving, possessive aristocracy: "Und wenn der Mensch erst an sein Geld denkt, ist er verloren."[1] On the basis of this generalization, the narrator has led the discussion of Polish political events back to one of the main themes of the work, namely money and possessions. For these and to avoid the shame of being divested of them, Hradscheck will commit murder the same night. It is no accident therefore that Kunicke is immediately let mention Hradscheck's name to support his counter-argument that everyone thinks of his money. As soon as possible Hradscheck steers the conversation away from Szulski's condemnation of those who are always anxious about money and back to the Polish question with a query about the veracity of the anecdote about Constantine and the eleven tallow lights. In this anecdote, the Russians again take a beating from Szulski in the person of Prince Constantine, the Russian regent in Poland, whose trick on Polish guests misfired, so that he himself had to eat one of the tallow lights intended for the others. Both of Szulski's anecdotes condemn the Russians from different points of view. In the first, Russian brutality is brought out by the beautiful Polish woman's throwing herself in the Vistula. In the second, the Russians are no longer victorious, but a laughing stock, since Prince Constantine's cunning redounds upon himself.

By choosing a pseudo-Pole to present by way of anecdotes the Polish question, Fontane adds an extra dimension to the situation in Chapter 5, namely irony and humour, which could hardly have been the case had he chosen a character who was both a real Pole and a genuine revolutionary.[2] It is not so much the anecdotes themselves

1 NyA III, 340.

2 Perhaps the ambiguity of the presentation of the Polish revolution in Chapter 5 is also connected with Fontane's ambivalent attitude towards revolution. Chapter 12 of "Meine Kinderjahre" gives a lively picture of the precocious eleven-year-old Fontane avidly reading accounts of the 1830 revolutions in the newspapers. The passage draws attention to his divided sympathies in the political field, which still obtain in the 1890's. In spite of sumpathy for the revolt of oppressed peoples which springs from his love of freedom, his 'sense of order' lets him experience "ein gewisses Engagement zugunsten der geordneten Gewalten, auch die russische nicht ausgeschlossen". (NyA XIV, 115)

here which lend an ambiguous note to the Polish problem, as their presentation by the chauvinistic Szulski. His generalization: "Kein Pole schneidet auf"[1] is gainsaid by his own manner of narration. The lack of a developed consciousness on the part of the listeners in this narrational situation is underlined by the slight role played by the peasants here. The conversation threatens to trail off into the realm of the ambiguously prurient already after the Dlugastraße anecdote and after the anecdotal element is replaced by the rousing song "Die letzten Zehn vom vierten Regiment", the peasants return to this area of entertainment.

Chapters 6 and 19 are concerned with the after-effects of the murder of Szulski – the Hradschecks' attempts to cover up, Abel's arrest and vindication through the 'finding' of the Frenchman's skeleton, Ursel's death brought about through fear and guilt, Hradscheck's embarking on a new life and his final attempt to remove all traces of the crime, which ends in his own death. The delineation of the psychological make-up of Hradscheck and Ursel as well as of the fluctuations of public opinion during this part of the work is admirably executed by Fontane. Anecdote functions between Chapters 13 and 19 to indicate the attitude of the Tschechiners towards the problem of the murder and to Hradscheck in his new social position as a widower. Besides this, Hradscheck's own anecdotes reveal his psychological state. In Chapter 13 different versions of an anecdote concerning the fate of the French soldier, who lies under the pear-tree, serve to clarify the mystery of the Tschechiners' loss of interest in the case of Szulski to the advantage of the Frenchman. "Denn Unglücksfälle wie der Szulskische waren häufig, oder wenigstens nicht selten, während der verscharrte Franzos unterm Birnbaum alles Zeug dazu hatte, die Phantasie der Tschechiner in Bewegung zu setzen".[2] The contradictory versions of how the French soldier might have met his fate in Tschechin during the Wars of Liberation are the favourite conversation topic among the Tschechiners around this time. This alerts the reader to the callousness and lack of social commitment of the peasants in

1 NyA III, 339.
2 Ibid. 370-371.

abandoning interest in the real murder amongst them in favour of a surmised murder with perhaps erotic undertones of some twenty years earlier. Instead of clearing up satisfactorily a mystery in their own village, they prefer to surmise about the past.

The alienation which existed between Ursel Hradscheck and the local community is reflected in the peasants' inadequate condolences with Hradscheck after her death. The peasants' lack of real interest in his loss as well as their lack of sympathy for her fate are brought out in several little incidents in Chapter 15. These factors are also made clear through the Tschechiners' choice of topics of conversation, while sitting drinking on his premises during the evening after Frau Hradscheck's funeral. Their expressions of sympathy are interspersed with stories of remarriage and this shows a lack of tact and sensitivity. The best of these stories, the narrator tells us, is that about Hauptman von Rohr. The version used here in "Unterm Birnbaum" is a four-line condensed rendering of the marriage exploits of the self-styled "Hauptman von Capernaum",[1] (an ancestor of Fontane's friend, Mathilde von Rohr) which Fontane first related in "Die Grafschaft Ruppin".

Instead of objecting to this kind of conversation, Hradscheck is shown during the peasants' tales as "ruhig und kopfnickend".[2] It would seem that he shares their callousness and insensitivity, since he has expressly gone against Ursel's dying wish for masses for Szulski, not so much from Protestant scruples as from a desire to gain the respect of Pastor Eccelius and the admiration of the peasants for the costly cross upon which he spends the mass money. The narrator reports after the erection of the cross: "Ehe der dritte Tag um war, ließ Hradschek die Träumerei fallen und nahm das gesellige Leben

1 See NyA III, 386 and NyA IX, 303. Fontane's freedom as narrator allows more play of humour in the "Wanderungen" version than in the context of this 'Novelle'. However, although the Tschechiners are not given some of the pointed observations of the "Wanderungen" version, such as the mention of the repeated singing of the hymn "Lobe den Herrn meine Seele" at each wife's funeral, their choice of remarriage stories to console Hradscheck is obviously meant as a damning feature. Whenever he reused an anecdote Fontane was careful to give it a new face by avoiding repetition.

2 NyA III, 386.

wieder auf."[1] Although the narrator has earlier indicated that Hradscheck loved Ursel in his own way, her death does not appear to have any profound effect on him, and in the final chapters her name is not even mentioned. The social life alluded to above takes the form of visits to cities, a breaking of the confines of the village. It is not however to places of gambling that the game-loving Hradscheck goes, but to theatrical events in Berlin. To depict Hradscheck's sociableness, a detailed account is given of his re-enacting of Angely and Holtei scenes for the benefit of his customers, who are now joined by 'Schulze' Woytasch,[2] as well as singing for them popular songs from Berlin and recounting anecdotes from cheap anecdote collections, when his Glaßbrenner stories run out. Once again the naivete of the peasants appears in their reaction to these anecdotes from the "Brausepulver" collections:

> Ja, diese Büchelchen fanden bei den Tschechinern einen ganz besonderen Beifall, weil die darin erzählten Geschichten immer kurz waren und nie lange auf die Pointe warten ließen, und wenn das Gespräch mal stockte, so hatte Kunicke den Stammwitz: "Hradscheck, ein Brausepulver."[3]

Little was made until this point in the story of Hradscheck's talent as an anecdote narrator. It is mentioned at the beginning of Chapter 9 as a point in his favour in the eyes of the local community, but this does not prevent them from being suspicious of him with regard to the disappearance of Szulski. Until Chapter 17 however when Hradscheck gets over Ursel's death, starts to attend the theatre during his frequent visits to Berlin and lays plans for marrying Dittchen, his participation in conversations has been subordinate to that of others in the circle at the inn. With the sight of a new life at hand and the eradication of traces of his crime, his quality as anecdote narrator comes to the fore and the last three chapters

1 NyA III, 390.
2 Rudolf Schäfer in "Theodor Fontane: 'Unterm Birnbaum'; 'Frau Jenny Treibel' ." München 1974, p. 41 points out that the tacit acceptance of Hradscheck by the community is shown in the new presence of the formerly disapproving 'Schulze' Woytasch during these convivial evenings.
3 NyA III, 391.

before his death give examples of the flowering of his social talent.

Just as Polish and French political affairs add a background of greater European interest in Chapters 5 and 13, the introduction of the entertainment world enlivens the confined atmosphere of Tschechin in the last chapters. Throughout his career since the murder of Szulski, Hradscheck never despaired and indeed was able to turn even setbacks to his advantage, e.g. being arrested 'wrongly' brought him sympathy once he was vindicated through the alibi of the Frenchman's skeleton; Ursel's death is put to good account when he spends her money for masses on an impressive cross. Its effect on the locals is immediate: "Am meisten aber gefiel ihnen, daß er das teure Kreuz überhaupt bestellt hatte. Denn Geld ausgeben (und noch dazu viel Geld) war das, was den Tschechinern als echten Bauern am meisten imponierte."[1] His visits to Berlin and Frankfort in the spring of 1833 provide the basis of many a night's entertainment at his inn, during which Hradscheck reveals all his narrative powers and sense of humour, proving himself to be indeed "ein feiner Vogel und Spaßmacher",[2] as the peasants had called him during the time when he was being suspected of the murder.

Significantly, the narrator lets Hradscheck relate only anecdotes which indirectly reveal his deepest impulses – contempt for the representative of the law and fear of discovery. Thus the anecdotes in Chapters 17 and 19, which are given a political aura[3] are in fact the murderer's attempts to rationalize his fears by telling funny stories. Having had gratifying narrative triumphs with the Eckensteher story, he proceeds with the political anecdote of the policeman:

> Sein bestes oder doch das, was er persönlich dafür hielt, kam erst nach und war die Geschichte von einem der politischen Polizei zugeteilten Gendarmen, der einen unter Verdacht des Hochverrats stehenden und in der Kurstraße wohnenden badischen Studenten, namens Haitzinger,

1 NyA III, 389.
2. Ibid. 351.
3 The is another example of Fontane's predating practice. Hradscheck's tale about the policeman in Chapter 17 was a current anecdote in the Vormärz period. Cf. Aufbau IV, 562.

> ausfindig machen sollte, was ihm auch gelang, und einige Zeit danach zu der amtlichen Meldung führte, daß er den pp. Haitzinger, der übrigens Blümchen heiße, gefunden habe, trotzdem derselbe nicht in der Kurstraße, sondern auf dem Spittelmarkt wohnhaft und nicht badischer Student, sondern ein sächsischer Leineweber sei.[1]

The style of officialese here which apes the police serves to discredit the policeman's assiduity, since it merely emphasizes all the more the lack of accuracy in official suspicions about subversives. The narrator tells us expressly that Hradscheck considers this his best story of the evening, thus putting it on a level above the mere entertainment of the Glaßbrenner stories. Clearly, Hradscheck appreciates this story best because it discredits the police. On the superficial social level, he may do this with impunity, having been 'wrongly' suspected by the local policeman, Geelhaar, of Szulski's murder. Thus, he can round off his anecdote by informing his listeners that the policeman in the Berlin anecdote was called Müller II, otherwise he, Hradscheck, would have had to believe for the rest of his life that his name was Geelhaar! This sidelight brings the peasants with the exception of Woytasch into a state of amusement and agreement which ends in the decision to make a wine punch and the drunken procession to the cellar for the bottles. The narrator brings out the irony of this descent to Szulski's burial place by remarking: "als ob einer begraben würde"[2] and the chapter ends with the sound of the heavy trap-door resounding through the house. This is Kunicke's joke to show that the ghost referred to by Ede is now captured, but it prefigures the fatal crashing of the door on Hradscheck after the next convivial evening. The fact that Hradscheck gets such an enthusiastic reception for his anecdote of the over-eager policeman is a measure of his rehabilitation in the Tschechin community after his acquittal for the murder of Szulski. The object of his criticism, Geelhaar, is now the laughing-stock of the peasants, just as Mutter Jeschke, who continues to be suspicious of Hradscheck, remains an outsider in society, and even is indirectly castigated in public for her part in Geelhaar's

1 NyA III, 394.
2 Ibid. 396.

apprehension of Hradscheck.[1] Thus those members of society who are acting in the interests of order are viewed with suspicion and derision, while the murderer, Hradscheck, once his name is cleared through the false alibi, enjoys the admiration of the community.

While the significance of the policeman anecdote to Hradscheck's own situation is immediately apparent to the peasants, the relevance of his final anecdote in Chapter 19 is only appreciated by the reader. This story about the famous feat of the German acrobat, Wilhelm Kolter, is neatly introduced through Ede's attendance at the Gusow fair. This absence allows Hradscheck to prepare for the final removal of Szulski's body from the cellar. The presence of acrobats at Gusow allows him to expatiate on this topic that night at the inn. The use of the subjunctive mood in the narration of the Kolter anecdote immediately alerts the reader to the distance created by such a device between the narrator and Hradscheck.[2]

> Und da habe denn.....der König von Preußen zum Kaiser von Rußland gesagt: "Höre, Bruderherz, was du von deinem Stiglischeck auch sagen magst, Kolter ist doch besser, Parole d'honneur, Kolter ist der erste Springer der Welt, und was ihm auch passieren mag, er wird sich immer zu helfen wissen." Und als nun der Kaiser von Rußland das bestritten, da hätten sie gewettet, und wäre bloß die Bedingung gewesen, daß nichts vorher gesagt werden solle. Das hätten sie denn auch gehalten. Und als nun Kolter halb schon das zwischen zwei Türmen ausgespannte Seil hinter sich gehabt habe, da sei mit einem Male, von der anderen Seite her, ein anderer Seiltänzer auf ihn losgekommen, das sei Stiglischeck gewesen, und keine Minute mehr, da hätten sie sich gegenüber gestanden, und der Russe, was ihm auch keiner verdenken könne, habe bloß gesagt: "Alles perdu, Bruder: du verloren, ich verloren." Aber Kolter habe nur

1 This is done by the representative of morality and religion, Pastor Eccelius, when he pointedly addresses the end of his speech at Ursel's grave to Mutter Jeschke with the commandment: "Du sollst nicht falsch Zeugnis reden wider deinen Nächsten." (NyA III, 385)

2 Similarly, a distinct element of distance is created in "Unwiderbringlich" when Holk recounts in a letter the words of the Princess telling the anecdote about Gruntvig, a letter which is not even addressed to the recipient, Christine, but to her companion for reading aloud. Through this device the narrator throws a critical eye on the character's motive.

> gelacht und ihm was ins Ohr geflüstert, einige sagen, einen frommen Spruch, andere aber sagen das Gegenteil, und sei dann mit großer Anstrengung und Geschicklichkeit zehn Schritte rückwärts gegangen, während der andere sich niedergehuckt habe. Und nun habe Kolter einen Anlauf genommen und sei mit eins, zwei, drei über den anderen weggesprungen. Da sei denn ein furchtbares Beifallklatschen gewesen, und einige hätten laut geweint und immer wieder und wieder gesagt, " das sei mehr als Napoleon". Und der Kaiser von Rußland habe seine Wette verloren und auch wirklich bezahlt.[1]

The anecdote of the balancing act itself show a humorous balance between 'high' and 'low' spheres. Just as the Prussian monarch says affectionately to the Tsar 'Bruderherz', so the humble Russian acrobat calls his German colleague brother, when reminding him of the impossibility of performing the feat required by the potentates. Collegiality between the performers who satisfy the royal whim (which may cost them their lives) is also indicated by the suggestion that what Kolter whispered in Stiglischeck's ear might have been the opposite of pious!

Fontane apparently altered the date of the Kolter anecdote. Normally he holds to historical accuracy, but sometimes as here or in the example of the Saint Anthony anecdote in "Schach von Wuthenow", he takes poetic licence in order to make some special point or emphasize a certain nuance. Alfred Dreyfuß has pointed out the discrepancies between Fontane's version and other accounts of the Kolter incident.[2] These alterations affect time, place and the principal characters of the anecdote. Aachen 1818 becomes Vienna 1814 in Fontane's version, the English tightrope-walker, Jack Barred, becomes the Russian acrobat, Stiglischeck, and Fontane adds in this version a bet between Tsar Alexander I and the Prussian monarch, Frederick William III. Dreyfuß wonders which version is correct, Fontane's or that in the Kolter album of 1865[3] as well as in other

1 NyA II, 401.
2 A. Dreyfuß: 'Fontane und der Seiltänzer' in FBL, Heft 3, 1974, p. 220-222.
3 Published anonymously, according to Dreyfuß, at the author's expense in Reichenbach and printed by J.G. Koch. (See Dreyfuß: op. cit., p. 220)

works on the acrobatic world.[1] I suggest that the version in "Unterm Birnbaum" is Fontane's own. In this work, it suits him to take the year 1814 and the Congress of Vienna as the backdrop to the anecdote, because the Congress is a well-known and immediately identifiable political-historical occasion. Indeed, it is better remembered for its entertainments than for its achievements. The Congress of Vienna then, rather than the more obscure Congress of Monarchs, held in Aachen in 1818, is the setting chosen by Fontane for the Kolter anecdote in the fictional setting. The notion of entertainment associated with the Congress of Vienna was presumably in Fontane's mind when making this choice. The frivolity of the occasion is underlined by the bystanders' remark that Kolter's feat is "more than Napoleon".

Besides the competitive element between the acrobats, Fontane also adds an element of competitiveness on the national level between the Prussian king and the Tsar through the notion of the bet between them. The competitive element in the Kolter album version of the story rests merely on the fact that the Prussian king sent for Kolter to come from Neiße to Aachen in order to do better than the Englishman, Jack Barred. So that a Prussian-Russian contest takes place, Fontane must include the Tsar in the story and change the figure of Barred to that of a Russian acrobat, namely Stiglischeck. In view of the good relations between the two countries at that time, the two monarchs being quite friendly and Russia having been on the Prussian side against Napoleon, the amical atmosphere conjured up by such a bet is plausible. A further touch of congruity can be pointed out from within the framework of "Unterm Birnbaum". Russia was a source of great interest in

1 On account of the shortness of the historical Wilhelm Kolter's legs, an authority on this area, Signor Saltarino (i.e. Hermann W. Otto) does not accept that he could have possibly performed the feat recounted in the anecdote, i.e. leaping over the Englishman, Jack Barred, and returning to the tight-rope. (See Signor Saltarino: "Das Artistentum und seine Geschichte." Leipzig 1910, p. 163. Cf. also Günter Bose/Erich Brinkmann: "Circus. Geschichte und Ästhetik einer niederen Kunst." Berlin 1978, p. 159-160, where the story of Kolter's alleged feat is dismissed as a chauvinistic legend.)

Chapter 5 in the context of the Polish November revolution, and this story in Chapter 19 retains the Russian flavour. On being told that Tsar Alexander really paid up on losing the bet, Kunicke, the old verteran of the Wars of Liberation, congratulates Hradscheck for his anecdote and cries: "Der Russe bezahlt immer. Hat's ja."[1]

Hradscheck's listeners enjoy the anecdote for its own sake. Kolter's victory over the Russian, Stiglischeck, on the tightrope can be a source of national pride to the Tschechiners, and they are also amused at the little insight which the anecdote gives into the pastimes of the monarchs. However, these factors are merely similar to those which adhered to the original story. Beyond the level of the listeners in the inn, the tale has a symbolic significance within the narrative as a whole. It is not simply a matter of "familiar gossip"[2] in the community, but a correlative of Hradscheck's dangerous 'balancing' act in Tschechin. By staging his own arrest and thus leading to his own vindication, he has cleverly led the community to a reappraisal of himself as a character. What Frederick William III says of Wilhelm Kolter appears to be true of Abel Hradscheck: "und was ihm auch passieren mag, er wird sich immer zu helfen wissen." The anecdote provides both a parallel to Hradscheck's situation since the murder and an anticipation of his forthcoming downfall, and also links up with an earlier association in the work. In Chapter 4, Frau Mietzel criticises the Hradschecks' pretentiousness which is unfounded, in her view, since Ursel was before her marriage to Abel "merely a Catholic and perhaps a tight-rope walker".[3] From being a stranger and an object of suspicion and jealousy, Abel has earned a place in the Tschechiners' hearts as a 'Spaßmacher' and story-teller. Thus, just as he thinks he is facing a new life and is ready to eradicate forever the traces of the crime which saved him from the social disgrace of bankruptcy, he tells the tale of a famous feat of balancing. His crime may be a thing of the past, but as long as Szulski lies in the cellar and as long as Ede and Mutter Jeschke draw attention to that part of the house with their superstitions,

1 NyA III, 333.
2 Ibid. 401.
3 Lionel Thomas's phrase: op. cit., p. 200.

Hradscheck is walking a tightrope. It is significant therefore that he relates the Wilhelm Kolter anecdote on his last night alive, and with a final touch of irony, his death is brought about by an imbalance, when he removes the plank which props up the barrels in the hallway he seals his own fate, for the trapdoor springs to under the weight of a big barrel. Thus a tiny detail of seemingly insignificant description from Chapter 1 becomes of great importance for the hero's fate in Chapter 19.

The presentation of period in "Unterm Birnbaum" is almost totally dependent on the use of anecdote, which is responsible for the conjuring up of the atmosphere of the Polish-Russian confrontation of 1830 as well as that of the more frivolous world of popular theatrical entertainment in Berlin in the 1830's. In an interesting essay which was published four years after "Unterm Birnbaum", "Die Märker und die Berliner und wie sich das Berlinertum entwickelte" (1889), Fontane describes this decade of the great success of the Königstädtisches Theater (which Hradscheck visits frequently during his sojourns in Berlin and from which he brings back entertaining stories for the Tschechiners) as "die Herrschaftszeit der Mittelmäßigkeit, Verschwommenheit und Trivialität, die Herrschaftszeit des Witzes quand meme, des Witzes, dem jede Rücksicht auf anderes unendlich Wichtigeres untergeordnet wurde. Jeder Minister war langweilig, ledern und gleichgültig, aber Beckmann war ein Gott".[1] After one of Hradscheck's 'performances for the drinking peasants, 'Schulze' Woytasch exclaims: "Beckmann is gut, aber Hradscheck is besser"[2] – fine praise from the village leader for the village murderer! Fontane's shifting of the action from the 1842 discovery of the perpetrator of the murder of a commercial traveller by the innkeeper, Fitting, to the early 1830's allows the presentation of the political background outside of Prussia as well as of the frivolity of popular interest in the decade 1830-1840. It is against this backdrop that the isolation and lack of social commitment of the Tschechiners is thrown into relief. They are constantly ready to drop from the general level to the level of the ambivalent

1 NyA XIX, 754. The Aufbau editors draw attention to this essay in the notes on "Unterm Birnbaum". See Aufbau IV, 560-561.
2 NyA III, 391.

or insignificant, as was shown in the reactions to the anecdote from the Polish revolution in Chapter 5 and in their own anecdotes in Chapter 13. Rather than relentlessly uncovering the evil in their midst, they prefer to indulge in fantasies about the past. The narrator tells us in Chapter 13 that the Szulski affair is as good as forgotten. His juxtaposition of the present murder with that of the past which fascinates them brings out their essential frivolity. On the personal level, the Tschechiners' lack of acceptance of the 'Fremdlinge',[1] the Hradschecks, helped to alienate these from the community in general. The peasants' callous lack of sympathy for the widower is again shown in the anecdote of Hauptmann von Rohr's four wives. With glee they join in the murderer's spite against the policeman, Geelhaar, in the political anecdote in Chapter 17.

Only after the death of Hradscheck do the Tschechiners, represented by Kunicke, Woytasch and Eccelius, begin to question themselves about their past actions and attitudes since the murder of Szulski:

> Waren doch alle, mit alleiniger Ausnahme von Geelhaar, viel zu befreundet mit Hradscheck gewesen, als daß ein Gespräch über ihn anders als peinlich hätte verlaufen können. Peinlich und mit Vorwürfen gegen sich selbst gemischt. Warum hatte man bei der gerichtlichen Untersuchung nicht besser aufgepaßt, nicht schärfer gesehen? Warum hatte man sich hinters Licht führen lassen?[2]

As always with Fontane however, there is no black and white version in the apportioning of blame – the pretentiousness of the Hradschecks, in particular that of Ursel, makes them forfeit the peasant community's respect. Similarly, Geelhaar and Mutter Jeschke, whose constant concern about the murder and Hradscheck's

1 NyA III, 368.

2 Ibid. 405. During the investigation under the peartree held in the hope of finding Szulski's body, the local crowd are described thus: "Alles plapperte, lachte, reckte den Hals, und wäre nicht Hradscheck selbst gewesen, der, die Blicke seiner alten Freunde vermeidend, ernst und schweigend vor sich hinsah, so hätte man glauben können, es sei Kirmes oder eine winterliche Jahrmarktszene." (ibid. 364)

suspicious behaviour seems to ensure the ultimate carrying out of justice, forfeit respect because of their faults. No admirable character appears in the story.[1] By writing a crime story in which the crime itself is not actually of interest, but which is perpetrated by a seemingly jovial character, whose narrative powers hold his listeners spellbound, Fontane adds considerably to this genre. The motive force in the plot is social pressure – the Hradschecks are psychologically unable to come to terms with their financial situation and in order to retain their social position commit a murder. Throughout the work all shades of public opinion[2] are touched on so that the level of social acceptance of the criminal pair is constantly under review.

The apex of Hradscheck's popularity is reached when he gives free rein to his narrative powers during the convivial evenings in the final chapters, and ironically the solid peasants join with the murderer in condemnation of the local policeman. The element of ordinary suspense, i.e. lack of knowledge of the killer's identity which the reader expects from the common thriller is lacking here. But a rather more subtle kind of suspense is provided by the expectation of the discovery of the criminal. This is due to the fact that the narrator presents Hradscheck, the murderer, as so shrewd a planner and so plausible an entertainer. According as the crime recedes in time and he makes a new life for himself, this suspense grows and the emergence of Hradscheck in the final chapters as actor and raconteur par excellence feeds this suspense. The anecdotes recounted here, besides proving the claim made earlier in the 'Novelle' for Hradscheck as an entertainer, both provide externalizations of his inward experience and technically provide an element

1 In a letter to Friedlaender, Fontane himself draws attention to the lack of an admirable character in the work: "Daß keine schöne, herzerquickliche Gestalt darin ist, wer dies auch gesagt haben mag, ist richtig." "Briefe an Georg Friedlaender." Ed. by Kurt Schreinert, p. 25.

2 Hans-Heinrich Reuter points out that the nuances and oscillations of public opinion do not play as large a role in any comparable work of German literature, mentioning in particular Schiller's "Verbrecher aus verlorener Ehre" und Droste-Hülshoff's "Judenbuche". See Reuter: "Fontane". Band 2, p. 633.

of retardation in the plot. The fact that Fontane was not obliged to create a rather archaic atmosphere as in "Grete Minde" and "Ellernklipp", lends "Unterm Birnbaum" flexibility with regard to the use of anecdote. Fontane had no difficulty in reconstructing a historical period with which he himself was so familiar, and he did so to no small degree in this work through the use of anecdote. Both the private level (the psychological state of the murderer) and the public level (the delineation of political events outside the narrow horizons of the Oder village) are depicted to a large extent in this story by anecdotes.

4. "Unwiederbringlich" (1891)

The eighteen-nineties saw the publication of four novels by Fontane in which the anecdote plays a varying but important role: "Unwiederbringlich", "Frau Jenny Treibel" (1892), "Effi Briest" (1894) and "Der Stechlin" (1898). In the first of these, Fontane departs, as he had done in the immediately preceding work, "Quitt" (1890) and the earlier "Graf Petöfy" (1884), from his favoured Berlin setting. The new background called for a store of anecdotal material which was non-German and non-Prussian. In the case of "Unwiederbringlich" with its background in Schleswig-Holstein and Denmark, the store drawn on was Nordic-Scandinavian.[1] The two settings in "Unwiederbringlich", Holkenäs in Schleswig and Copenhagen offer two contrasting atmospheres which mirror tensions in the plot. Fontane uses anecdote in this novel in several ways: to build up atmosphere, to aid characterization, to provide subtle pointers at important junctures and to indicate at another

1 Fontane was of the opinion that he had successfully caught the Nordic atmosphere, as a letter to Julius Rodenberg of 18.11.1890 shows: "Täusche ich mich nicht, so ist zweierlei gut: die eigentliche, mir überlieferte Geschichte und das Kolorit. Für letztres wird ein auch im Norden so Befahrener wie Sie ein Auge haben." "Briefe and Julius Rodenberg". Ed. by Hans-Heinrich Reuter. Berlin, Weimar 1969, p. 40.

level realities behind the action and conversations which are never otherwise explicitly manifested.

The Denmark to which Holk turns from Holkenäs is fun-loving, light-hearted, frivolous, and not destined to last. The war of 1864 with Prussia ended with the victory of Prussia and the annexation of Holstein. The novel continually plays on this situation which evolved less than five years after its own setting in 1859-1860. Fontane was familiar with the Danish scene from journies there, which he had documented in his "Reiseberichte" 1864-1865 and from his preparation for the book "Der Schleswig-Holsteinische Krieg im Jahre 1864". It is interesting to note that in "Unwiederbringlich" even in the slightly removed setting of Denmark, Fontane remained true to the theme which fascinated him so much, the old and the new. Unlike the dawning of the democratic age in "Der Stechlin", there is no new era posited for Denmark in "Unwiederbringlich".

The Copenhagen court setting offers Graf Holk social distraction, piquant conversation and ambivalent situations. All of this attracts and fascinates the side of him which rejects a quiet life on his estate in Holkenäs with the serious and pious Christine. Several of the Copenhagen characters are described as lovers of conversation and anecdote. Holk's landlady, Frau Hansen, and her daughter, Brigitte, are said to be a "Nachschlagewerk für alle Kopenhagener Geschichten",[1] while the courtier, Pentz, who makes this pronouncement, is himself described by the narrator as "ein lebendiges Nachschlagebuch für die hauptstädtische Chronique scandaleuse". [2] Ebba von Rosenberg describes the Danish princess rather tartly as playing the role of the eighteenth-century lady with her anecdotes and quotations.[3] Ebba herself is depicted as a brilliant conversationalist, who has a deep interest in stories of any kind, particularly the more piquant variety, but like most of Fontane's important female characters, she does not relate any anecdotes. The presence of the archaeologist, Worsaae (1821-1885), at Pentz' day-long breakfast in Chapter 16 is said to be indispensable

1 NyA V, 66.
2 Ibid. 104.
3 Ibid. 84.

because of his talents as a narrator of anecdotes.[1] Pastor Schleppegrell entertains the courtly gatherings at Fredericksborg with his anecdotes, and Holk likes to converse in the same setting with Doktor Bie, because of the latter's store of informative stories about Greenland.

The emphasis is therefore mainly placed on conversational arts in the Copenhagen setting, and a person's ability to narrate gripping tales is a measure of his suitability or adaptiveness to that society. Since the anecdotes in "Unwiederbringlich" are narrated only in the Copenhagen setting, the narrator ensures that story-telling is associated only with the free and easy atmosphere of the Danish capital – and by extension with the laxer side of Holk's characer. Although they do not see eye to eye on political matters, Christine looking towards Prussia and Germany politically, and Holk looking backwards to the older Denmark of the eighteenth century, both Christine and Holk can be said to stand on the side of the old. Similarly, the Danish court life portrayed in the novel is a vestige of the older regime: the Princess is clearly associated with the eighteenth century and King Frederick VII is aligned through his hobby of archaeology with the old and appears to take more interest in his mistress and tavern life than in affairs of state.

On the other hand, the barrenness and rigidity of life at Schloß Holkenäs is shown in the fact that not a single anecdote is narrated there. The aged Pastor Petersen attempts to tell an anecdote from the Congress of Vienna about the game of whist, a story which he claims to have heard from the Danish sculptor, Bertel Thorvaldsen, and originally from Wilhelm von Humboldt. But this narration is interrupted by a call for him to attend to the card-game on hand among the men and Fräulein Dobschütz starts reading aloud from the newspaper for Christine's benefit. This interruption of the narration is unlikely to be merely adventitious in the case of a writer who is as aware as Fontane. His care in the introduction and setting of anecdotes im general makes the reader suspect that this little incident is included on purpose to point up the fact that

1 NyA V, 100.

converation is rather strained in Holkenäs. The easy-going atmosphere of Copenhagen, which affects both conversation and morals and both court and lower strata of society (represented by the Hansens), is set off against the restrictive and pietistic atmosphere created by Christine in Holkenäs. Thus, the presence and the lack of anecdote can play a role in the subtle manifestation of an underlying but profound divide between the marriage partners, Holk and Christine. This is not to say that Christine is unable to appreciate any kind of conversation or even of anecdote. Her emphasis however on subjects of serious content and her pietistic outlook makes relaxed conversation in her presence difficult, even within the famliy setting. In essence, the underlying friction between her own and her husband's more ambivalent outlook creates the lack of ease so notable in Holkenäs. Her brother in commenting on her character and marriage in Chapter 5 tells Schwarzkoppen of his attempts to help the situation: "Ich versuche mitunter, zum Guten zu reden und ihr klar zu machen, wie sie sich anpassen und ihrem Mann zuhören müsse, wenn er was aus der Welt erzählt, einen Witz, ein Wortspiel, eine Anekdote."[1] Through several incidents the narrator indicates that Christine is quite interested in anecdotes but on each of these occasions, the anecdote in question is either never related or in some way adds to the existing friction. Anecdote is not connected with Christine in the interests of providing an enjoyable social atmosphere, but rather as a further proof of her seriousness and overriding interest in religious affairs. The first incident in this connection is the already-mentioned scene in Chapter 3, where her companion read aloud to her from the newspaper. Having rejected the possibility of items of political or military interest, Christine settles for an article on the ailing Frederick William IV, giving the following explanation for her choice: "Die rein menschlichen Dinge, zu denen, für mich wenigstens, auch das Religiöse gehört, interessieren mich nun mal mehr. Dieser unglückliche König in seinem Charlottenburger Schloß; ..... ein so heller Kopf, und nun umnachtet in seinem Geiste."[2] Christine

1 NyA V, 28.
2 Ibid. 19.

shows here an unattractive degree of formality and self-consciousness. Her companion of many years standing is of course already aware that Christine is extremely interested in religion! Here, the narrator clearly wants to show that for Christine religion is anchored wholly in the 'human' sphere – she hopes for something from the newspaper article on the Prussian king which would throw light on his attitude to religion. Religion for Christine is, if not a subterfuge, an 'Ersatz', certainly not a spiritual force. Hence her preference for the anecdote under the guise of interest in religion. This scene, and especially Christine's above-quoted statement indicates her lack of self-knowledge, which is an important motif in the novel and which provides motivation of the tragic end.[1] Christine is not aware of the contradiction in her turning towards Prussia. She wishes to see in it an upholder of Lutheran ideals, and prefers not to dwell on its importance as a military power. Not by superiority of moral virtue, but by virtue of its military strength will it be in a position to dictate to Denmark in 1864, a situation which is anticipated in the newspaper article read out to Christine in Chapter 3. Christine however turns away from the article when it transpires that it concerns Prussian military affairs, the Prince Regent's policy of achieving military preparedness, rather than details of Frederick William IV's madness. Only when what seemed anecdotal threatens to have political consequences, does she lose interest in the subject, and the precise link made in the article between this Prussian 'Wehrhaftmachung' and Schleswig-Holstein is rejected by Christine in her attack on prophecies. Somewhat later, Holk is described as an ostrich with his head in the sand by his brother-in-law, who represents the common-sense point of view in the novel, for his failure to see a threat to Denmark from the Prussian quarter.

Later in the novel an anecdote about the Danish theologian,

1 Heide Eilert interprets Christine's suicide in the context of Freud's concept of the "cultural sexual morality" of the Victorian age. See H. Eilert: ' "...und mehr noch fast, wer liebt". Theodor Fontanes Roman "Unwiederbringlich" und die viktorianische Sexualmoral' in ZsfdPh, Band 101, 1982, 4, p. 527-545.

Nicolai Gruntvig (1783-1872) throws further light on the characters of Holk and Christine and on the deterioration of the relationship between them. This time the anecdote is actually narrated, but in a manner which backfires on its narrator, Holk. In Chapter 23 the reader finds him musing on Pastor Schleppegrell, the Princess and Ebba, and only incidentally is Christine's illness mentioned in a reference back to a letter received the previous day from Fräulein Dobschütz. Reference is also made to Holk's disbelieving attitude towards the reported illness. In order to fill out his letter to Holkenäs (addressed not to his wife, but to her companion for reading aloud!), he adds a postscript with the Gruntvig anecdote which the Princess had related the day before. The lack of intimacy and immediacy in this anecdote narration is striking. Holk relates to his wife's companion a story which he has heard from the Princess:

> Die Prinzessin (...) sagte: "Gruntvig ist ein bedeutender Mann und so recht angetan, ein Dänenstolz zu sein. Aber einen Fehler hat er doch, er muß immer etwas Apartes haben und sich von dem Rest der Menschheit, auch selbst der dänischen, unterscheiden, und wiewohl ihm nachgesagt wird, er stelle Dänemark so hoch, daß er ganz ernsthaft glaube, der liebe Gott spräche Dänisch, so bin ich doch sicher, daß er von dem Tag an, wo dies ganz allgemein feststände, mit allem Nachdruck behaupten und beweisen würde, der liebe Gott spräche Preußisch. Gruntvig kann nicht ertragen, mit irgend jemandem in Übereinstimmung zu sein."[1]

More than anything else, the distance between the marriage partners is underlined by such a narrative situation. Here there is nothing of the affectionate communication which used to temper their correspondence during earlier instances of separation. This phenomenon was purposely alluded to by the narrator earlier in the novel.[2] Perhaps unwittingly, Holk unwisely refers to his wife's interest in "Pastoralanekdoten und theologische Streitigkeiten" as the

1 NyA V, 153-154.
2 Ibid. 119 (Chapter 18)

motivation for his inclusion of the story in his letter. In the strained atmosphere of the correspondence any allusion to Christine in connection with quarrels is dangerous and reminds the reader, even though Holk is specifically referring to theological disputes, of the passage in Chapter 4, in which the narrator informs the reader that everyone present is aware that Christine lacks peace, even though it is her devout wish to possess it.[1] A further factor showing the distance between Holk and Christine in this anecdotal situation is the rather flippant manner in which he refers to God's language,[2] given the seriousness of his wife with regard to such matters.

One of the features which marks Holk as being excessively bound to the past is his interest in "anekdotisch Genealogisches".[3] It is on this subject that the narrator gives us one of his partial portraits of Holk in Chapter 13 which helps to explain a great deal in Holk's character. Here, Holk is described as extremely proud of his aristocratic pedigree feeling himself in this respect as superior even to royal houses. It is this interest in genealogy which brings him to his first faux-pas in the Copenhagen setting. His expatiations in Chapter 13 in his first conversation with Ebba von Rosenberg which contains anecdotal elements are brought to an abrupt halt by her revelation of her Jewish origin. In this early conversation between the future lovers therefore Holk's lack of social perception and also a certain lack of contact with reality are indicated. But more importantly, the lack of real communication between this pair is here foreshadowed. Holk's enthusiasm for his genealogical hobby blinds him to the possibility that Ebba's name is Jewish rather than Germano-aristocratic, just as his passion for her later blinds him to

1 NyA V, 26. Frances M. Subiotto draws attention to the role of the anecdote and enclosures in Holk's letters home and indicates that he is fobbing Christine off with stories in which he himself has no more than a passing interest. See F. M. Subiotto: 'The Function of Letters in Fontane's "Unwiederbringlich" ' in MLR 65, 1970, p. 312-313.

2 Fontane also relates the anecdote in "Reiseberichte aus Dänemark" (NyA XVIII, 310) in connection with the alleged self-confidence of the people of Copenhagen.

3 Ibid. 87.

the reality that she neither loves nor wishes to marry him. Indeed, Ebba's overall negative opinion of Holk is revealed to the reader through various conversations during which his character is discussed. Thus her eventual refusal to marry him no longer surprises the reader, while Holk himself is at the time shattered by it. Ebba's view that Holk lacks wholeness, that he is half moralist and half man of the world is corroborated in the plot by his oscillation between the poles of Pietism and frivolity. The frivolous aspect is adequately portrayed in the manner in which he first succumbs to the impression made on him by Frau Hansen's story of her daughter's alleged triumph in Siam. This story in Chapter 11 sets the tone for further instances of gullibility on Holk's part. Although he entertains ironical thoughts about Frau Hansen's 'fairy-tale', he reaches this point of sophistication only when his attentions are already turning in the direction of Ebba. In Chapter 15 he had already related the story without expressing any doubts about its veracity in a letter home. The motifs in the story about the Siamese Emperor's attentions to Brigitte, adventure, jealousy and infidelity, mirror the main plot of the novel.[1] The measure of Holk's adaption to the nonchalant atmosphere of the court and capital is shown in his differing reactions to arch remarks made about the Hansen women. By the Christmas at Fredericksborg, he can laugh at Pentz' observation with regard to Brigitte Goje, Brigitte Hansen's namesake, that all Brigittes have something strange about them. This increasing adaption anticipates the further action of the intimacy between Ebba and Holk and his subsequent delusion that they can have a permanent union.

It is one of the remarkable features of "Unwiederbringlich" that Fontane manages to continually portray the decline of the marriage relationship, even though the married partners are apart for most of

1 Dieter Lohmeier has pointed out how many strands of the novel offer a variation on the motif of the "Reiz des Illegitimen", including the references to historical figures like Christian II and Düveke, Christian IV and Kirsten Munk, Friedrich VII and Countess Danner. See D. Lohmeier: 'Vor dem Niedergang. Dänemark in Fontanes Roman "Unwiederbringlich" ' in "skandinavistik" 2, 1972, p. 35.

the novel. This is done not only by means of showing their alienation in correspondence, but also through the inserted anecdotes. In Chapters 21 and 22 reference is made to the hollowed stone at Fredericksborg bearing the incription "Christian IV, 1628". In the first of these chapters, the Scheppegrells, Ebba and Holk pause at the stone on their way back to the castle. The anecdote becomes a cause of curiosity to Schleppegrell's listeners in Chapter 21, and his refusal to tell the story on grounds of lack of time retards its impact. When it is finally related in Chapter 22, there are two versions about the reason for the inscription on the stone. The first is innocuous: Schleppegrell claims it marks the first pay-day on renovations of the castle, when Christian IV (1577-1648) personally paid the workmen. The second version, which is more piquant, tells that the king inscribed the stone in 1628 to mark the day on which his morganatic wife, Christine Munk, for no apparent reason sulked and later refused to let him enter her bedroom. Two factors about the dispositions of the characters in the anecdote are brought out in Schleppegrell's second version of the anecdote: Christian IV was more "gnädig und liebenswürdig"[1] than ever before and Christine Munk was normally one of the best-humoured and most affectionate of women. In connection with this anecdote, Ebba taunts Holk for his "Vorliebe für das Große",[2] and her historical references here prove that greatness can be allied with having mistresses and being interested in small things, such as this story about Christian IV and Christine Munk's mood. The discussion which follows the narration of this anecdote characterizes those taking part. Holk's lack of finesse in his own marriage is mirrored in his complaint that the story is trivial. It is not accidental that the tale comes after Frau Schleppegrell's statement about the essence of marriage being a couple's helping each other and seeing the justice of each other's point of view. Although the narrator comments on her ignorance of the thoughts arising in Holk on this occasion, it is clear from the context of the other chapters here that her piece of wisdom about

1 NyA V, 149.
2 Ibid. 150.

life is really falling on deaf ears. Holk's disdain for the pastor's wife as ordinary and unexciting fits in with his aristocratic pride and his lack of judgement in human relationships. He does not share the view that boring people are just as nice and entertaining as interesting people. Ebba makes the claim that all people of high station who have wit and intelligence share this experience.[1] Holk's lack of pondering on Frau Schleppegrell's talk is shown in Chapter 23 in his letter home, a letter which could have well taken the form of an application of Frau Schleppegrell's idea to his own marital relationship, instead of using the Gruntvig anecdote and condescending remarks about pastors' marrying princesses to fill out his letter. His brother-in-law's letter in the same chapter draws attention to the futility of his trying to conceal his "Nüchternheit hinter Stadtklatsch und Hofklatschgeschichten".[2] The use of the subjunctive mood to report Holk's observations on the Christian IV anecdote alerts the reader to the narrator's distance from Holk's position. Holk's failure to appreciate the anecdote in which the king is shown in a situation like any ordinary human being (in which being royal does not give him any advantage) reveals a lack of interest in the historically marginal (which would be untypical of Fontane himself) and also reflects the serious lacks in his personal relationships with women. The fact that a woman determines the scene in which a king is rebuffed gives an unusual perspective to an historical personage,[3] one that Holk is not able to cope with, when he rejects the whole thing as being "zu kleinen Stils".[4] When Schleppegrell adds the detail about

1 NyA V, 144.

2 Ibid. 156.

3 Cf. Norbert Frei's comment on this anecdote: "Geschichte ist auch die der Frauen, und letztlich die bessere, weil menschlichere." (N. Frei: "Theodor Fontane. Die Frau als Paradigma des Humanen". Königstein/Ts. 1980, p. 86)

4 NyA V, 149. No doubt Fontane made the mental connection between two anecdotes about kings being left outside bedrooms by their women, both of which he used in his works, this one about Christian IV and the one about Henry IV of France and Gabriele d'Estrées. As in this passage in "Unwiederbringlich", in "Vor dem Sturm" another somewhat shocked character reacts to a royal indiscretion on the part of Henry IV. Krach finds the story about Henry commenting on his own tendency to take people's things that if he

the historical couple's temperament, gracious and amiable on the man's part, good-humoured and affectionate on the woman's, this strengthens the impression that the anecdote is one which hinges on the element of timing. Christian and Christine do not normally have rows because of ill-humour and sulks, and this exception, important enough to Christian that he should mark the occasion with the hollowed stone, proves the rule. Obversely, Holk's disastrous relationships revolve around scenes in which bad timing and lack of communication lead him to make moves which he later regrets, e.g. the Christmas scene where Christine's lack of gaiety leads him to rationalize his wish to leave her, and the proposal scene in which Ebba quickly shatters his illusions. Clearly, the story about Christine Munk prefigures the Christmas scene with Christine Holk, and reflects the Holks' marriage as a whole, while being itself an exception in the lives of the seventeenth-century couple.

The alienation of husband and wife is clearly indicated in "Unwiederbringlich" through the use of anecdote. Weaknesses on both sides are displayed in their employment and reception of anecdotes. Holk's tendency towards adventurousness, his lack of psychological insight and his callousness with regard to his wife's feelings are thereby well brought out. On the other hand, Christine's excessive piousness and seriousness are also indicated through the anecdotes. The anecdote is a significant part in the conversations which give the flavour of the Danish setting. Through the use of Nordic material, the atmosphere of Copenhagen and its past is built up by Fontane. Lightness of touch, wit and nonchalance characterize the court conversations, together with a good deal of irony at the expense of Holk, the Schleswig-Holsteiner.The anecdote about Christian IV and Christine Munk is a good example of the

had not been king, he would have been hanged 'unköniglich' and 'frivol' (NyA I, 157). The human frankness of the king figure in both cases shocks the character who feels that kings should also do and say things in the grand style, i.e.. present a public pose. The great satire on this grand style comes of course from the pen of that admirer of both Henry IV and Fontane, Heinrich Mann, in his exposé of the public pose of William II and the posturings of the Wilhelmine Era in "Der Untertan".

narrator's eliciting reader attention. Holk's reaction to the story, i.e. that it is too trivial for a king, shows the inappropriateness of his own yardstick. The human element (which the hollowed stone story demonstrates) is the raison d'être of all anecdotes and Fontane's own love of the small and marginal, when it shows the human factor,[1] bears witness to this fact. That Holk does not appreciate the story is in keeping with his failings with regard to apparently trivial things like letter-writing, or his lack of perspective in judging a character like Frau Schleppegrell, who on the occasion that Holk sees the hollowed stone makes the observation about marriage which, had he actively incorporated into his own life, might have saved his marriage. However, Holk in his unconscious arrogance, finds both Frau Schleppegrell and Christian IV's action too insignificant to learn anything from them. While the anecdotes in "Unwiederbringlich" fulfil useful functions with regard to characterization of the main figures and their relationship and with regard to the adding of local colour and historical background, they still remain within the sphere of the private plot, and do not successfully merge the private and the public level.

In the four works, "Vor dem Sturm", "Schach von Wuthenow", "Unterm Birnbaum" and "Unwiederbringlich", which present period and also incorporate the anecdote, different degrees of sophistication can be discerned in its use. "Vor dem Sturm" still shows a certain naïveté with regard to the technical introduction of anecdotes: the narrator introduces them in an en bloc characterization; characters refer to sources for some anecdotes; in two chapters an excessive amount of anecdotes is strung together and has to carry the conversation almost totally; characters make very conscious use of anecdotes to win arguments, a device which seems rather flat and one-dimensional; a character tells anecdotes with which the listener is already familiar; and two anecdotes in the novel are clearly unnecessary. Yet, on the whole Fontane is at pains to integrate anecdotes with the major themes of the novel, and in cases like the

1 Cf. Professor Wilibald Schmidt's observations on the human element and 'das Nebensächliche' in connection with the anecdote in Chapter 7 of "Frau Jenny Treibel".

green coffins anecdote and the anecdote about the Kunersdorf officer, the anecdote reaches a degree of artistic sophistication which heralds Fontane's later success with the interpolation of anecdotes into his fiction. "Schach von Wuthenow" shares with Fontane's first novel the very conscious use of anecdotes by characters in order to win arguments, but this is done with much more artistry than in the first novel, and the narrator refrains from telling any, thus mirroring in this regard his reticence in the work as a whole as opposed to his prominence in "Vor dem Sturm". The pictorial presentation of Frederician anecdotes in one chapter represents a step forward in subtlety as against the presentation of Frederician anecdotes in "Vor dem Sturm". Although anecdotes are again consciously used by characters to win arguments, they are all clearly linked to the presentation of the main character and of the Prussia of 1805-1806, and thus this work shows a greater internal unity between the anecdotes it uses than was the case in "Vor dem Sturm". "Unterm Birnbaum" succeeds in using anecdotes which are relevant to characterization, to technical elements like pre-figuration of aspects of the plot, and to the presentation of the decade of 1830-1840. This work shows a very advanced level of sophistication in the artistic use of the anecdote, unlike "Unwiederbringlich", chronologically the last of the four historical works which make use of the anecdote. In "Unwiederbringlich", the anecdotes, while they fulfil useful functions in connection with characterization, pre-figuration and the creation of local colour and atmosphere, are not subtly worked into the whole texture of the novel, as is the case with "Schach von Wuthenow" and "Unterm Birnbaum" of the eighteen-eighties, or "Frau Jenny Treibel", "Effi Briest" and "Der Stechlin" of the eighteen-nineties.

III. "Anekdoten aus allen fünf Weltteilen":

World-wide Associations

1. "Der Stechlin" (1898)

Fontane did not feel constrained to construct a tightly-knit plot in the two works last published during his lifetime, "Die Poggenpuhls" and "Der Stechlin". "Die Poggenpuhls", published in 1896 is in several ways the forerunner of "Der Stechlin", but does not make use of the anecdote. This is not merely due to the extremely economical nature of the book,[1] but also to the fact that the Poggenpuhl family is isolated from society in general. Social gatherings which would show the family interacting with its peers are lacking. This is because poverty has isolated the Poggenpuhls from that stratum of society to which they feel entitled to belong by virtue of their noble birth and tradition of service to Prussia. Although the family's ultimate financial saviour, General Eberhard von Poggenpuhl, is described as a lover of anecdotes, like Graf Adam in "Graf Petöfy", he does not relate any.

The main character, Dubslav, in "Der Stechlin" is characterized very early in the novel as a lover of conversation, not indeed as a monopolist of conversation, but one who also likes to hear others talk.[2] Nor does Dubslav monopolize the anecdotes, because even rather minor characters have the telling of some of the most important anecdotes in the novel. It seems as if Fontane were distilling his own thoughts into the many conversations which comprise the bulk of this book,[3] whether the speaker be Dubslav or

1 "Die Poggenpuhls" comprises only 86 pages in the NyA.

2 "Er ließ sich gern was vorplaudern und plauderte selber gern."(NyA VIII, 8)

3 Julius Petersen makes the point that Fontane seems to be playing Eckermann to himself in this novel. Contemporary reviewers also noted the deep inner connection between the book and the person of the author. See J. Petersen: 'Fontanes Altersroman' in "Euphorion" 29, 1928, p. 3.

Woldemar, Lorenzen, Melusine, Armgard or Graf Barby. This is not to say that they all speak with one voice, but they are all allowed, even a somewhat unattractive character such as the churchman, Koseleger, to contribute conversationally to the important ideas of the novel. In spite of the novel's loose structure it does not contain an excess of anecdotes. A work less than one-third of its size, "Schach von Wuthenow", carries as many as two-thirds of the anecdotes which appear in "Der Stechlin". The interweaving of the old and the new which was reflected in many of Fontane's works before "Der Stechlin" becomes in this novel the umbrella theme which covers several sub-themes: heroism, love/caritas, Prussian lack of self-confidence, and revolution. The following list shows the matching of themes with anecdotes in the novel:

The old and the new	The rats (Chapter 3) Frederick William IV (Chapter 4) Russian teacher (Chapter 5) Dr. Heim and Queen Luise (Ch.6) Joao de Deus (Chapter 15) Bismarck (Chapter 19) Johanna Knothe (Chapter 20) Siamese Princess (Chapter 20) Frederick II (Chapter 22) Madame Rachel (Chapter 27) William I (Chapter 32) Greely (Chapter 38)
Heroism	Russian teacher (Chapter 3) João de Deus (Chapter 15) Greely (Chapter 38)
Revolution	The rats (Chapter 3) The 1848 anecdote (Chapter 5) Johanna Knothe (Chapter 20)
Self-confidence	Frederick II (Chapter 22)
Love/caritas	William I (Chapter 32)
Revaluation/restitution/regeneration/ reversal (includes the overthrow of set notions of the appropriate)	Russian teacher (Chapter 5) Siamese Princess (Chapter 20) Madame Rachel (Chapter 27) William I (Chapter 32) Greely (Chapter 38)

The important theme complex of the old and the new is consistently elaborated by the use of anecdotes. With extreme subtlety Fontane marshals the subjects which are aligned with this theme complex. One of the more negative aspects of contemporary Prussian society which Fontane describes in the novel is the existence of the influential new-rich entrepreneurial class whose heyday had been reached during the expansionary period of the 'Gründerjahre'. These are represented in "Der Stechlin" by the conservative, recently-ennobled Gundermann couple. The lack of refinement, the materialism, pretentiousness and reactionary fear of progress which were characteristic of this class are reflected admirably in the conversations of this couple, whom Dubslav is compelled to invite to his dinner-party in Chapter 3 for want of company. The behaviour of Frau von Gundermann on this occasion confirms Dubslav's doubts as to whether the Gundermanns would be suitable company for his dinner-party. Frau von Gundermann's dinner-table conversation with Czako revolves mainly around complaints about her life in the country, social isolation, trouble with maid-servants. She speaks with animation only when reaching the subject of her youth in a Berlin suburb. Her reminiscences here concern games she and her companions played with rats in the flooded street channels, reaching a climax in her account of a boy being bitten by a rat. Although she does not understand Czako's reference to an "Oeil de Boeuf",[1] one of her complaints is the lack of people in the region with whom it is possible to have a cultured conversation! Her reminiscences on rats and rat-bites hardly fit into this category, and her eager reception of Czako's personal anecdote of a great rat-hunt in Paris, when he went through the sewers in a boat with ratters also says little for her breeding.

The anecdote indicates a great lack of poise and education on the part of Frau von Gundermann, who is being both teased and humoured by Czako. However, the rats anecdote told in the first social gathering in "Der Stechlin" represents one of the novel's several variations on the important theme of revolution. The notion

1 NyA VIII, 30.

is included here of a descent to the 'underworld' of the 'Eldorado'[1] of the rats. The threat of rats which number as many as the humans above ground is dwelt on by Czako in the little flourishes added to his anecdote. The idea of revolution has already been mooted by Dubslav's account of Lake Stechlin with its seismographic sympathy for revolutions all over the world. Irony is contained in the narrative situation of the rat anecdote. Frau von Gundermann unwittingly applauds the story which hints at revolution and social change, a position which would be exactly the opposite of her conscious parti pris. Thus, on the anecdotal level, as in her reference to the "Oeil de Boeuf", a discrepancy is again apparent between what she says and what she is. This kind of subtlety is typical of Fontane's narrative art. This seemingly insignificant personal anecdote appears at first sight to indicate merely what the reader has already guessed, namely, Frau von Gundermann's lack of refinement. However, with it one of the novel's major themes is discreetly indicated. Frau von Gundermann's fears of revolution have their counterpart in her husband's obsession with Social Democracy. Much later, in Chapter 20 at the Rheinsberg-Wutz Conservatives' election dinner, Herr von Gundermann compulsively returns to his favourite topic, the threat of Social Democracy. He starts his post-prandial speech with the anecdote of the execution of Frau Johanna Knothe which took place in 1864. This plumber's wife and her lover, the plumber's apprentice, had murdered her husband. Gundermann uses the climax of the story, (Frau Knothe's last words to the young men watching the execution: "Ja, ja, meine jungen Herrens, dat kommt davon") to lay the blame on the Social Democrats for the reversal of the proper order of things.[2] A society in which Dubslav's coachman

1 NyA VIII, 31. For the relevance of the Paris rats to the Commune and thus to the indirect allusions to revolution in "Der Stechlin", see P.- P. Sagave: 'Theodor Fontane et la France 1870/1871' in IASL 1, 1976, p. 174 f. This aspect shows that both Gundermanns are included for the same purpose: to show the fear of the new rich of being undermined from 'below'. Cf also J.J. Sheehan: "The Career of Lujo Brentano. A Study of Liberalism and Social Reform in Imperial Germany". Chicago 1966, p. 47-48.

2 NyA VIII, 179

may replace Dubslav as a candidate in the Reichstag has its priorities wrong, in Gundermann's view.

The irony in this speech situation resides in the fact that the new-rich, newly-ennobled Gundermann is even more opposed to social and political progress than the traditionally privileged class represented by von Molchow, whose verdict on the speech is pithily expressed: "Gundermann ist und bleibt ein Esel."[1] Herr von Molchow's analysis of the conservatives' position shows him at least to be aware of political realities, whereas Gundermann's outlook, characterized in his anecdote and speech, is one of simplistic horror of democratic voting procedures. Both anecdotes connected with the Gundermanns therefore bring out their lack of refinement – rats and executions at the dinner table – while at another level indicating the theme complex of the old and the new. The social democratic element belongs to that which is new, and it is a subject to which Fontane returns again and again in the novel, not just in the parts immediately concerned with the Rheinsberg-Wutz election in which Dubslav runs as the Conservative candidate.

The contrast of the old and the new is continued throughout the novel. The most obvious believer in the values of a new order is Pastor Lorenzen, "beinah Sozialdemokrat",[2] who, in spite of his love of old families, believes that the aristocratic world has collapsed and that the new age will be democratic: "Eine neue Zeit bricht an. Ich glaube, eine bessere und eine glücklichere. Aber wenn auch nicht eine glücklichere, so doch mindestens eine Zeit mit mehr Sauerstoff in der Luft, in der wir besser atmen können. Und je freier man atmet, je mehr lebt man."[3] This "revolutionary discourse" in Chapter 29 contains Lorenzen's views on the development of Prussian history up to the present time. The notion of a watershed having been reached in political development in the world is also shared by the much-travelled and broad-minded Graf Barby. He expresses similar views

1 NyA VIII, 180.
2 His pupil Woldemar von Stechlin says this of him in Chapter 13 (NyA VIII, 124).
3 Ibid. 254. See also ibid. 47.

in a different way to Baron Berchtesgaden in Chapter 14,[1] in reply to the latter's assertion that the Vatican will prevail in the struggle between church and state in Italy. For Lorenzen in the revolutionary discourse, the aristocracy is losing the people's sympathy and he uses for it the metaphor of the old stone roof which can no longer afford protection.[2]

The novel's central character however and the one who earns the narrator's greatest sympathy is Dubslav for whom the new era means a lowering of standards generally, in spite of his relativism and of his almost progressive notions of the necessity of an improvement in the living standards of the ordinary people. In spite of the fact that the narrator dwells lovingly on this figure, his defeat as a Conservative candidate in the election, as well as his expression of some of his more antiquated ideas, suggest that Dubslav's political stance is not in tune with developments in modern Prussia. The sympathetic portrayal of Dubslav bears out Fontane's statement in "Von Zwanzig bis Dreißig" of his continuing attraction to the Junkers, an attraction to their human qualities.[3] Dubslav can be seen as demonstrating the best moral features of Fontane's conception of positive Prussianism. Not surprizingly, those anecdotes connected with the figure of Dubslav frequently imply a certain superiority of the old values. He is an old man and he himself humorously remarks that even his jokes tend to be those of the era of the Congress of Vienna rather than of the present.[4] His only anecdote in the novel

1 "Das moderne Leben räumt erbarmungslos mit all dem Überkommenen auf. Ob es glückt, ein Nilreich aufzurichten, ob Japan ein England im Stillen Ozean wird, ob China mit seinen vierhundert Millionen aus dem Schlaf erwacht und, seine Hand erhebend, uns und der Welt zuruft: "Hier bin ich," allem voran aber, ob sich der vierte Stand etabliert und stabiliert – denn darauf läuft doch in ihrem vernünftigen Kern die ganze Sache hinaus – das alles fällt ganz anders ins Gewicht als die Frage "Quirinal oder Vatikan". Es hat sich überlebt."(NyA VIII, 131)

2 Ibid. 254. Cf. Fontane's letter of 6.5.1895 to Friedlaender about his increasing hatred for "alles, was die neue Zeit aufhält". ("Briefe an Georg Friedlaender", p. 284)

3 The composition of "Von Zwanzig bis Dreißig" and "Der Stechlin" overlaps in the mid-nineties.

4 See NyA VIII, 47.

is nearly fifty years old, and Fontane had already related it in the first volume of his "Wanderungen durch die Mark Brandenburg" in the Rheinsberg section of the Ruppin volume, first published in 1861. A comparison of the early and late versions helps to clarify Fontane's art in remodelling old anecdotes which he has previously used in his own works, and enables the reader to draw some conclusions about the variations which he includes in the fictional version.

The "Ruppin" version (1861)	The fictional version (1898)
Friedrich Wilhelm IV. kam nie nach Ruppin oder Rheinsberg, ohne der alten Marquise auf Köpernitz seinen Besuch zu machen. Es traf sich, daß sie, bei einem dieser Besuche, ganz wie zu Zeiten der Remusinsel-Diners, durch ihre Kochkunst glänzen und den König durch eine Trüffel- oder Zervelatwurst überraschen konnte. Friedrich Wilhelm IV. erbat sich dann auch etwas davon für seine Potsdamer Küche (natürlich nicht vergeblich), und zum Weihnachtsabend erschien das königliche Gegengeschenk: ein Kollier aus goldenen Würstchen bestehend, die Speilerchen von Perlen, und begleitet von einem verbindichen Schreiben mit dem Motto: "Wurst wider Wurst". Geschenk und Gegengeschenk wiederholten sich mehrere Male, so daß sich zu dem Kollier ein Armband und zu dem Armband ein Ohrgehänge gesellte; zuletzt erschien eine Tabatiere in Form einer kurzen, gedrungenen Blut- und Zungenwurst, äußerst wertvoll, oben und unten mit Rubinen besetzt. Die Freude war groß, aber es war die letzte dieser Art. Aus den Zeitungen ersah die	Da war also drüben in Köpernitz diese La Roche-Aymon, und weil sie noch die Prinz-Heinrich-Tage gesehen und während derselben eine Rolle gespielt hatte, so zählte sie zu den besonderen Lieblingen Friedrich Wilhelms IV. Und als nun – sagen wir ums Jahr fünfzig – der Zufall es fügte, daß dem zur Jagd hier erschienenen König das Köpernitzer Frühstück, ganz besonders aber eine Blut- und Zungenwurst, über die Maßen gut geschmeckt hatte, so wurde dies Veranlassung für die Gräfin, am nächsten Heiligabend eine ganze Kiste voll Würste nach Potsdam hin in die königliche Küche zu liefern. Und das ging so durch Jahre. Da beschloß zuletzt der gute König, sich für all die gute Gabe zu revanchieren, und als wieder Weihnachten war, traf in Köpernitz ein Postpaket ein, Inhalt: eine zierliche kleine Blutwurst! Und zwar war es ein wunderschöner, rundlicher Blutkarneol mit Goldspeilerchen an beiden Seiten, die Speilerchen selbst mit Diamenten besetzt. Und neben diesem Geschenk lag ein Zettelchen: "Wurst wider Wurst".

die Marquise bald darauf, daß einer der Hofschlächtermeister zu Potsdam, als Gegengeschenk für eine große Fest- oder Jubiläumswurst (und sogar unter Beifügung desselben Mottos: "Wurst wider Wurst") in gleicher Weise durch eine Tabatiere geglückt worden war, und die Sendungen in die Königliche Küche hörten von diesem Augenblick an auf.[1]

The style of the earlier version suits that of the objective report, while that of the novel version dwells on the personal and subjective element e.g. the countess was one of the king's favourites because she had known Prince Henry, the little detail of the packet arriving by post in Köpernitz is mentioned, the king is "der gute König" and the countess's presents to him are "all die gute Gabe". Dubslav's version also varies the time sequence – in his story the countess delivers sausages to the royal kitchen for several years before receiving the royal recompense. In the early version, each year's sausage gift is returned with a different piece of jewellery which is described in detail, because this is presumably of interest to the "Wanderungen" reader. Dubslav ends his account with the dictum: "Wurst wider Wurst", while the "Wanderungen" report offers the very interesting sequel of the countess's disappointment at the repetition of the royal joke and generous gesture for another – this time the Potsdam butcher. Her abrupt stoppage of sausage gifts for the royal kitchen is in consequence not mentioned in Dubslav's version. The reader asks himself why this anecdote is related by Dubslav, and above all why it is different from Fontane's earlier version? It is Fontane's practice in any case to alter an anecdote on the second telling, but the change in the second version of the sausage anecdote appears to have a significant political ring to it. Given the honesty of Dubslav's character, we may presume that he is not deliberately supressing part of the story from his listener, Czako, indeed the most interesting

1 NyA VIII, 38-39 and NyA IX, 295.

part! To state, as Hans-Heinrich Reuter does, that this is an example of Fontane's indirect self-citation is not a satisfactory solution to the problem of the ending of this anecdote.[1] The anecdote purports to be about Frederick William IV, as indeed it was in the "Wanderungen" version, but in fact in the novel it is not. Dubslav's stated purpose in telling it to Czako is a social one; he likes to exchange stories as others do photographs. Thus, as Cornelie Ueding points out, he substitutes a living, changing form for a fixed image, which presents the public pose as a valid image of the person.[2] The storytelling is supposed to remind Czako in the future of Dubslav, not of Frederick William, just as a photograph should have reminded him of his host. The photograph, that modern invention, however, could never be as vivid an experience as the memory of the old man telling the story, a situation as old as society itself. Even in this brief scene, therefore, the old and the new are intertwined in a most unobtrusive way.

Dubslav's version of the sausage anecdote is admirably suited to his characterization in the novel. The story is short, winning and amusing. It is also however clearly employed in order to make at an early stage of the work an important point about Dubslav's political position. With an indirect subtlety, this anecdote, or rather Dubslav's own attitude towards it, shows in a pleasant narrative manner, which is not at all abstract or studied, how much he lives in the past. He continues as an aftermath to the story to claim that the anecdote means more to him than a constitution and that he is sure that the king thought so too! From the point of view of the theme of the old and the new, this statement provides the relevance of the inclusion of the sausage anecdote in the novel, and indeed of the truncated version, not the "Wanderungen" version which, with its implied critique of the monarch, would have been unsuitable for Fontane's

1 H.-H. Reuter holds that a clear explanation of the change on both Fontane's and Dubslav's part is not to be given – it is due not to forgetfulness or craftiness, nor to the fact that Fontane wants to introduce Dubslav's 'confessions', but can be seen as an example of Fontane's art of indirect self-citation. (See. H.-H. Reuter: "Fontane", vol. 1, p. 379.)

2 See Cornelie Ueding: op. cit., p. 243.

purposes in the novel. The inclusion of an approximate date in Dubslav's version supports such a political interpretation: the apparently casual reference "sagen wir um Jahr fünfzig"[1] locates the tale in the immediate aftermath of the unsuccessful 1848 revolution and in the year of the actual granting of the Prussian constitution, while, significantly enough, Fontane's version in the "Wanderungen" does not specify a date for the occurrence. The traditional aspect of the anecdote, the giving of an insight into the lives of the famous, is retained in this anecdote through its emphasis on the generosity and humour of Frederick William IV. A comparison of it with the earlier, more critical version, and especially the connection with the issue of the constitution (and only the latter factor, of course, is internal to and new in the novel) give this apparently harmless and traditional anecdote a political significance.

Dubslav, although he is not characterized as being 'antediluvian' like his sister, Adelheid, tends to live – politically speaking – in the past. The rest of the conversation of which the anecdote was the climax adequately proves this. Dubslav returns in memory to the days of the Holy Alliance and regrets that his country has lost its old friendship with Russia. Czako, who humours his partners in conversation (as was already shown in his conversation on rats with Frau von Gundermann) beats a retreat here into embarrassed silence, even though he has stated that he supports Dubslav's preference for a story like the sausage anecdote to a constitution. The narrator

1 C. Ueding writes in connection with Fontane's dating procedure here: "sagen wir ums Jahr fünfzig – es hätte alles auch ein wenig früher oder später oder ein wenig anders verlaufen können." (C. Ueding: op. cit., p. 242) While it is true to say that Fontane is not too worried about historical accuracy, he sticks to historical accuracy, unless he has a 'higher' purpose. His antedating practice with regard to anecdotes is invariably used in order to make a political point. This is also the case with the Frederick William IV anecdote. In other words, he is worried about the accuracy and sense relevance of the dating which h e applies within the fictional context. What is of interest here is that the date given in the fictional context is 1850, i.e. in the context of the failed revolution of 1848 and an unsatisfactory constitution. The impact of the Frederick Willaim IV anecdote is made precisely by the date, the apparently so casual reference to 1850.

makes sure that the point is not lost on the reader by informing him that Czako is a "ganz moderner, stark politisch angekränkelter Mensch",[1] one who is critical of such manifestations of eccentricity as Dubslav is now revealing with his mid-nineteenth century brand of Prussian enthusiasm for Russia.

The sausage anecdote is included very plausibly in Chapter 4 under the guise of local history. It is quite convincing that Dubslav should tell his guest an anecdote about Countess Caroline Amalie de la Roche-Aymon, who is buried nearby in Köpernitz. However, as we have seen, the anecdote holds an early and key position in the novel for the depiction of Dubslav's political stance. His own charm, his humour and his love of the personal, human element come out in his telling of the tale, but it has far wider ramifications than merely those of characterization or depiction of social situation. Dubslav has some enlightened sentiments about improvement of the peasants' conditions, improvements which even Lorenzen calls "die reinste Neulandtheorie".[2] When after his defeat in the election, he meets the inebriated Tuxen, their exchange concerns the "Tüffelland"[3] (land on which to grow potatoes) promised by the successful Social Democratic candidate, Torgelow, to the agrarian labourers. Fontane is aware that Dubslav's almost social democratic notions would be the essence of genuine Prussian paternalism. In spite of all this however Dubslav fails to see that the coming of democracy cannot be restrained any longer. It is already clear in Chapter 4 that the era of the reactionary Holy Alliance and Frederick William IV's anti-constitutional stance present a political outlook which is more congenial to Dubslav than the contemporary political movement away from paternalism. Later, in Chapter 5 he gives a blanket condemnation of the decline he thinks has taken place since the early

1 NyA VIII, 40.
2 Ibidem.
3 The double irony here consists in the fact that Prussian paternalism at its best contained a good dose of social democracy, while Social Democracy in fact failed to look after the agrarian labourer. See Eda Sagarra: ' "Eingepökeltes Rindfleisch oder Spargel und frisches Gemüse" – the Christian Social Background to "Der Stechlin" ' in "Formen Realistischer Erzählkunst". Nottingham 1979, p. 578.

nineteenth century: "Ja, herabgestiegen ist alles, und es steigt immer weiter nach unten. Das ist, was man neue Zeit nennt, immer weiter runter."[1] All Dubslav's good human qualities, and they are many, do not hide the fact that politically he is rather out of date, and it is no accident that much of the novel is concerned with his death. The pervading impression is given also of the fall of his whole class – the landed aristocracy, which is in Lorenzen's terms the roof which no longer affords protection to the building. Small wonder then that Dubslav's preference is for jokes and anecdotes of bygone eras. But Dubslav is at least aware that he is old-fahsioned, and stresses the fact with the humour and self-irony which characterize many of the most attractive Fontane figures.

Frequently with Fontane a person is not just characterized by what he says, and by what is said about him either by the narrator or by other characters, but also by what is said to him. This is the case in Chapter 33, after the wedding of Armgard and Woldemar, when Dubslav and Court Preacher Frommel converse together. It is clear from the passage that the conversation is included in the novel simply in order to lead up to the anecdote told by Frommel about Kaiser William I in Gastein. Many details of the conversation leading to the anecdote both pave the way for it by means of association and sound chords reminiscent of the major preoccupations of the novel: world-wide connections (captains who sail in ships from New York to Bristol are few in Berlin), the rough surface of a lake, a hotelier's wife, who was once courted by a king or Kaiser. These apparently random associations of Dubslav all inevitably lead to an anecdote with a hotel-setting concerning the Kaiser. Emil Frommel[2] (1828-1896) is the only historical character given a part in the novel, and he appears to be included simply that he may relate this story to Dubslav, for he does not appear in the novel except at the wedding. Since Frommel's anecdote already existed in printed form

1 NyA VIII, 47.

2 The following quotation from the 1923-1939 edition of "Der Große Brockhaus" indicates those qualities which might have attracted Fontane to this figure: "Frommel war als Prediger, Seelsorger und Erzieher feinsinnig und volkstümlich, nie Parteimann, von unabhängigem Urteil" (op. cit., vol. 6, p. 642).

in Frommel's complete, works, Fontane could use this version as the basis of his own.[1] A comparison of Frommel's with Fontane's version shows the tiny but artistically significant modifications which Fontane made in order to make the story suit the context of the novel.

The historical version (1878)

Das "Badeschloß", in dem der Kaiser sein Absteigequartier hatte, war damals noch kein Hotel, es wohnten aber andere Kurgäste noch mit dem Kaiser zugleich in demselben. Das war auch die Ursache zu der nachfolgenden Geschichte, die so ganz den herzgewinnenden Sinn des hohen Herrn bezeichnet. Es lag unten ein kranker Badegast im Erdgeschoß. Es gab Tage in Gastein, wo es mit Kübeln goß, so daß an ein Ausgehen nicht zu denken war. Und doch sollte der hohe Herr sich Bewegung machen. Er benutzte darum die ganze Flucht von Zimmern, um auf und ab zu gehen. Als der Kammerdiener den Kaiser nicht mehr auf und ab gehen hörte, ging er hinein, um etwas zu bringen. Aber welch Bild entrollte sich ihm! Der Kaiser legte, sich bückend, einen Teppich neben den andern im Schweiße des Angesichts. "Aber, Majestät, was tun Sie da, warum lassen Sie mich das nicht tun?" Lächelnd sagte der Kaiser: "Ja, das habe ich nun einmal selber gemacht. Da unten wohnt ein schwerkranker Badegast, der zu Bette liegt und wenig schlafen kann. Da

The fictional version (1898)

Eine ganz kleine Geschichte; aber das sind gerade die besten. Da hatten wir mal einen schweren Regentag in Gastein, so daß der alte Herr nicht ins Freie kam, und statt draußen in den Bergen, in seinem großen Wohnzimmer seinen gewohnten Spaziergang machen mußte, so gut es eben ging. Unter ihm aber – was er wußte – lag ein Schwerkranker. Und nun denken Sie sich, als ich bei dem guten, alten Kaiser eintrete, seh ich ihn, wie er da lange Läufer und Teppiche zusammenschleppt und übereinander packt, und als er mein Erstaunen sieht, sagt er mit einem unbeschreiblichen und mir unvergeßlichen Lächeln: "Ja, lieber Frommel, da unter mir liegt ein Kranker; ich mag nicht, daß er die Empfindung hat, ich trample ihm da so über den Kopf hin..."[2]

1 Emil Frommel: "Gesammelte Schriften". 11 Bände. Berlin 1873-1897, Band 10 (1878) p. 37-38.

2 NyA VIII, 272.

habe ich die Teppiche alle zusammengelegt, damit der Mann mich beim Gehen nicht hört; da geht's sich doch leichter, und man macht so was am besten selbst..."

Fontane's version is pithier and livelier. The use of Frommel himself as the Kaiser's intelocutor instead of the nameless servant makes for immediacy. Unnecessary detail is excluded, such as that about the hotel. Instead, the conversation in Chapter 33 starts off as a conversation about hotels. The Emperor's explanation about his action is cut to the minimum. Frommel's old-fashioned phrases: "der hohe Herr", "welch Bild entrollte sich ihm", and the Biblical "im Schweiße des Angesichts" are omitted. The Kaiser is referred to as "der gute alte Kaiser" and "der alte Herr", and speaks rather like a character of Fontane. Frommel relates the anecdote in the novel in response to Dubslav's request for a story which will show him what the Kaiser was really like during the quiet days at the spa. In Dubslav's view, Kaiser William I was the last monarch who was also a real human being.[1]

On its most superficial level, this anecdote fulfils the traditional function of the anecdote about a famous personage: it gives a view into the character of the Kaiser. The historical Kaiser's great human

1 There is a discrepancy here between the Aufbau and the NyA reading of Dubslav's statement. The NyA reads: "Sie waren ja mit unserm guten Kaiser Wilhelm, dem letzten Monarchen, der noch ein wirklicher Mensch war, immer in Gastein zusammen." (NyA VIII, 272) The Aufbau version gives: "dem letzten Menschen, der noch ein wirklicher Mensch war". (Aufbau VIII, 313) "Menschen" appears in the first printing of "Der Stechlin" in the periodical "Über Land und Meer" and in all the subsequent book editions, but is obviously based on a mistake in the manuscript. Cf. NyA VIII, 396. "Monarchen" makes more sense in the light of the Frommel anecdote. Dubslav asks for a story about something "woran man ihn so recht eigentlich erkennt". Compare also Dubslav's remark about the three nineteenth-century Tsars called Alexander in his sequel to the sausage anecdote: "alle drei große Herren und alle drei richtige Kaiser und fromme Leute, oder doch beinah fromm, die's gut mit ihrem Volk und mit der Menschheit meinten, und dabei selber richtige Menschen..." (ibid. 40)

simplicity was one of the reasons why he became during his lifetime almost a symbolic figure.[1] In Fontane's novel, both teller and listener agree as to the interpretation of the tale namely that it proves the real character of the Kaiser. Dubslav's claim, however, that such a monarch will not be found again in Prussia, brings the story onto another level and demonstrates that the anecdote mirrors the theme complex of the old and the new. The conversational lead-up to the anecdote also foreshadows this, when Dubslav once again expresses his scepticism about the new era:

> Jetzt hat man statt des wirklichen Menschen den sogenannten Übermenschen etabliert; eigentlich gibt es aber bloß noch Untermenschen, und mitunter sind es gerade die, die man durchaus zu seinem "Über" machen will. Ich habe von solchen Leuten gelesen und auch welche gesehn. Ein Glück, daß es, nach meiner Wahrnehmung, immer entschieden komische Figuren sind, sonst könnte man verzweifeln.[2]

It is clear from the overall characterization of Dubslav in the novel that his conservatism is not doctrinaire – it does not share that rigidity of opinion which Fontane found distasteful in any sphere of life. Even the very contrast with his sister, Adelheid, suggests that Dubslav's political outlook is mild and conciliatory. Although he theoretically opposes the new, he is ready to concede that it may have something to recommend it: "all das dumme Zeug, das Neue (dran vielleicht doch was war)."[3]

The close analysis of the sausage anecdote and the Frommel anecdote throws light on Dubslav's political outlook. That essential humanity which is the main point of Lorenzen's speech at Dubslav's funeral permeates all of Dubslav's thinking and his utterances. This humanity makes Dubslav a wise and kindly person, who would care like a father for the tenants on his estate and for his constituents, if he were successful in getting elected as a Conservative member of the Reichstag. Dubslav appreciates Frommel's anecdote about

1 See the entry on William I in "Der Große Brockhaus" (15th ed., 1935).
2 NyA VIII, 272.
3 Ibid. 209.

William I because it expresses two features which exactly correspond to his own outlook on life and politics. The first is the Kaiser's humanity in saving the sick man from discomfort, while doing this good deed by himself and not calling a servant. The second feature arises from Dubslav's interpretation of the anecdote as a sign of the times he lives in, namely, that this humanity is on the decline, even among monarchs.

It is this latter aspect which makes a connection between both anecdotes. Dubslav's return to the subject of the sausage[1] in Chapter 23 shows that he is not at all as laudatory of Frederick William IV as had seemed to be the case in Chapter 3. His narration of the anecdote to Czako ended with his interpretation that the story was as good as a constitution. The opinion, thus stated, must rest on belief in the benevolence of all authority, the belief, in other words, that the authority will be as just and caring for those subject to it as Dubslav himself is. Each time the sausage anecdote is referred to, Dubslav's listeners are embarrassed by his professed love for the earlier part of the nineteenth century when Prussia and Russia were close allies. In each case, without actually saying as much, the narrator thus shows that Dubslav is regarded as politically out of date by his contemporaries, whether "politisch angekränkelt" like Czako or Christian Social like Lorenzen. In fact however Dubslav's conservatism does not exclude criticism. His return to the subject of the king's tobacco-box in Chapter 23 shows that he has a mind of his own. His critical opinion, which is only barely alluded to, resides in the fact that he sees such royal presents as being almost bribery. The implication is that there may not have been a proper constitution, but there were 'presents'. The criticism implied in the Frommel anecdote is not just that of the decline in the era, but the Emperor is called the last monarch, who was also a real human being. This seems to be specific criticism of William II, criticism which would be in accord with Fontane's revised views about William II in the latter part of the eighteen-nineties.

1 The reader can only be sure that Dubslav is referring back to the sausage anecdote (in connection with the topic of 'Bestechung') from his use of two words in this passage in Chapter 23: "solche Tabatiere". (NyA VIII, 208)

Dubslav's veiled criticisms in connection with both anecdotes and his 'almost Social Democratic' ideas about living standards for the people show that his politics are far removed from those of other Conservatives in the novel, e.g. of Gundermann. While Dubslav's political outlook is therefore not at all rigidly dogmatic, it is not at the same time likely to help him win the election. His adamant preference for the 'old days' makes him appear particularly old-fashioned. It is a typically Fontane-esque paradox, however, that those stories which most seem to brand Dubslav as an arch-conservative on closer reading provide proof that Dubslav subjects authority to criticism even though he does so in a very private way in conversation with Frommel and Lorenzen. Dubslav's love of 'old' values is sincere and rests on his humanity, while at the same time he is willing to accept a revaluation of these, e.g. his reaction to Lorenzen's Greely anecdote, which we shall discuss later. Indicative of Dubslav's political position, which although not progressive is not rigidly conservative either, is the fact that he is always shown as harmonizing with Lorenzen, even though he programmatically expresses disapproval of Lorenzen's views. Not Dubslav, but Adelheid is the opposite pole to the clergyman. While Lorenzen is described as an "Excelsior-, ein Aufsteigemensch",[1] she is associated with images of rigidity and petrefaction. Her narrow politics and doctrinaire insistence on the superiority of the Brandenburg aristocracy contrast with the humanity and open-mindedness of Dubslav, who is an example of the best kind of nobleman, one who is noble not just by birth but in outlook as well.

The politics of Dubslav's son, Woldemar, and his position vis-a-vis the old and the new are rather difficult to define, as far as his figure in the final version of the novel is concerned. Whereas in the final version of the novel the measure of Woldemar's conservatism or progressiveness remains uncertain, his position in relation to the theme of old and new is emphatically declared in a passage originally planned by Fontane for Chapter 21 as a reflection on the election results:

1 NyA VIII, 143.

> Das Alte mußte fallen, nicht weil es schlecht war, es war nicht schlecht, sondern bloß weil es alt war. Auch dann noch mußte es fallen, wenn es besser ist als das Neue. Eine Generation stößt die andre ins Grab; die, die vom Schauplatz abtritt, war vielleicht die bessere, die klügere, aber sie muß fort, weil jedes Leben, auch das beste, ein bestimmtes Zeitmaß hat.[1]

The open-ended nature of the novel's conclusion with its quotation of Melusine's letter to Lorenzen shows however that too much attention should not be paid to the question of Woldemar's continuing political outlook: "es ist nicht nötig, daß die Stechline weiterleben, aber es lebe d e r S t e c h l i n."[2] It is the 'Gesinnung' factor which is to be of abiding importance, and the fact that Woldemar and Armgard are linked with the caritas theme proves that – with or without progeny, with or without progressive politics – the future is assured as long as that openmindedness and lack of narrow rigidity, symbolised by the lake, are retained. "Der Stechlin" does not present a cut-and-dried laudatio of modern tendencies and a rejection of traditional values. The intertwining of the old and the new during the very process of change in society is the intention behind the novel. Lorenzen, the exponent in the novel of the Christian Social element, warns his ex-pupil, Woldemar, already in Chapter 3 against unconsidered enthusiasm for that which is new: "Lieber mit dem Alten, soweit es irgend geht, und mit dem Neuen, soweit es muß."[3] In a letter to Friedrich Paulsen, Fontane indicated in 1897 that his new novel was 'patriotic', although this element was approached in it from a different angle: "Er ist patriotisch, aber schneidet die Wurst von den andern Seite an und neigt sich mehr einem veredelten Bebel- oder Stöckertum, als einem alten Zieten- oder Blüchertum zu."[4] As has already been seen, even the anecdotes connected with Dubslav which on one level associate his figure with 'old' values, also show his critical approach. He is not a 'Fondeur'. He is repelled by 'Fronde' and finds it inappropriate for the nobility.

1 Aufbau VIII, 435.
2 NyA VIII, 361.
3 Ibid. 27.
4 "Briefe an die Freunde". Letzte Auslese. p. 612.

However, with a relativization which characterizes so much of what Dubslav says, he adds about 'Fronde' in this passage which follows the Frommel anecdote: "Bloß mitunter, da paßt sie doch vielleicht."[1]

One of the important themes of "Der Stechlin" is that of heroism. We shall see how this theme, even through the medium of anecdote alone fits into the more comprehensive and more important theme of the old and the new. The phenomenon of heroism was of interest to Fontane from his earliest days as a writer. His lyrical subjects were often Prussian military heroes, such as in the ballads on Derfflinger, Blücher, Zieten, Seydlitz and Frederick the Second. With such ballads he won the applause of his literary colleagues in the 'Tunnel' club, and this situation is echoed in the 'Castalia' club meetings in "Vor dem Sturm", where the heroism theme is also touched on. The anecdotes in "Der Stechlin" which deal with heroism have, however, little in common with the traditional Prussian anecdote of valour on the battlefield, of a stroke of luck or bravery which wins the day or brings about a turning-point in an encounter.

In Chapter 5 of "Der Stechlin", Czako tells the Stechlins and his companion, Captain Rex, an anecdote about a Russian schoolmaster who, on being conscripted, refuses even to practise shooting because of his belief that this constitutes preparation for killing and murder. For this, the teacher suffers in the army and finally dies as a result.[2] Captain Rex, characterized in the novel by his political and religious rigidity, condemns the teacher's action as empty show, and even Dubslav, usually so tolerant, takes it as proof of his pet theory that all teachers are crazy. Technically, the narrative reason for the introduction of the anecdote and of Dubslav's reaction to it is that Dubslav is thereby allowed to introduce the figure of the eccentric local teacher, Krippenstapel, to the breakfast conversation. It is not without significance that the anecdote is related directly following Dubslav's account to his guests of Pastor Lorenzen's political ideas: the aristocratic age is in a state of collapse, the democratic era is

1 NyA VIII, 273.
2 Ibid. 48.

dawning.[1] The anecdote of the teacher's sticking to his pacifist principles even to the point of death, though lost on the unsympathetic listeners, is a foretaste already in Chapter 5 of the revaluation of the phenomenon of heroism, which is such a marked characteristic of the latter part of the novel. It is also hardly accidental that the anecdote follows a reference to Lorenzen's ideas, since he above all is associated with the notion of revaluation and with the demand for a revitalization of society in general. Later, as we shall see, Lorenzen carries the theme of heroism very powerfully, not merely in theoretical conversation, but also through the more concrete and memorable medium of the anecdote.

Two of the conversation partners from Chapter 5 meet again in Chapter 22, where the theme of heroism again appears in the guise of a Prussian anecdote. At first sight, this story may appear to remain much in the vein of the traditional Prussian anecdote about military valour. The narrator is Woldemar, the listener, Czako. The content of the anecdote and Woldemar's narrative purpose do not so much concern the traditional value of a particular feat of heroism on the battlefield as the necessity of having a certain attitude of mind. Albeit expressing himself humorously as usual, especially when referring to himself, Czako complains that he will never achieve promotion in the Prussian army because of his Slavic-sounding name. Woldemar treats the problem seriously, and in order to boost his friend's morale tells a Frederician anecdote. In fact, with a generalization he includes all his countrymen, who in spite of their victories, or maybe because of them, lack a certain self-confidence. Woldemar is of the opinion that success is ultimately due to the nature of one's self-judgement. Therefore, he can quote with approval Frederick's encouraging words to an officer in distress: "Denk Er nur immer, daß Er hunderttausend Mann hinter sich hat."[2]. In order to build up Czako's self-confidence and in the belief that it is a good example to

1 NyA VIII, 47.

2 Ibid. 198. Fontane had already used this anecdote in "Wanderungen durch die Mark Brandenburg". See "Spreeland", NyA XII, 188. Cf. Fontane's own sense of a lack of confidence in the land. Cf. Joachim Remak: "The Gentle Critic". New York 1964, p. 76-77.

his country in general, Woldemar tells a traditional Prussian anecdote from the military sphere. This holding up of Frederick's words to the modern age is not a contradiction of Woldemar's apparent espousal in "Der Stechlin" of the 'new' values. It is not unusual in Fontane's narrative works that a traditional anecdote be used for the purposes of a didactic reminder for the present. In "Schach von Wuthenow", as we have seen, even as ardent a critic of contemporary Prussia as Bülow tells a Frederician anecdote for the precise purpose of pointing out a present fault in his countrymen's outlook. The narrator in "Schach von Wuthenow" indirectly does the same thing by having the hero in a moment of indecision and suffering look at illustrations of Frederician anecdotes, which depend for their effect on the bravery and sangfroid of the monarch.[1]

The emphasis in Woldemar's anecdote in Chapter 22 is not in any case on a specific example of battlefield heroics, but rather on a general mental attitude of self-confidence. Even Dubslav, a professed lover of the battlefield type of heroism, has to admit early in the novel that the phenomenon is something exceptional and that usually a person is forced into it through circumstances.[2] The revaluation of heroism, which has been steadily prepared for at earlier stages of the novel, finally is teased out in detail in the latter part, between Chapters 28 and 38. In Chapter 28, Melusine's conversation partner, the village mayor, Kluckhuhn, entertains her with conversation about the Danish warship, Rolf Krake, and the action of the Prussian military engineer, Klinke, in the storming of the Düppel redoubt during the Schleswig-Holstein war of 1864. Kluckhuhn is at pains to draw a distinction between what he terms a moral kind of courage and ordinary heroism. Real heroism is to be found in little acts performed by the individual on his own, not in mere participation in the concerted effort of a group of soldiers:

> immer bloß das Kleine, da zeigt sich's, was einer kann. Wenn eine Bataillon 'ran muß un ich stecke mitten drin, ja, was will ich da machen? Da muß ich mit. Und baff, da lieg ich. Und nu bin ich ein Held. Aber

1 See above p. 120-123.
2 NyA VIII, 25.

eigentlich bin ich keiner. Es ist alles bloß 'Muß', und solche Mußhelden gibt est viele. Das is, was ich die großen Kriege nenne. Klinke mit seinem Pulversack, ja, war bloß was Kleines, aber er war doch groß.[1]

Klinke's making a breach in the Düppel redoubt by blowing himself up voluntarily with it may not have been a major event in the war, but it was an individual act which allowed the Prussians to storm the redoubt and constitutes, in Kluckhuhn's view, proof of Klinke's greatness. Just as the paradox of the little action being in reality a great one lies at the bottom of Kluckhuhn's conception of real heroism, so too in Lorenzen's conception of this subject a reversal of conventional opinion is essential. Lorenzen's more theoretical approach to this theme comes in the revolutionary discourse with Melusine in the chapter directly following her conversation with Kluckhuhn. In this second conversation, Lorenzen gives a comprehensive account of his views on the development and present state of Prussia. He claims that people have lost interest in battles and that heroism has declined as a value, although the régime attempts to boost it artificially. The heroes of the new age which Lorenzen welcomes, are not warriors but inventors.[2] In this conversation, the theme of heroism is not carried further than this, but it returns in Lorenzen's important second last conversation with Dubslav in Chapter 38. After this talk, Dubslav has a good night, although he is very near his end: "Wenn man mal so was andres hört, wird einem gleich besser."[3] The final summing up of Lorenzen's outlook on heroism comes in the form of an anecdote about the Arctic explorer, Lieutenant Adolphus Washington Greely (1844-1936). Dubslav requests that Lorenzen entertain him with something nice and amusing, drawing attention to his wonderful memory for "anecdotes from all five continents",[4] although he expects and would welcome an anecdote from Prussian history, about Frederick the Second, Blücher or Wrangel. Lorenzen is

1 NyA VIII, 244. The Klinke story is not historically accurate.
2 Cf. NyA VIII, 253.
3 Ibid. 319.
4 Ibid. 316.

obviously an expert in this area of anecdotal material, but the mention of Prussian military figures and of Dubslav's love of heroism gives him the cue to re-examine the meaning of heroism and the cult of heroes. To the heroism of the battlefield, Lorenzen prefers heroic acts which do not reach the light of day: "Alles vollzieht sich stumm, einsam, weltabgewandt".[1] In part-echo of his talk with Melusine, Lorenzen claims as real heroes inventors, climbers, divers and explorers and that, for him at any rate, real heroism "steht immer in Dienst einer Eigenidee, eines allereigensten Entschlusses".[2] This emphasis on individual decision and action is borne out by Lorenzen's anecdotal account of an incident from the Lady Franklin Bay expedition of 1881-1884. The incident in question was the execution of a soldier, Private Charles B. Henry on 6 June 1884. On that day, Henry was shot on Greely's orders, for having once more in spite of a stern warning stolen from the expedition's food store. The surviving members of the expedition were rescued from imminent death due to starvation and frostbite by the rescue ship Thetis under the command of Captain Schley on 22 June 1884. On the return of the party to the East Coast of the United States, a controversy broke out about the conduct of the expedition. One of the controversial aspects was the execution of Private Henry. Fontane's fictional version of this aspect of the expedition differs in several respects from the historical Greely's version.[3] Lorenzen relates as follows:

1 NyA VIII, 317.

2 Ibidem.

3 These discrepancies can be briefly summarized as follows: in reality, seven men survived as opposed to Lorenzen's five. No names are given in Lorenzen's account, not even that of Henry (a deserter of German origin, who had re-enlisted under this alias, his real name being Charles Henry Buck). The situation in each case is different: in the novel, the party is still travelling on foot, having left the ship. In reality, they had broken camp at Fort Conger on Ellesmere Island and proceeded according to pre-arrangement southward to Cape Sabine, since the expected relief and supply ships had failed to reach Lady Franklin Bay. At the time of the June execution, the party had been stationary since the previous October, awaiting either rescue or death from starvation and exposure. Henry was not the provisions-bearer (there was in reality no moving procession), but this adds a touch of

... Also zuletzt nach langer Irrfahrt, waren's noch ihrer fünf: Greely selbst und vier seiner Leute. Das Schiff hatten sie verlassen, und so zogen sie hin über Eis und Schnee. Sie wußten den Weg, soweit sich da von Weg sprechen läßt, und die Sorge war nur, ob das bißchen Proviant, das sie mit sich führten, Schiffszwieback und gesalzenes Fleisch, bis an die nächste menschenbewohnte Stelle reichen würde. Jedem war ein höchstes und doch zugleich auch wieder geringstes Maß als tägliche Provision zubewilligt, und wenn man dies Maß einhielt und kein Zwischenfall kam, so mußt es reichen. Und einer, der noch am meisten bei Kräften war, schleppte den gesamten Proviant. Das ging so durch Tage. Da nahm Leutnant Greely wahr, daß der Proviant schneller hinschmolz als berechnet, und nahm auch wahr, daß der Proviantträger selbst, wenn er sich nicht beobachtet glaubte, von den Rationen nahm. Das war eine schreckliche Wahrnehmung. Denn ging es so fort, so waren sie samt und sonders verloren. Da nahm Greely die drei andern beiseit' und beriet mit ihnen. Eine Möglichkeit gewöhnlicher Bestrafung gab es nicht und auf einen Kampf sich einzulassen, ging auch nicht. Sie hatten dazu die Kräfte nicht mehr. Und so hieß es denn zuletzt, und es war Greely, der es sagte: "Wir müssen ihn hinterrücks erschießen." Und als sie bald nach dieser Kriegsgerichtsszene wieder aufbrachen, der heimlich Verurteilte vorn an der Tete, trat Greely von hinterher an ihn heran und schoß ihn nieder. Und die Tat war nicht umsonst getan; ihre Rationen reichten aus, und an dem Tage, wo sie den letzten Bissen verzehrten, kamen sie bis an eine Station. ... Ich weiß nicht mehr, ob Greely selbst bei seiner Rückkehr nach New York als Ankläger gegen sich auftrat; aber das weiß ich, daß es zu einer großen Verhandlung kam. ... In dieser wurd er freigesprochen und im Triumph nach Hause getragen.[1]

irony to the fictional version. The execution, which seems surprizingly sudden in Lorenzen's version, has a longer lead-up to it in the published version of Lieutenant Greely's journal: "Three Years of Arctic Service". New York 1886. Already in May, Greely mentions the necessity of "severe action" (p. 315) being taken if stealing from the provisions continues. On 5 June, he cautions Henry sternly, when the latter admits to further thefts. The same day, Greely writes a preliminary order that Henry is to be executed if apprehended once more. On 6 June, Henry makes bold admissions about his stealing, showing no remorse, and Greely gives a written order for him to be shot, taking care to be absent during the execution. (See Greely: op. cit., p. 315-319. The book was translated into German by Reinhold Teuscher under the title "Drei Jahre hoch im Norden". Jena 1887.)

1 NyA VIII, 318-319.

In Fontane's version, the offender is ennobled by not being branded as he is in Greely's published works, as a thief, liar and insubordinate soldier. The historical Greely is at pains to stress the military nature of his decision as a commanding officer, while in Lorenzen's version the action is made to seem more individual. It is an individual's decision made in the loneliness of a moral dilemma. A further more human, or more individual element in Lorenzen's version is the inclusion of a consultation by Greely with subordinates. In the original, two of them are simply given the written order to execute, while the whole party confers on the matter after the shots are fired, agreeing that in the circumstances the action was proper. Further emphasis on individual action is placed in Lorenzen's version by the fact that Greely performs the action himself, graphically stepping out of line and shooting Henry in the back. The fictional story appears to receive immediate 'proof' that the action was right, in that the day the last morsel is consumed they reach a station. The many differences between the fictional version and reality tend to be in the interests of a more dramatic situation, in which the individual element is more strongly emphasised than in the original.[1] No doubt

1 Further fictional elements besides the consultation in a military tribunal are the lack of warning to the offender, the carrying out of the execution by Greely himself, and the shooting from behind. Theodore Powell, who had access to the papers of all members of the expedition, notes that the two officers charged with the execution decided not to shoot Henry in the back, but to give him a chance to say his prayers. Before being shot, he tried to attack them with an axe. See Theodore Powell: "The Long Rescue". London 1961, p. 272-273. The "große Verhandlung" mentioned by Lorenzen did not take place. Greely requested one in New York, but the army authorities decided it was not necessary, because they deduced from his own journal and from the journals of his subordinate officers that no blame attached to him for his action. In "Der Stechlin" no mention is made of the fact that the 'hunters' of the party were risking their lives every day to get foxes and shrimps, when Henry committed the crimes of stealing from the provisions. Lorenzen mentions nothing of stealing being something of a commonplace on the expedition, nor anything about the offender's being a thief of other items besides food. In reality, the party did not come to a station on the day that the last item of food was consumed, but hung on with ever-dwindling supplies until the arrival of the rescue ship.

some of the discrepancies between reality and fiction here are due to lack of knowledge or to lapses of memory on Fontane's part. While he would have been familiar with the reportage of the Greely controversy in the German newspapers,[1] he made unsuccessful attempts during the writing of the fictional version to find out exact details about the Greely expedition from Paul Meyer, Friedrich Fontane's friend.[2] Hence the words put into Lorenzen's mouth that his memory may not be totally reliable as regards the details of the story.

Greely's decision is not covered by the normally accepted rules of moral behaviour; there even appears to be an element of criminality about the affair.[3] This explains the necessity of an investigation of the historical Greely's conduct. Precisely this apparent criminality appeals to Lorenzen as constituting a fruitful example of how the notion of heroism can be re-interpreted. The very closeness of Greely's action to the taint of scandal makes his decision all the more difficult and his action all the more admirable.

1 For example, the report on the rescue of the expedition party in the "Illustrirte Zeitung. Wöchentliche Nachrichten über alle Ereignisse, Zustände und Persönlichkeiten der Gegenwart". Leipzig, Berlin, Nr. 2150, of 13. 9. 1884, p. 226.

2 See "Erinnerungen an Theodor Fontane 1819-1898". Aus dem Nachlaß seines Freundes und Testamentvollstreckers Justizrat Paul Meyer. Berlin 1936, p. 20-21.

3 Just as controversial, if not more so, in historical reality was the circumstance that partially-eaten corpses of some expedition members were discovered by the relief-party near the survivors' tent. (See the abovementioned article on the relief of the expedition party in the "Illustrirte Zeitung", p. 226 and Theodore Powell: op. cit., p. 300-301.) Greely does not allude to the suspicion of cannibalism either in his book on the expedition or in his autobiographical work: "Reminiscences of Adventure and Service". New York, London 1927. He claimed to the military authorities that, as leader of the expedition, he had had no knowledge of any cannibalism among his party, and he was exonerated from any blame for it as in the case of the execution of Private Henry. A reference on Fontane's part to this other controversial aspect of the expedition would of course have destroyed the anecdotal form, which is restricted to one incident, and would have spoiled the impact of a story about a man being shot for stealing bacon and biscuits.

The scales of normal assessment of moral acts might weigh against him. His decision balanced the salvation of all his men not only against the obnoxiousness of the solution itself, but also in case of survival against the risk of life-long opprobrium from society as a whole. Lorenzen interprets the ambivalence of Greely's moral dilemma thus in a comment on his own anecdote: the quarter-master's action, in itself something trifling, was in the circumstances a terrible crime, while Greely's decision, reached in apparent contradiction of law, honour and divine commandment, denotes true heroism: "Schmach und Schimpf, oder doch der Vorwurf des Schimpflichen, haben sich von jeher an alles Höchste geknüpft."[1]

The choice of a "Yankee pur sang"[2] for Lorenzen's revaluation of heroism makes another link between that revaluation and the major theme-complex of the old and the new in the novel. Not only is there a contrast of the old and the new in his interpretation of Greely's action: the 'new' heroism is a less easy one to practise than traditional battlefield heroism, where the modalities of action were clearly defined, but also the status factor undoubtedly plays a part in Lorenzen's choice of hero. The great distinguishing feature of the new democratic age, according to Lorenzen in the revolutionary discourse, is its disregard of the old clichés attached to inherited status and the concomitant freedom of the individual to change his status by his own efforts.[3] This gives a clue to one reason why Lorenzen's heroes are explorers and inventors. The courage and intelligence needed for Lorenzen's heroes are not restricted to the 'old families'. "To be an explorer was a choice open to all."[4]

1 NyA VIII, 319.
2 Ibid. 318.
3 "Der Hauptgegensatz alles Modernen gegen das Alte besteht darin, daß die Menschen nicht mehr durch ihre Geburt auf den von ihnen einzuhehmenden Platz gestellt werden. Sie haben jetzt die Freiheit, ihre Fähigkeiten nach allen Seinen hin und auf jedem Gebiete zu betätigen." (Ibid. 251-252)
4 So writes the doyenne of the history of Arctic exploration, Jeannette Mirsky in "To the Arctic: The Story of Northern Exploration from Earliest Times to the Present". New York 1948. Reprint with a new introduction, Chicago 1970, p. xxi.

Three military stories, that of the Russian schoolteacher, of Klinke and of Lieutenant Greely form a complex of little narratives which links thematically chapters from different partsof this large novel in conversations which appear at first sight to be casual and unrelated, but which actually present a revaluation of the value of heroism.[1] This revaluation is heralded in by no less a person than Dubslav himself with his early statement that heroism is mostly the product of a constrained position. There is no logical contradiction between Dubslav's recognition in Chapter 3: "Heldentum ist Ausnahmezustand und meist Produkt einer Zwangslage"[2] and his statement in Chapter 38 which prompts Lorenzen to tell the Greely anecdote: "Ich spiele mich persönlich nicht auf Heldentum aus, Renommieren ist ein elendes Handwerk; aber ich darf sagen: ich liebe das Heldische. Und Gott sei Dank kommt dergleichen immer wieder vor."[3] The word 'Renommieren' here shows a conscious linking on the narrator's part with the anecdote about the Russian schoolmaster, because the conversation about that story revolved arund the notion of 'Renommisterei'.

1 Hugo Aust has denied the validity of the reader's taking Lorenzen's Greely anecdote as representing the view of Fontane himself, claiming that Lorenzen is merely one of Fontane's characters who happens to hold this particular view. Aust takes exception to Richard Brinkmann's assumption in "Theodor Fontane. Die Verbindlichkeit des Unverbindlichen". München 1967, p. 112, that the narrator and Fontane himself share Lorenzen's interpretation of Greely's action. See Hugo Aust: "Theodor Fontane. 'Verklärung'. Eine Untersuchung zum Ideengehalt seiner Werke". Bonn 1974, p. 306-307. From the examination of the Greely anecdote in the context of Lorenzen's place in the novel as a whole and of his important role in Fontane's earlier conception of the novel, as well as in the context of other fictional references to the heroism theme e.g. the Barfus story in "Frau Jenny Treibel", it would certainly appear that Lorenzen's interpretation of the Greely anecdote d o e s concur with that of Fontane.

Quite clearly, the anecdotes in these cases, as in the case of the Barfus anecdote in "Frau Jenny Treibel", are conceived by Fontane in order to give flesh and blood of a story from reality to an idea: what constitutes true humanity, revaluation, heroism.

2 NyA VIII, 25.

3 Ibid. 316.

The fact that Dubslav pauses before accepting the Greely anecdote as an example of true courage and 'modern' heroism does not invalidate it as an example of this value. After all, he is the representative of the old in the novel, and indeed of the good, old values. After initial hesitation he endorses Lorenzen's unorthodox view of heroism, and that is why Dubslav is chosen as the character who first pronounces that battlefield heroism is often a matter of constraint rather than a true choice. The Greely anecdote is important for, and relevant to, not simply the revaluation theme (in connection with heroism), but also the novel as a whole. This anecdote's apparent dubiousness makes it an excellent Fontane-esque vehicle to convey "den großen Zusammenhang der Dinge", a great theme of "Der Stechlin".[1] Dubslav, susceptible like Lorenzen to admiration for explorers, feels initially that the Prussian army's action at Saint Privat during the Franco-Prussian war is of greater value in terms of heroism than anything an explorer might suffer. However, after Lorenzen's narration of the Greely anecdote and in particular after Lorenzen's interpretation of Greely's action as being morally right in spite of the generally accepted laws of God and man, Dubslav is won over to this new concept of what constitutes heroism. This is the "something different" which improves his condition in Chapter 39.

Lorenzen's revaluation of the value of heroism is in keeping with his tendency throughout the novel to welcome the advent of a new era with new tendencies and new directions. In this context, his brand of Christianity appears to be new, but he is himself at pains to

1 In passing, Horst Turk points out that the close of this conversation in Chapter 38 on heroism differs even in the form of language from other conversations in the novel. See H. Turk: 'Realismus in Fontanes Gesellschaftsromanen' in "Jahrbuch der Wittheit zu Bremen", Band 11, 1965, p. 454. There is certainly an unusual air of finality and agreement on a principle in Dubslav's gesture of taking Lorenzen's hand with the words: "Sie sollen recht haben". (NyA VIII, 319) For Charlotte Jolles heroism is "ein Thema, das den ganzen Roman durchzieht und in der Greely-Anekdote eine 'Umwertung' des Begriffs in seiner letzten Konsequenz zeigt". (C. Jolles: ' "Der Stechlin": Fontanes Zaubersee' in "Fontane aus heutiger Sicht". Edited by Hugo Aust, p. 246.)

show that it is merely the application of the old, but true Christian principles. Lorenzen, while he appreciates much of Prussia's past,[1] is aware of a certain decline in standards, a certain petrifaction which consists in adamant defence of everything traditional, because it is traditional. He himself, on the other hand, welcomes the opportunity of embracing that which is new, in cases where tradition fails. Thus, Lorenzen is obliged to judge the Prussian aristocracy on the whole as no longer fulfilling the function of being a bulwark of society in the new democratic age. Such views, which are put forward in theoretical fashion as late as Chapter 29, have in fact been prepared for well in advance in the novel. Already in Chapter 5, Dubslav informs his guests that the absent Lorenzen's view of the present-day situation is that the aristocratic world is in collapse and that the democratic age is dawning. Lorenzen's welcoming attitude to the new era does not however mean that he accepts the new as being good simply because it is new. His words to Woldemar in Chapter 3 prove that this is not the case: that which is old may and should be adhered to, as long as it is good, but rejected if the opposite obtains. This openness to the traditional a n d the new is reflected in the characterization of Lorenzen and in his relationship with Dubslav and the younger generation. Both Melusine and Dubslav approach Lorenzen as someone who will be an important mentor in the future for the continued upholding of their ideals. This factor is shown in the form of their requests that he continue to watch over Woldemar von Stechlin's development. Lorenzen's conscious revaluation of traditional concepts reflects Fix's demand for an 'Umwertung'[2] (in the mouth of Fix merely a cliché), which is the subject of Adelheid's disquiet in Chapter 9. It is interesting to note that Fontane viewed the clergyman as an opposite pole to Adelheid, even during the early stages of his conception of the novel.[3] While she is characterized as being rigidly caught up in the traditional values of the Prussian aristocracy, more especially in its

1 Dubslav calls him a "Friederikus-Rex-Mann" (NyA VIII, 316).
2 NyA VIII, 89.
3 In an early manuscript note Fontane writes about the original Lorenz: "Ganz widerstrebend ist ihm Adelheid." (Aufbau VIII, 432)

prejudices, Lorenzen is the first one in the novel to point out expressly that the highest sphere of Prussian society naïvely believes everything Prussian is a higher form of culture.[1] This theme is moreover subtly indicated again and again in the novel in connection with the opposite suggestion of the necessity of being open to the influence of the world at large, but only on very few occasions is the case put as baldly as this by any of the characters. Koseleger's anecdote about Madame Rachel can be interpreted as fitting into the same theme-complex, as indeed do the other anecdotes related with the England theme.

The enthusiasm shown by Woldemar, Dubslav, Melusine and Armgard for Lorenzen stems from an appreciation of his gentleness of character and the loftiness of his ideals, although Dubslav, because of his own make-up and background, is slightly uneasy about Lorenzen's political stance. Lorenzen loses the pride of place originally intended for him in the novel, presumably in keeping with the shift in emphasis from his pupil, Woldemar, to the ageing Dubslav in the final version. Fontane goes so far as to call Lorenz a main character in one respect in an early note on the original pastor figure.[2] This particular respect is important for it links the original Lorenz with Fontane's intention for the symbolic undertones attached to Lake Stechlin. While Lorenzen is not a major figure in the final version of the novel, he is still an important figure because he is very closely linked with the theme of the old and the new.

1 NyA VIII, 251.

2 Fontane writes: "Pastor Lorenz ist in einer Beziehung eine Hauptfigur: die Geschichte mit dem Stechlin-See – die den gedanklichen Kern des Ganzen bildet – wird durch ihn vertreten; was an der Stechlin-Geschichte Symbol und Zeichen ist, das wird durch ihn beständig gedeutet. Er entwickelt beständig den Gedanken, für den der Stechlin-See das Symbol ist. Er ist ein Christlich-Sozialer von der freieren, beinah freiesten Richtung, und die Gespräche, die er führt, mit Woldemar, Melusine, dem alten Stechlin, vielleicht auch mit Adelheid drehen sich alle um das Programmm der "Jungen". Dabei ist er voll Liebe zu dem alten Stechlin." (Aufbau VIII, 432) For reflections in the figure of Lorenzen of the programme of the "Jungen", the more radical group of the Christian Socialists, see Eda Sagarra: op. cit.

Woldemar goes up in Melusine's estimation, when he tells the company in Chapter 15 of Lorenzen's enthusiasm for the Swedish singer, Jenny Lind (1820-1887), and the Portuguese poet, João de Deus Nogueira de Ramos (1830-1896). The very fact that Lorenzen's preferences hail from countries outside Prussia is telling. Here again openness to outside influences is being subtly indicated. Indeed, this whole conversation on Lorenzen is introduced with a Swedish punch, which Woldemar claims as part of his own enthusiasm for Scandinavia. In Chapter 14 then Scandinavia and indirectly Portugal provide a foretaste of the place occupied by England seven chapters later. Just as Adelheid provides an amusing example of the wrong kind of Prussian – aristocratic rigidity and refusal to see good in other cultures – so too the figure of Dr. Wrschowitz, the Wagner enthusiast, who has an irrational hatred of everything from Scandinavia, even of the composer, Niels Gade, is included in the novel in order to play this theme in a minor key. It is no accident that the chapter which provides the amusing encounter between Woldemar and Wrschowitz at the Barby's house is also the chapter in which Woldemar gives Armgard and Count Barby the account of the special peculiarities of Lake Stechlin. The narrow Scandinavian stance of Dr. Wrschowitz is thus indirectly contrasted with the sensitivity of the lake's waters to events in far-off corners of the earth. Having introduced this contrast in Chapter 13, Fontane continues the Scandinavian theme from the positive side in Chapter 14, as a means of focussing on Lorenzen's character. The pastor's innocent enthusiasm for the Swedish singer has its counterpart in Chapter 15 in Woldemar's narration of the anecdote about the funeral of João de Deus. Woldemar chooses this story (which is really Lorenzen's story) in order to characterize his former tutor for the Barby girls and Baroness Berchtesgaden. But this is not merely a case of an anecdote being included for the sake of characterization. The fact that Lorenzen is so moved by the story is of course telling: it reveals his own penchant for all that is innocent, good and highly-motivated, for the concept of service and self-sacrifice. According to Woldemar's account, however, Lorenzen's remarks about the anecdote show that he places it in the context of his whole criticism of society and his demand for a new order based on selflessness and love

> Unsre ganze Gesellschaft – und nun gar erst das, was sich im besonderem so nennt – ist aufgebaut auf dem Ich. Das ist ihr Fluch, und daran muß sie zu Grunde gehen. Die zehn Gebote, das war der alte Bund, der Neue Bund aber hat ein andres, ein einziges Gebot, und das klingt aus in "Und du hättest der Liebe nicht ... "[1]

Lorenzen sees the life of João de Deus as a putting into practice of all he himself has ever striven for. A comparison of Woldemar's anecdote about João de Deus with Fontane's source shows to what extent he tightened and altered the narrative in order to improve the story and make it more appropriate. His source is an article published in February 1896 by Hedwig Wigger in "Das Magazin für die Literatur des In- und Auslandes".

Hedwig Wigger's article (1896)	The novel version (1898)
"E' um santo", (er ist ein Heiliger) hörte ich vor Jahren, als ich selbst in Lissabon lebte, oft sagen, ohne damals die ganze Größe dieses schlichten Mannes zu fassen. Heute freilich wiederhole ich: "e' um santo", ich weiß, daß Volkes Stimme Gottes Stimme ist. Nun ist er tot, hat das Aufraffen aus der Schlaffheit und Ohnmacht seines geliebten Vaterlandes nicht mehr erlebt. Aber er hat erlebt, was zuvor seinem Sterblichen in seinem Vaterlande widerfahren ist: das Nationalfest an seinem letzten Geburtstag am 8. Marz 1895. An diesem Tage bereiteten ihm alle Akademien, alle Schulen, ja die ganze Nation eine glorreiche Apotheose, eine Feier, vor welcher der bescheidene Sinn des Weisen sich	

1 NyA VIII, 145.

scheu versteckte. Arm ist er gestorben, wie er gelebt hat, und eine Begräbnisfeier ist ihm zu teil geworden, die nicht nur den Dichter, sondern auch das Volk ehrte, das er durch sein Leben und Schaffen so hochgeehrt hat. An dem Tage der Beisetzung, die in dem Hieronymustempel stattfand, dem Pantheon der großen Könige, in welchem auch die Urnen Camoes', Vasco da Gama's und Alexandre Herculano's ihren Platz haben, waren alle Schulen des Landes, alle Fabriken und Läden Lissabons geschlossen. Der Minister, der Staatsmann, der Gelehrte, der Handwerker und der Arbeiter gingen schmerzerfüllt hinter dem Sarg her. Schluchzend suchte die arme Fabrikarbeiterin ihrem Kinde zu erklären, daß es dem Toten alles zu verdanken habe.[1]

... Und als er nun tot war, der Joao de Deus, da gab es eine Landestrauer, und alle Schulen in der Hauptstadt waren geschlossen, und die Minister und die Leute vom Hof und die Gelehrten und die Handwerker, alles folgte dem Sarg dicht gedrängt, und die Fabrikarbeiterinnen hoben schluchzend ihre Kinder in die Höh' und zeigten auf den Toten und sagten: Un Santo, un Santo. Und sie taten so und sagten so, weil er für die Armen gelebt hatte und nicht für sich.[2]

The physical proportions of the two accounts show that the novel version is more economical. The first paragraph of the extract from Wigger's article has its quotation "E' um santo" altered in the novel version into the climax of the anecdote. This is presumably the aspect which interested Fontane most: that veneration for the poet[3]

1 H. Wigger: 'Joao de Deus' in "Das Magazin für die Literatur des In- und Auslandes", Jahrgang 65, Nr. 9 (29.2.1896), p. 297. Wigger's account of the celebrations for the poet's sixty-fifth birthday is included here, because Fontane borrows the Portuguese words "um santo" from it for his ficitonal version of the poet's funeral. He changes, perhaps inadvertently, the Portuguese form of the sentence "E' um santo" to "un Santo".

2 NyA VIII, 145.

3 If Fontane claims that he could never resist historical anecdotes, the same holds for anecdotes about writers. The João de Deus anecdote employed in "Der Stechlin" is a positive counterpart to several anecdotes in Fontane's works about poor treatment of writers. A further irony of which he was no doubt aware was the fact that João de Deus was not known to every

should penetrate all classes of society[1] and that his goodness should be publicly recognised by everyone. The enumeration of all classes could not be simpler than the mention of the different professions, high and low: "Minister" ... "Leute vom Hof" (a significant addition by Fontane!)[2] ... "Gelehrte" ... "Handwerker" ... "Fabrikarbeiterinnen". Fontane's version emphasizes more strongly and less verbosely the closeness of all classes in Portugal in their grief for the dead poet, particularly in the phrase not found in Wigger's article: "alles folgte dem Sarg dicht gedrängt". Hedwig Wigger's phrase about the poet's poverty in life as in death, which introduces the funeral scene in the article, is given more point in the novel version by being placed at the end, where it receives causal significance for this very great manifestation of grief and veneration: "und sie taten so und sagten so, weil er für die Armen gelebt hatte ... ". The final phrase in Fontane's version, which is italicized for further emphasis, appears nowhere in the article, although its meaning permeates it: "und n i c h t f ü r s i c h". The novel version makes the situation very simple: he was regarded as a saint, because he lived for the poor and not for himself. Fontane's version avoids all the more pompous aspects of the original, such as the long sentence on famous persons who are laid to rest at Saint Jerome's Cathedral in Lisbon. He also cuts out the birthday celebrations. Certain phrases used by Lorenzen and Woldemar at their 'last meeting' and on the excursion ensure

Portuguese because of his poems, but because of his part in the reform of the primary school system with the work "Cartilha maternal".

1 The emphasis on all classes in this anecdote told originally by Lorenzen, who is associated with Christian Social ideas in the novel, links most probably with the Christian Social thinking that social conflict and alienation was the central problem of contemporary Germany, i.e. in the eighteen-nineties, and that their contribution to society could and should be to the establishment of social harmony.

2 Fontane's inclusion among the mourners of people from the court broadens the already broad spectrum of society used by Hedwig Wigger in her factual account of the funeral. It also provides an ironical counterpoint to lack of appreciation of himself in the corresponding Prussian sphere. In this connection, he bitterly quotes the anecdote of the Persian poet, Firdausi, in a letter of 30 November 1876. ("Briefe". Ed. Schreinert, vol. 3. p. 174)

that the João de Deus story relates specifically to the important theme of the novel: the old and the new. Woldemar says João de Deus is "kein alter Dichter, sondern ein neuer".[1] "Die zehn Gebote, das war der alte Bund, der Neue Bund aber hat ein andres, ein einziges Gebot ... "[2] Thus the João de Deus anecdote, introduced in Chapter 15, apparently as a means of characterizing Lorenzen, is in fact used for the further and more important purpose of demanding and welcoming a new order, an order which, in Lorenzen's view, should be based on the ancient principle of caritas.

Under the influence of the moving anecdote and of Lorenzen's interpretation of it, the ladies join hands with Woldemar in veneration of the Portuguese poet and admiration for Lorenzen. It is presumably not accidental here, while the other characters and the reader are still wondering which of the Barbys Woldemar will choose as his bride, that the Baroness makes Woldemar join hands first with Armgard.[3] When the circle is complete, Baron Berchtesgaden asks if this is meant to signify an engagement. Fontane excels at such subtle means of anticipation, and it can be said in this context that the coming together of Armgard and Woldemar takes place to a certain extent here already in their mutual admiration for the ideals of Lorenzen. Armgard later on states her preference for Saint Elizabeth of Hungary as against either Elizabeth I of England or Mary Stuart,

1 NyA VIII, 145.

2 Ibidem.

3 Hands are joined in a special gesture of agreement three times in connection with Lorenzen's ideals. In Chapter 3 it happens when Woldemar assumes Lorenzen's version of "innere Mission" should be "mit dem Neuen" (quickly corrected by Lorenzen to the phrase suggesting an interweaving of old and new: "Lieber mit dem Alten, soweit es irgend geht, und mit dem Neuen nur, soweit es muß." (NyA VIII, 27) In Chapter 15 Lorenzen's João de Deus enthusiasm is appropriated by the Barbys, Woldemar and the Berchtesgadens and marked by the crossing and joining of hands. Finally in Chapter 38, after the narration and interpretation of the Greely anecdote by Lorenzen, the last anecdote in the novel, Dubslav shakes hands with Lorenzen with the words: "Sie sollen recht haben" (ibid. 319). The gesture gives added significance each time to the allusions to the old and the new and the necessity of revaluation.

giving as the motivation for her choice the opinion that happiness resides in living for others and giving to the poor.[1] This formulation is simply another way of expressing the sentiment in the João de Deus anecdote. Through the subtle touching of the caritas theme in the conversation about queens another delicate move is made in the relationship between Woldemar and Armgard. This is expressed in the form of their tacit engagement at the end of Chapter 25. The t a c i t n e s s of this act of engagement is proof of the importance to be attached to the value of caritas in the novel, which is concretely illustrated with the story of João de Deus and made theoretically relevant to modern Prussian society by Lorenzen's exposé of that society in terms of the one commandment of the New Testament.

It is clear therefore that caritas like heroism is an 'old' value which must be re-interpreted to be appropriate in the new age. Lorenzen understands his values to be simply a return to original Christianity with its emphasis on the basic value of love. Lorenzen is characterized as someone who has reflected much on Prussian history and on the contemporary situation in Prussia. His espousal of Christian Social principles marks him as a progressive-minded pastor, but he is not explicitly allied to any party, in spite of the Stechlins' allusions to his democratic ideals and his "Ritt ins Bebelsche".[2] In view of this characterization, it is appropriate that Lorenzen should be one of the main vehicles for the expression of the theme of old and new. From the João de Deus and the Greely anecdotes, we see that Lorenzen is able to ponder on old values and give them a new face in new times. The enthusiasm of the common people in Portugal for a poet, who based his actions on the principle of charity, earns Lorenzen's enthusiasm, just as the life of that poet seemed to him to represent all he himself would like to stand for. In the case of the Greely anecdote, the independence of the

1 Heiko Strech points out the simplicity of the language in both the Portuguese anecdote and Armgard's statement about happiness, emphasizing that in both passages the simple expression of feeling is completely free of irony or virtuosity in the use of language. See. H. Strech: op. cit., p. 127.

2 NyA VIII, 340.

explorer's moral judgement in a difficult and extreme situation which is not covered by the rules of normal conduct is the factor which earns Lorenzen's respect. Lorenzen's lack of conventional pastoral care is reflected in the final chapters in his treatment of Dubslav. Unlike Ermyntrud Katzler and Koseleger, Lorenzen does not try at the last to interfere with or even influence Dubslav's spiritual life, just as he will not interfere with the further development of Woldemar, as is clear from his final conversation with Dubslav about the future of his son. This will be the case, even if Woldemar departs from the principles he has picked up from Lorenzen and returns to the 'old paths'.[1] Freedom from narrow rigidity of any kind coupled with a positive adherence to ideals such as charity and the improvement of society at all levels are the hallmarks of Lorenzen's outlook. This outlook is expressed in the novel not merely through Lorenzen's conversations with others,[2] or in the conversations of others about him, but most tangibly in the anecdotes associated with him. These are just two in number, and he is no "biederer Anekdotenerzähler",[3] but their impact is powerful and their status within the intellectual framework of the novel as a whole is of great significance.

The criticism of the aristocratic class in Lorenzen's revolutionary discourse is stated in clear and direct terms. Throughout "Der Stechlin" however such criticism is reflected with varying nuances through Fontane's art of indirect allusion. The chapters concerning the Rheinsberg-Wutz election provide an amusing and indirect commentary on the aristocratic Conservatives. Chapter 19 contains an anecdote about Bismarck which carries some of the

1 NyA VIII, 343-344.

2 In the final version of the novel, Lorenzen is not shown as a conversationalist in the way that Dubslav is, the way in fact which characterizes many of Fontane's important figures. The reader is let know expressly that Lorenzen is not: "Er ist ein Schweiger" (NyA VIII, 235) and again: "aber er war kein Damenmann, noch weniger ein Causeur" (ibidem). The fact that he is often taciturn lends even more interest and importance to the anecdotes which a r e associated with him.

3 Julius Petersen: op. cit., p. 38.

criticism of the nobility. While waiting for the election results Gnewkow, Molchow, Stechlin, Krangen, Beetz and Nonne kill the time by visiting the grounds of Rheinsberg Castle. Molchow points out their luck that an election day like this gives them an opportunity to turn to historical and cultural matters! To illustrate the point, he tells the story of Bismarck's reply to an American lady whom he had accompanied around the Berlin Bildermuseum, when she thanked him for this service about forty years later. With a mixture of "chivalry and embarrassment", he told her he was in her debt, as he would probably never otherwise have seen the inside of the art gallery.[1] From the context, it is clear that the narrator means this anecdote to be taken as a sign of a lack of culture. Only when these nobles have nothing better to do, and when they are forced to wait for the political news, do they think of doing something 'cultural'. Even Dubslav can mention the name of only one Egyptian king.[2] Lorenzen's later argument that the aristocratic class can no longer be depended on to provide leadership in Prussia is here anticipated on the less theoretical but more memorable narrative level with the Bismarck anecdote. From the point of view of culture it seems that the Conservatives here, in spite of their privileged birth, are no better than any other section of society. This point is ironically supported in an amusing way by evidence from the very mouths of these representative Conservative aristocrats. If they are offering neither cultural nor political leadership, and share in the egotism rampant in society (Lorenzen's view, though of course Dubslav himself does not share this egotism), then it comes as no

1 NyA VIII, 172.

2 Ibid. 171. Katherina Mommsen considers that the Bismarck anecdote indicates a general fall in standards of education among the nobility since the early nineteenth century in Germany. (See K. Mommsen: op. cit., p. 32) Exceptions apart, Prussian aristocrats were however even in the early nineteenth-century not distinguished for their cultural interests. The Austrian nobility, which had backed out from the political and military forefront, made up for this in other spheres. Fontane's point in this chapter of "Der Stechlin" seems to be that the Prussian aristocrats were quite clearly unfit to make good – from the cultural point of view – the decline in leadership qualities.

surprise that the Conservative Party of which these men are the bulwarks is defeated in the Rheinsberg-Wutz election. The oblique nature of Fontane's criticism is remarkable in this example, as in the case of so many of the other anecdotes in "Der Stechlin". At first sight, the Bismark anecdote appears to be simply an amusing story which gives an inside view into the life of a famous personality. It could be almost a tribute to the great Chancellor, and thus merely an uncritical, affirmative anecdote set squarely in the tradition of régime-boosting anecdotes. However, when fitted into the overall context of the many perspectives put forward in the novel on the political and cultural situation in late nineteenth-century Germany, the anecdote show its extra dimension. The characters who enjoy the story are themselves the butt of its gentle and oblique satire. Fontane's manipulation of this Bismarck anecdote in "Der Stechlin" is a subtle reflection of his complex attitude towards Bismarck as a man and as a statesman.[1]

Besides the Bismarck anecdote in Chapter 19, a further story told in the following chapter can also be related to the general level of Prussia itself. Herr Thormeyer tells in connection with a piece of local gossip the anecdote of the Siamese princess, whose virginity was "restored" on her return from captivity in the harem of a prince of Assam by means of a ritualistic bath in buffaloes' blood. The story is given in detail and is the main subject of conversation in Chapter 20. It is obviously the raison d'être of this chapter. As is the case with many of Fontane's anecdotes, teller and listeners are characterized by the stories they narrate and listen to. The Conservatives listening to this anecdote as part of the post-prandial conversation after the bye-election receive it on the level of titillating conversation in much the same way that the Tschechiners reacted to such snippets in "Unterm Birnbaum". However, the anecdote of the restoration of virginity is not included simply in order to show these noblemen amusing themselves on election day.

1 See Walter Müller-Seidel's investigation of this attitude in 'Fontane und Bismark' in "Nationalismus in Germanistik und Dichtung. Dokumentation des Germanistentages in München vom 17. bis 22. Oktober 1966". Hrsg. von B. von Wiese und R. Heuß. Berlin 1967, p. 170-201.

Fontane sometimes uses tales from exotic or far-off places in order to comment on a situation close at hand, e.g. the Ming Dynasty and Saint Anthony anecdotes in "Schach von Wuthenow". This fact, the election setting and the care with which the anecdote is related make a background in contemporary Prussian politics likely, but even here the anecdote is open to variant interpretations. Two phrases, one from a listener and the other from the narrator, make the link with contemporary Prussian politics: Herr von Zühlen's remark: "Wir reden jetzt so viel von großen Mitteln",[1] and the sentence with which Herr Thormeyer leads up to the narration of the Siamese anecdote: "Sie begegnen diesem Hang nach Restitution überall".[2]

In his plans for the novel Fontane calls this story 'most interesting'.[3] It is clear from the context of this remark that at the time of making it, Fontane still did not know where the story should be included in the novel. This suggests that he saw it as reflecting one or more of the major themes. Its final position in Chapter 20 during the conversation of the Conservatives seems therefore all the more significant. The phrase "Blut sühnt"[4] which the Conservatives make much of in their discussion may be connected with the idea of a blood-bath. Fontane alludes in a letter of 6 May 1895 to the possibility of a "furchtbare Schlacht" in connection with the breakdown of the old order and the establishment of the new.[5] If the Siamese princess in the story were meant as an allegorical reference to Prussia herself, then Fontane might also have had in mind a real political counterpart to the anecdotal ritual blood-bath of the ravished princess. Vincent Günther has suggested that the restitution mentioned by Herr Thormeyer and suggested in the anecdote is meant to apply to Prussia herself. The story could then be seen in the context of the theme of the old and the new. The new Prussia must be one which has been restored and brought from a period of decline to a more positive condition. "Die Katastrophe

1 NyA VIII, 184.
2 Ibid. 182.
3 Aufbau VIII, 432.
4 NyA VIII, 182.
5 "Briefe an Friedlaender", p. 284.

wird kommen und muß kommen, aber sie wird nur ein Übergang sein zu einer neuen Reinheit und Freiheit, die die gegenwärtige befleckte Gesellschaft nicht allein erreichen kann."[1] Günther's interpretation suggests a somewhat all-too-clear and flat parallel between the restoration of the princess's virginity and a future, supposedly unbesmirched society. Edward Frank George suggests that the Siamese story tells of the need to embrace change, since ignoring or resisting it would be tantamount to ignoring or resisting life itself.[2] Alan Bance sees the story as suggesting the triumph of the imagination over factualness, thereby implying a parallel with Prussia's difficulty "in coming to terms with its own abrupt changes in the last third of the nineteenth century, in 'living down' its military successes, and evolving social structures (progressive and yet in the best sense regressive, i.e. 'altpreußisch', at the same time) commensurate with the dynamic forces of its modernisation and industrialisation".[3] The variant interpretations are perhaps proof of the different layers of meaning in this anecdote. As in the case of the Bismarck story, this anecdote operates on at least two levels. Firstly, what does it signify to its narrator and his listeners, the Conservative stalwarts?

The narrator, Thormeyer, headmaster of Rheinsberg Gymnasium, is based on Friedrich Thormeyer (1765-1837), the autocratic headmaster of the Neuruppin school which Fontane attended in 1831-1832.[4] In introducing Thormeyer in Chapter 20, the narrator

1 V. Günther: "Das Symbol im erzählerischen Werk Fontanes". Bonn 1967, p. 123. Günther's interpretation brings the anecdote rather too closely into connection with individual characters in the novel, in making the parallel with the modesty of Armgard, and finally suggesting that restitution can not come from society, but only from the individual. (See ibid. p. 130.)

2 E. F. George: 'The Symbol of the Lake and Related Themes in Fontane's "Der Stechlin" ', in FMLS 9, 1973, p. 150.

3 A. Bance: op. cit., p. 241-242. This comment is the most satisfactory offered to date in the critical literature.

4 The description of the historical Thormeyer is one of the highlights of "Die Grafschaft Ruppin", which contains in its summary the following sentence on Thormeyer's exercise of and reaction to power: "Ein Donnerer in den Klassen, erwies er sich als 'devotest ersterbend' jeder vorgesetzten

calls him a "dyed-in-the-wool conservative" and ridicules him, as later at Dubslav's funeral, for his decorations, going so far as to discount the notion of Thormeyer's being well thought of in high places. "Man kannte ihn 'oben' ganz gut."[1] The Conservatives' close mental linking of the circumstances of the Siamese story with Prussian politics is clear from Thormeyer's sarcastic parallel between the lower-class abducting prince and the 'candidate', i.e. Torgelow of the Social Democratic Party. The lower-class candidate, Torgelow, has won the bye-election (i.e. run off with the prize) against the higher-class Conservative, Stechlin. The references to "großen Mitteln", a holy war, fire and sword, triumphal return home, may suggest a future reversal of the growing Social Democratic trend in Prussia on the part of these Conservative Party members, as indeed the references to the blood-bath may be an indirect allusion of the conservative narrator, an allusion which would find favour with his listeners, to the notion of 'Umsturz' in the 1890's, i.e. that by continuous harping on the possibility of a revolution, it was hoped to retain the status quo.

The Siamese anecdote must not however be reduced to what it means to the teller and the listeners. The whole thrust of the novel provides the setting which allows the larger interpretation of this anecdote as indicating change and renewal, interweaving the old and the new, and integrating change into that which was old and good. 'Good old Prussia' could be reconstituted in a new democratic age, whose ozone Lorenzen welcomes. It is ironical that the story which the Conservatives tell among themselves on the day of the lost election, is one which has indirect relevance to the criticism made of contemporary Prussia throughout the novel and in particular to

Behörde gegenüber, diese mochte sein, was und wie sie wollte." (NyA IX, 177) In the "Wanderungen" context, Fontane dwells on the description of Thormeyer in order to show "the extraordinary difference between then and now" (ibid. 176). The exclusive emphasis on authority then contrasts with the new sense of beauty and freedom, without which education has no value. No doubt Fontane saw in Thormeyer a representative of an old order that should die out.

1 NyA VIII, 176.

Lorenzen's criticism in Chapter 29, which clarifies so many of the allusions in the novel. The upholders of the old order, the representatives of those who think "daß es ohne sie nicht gehe",[1] tell a story which, while it appears to mean one thing to them, means something much different in the context of the novel as a whole.

A further anecdote told in the novel, that of the London beautician, Madame Rachel, returns to the theme of restitution, as as will be seen later, this anecdote from another country outside Prussia has relevance also to a critique of Prussia. Placing the Madame Rachel anecdote in context leads to a discussion of the role of England in "Der Stechlin" and gives an example of the intricate interweaving of themes and allusions in the novel. In Fontane's original conception of the novel, the section dealing with Woldemar's experiences in England is allowed to play a much larger part than it actually does in the final version.[2] With the displacement of interest from the young man to his father as the central figure, the English element shrank to relative unimportance, as far as the superficial level of plot is concerned. However the plot is not in the forefront of the author's interest in this novel as has been widely recognised. The reader does not see Woldemar actually in England in the novel; he merely reads of the journey and of Woldemar's experiences through the medium of telegrammes and conversations. Fontane's originally-planned four to five chapters set in England are replaced in the final version by the section "In Mission nach England", which comprises four chapters placed between the section on the Rheinsberg-Wutz election and the engagement story. The chapters concerning England provide therefore an element of retardation of

1 NyA VIII, 253.

2 On the importance of England in the works of Fontane see Charlotte Jolles: "Theodor Fontane and England. A critical study in Anglo-German relations in the nineteenth century". Master of Arts Thesis, London 1947; Herbert Knorr: "Theodor Fontane und England". Diss. Göttingen 1961; C. Jolles: ' "Und an der Themse wächst man sich anders aus als am 'Stechlin' ". Zum Englandmotiv in Fontanes Erzählwerk' in FBl 1, 1957, Heft 5, p. 173-191; and H.-H. Reuter: 'Die englische Lehre. Zur Bedeutung und Funktion Englands für Fontanes Schaffen' in "Formen Realistischer Erzählkunst". Nottingham 1979, p. 282-299.

the novel's plot. The experiences in England, not necessarily those of Woldemar only, for many characters join in to build up this theme, are related mainly through the medium of anecdote. More reflections on the important theme of openness to the world and of the relatedness of things on a world-wide scale are provided through the medium of anecdote in the section "In Mission nach England".

In a letter of the early summer of 1897 Fontane writes a short summary of the novel's content to Adolf Hoffmann, which is restricted to the wide-ranging relationship between the insignificant Prussian lake and other natural phenomena, such as earthquakes and volcanic eruptions in places like Java and Iceland.[1] Woldemar's words about Lake Stechlin's "Weltbeziehungen, vornehme, geheimnisvolle Beziehungen"[2] imply that it is a mistake to shut oneself off from the outside world. The apparently unimportant Prussian lake can be deeply affected by disrupting events which take place thousands of miles away.[3] It is in the interests of these world-wide connections, indicated primarily in the novel by this central symbol of the lake, that the passages on England are also included. Fontane's experiences in England in the eighteen-forties and fifties consolidated his natural propensity to look beyond the confines of his own country in cultural and political matters. In this novel the anecdotes concerning England provide a broader backdrop to the events which take place in Berlin and Rheinsberg-Wutz and give a sense of wider perspective. A letter of 14 May 1898 to Gustav Keyßner gives a further indication of Fontane's outlook in this connection. Speaking of a certain attitude of cultural superiority recently displayed during debates in the Bavarian Parliament, he comments that the same attitude prevails in the Reichstag and connects this whole question with his intention in writing "Der Stechlin". He summarizes that the Germans do not, as they think, stand on very firm ground with

1 See Erler: "Briefe", vol. 2, p. 426.

2 NyA VIII, 124.

3 E. F. George: op. cit., p. 149 describes the symbol of the lake in the following terms: "The lake signifies a repudiation of the tendency to become insular, to withdraw into a narrow, circumscribed environment, and thereby to divorce oneself from the wider issues of life."

regard to their claim to a culture which is superior to that of other countries.[1]

The relegation of the English setting from the direct level of action in the original plan to the indirect level of conversation in the final version is appropriate to the novel's lack of a tightly-knit plot. Had the section been included as originally planned, Fontane would have had to employ a great deal more material to provide a convincingly realistic picture of Woldemar's experience abroad. Such a procedure might have made the novel even more expansive than it finally turned out to be. The point made by the minor character, Herbstfelde, in Chapter 21 about the variety of possible experience in London was one noted by Fontane himself during his English sojourns: "Alles Mögliche, wovon wir hier gar keine Vorstellung haben, vollzieht sich da mitten auf dem Straßendamm."[2] Herbstfelde's stories about his friend's prowess in foreign languages and his own efforts at reaching an understanding with the English chambermaid (the Chinese acrobat anecdote) are amusing and suit the barrack atmosphere, but such stories are included merely as impressions and could be put in the mouth of any minor character.

The multiplicity of experience hinted at in a somewhat trivial way here would most likely have been portrayed on a rather more elevated level, had Fontane actually adhered to the original plan of setting part of the novel in London itself. However such trivial

1 "Mein neuer dickleibiger Roman ... beschäftigt sich fast ausschließlich mit dieser Frage; Dynastie, Regierung, Adel, Armee, Gelehrtentum, alle sind ganz aufrichtig davon überzeugt, daß speziell wir Deutsche ein hohe Kultur repräsentieren; ich bestreite das; Heer und Polizei bedeuten freilich auch eine Kultur, aber doch einen niedrigeren Grad, und ein Volk- und Staatsleben, das durch diese zwei Mächte bestimmt wird, ist weitab von einer wirklichen Hochstufe." (Erler: "Briefe", vol. 2, p. 438) Cf. also Lorenzen's criticism of the Prussian outlook in Chapter 18 of "Der Stechlin". Already in a letter of 1875 from Italy to Emilie, Fontane shows his consciousness of this problem: "Nicht nur, daß man Schritt um Schritt empfindet, wie sehr uns diese alten und reichen Kulturlande voraus sind, nein, man taxiert uns auch in diesem Sinne. Man will von uns nichts wissen." (Erler: op. cit., vol. 1, p. 426)

2 NyA VIII, 195.

stories reflect in a minor key an important theme of the novel and have their parallel later on a higher level in the more symbolic tale about the London cosmetician, Madame Rachel. This is narrated in Chapter 27 to the Barby visitors and the Stechlins by 'Superintendent' Koseleger. Although Koseleger has never been to England, he provides in this chapter the generalizations which indicate the relevance of the England motif to the great theme of the old and the new:

> Wenn irgendwo das vielzitierte Wort von dem "in einem Tag mehr gewinnen, als in des Jahres Einerlei", hinpaßt, so da drüben. Alles modern und zugleich alles alt, eingewurzelt, stabilisiert. Es steht einzig da; mehr als irgendein andres Land ist es ein Produkt der Zivilisation, so sehr, daß die Neigungen der Menschen kaum noch dem Gesetze der Natur folgen, sondern nur noch dem einer verfeinerten Sitte.[1]

The first of these sentences echoes the tenor of the barrack conversation about England, where the topic of multiple experience is supported by the Chinese acrobat anecdote. Furthermore, Koseleger's statement supports in retrospect (without his knowing it) the impressions recorded in the conversations between Woldemar and the Barbys on the subject of England both before and after his sojourn there. One can speak of the anecdote about Madame Rachel as being the culmination of this whole section, and indeed as being one of the highlights of "Der Stechlin". The story is introduced by Koseleger in direct response to Adelheid's assertions about the inferiority of life in England, her fatuous statements having ranged from her assumptions about the constant pregnancy of Englishwomen to an alleged swing back to Catholicism in the country as a whole. According to Koseleger's story, an English duchess lost a court-case against a London beautician, Madame Rachel, who had presented the lady with an allegedly exhorbitant bill for services rendered. The court decided in favour of the defendant, Madame Rachel, on grounds of her evidence that her cosmetic achievement was, in contrast to that of other cosmeticians, "beautifying for ever".

1 NyA VIII, 236.

This anecdote must have been one of Fontane's favourites. The key-phrase "beautifying for ever" appears to have become a household-word with the Fontanes and seems to have been known even to their friends.[1] Fontane had returned home from London in January 1859, and during the years 1859 and 1860 was putting together all the essays which he had prepared in England and which had appeared in newspapers.[2] No doubt the action brought by the beautician, Madame Rachel Leverson, against the Honourable Mrs. Carnegie in 1862 was of considerable interest to him, and accounts of it were published in both the English and German newspapers. Since he quotes the key-phrase in English, he must have read an English newspaper version of the court-proceedings. A report of the case was contained in "The Times" of 20 June 1862. "Das Morgenblatt für gebildete Leser" published a report of the case on 16 July 1862. In the press versions the high-point of Rachel's testimony runs as follows:

"The Times"

My process is called by the ladies enamelling, but it is not so. After the process I use, the skin itself becomes so white that it resembles painting on ivory. Mine is a process of cleansing the skin and rendering it transparent. It is not closing up the pores by plastering the skin over. She was so delighted with her appearance after the second and third application that she wished to be made beautiful for ever. I am positive that the services I have rendered are permanent ... I have made her beautiful for ever.[3]

"Das Morgenblatt"

Im eigentlichen Sinne des Wortes wird nicht emaillirt. Ich entferne bloß jede Unreinigkeit von der Haut und lege dann gewisse Kräuter auf. Ich schminke nicht. Mein Prozess öffnet die Poren, statt sie zu verstopfen, und ist eine höhere Art von Waschen. Die Haut wird alabasterweiß und bleibt so. Sie gleicht Elfenbeinmalerei. Ich habe sehr viele Kunden. Madame Carnegie war so zufrieden mit mir, daß sie mich den Prozess oft wiederholen ließ. Ich habe sie ewig schön gemacht.[4]

1 See e.g. "Briefe an G. Friedlaender", p. 2 (5. 12. 1884).
2 Many of his articles on Scotland appeared in "Das Morgenblatt" from 1859.
3 "The Times" of 20. 6. 1862, p. 11, column A.
4 "Das Morgenblatt für gebildete Leser" of 16. 7. 1862, p. 694.

Given the likelihood of Fontane's familiarity with more than one newspaper account of the court case, the divergences between the version in "Der Stechlin" and other accounts raise several questions.

The most important of these divergences is that Madame Rachel Leverson, the plaintiff and n o t the defendant as in the novel, did not emerge victorious, as Koseleger claims, but lost. "The Times" states: "His Lordship summed up, leaving it to the jury to say whether the defendant[1] had authorized his wife to employ Madame Leverson the plaintiff in the way she had been employed, when the Jury immediately found a verdict for the defendant,[2] while "Das Morgenblatt' reports: "Der Gatte behauptete dagegen, seine Frau sey keineswegs verschönt und ihre Körperschäden seyen eher schlimmer geworden; und das Gericht war unbillig genug, die Klägerin abzuweisen."[3] Did Fontane in the intervening time-lapse of over thirty years forget the parties and the outcome, or did he knowingly change these, in order to make some point? It is necessary to look first at other changes made by Fontane against the probable sources. Several aspects of his version lend ennoblement to the figure of Madame Rachel, and raise the tone of the story as a whole. She is shown as dignified and impressive in court. She is always referred to as a "Künstlerin", an artist, and even calls the other cosmeticians who appear in court her "Mitkünstlerinnen", fellow-artists, while Koseleger, the narrator of the anecdote, calls them her"Konkurren–tinnen", rivals. These witnesses do not appear in the newspaper versions quoted, and thus Rachel, with her vindicated claim in Fontane's version, becomes an undisputed queen among artists. Her client in Fontane's version is a beautiful duchess who is mindful of the effects of the passage of time upon her face, whereas in reality, she was merely the Honourable Mrs. Carnegie, who although still young, had 'faded' according to Rachel's testimony in "The Times", and had also suffered the extra disfigurement of a breast operation, whose scars Rachel had to camouflage. The phrase

1 i.e. Captain Carnegie, the society lady's husband.

2 "The Times". ibidem.

3 "Das Morgenblatt" ibidem.

"beautifying for ever" or "ewig schön machen" in now way clinches the argument (as it does in "Der Stechlin") in the accounts in "The Times" and "Das Morgenblatt". In these the English law which makes a man responsible for his wife's bills is shown as important, implicitly in the judge's summary in "The Times", explicity in "Das Morgenblatt". The balance of the case hinges on whether or not Captain Carnegie authorized his wife to employ Madame Rachel "in the way that she had been employed", a much more mundane factor than the swaying of the "hohen Gerichtshof"[1] in Fontane's version by Rachel's impassioned statement that only h e r services constitute "beautifying for ever". Fontane's version excludes the details of the facial cleansing and scarring operation, the exact sum of Rachel's bill and the husband figure.[2] He includes the other beauticians, emphasizes Rachel as an artist, provides her with a very dignified self-defence with its theoretically convincing juxtaposition of references to "helfen auf Zeit" and "beautifying for ever", and has the judge pronounce in her favour. All these aspects, both the inclusions and the exclusions, make the story seem unusual and noteworthy in Fontane's version. Koseleger interprets his own anecdote in a way which not only refutes Adelheid's diatribe against England but also fits in with the theme of openness to other cultures and of the multiplicity of experience possible in England and with the theme of the old and the new in the novel. When Koseleger describes the scene of his first experience of this court-case in the Dutch town of The Hague in the 1860's with himself, a young German, reporting on the English court case daily to Her Imperial Highness, the Russian Princess Vera, the reader is reminded of the world-wide connections which Lake Stechlin itself symbolizes. While he agrees with Adelheid on the existence of the 'natural human being bordering on the savage in England, he also argues that this

1 NyA VIII, 239.

2 The bill presented by Madame Leverson to Mrs. Carnegie amounted to 928 pounds sterling according to "The Times", and 935 pounds according to "Das Morgenblatt". The husband, Captain Carnegie, is characterized in "Das Morgenblatt" as extremely rich and mean.

phenomenon exists side by side with an extreme refinement of life and society in England which to him is the highest expression of culture.[1] The Madame Rachel case, in his view, is an expression of that refined, perhaps over-refined culture. In any case, he sees it as something that could not happen in Prussia, because there that degree of culture and refinement is lacking.[2] In Prussia and especially in the Mark Brandenburg, only the grotesque or laughable side of such a case would be apparent to people, and not the high degreee of civilisation which is necessary for such an incident to occur in the first place.[3] The variety and multiplicity of experience, the refinement of custom, the stability of institutions, the interweaving of the old and the new: these positive points in Koseleger's appreciation of England are by implication not as strong or are threatened in contemporary Prussia.

Fontane hardly forgot the real outcome of the celebrated court-case of 1862. He would presumably have consulted the sources on writing the novel, as he had tried to do in the case of Greely's story. Had he reported the outcome of the case as it had happened in reality, with a loss for Madame Rachel, he would have been constrained to tell a story which is after all not so extraordinary. The normally expected course of events is not reversed in reality. In the fictional version the outsider beautician, emphasized as an artist, gains justice and recompense against a member of the aristocratic establishment, and her claim to provide beautifying services which last forever is vindicated by the objective authority of the court.

A further aspect of the reportage of the Leverson versus Carnegie case in Germany deserves comment. A striking feature of the "Morgenblatt" report is its ani-Jewish note. This version devotes over half of its total length to a sarcastic diatribe on an alleged vision by Madame Rachel (in which an angel was supposed to have given her the secrets of her art) and on her subsequent roaring trade. The

1 See NyA VIII, 237.
2 Ibid. 238.
3 Ibid. 239.

"Morgenblatt' version uses phrases such as "träumte einer in London wohnende Bürgerin des auserwählten Volkes" and "Mit dem Instinkt ihrer Race kam die junge Hebräerin – Leverson ist ihr Name – sofort auf die Idee, das wunderbar erschlossene Geheimnis kaufmännisch zu verwerthen."[1] On the jury's verdict the "Morgenblatt' version comments: "Hätte sie nicht in einer Anwandlung von falscher Bescheidenheit den himmlischen Ursprung ihrer Geheimmittel und ihres Emaillirungsprocesses verschwiegen, das Resultat wäre vermuthlich ein anderes gewesen."[2] Fontane's version omits all references to Rachel's Jewishness and avoids the Jewish surname by using her professional name only. The polemical tone of the "Morgenblatt" article includes within the orbit of its condescending remarks the 'fair sex' who sought the beautician's services and fell for the story of the celestial origins of her art. "The Times", on the other hand makes no reference to Rachel's race, restricting itself to the testimony given. Perhaps the strong polemical element in the "Morgenblatt" version prompted Fontane to put into the mouth of Koseleger the criticism that Prussians would only be able to see the ridiculous and grotesque aspect of such a case. Koseleger has been seen by most critics as an unattractive figure whose main motivating force is his ambition to rise in the Church. It must be pointed out however that two positive functions, which are allied to each other, are allotted to him in the novel. In Chapter 38 Dubslav complains on his death-bed that Baruch Hirschfeld, the Jew who has lent him money all along, now suddenly requires repayment or else the estate. From this particular instance Dubslav generalizes when he claims that this incident shows the cloven hoof, meaning that in the heel of the hunt, all Jews will demonstrate avariciousness. Koseleger, who has come to 'save' Dubslav's soul, and is thus in one way satirized by the narrator, counters this suggestion with the sensible remark that this (greed for money) is much less a question of race than of profession.[3] The class which Koseleger probably has in mind here is

1 "Das Morgenblatt" of 16. 7. 1862, p. 693.
2 Ibid. p. 694.
3 NyA VIII, 300.

that of the new-rich Prussian industrialists, some of them newly-ennobled, which Fontane had already satirized in "Frau Jenny Treibel". For Koseleger follows this generalization with an apparently random remark about Frau von Gundermann's inability to get along with a servant. The Gundermanns are the Christian representatives of that entrepreneurial class in the novel. Besides this very subtle defence of Jews in Chapter 38, Koseleger is the defender of England and what it stands for in the novel, as we have seen, when even the cosmopolitan Barby girls are outtalked on the subject in Chapter 27 by the xenophobic Adelheid von Stechlin. Thus the unattractive mixture of egotism and ambition which is displayed in Koseleger's conversation with the unworldly Lorenzen in Chapter 18 has its positive counterpart in his defence of 'otherness' in the novel. He is shown as broadminded and open to other cultures in his assessment of the Jews and the English. While contemporary readers of the 1862 newspaper reports of the court-case would have been aware of the Jewish aspect (especially the German readers who were reminded by "Das Morgenblatt"), it is unlikely that most readers of "Der Stechlin" at the end of the century would remember such a detail. Anti-Jewish sentiment was then a much more powerful force than in the 1860's. For today's reader the anti-Semitic element attaching to the Rachel anecdote is completely lost because Fontane himself omits it, and only acquaintance with the sources reveals it. By omitting even the beautician's surname Fontane does not let this aspect surface at all in the "Stechlin" account. Balance is created in the naming process when her client becomes an unnamed duchess in Fontane's version. While it is true that Fontane sometimes criticises Jews in private,[1]

1 In his article: 'Theodor Fontane: The Philosemitic Antisemite' in "Publications of the Leo Baeck Institute: Yearbook XXVI", 1981, p. 303-322, Wolfgang Paulsen claims the existence of a strong anti-Semitic streak in Fontane, referring in the main to Fontane's letters. In his section on "Der Stechlin" Paulsen draws attention to Koseleger's remark in Chapter 38 that Dubslav is supposed to have a philosemitic streak. (See Paulsen: op. cit., p. 318-320.) Paulsen fails however to draw attention to Koseleger's defence of the Jews, when Dubslav, having objected to the (Jewish) doctor,

it is also true that his criticism must be seen against the overall background of his abhorrence of the vulgarity and ostentatiousness of the whole new-rich class which emerged after the foundation of the German Empire in 1871.[1]

The materialism of contemporary life was not something which Fontane noted with distaste merely in Prussia. It is this aspect which provides the negative side of the picture of England in "Der Stechlin" and thus the possibility is avoided that the image of England smacks of ill-considered enthusiasm. This is a criticism which might have been voiced by Adelheid, would it not have lent her too much perspicacity. The criticism is made fleetingly and it prevents the picture of England from being too flat or one-sided. Two phrases are used by Lorenzen which were favourites of Fontane himself in descriptions in his letters about England, namely, the "cult of the Golden Calf" and "they say Christ and mean cotton".[2] It is fitting that Lorenzen should voice this criticism, since he was both once an uncritical admirer of England and he also stands for a sincere putting into practice of Christian ideals, especially that of love from the New Testament. Had Adelheid expressed the criticism of England's late nineteenth-century materialism, it would seem to be merely a part of her xenophobia and chauvinism.

Peter Demetz claims that the experiences connected with

Moscheles, goes on to criticise Baruch Hirschfeld in the scene referred to above (p. 208). Paulsen does not point out that it is Moscheles' strong support of the Social Democratic Party, symbolized by his red socks, which appears to be the butt of Dubslav's criticism, and not his Jewishness. The very fact that Koseleger turns Dubslav's attention away from Hirschfeld towards Frau von Gundermann suggests a deflecting of criticism from Jews in particular towards the new-rich in general.

1 Wolfgang Paulsen does concede this background to Fontane's criticism of Jews, and draws attention to the member of Fontane's own family, his sister Jenny, who became a member of the new-rich class and lent her name to Frau Jenny Treibel. (See W. Paulsen: op. cit., p. 313-314.) In "Frau Jenny Treibel", incidentally, another 'hidden' defence of Jews is to be found in Schmidt's conversation with Distelkamp in Chapter 6 about Etienne Friedberg.

2 NyA VIII, 208.

England in "Der Stechlin" are indirectly related by means of anecdote, and not shown directly in the action, in order to indicate that Woldemar will eventually follow in his father's footsteps instead of keeping in line with the cosmopolitan Barbys.[1] This claim does not really tally with the impression given in the novel that the future may hold both of these possibilities. If Woldemar continues to be influenced by Lorenzen, it would appear that he will remain open to what is new, while at the same time appreciating the positive elements in tradition. Dubslav's vision of his son shows him mixing in future with people of all shades of political opinion. The fact that the England experiences are condensed into anecdotes does not prove anything about Woldemar's future development which, as the last sentence of the novel shows, is not a matter of importance. Through the use of anecdotes in "In Mission nach England" Fontane was able to subsume many strands of his own thought about and experience in and of England under the heading of the contrast it offered to contemporary Prussia. Instead of creating a second and completely different atmosphere (which would have necessitated an amount of action that might have been out of proportion to the lack of action in the Prussian background), Fontane ensured that all the necessary points of the picture of England were brought forward and made particularly memorable through the use of anecdotes. The choice of this procedure is in harmony with the rest of the novel in which so many ideas are made concrete through their representation in the form of stories exchanged by the characters.

Openness to other cultures outside Prussia, moving away from arrogance and narrowness, the interweaving of the old and the new – all these features are contained in the associations included in the novel in connection with England. When Koseleger and Melusine exchange a meaningful glance after Adelheid's tirade

1 See P. Demetz: "Formen des Realismus", p. 181. It is difficult to see the logic behind this statement. Even assuming that Demetz were right, the fact that something is said indirectly is no proof of a negative intention. In fact, most of the best insights in the novel are reflected indirectly through one or more anecdotes, apart altogether from other indirect modes of portrayal.

against England in Chapter 27, this is clearly an unspoken alliance of liberals and cosmopolitans against a reactionary, blinkered Prussian. Significantly this glance is exchanged just when Adelheid has declared that there is no proper aristocracy in England. The nobility represented by Adelheid is precisely not that seen as worthy of respect in "Der Stechlin", for she lacks openness and nobility of soul. Her pride in old families is based on their birthright, a factor which is not necessarily a guarantee that they are capable of giving leadership in the modern world, as we hear from Lorenzen in Chapter 29. Hence the emphasis on new forms of heroism and leadership given by members of 'new' families, such as inventors and explorers. Outsiders like Greely in the given situation and Cooper's Spy[1] (who hazards all for the cause of American independence: reputation, possessions, life itself) risk losing all in society, but are ultimately justified after potentially disgraceful actions. It is no accident that Armgard's letter referring to Lake Trasimeno's effluent called Emissario, which amuses her,[2] and the Greely anecdote are contained in the same chapter. This is an example of Fontane's art of allusion, whereby associations and links

1 The main character of the American novel "The Spy. A Tale of the Neutral Ground." (New York 1821) by James Fenimore Cooper is admired by Lorenzen.

2 Armgard's amusement stems from her (tacit) translation of the Latin 'emissarius' as 'spy'. 'Emissarius' means primarily however 'messenger', while 'emissarium' is an 'outlet for water'. In modern Italian 'emissario' means both 'messenger' and 'effluent', not 'spy'. The narrator wishes to ensure that only the 'spy' meaning remains in the reader's mind, hence the play on the incorrect Latin form, 'emissarius'. Lake Trasimeno which Fontane saw on 15 October 1874 has in fact two effluents called 'Emissario', one dug by the ancient Romans, and the second dug during the composition of "Der Stechlin" in 1896, and opened in 1898. Both effluents link with Torrento Caino, an effluent of the Tiber. Thus the provincial Umbrian lake is indirectly linked with Rome itself, a phenomenon which would surely not have been lost on the author of "Der Stechlin". With good reason, Armgard chooses 'Emissarius' (spy), for this creates the connection with Cooper's "Spy", mentioned by Lorenzen in his introduction to the Greely anecdote, in order to clarify his ideal of heroism as independent personal decision and action.

between apparently disparate and unrelated scenes are established and seep without effort into the reader's consciousness. Lorenzen's two stories about João de Deus and Lieutenant Greely celebrate unselfish values and support the major theme of the interweaving of the old and new. The link of the New Testament makes it quite clear that this is what Fontane has in mind with the João de Deus anecdote. The Portuguese poet's example stands out in an egotistic society. The changes wrought by Fontane against the original material are in the interest of supporting the major theme: the Portuguese poet is an example because he lived for the poor and not for himself. His very life is told by Lorenzen in such a way that the reader becomes conscious that the poet is an embodiment of Lorenzen's own philosophy and of the thrust of the novel. That which is really old, the principle of love, enshrined in the New Testament, should be the basis of the new democratic society, as the poet's love of his countrymen, especially the poor, was the motivating factor of his life of sacrifice and selflessness. Fontane's version of the Portuguese story pares down the material to what is essential and to what pertains to the novel. The new form which he creates from the literary article by Hedwig Wigger is anecdotal because of its limitation to a single incident and its shifting of the key-line "E' um santo" to the end of the story where it gains extra emphasis. The addition of the phrase "und nicht für sich" (and not for himself) underlines Lorenzen's real interest in the story, and contains within itself the reason for the anecdote's inclusion in "Der Stechlin". The life of João de Deus reaches a level of charity which may be said to reach out into the heroic, thus creating another link between themes of a novel which is particularly rich in allusions and hidden associations.

When Greely decides to kill his thieving colleague, he risks not only his future career in the army, but also even his freedom, should a subsequent court of enquiry find him guilty. The balance hangs between the faint hope of survival through the killing and the certainty that civilised society will be shocked and vengeful when the story is revealed. The geographical isolation of the setting emphasizes the psychological independence of the moral decision. The link with the Barfus anecdote from "Frau Jenny Treibel" is this:

in both stories the main character takes a difficult decision which is not palatable to their milieu. Characteristically Fontane-esque is the curious fact that exactly the opposite characteristic is lauded in each case. In the sixteenth-century story the quality pleaded for is leniency, while the contemporary explorer has to act with a severity fatal to the life of the offender. No quarter is shown to the thieving soldier, while the cowardly officer is given a chance to show his valour and power of self-sacrifice on another occasion. In both anecdotes, the characters think for themselves, either directly countermanding the accepted modus operandi or making a totally lonely moral decision without precedents or guidelines. Heroism is not a cut-and-dried value displayed by soldiers rushing into battle as they have done since time immemorial. Modern heroism is more subtle and can manifest itself completely outside of the military sphere. The very fact that in these military stories about Barfus and Greely the heroic decision is taken out of the context of the military or reached against the traditional military thinking points to the lifting of the value of heroism out of its traditional context into a newer, broader setting. In this light the career of João de Deus can be seen as a combination of the principal virtues alluded to in the novel, love and heroism, themselves simply old values but revalued and shown as aspects of the new.

"Der Stechlin" represents the peak of Fontane's art in embedding foreign anecdotal material in the larger fictional framework. This peak is reached through the consistent linking of anecdotal material from very disparate sources with the overall purpose of the novel. Even where inserted stories serve to characterize individual figures or a group, they also have a general relevance to the interpretation of the work as a whole. As far as its use of the anecdote is concerned the novel does not suffer at all from the discursiveness and formlessness which have been attributed to it by some critics, especially since Conrad Wandrey's remarks in this regard. At no stage in "Der Stechlin" is an anecdote used in an arbitrary manner, simply for the purpose of entertainment or as an independent subject of conversation. The interrelationship of all the inserted stories with the major aspects of thematic interest is one of the remarkable features of this large novel. Undoubtedly the fact that Fontane dispensed with the predominance of the plot element, thereby giving himself free rein with conversation and association, greatly aided the introduction of anecdote. Little stories could be introduced easily through the medium which was Fontane's forte, dialogue, while at the same time the novel is not restricted by the exigencies of a complex plot. In those novels in which the plot is an important factor, anecdotes often have to be introduced in relation to some plot element, which may mean some constraint on the writer.

Even apparently minor anecdotes in "Der Stechlin" show on examination their relationship with an important theme. In Chapter 6 Woldemar reports to Rex and Czako an anecdote about Doktor Heim and Queen Luise which was told by Dubslav to the former Princess Ermyntrud, now plain Ermyntrud Katzler. Extra value is gained from the scene within the scene within the scene: Woldemar tells of Dubslav's relationship with the Princess by relating an early nineteenth-century Berlin anecdote of Heim's ticking off the queen after the sixth or seventh birth with the notion that a fallow period is necessary![1] Queen Luise's many pregnancies provide a parallel for Ermyntrud's fertility, but the parallel ends when the reader learns that having many children is a fetish adopted by Ermyntrud as part of her attempt to become an out-and-out bourgeoise. With an irony typical of the narrator this anecdote does not flatter Ermyntrud, as she imagines, but indicates at one and the same time her excessive class-consciousness and her exaggerated sense of duty, which has become the plague of her husband's life. This apparently insignificant anecdote thus is a further reflection of the negative aspects of Prussianism demonstrated in the novel. It has a situational function also in that it provides interest for the conversation between the three officers on their journey from Stechlin to Wutz. It describes the relationship between Dubslav and Ermyntrud, and the reactions of the listeners to the tale are also significant: Rex reacts with an effusive Byzantinism and Czako with some scepticism. In Chapter 5 Krippenstapel jokes about his relationship with his pupils by drawing on the 1848 anecdote about

1 NyA VIII, 69.

the town-mayor, who intended to maintain law and order by simply putting his own boot in the window. This little story, which fits in well with the episode in Krippenstapel's school, is a further link in the chain of references to revolution in the novel, and therefore is a further reflection of the theme of the old and the new. Fontane attributes the anecdote to the 1848 period in order to make it more relevant to his theme, although it had already appeared in literary works of the Romantic period. In Chapter 19, the Conservatives have a guffaw at the anecdote about Prince August of Prussia (1779-1843), the womanizer and one-time lover of Mme Récamier who, according to Berliners on the occasion of his death, was refused admittance to heaven, until Saint Peter had brought the eleven thousand virgins to safety! The Conservatives themselves make the connection with 'Fronde' – Prince August's behaviour was a revolt against morality – thus touching in humorous vein on a major theme of the novel. The triviality of the story is another indirect comment on the level of conversation among the Conservatives here.

The individual analyses of anecdotes in "Der Stechlin" showed how they are linked with the portrayal of Prussian society in the eighteen-nineties. This portrayal is loving but critical, making the novel a fitting monument to Fontane's life-long study of his country's culture and its problems. Clearly the old and the new is the theme which most excites Fontane's imagination, and it is referred to in hundreds of other allusions besides anecdotes. Typical of the narrator's humorous approach even in dealing with this serious topic are, for example, the calls from the Conservatives at the election dinner demanding "Was Neues"! (Something new!) when Gundermann is boring them with his anti-Social Democratic gloss on the anecdote about Johanna Knothe's execution. The most outstanding feature of Fontane's success in employment of the anecdote in "Der Stechlin" is the ease with which these extraneous stories are embedded in the fictional text. Although the anecdotes are actually employed by the author to carry ideas and an interpretation of the society in which he himself lived, there is nothing forced or artificial about them. Many essentially abstract throughts are put forward in a most concrete and sociable manner as part of the give-and-take of normal conversation.

IV. "Bruchstücke sind besser als Ganzes":

Anecdote and Autobiography

1. "Aus den Tagen der Okkupation (1871)

In terms of his development as a creative writer Fontane was still somewhat immature at the time of composition of those autobiographical works which have as their raison d'être his experiences during the Franco-Prussian War and German occupation of France in 1870-1871. The first novel "Vor dem Sturm" appeared only eight years after these autobiographical works and Fontane himself saw his breakthrough in the craft of writing as coinciding with the publication of this novel and of the war book "Der Krieg gegen Frankreich" (1876),[1] of which "Kriegsgefangen. Erlebtes 1870" (1871) and "Aus den Tagen der Okkupation" were for him "die feuilletonistischen, schellenläutenden Vorläufer".[2] It is to be expected that among other things the art of the anecdote will show some weaknesses in the case of a writer just leaving the apprenticeship stage. As in "Wanderungen durch die Mark Brandenburg" there is sometimes in these two works a tendency for a good passage to dissolve into an atmospheric scene. Some anecdotes appear to be included for their own sake and not because they are rendered absolutely necessary by the context or by some compelling link of the writer's imagination with the reality perceived. In fact taking the date of publication of the "Kriegsgefangen" and "Aus den Tagen der Okkupation" into account, it is surprising to see

1 His experience in war reportage must be a record for a creative writer: Conrad Wandrey reckons Fontane's production by 1876 in terms of some 3,500 lexicon-sized pages on the Prussian wars. (See Wandrey: op. cit., p. 332.).

2 This is how he describes them in a letter of 5 December 1871 to Rudolf von Decker. (See Brinkmann/Wiethölter: "Theodor Fontane", vol. 2, p. 88.)

already the characteristic feature of Fontane's efforts in the field of the anecdote clearly discernible, i.e. the intention of marrying it with the major preoccupations of the works as a whole. The extent of his success is remarkable, given the above-mentioned reservations. This success can be attributed perhaps to the clarity and unity of the subject-matter in both works. Both have rigid restrictions in that they simply report his experiences of a limited period of time during which one large topic dominates, i.e. the Franco-Prussian war in so far firstly as it affected his own life without his wishing it i.e. through imprisonment, and secondly by his own volition, i.e. his attempt to re-create the story of the war, not systematically, but through visiting battlefields and so on. This unity of experience is allied with a unity of approach.

The semi-official nature of the actual "Kriegsbücher" as opposed to the autobiographically inclined "Kriegsgefangen" and "Aus den Tagen der Okkupation" meant that Fontane had to drop the anecdotal style he had favoured for the"Wanderungen durch die Mark Brandenburg" since the early eighteen-sixties, and adhere to a more factual style required for descriptions of military operations. The relative ease of composition in the autobiographical "Kriegsgefangen" and "Aus den Tagen der Okkupation" contrasts with the toil which Fontane put into the war books proper, toil which was not really recompensed by the Prussian authorities, as he often remembered in his more bitter moments.

The approach in "Kriegsgefangen" and "Aus den Tagen der Okkupation" frees Fontane for the first time from the difficult task of factual and comprehensive reportage of military affairs, although the war situation is of course the necessary basis of the two works. The fact that in "Kriegsgefangen" and "Aus den Tagen der Okkupation" Fontane's personality and his experiences are of such importance ensures both the originality and the anecdotal mode of procedure in these two works. The partly compilatory nature of the semi-official war-books, which Contrad Wandrey found unoriginal,[1] survives to a certain extent in the reports by German officers whom

1 See C. Wandrey: op. cit., p. 333-337.

Fontane met in captivity. This compilatory aspect is evident in three chapters of "Kriegsgefangen".[1] This is approximately one-eleventh of the whole, and consists of material otherwise unpublished at the time. It has been justifiably claimed that the best parts of "Aus den Tagen der Okkupation" are those in which the anecdotal element takes precedence over general discussion.[2]

Fontane always preferred to extract a human element from his material, and the reader senses immediately that the scope offered to him for this in the war-time autobiographical work was much more congenial to his nature as a writer than that in the more official war-books. Conrad Wandrey comments on the dilemma in which Fontane found himself in trying to compose the 'official' war-books, where he had to, so to speak, fall between two stylistic schools: "... der notgedrungene Verzicht auf seine subjektiv-gemütliche Darstellungensweise mag es mitverschuldet haben, daß Fontane über das stoffliche Referat kaum hinauskommt. Reine Objektivität 'in historicis' aber, ohne Anekdotenwürze, war fur ihn gleichbedeutend mit Langeweile. Und ein gehobener Stil, der diesen Ausfall hätte wettmachen, das ewige Einerlei der Gefechtsschilderungen pathetisch beleben können, verbot sich dem Gegner der Feierlichkeit und des patriotischen Traras von selbst."[3] No such dilemma obtains in the autobiographical war-books. Fontane himself is the centre-point of the experience and it is h i s experience as well as h i s attempts to find items of interest for the contemporary reader which put him in a sovereign position. Even the visits to battlefields are extremely personalized accounts, and more is learned about Fontane's experience and attitudes than about the military engagements. The 'Anekdotenwürze' mentioned in the above quotation from Wandrey is a very large ingredient in the autobiographical war-books, while the material is in any case palatable to the ordinary reader in a way

1 Chapters 10 to 12.

2 Günter Jäckel: 'Fontane und der deutsch-französische Krieg 1870-71' in FBl, 1970, Band 2, Heft 2, p. 103: "Die besten Stellen finden sich in dem Buch ... dort, wo der Historiker und Reporter aus der allgemeinen Erörterung ins Erzählerische ausbricht, ins Anekdotische."

3 C. Wandrey: op. cit., p. 333.

which the books on the 1864, 1866 and 1870 wars cannot be. The second of the two autobiographical war-books presents a greater variety of material and a much more comprehensive picture of Fontane's attitude to the war, the occupation and the situation of contemporary France, than the first. The range of experience open to Fontane was obviously much greater for the occupation book than for the book on his imprisonment. One senses, for example, a slight unease on the author's part, in "Kriegsgefangen", in recording this necessarily limited experience in an artistic way. Small sections, which are probably inserted in the interest of artistic balance, (e.g. the section "Sentinelle, Prenez Garde à Vous" with its echoes of "Hamlet") seem rather forced. "Aus den Tagen der Okkupation" is a richer book quite simply because its subject-matter covers a much larger area of interest, i.e. both Fontane himself and the contemporary situation in France. And the latter – in the case of a writer like Fontane – demands attention to the past. By the time he came to write "Aus den Tagen der Okkupation", Fontane also had the experience of writing "Kriegsgefangen" behind him, and the experience of composition within the genre must have been of assistance to him for the second book. Fontane's lack of a narrow nationalism is apparent in nearly all his works,[1] in spite of his being steeped in the history, culture and problems of his own country. His openness to the culture and outlook of other nations such as England and France, is clear in the literary works from "Vor dem Sturm" to "Der Stechlin".[2] Even a glance at the anecdote in these works bears out this. It remains a notable achievement, however, to have

1 One may mention as perhaps an exception in this regard his poem 'Jung-Bismark' written in 1885 for Bismarck's birthday.

2 Indeed, references to other countries and other ways of life can be for Fontane an indication of the necessity for receptiveness towards the good elements in other cultures and a warning against narrow nationally-conditoned prejudices and over-estimation of one's own culture. Cf. Charlotte Jolles: 'Und an der Themse wächst man sich anders aus als am Stechlin', p. 187 in connection with the England motif in "Der Stechlin": "England steht für Weltoffenheit, Weite des Horizonts im Gegensatz zur Enge und zum Eingemauertsein."

protected this sense of fairness and openmindedness from the inevitable nationalistic war-time propaganda of 1870-1871 and not to have pandered to any anti-French feelings on the part of either officialdom or of the ordinary German reader of the day.

In "Kriegsgefangen" and "Aus den Tagen der Okkupation", Fontane included personal anecdotes with the intention of showing that human nature is the same everywhere and of presenting to the victorious Germans a balanced view of the vanquished French. A letter to Mathilde von Rohr after the publication of "Aus den Tagen der Okkupation" shows how little Fontane expected from his countrymen by way of understanding for its broadminded approach to the French: "Über die Aufnahme, die das Buch beim Publikum finden wird, bin ich einigermaßen neugierig; in Petersburg, in Warschau, in New York, in der Schweiz, in Holland wird man es wahrscheinlich mit Zustimmung lese, hier wird man es wohl wieder zu 'franzosen-freundlich' finden, weil ich nicht ausgesprochen habe, jeder Franzose muß zur Strafe seiner Sünden lebendig gebraten werden."[1]

One of the personal anecdotes in "Aus den Tagen der Okkupation" concerns Fontane's discomfiture in the company of some Prussian officers in a train. Their attitude towards the French is summed up in the phrase "Alles Bande".[2] The youngest of these, still in his teens, declares: "Man muß ihnen den Daumen aufs Auge drücken."[3] It is precisely this kind of prejudice that Fontane's books on France oppose. Furthermore, his observations in France (over and above those he had already made during his sojourns in England) made him reject the notion that the level of education in Prussia was higher than in other European countries. In order to counteract such generalizations he simply records his own positive experience in encounters with the French.[4] While Fontane's 'good'

1 Letter of 19. 12. 1871. See "Briefe". Edited by Schreinert/Jolles, vol. 3 p. 113. Interestingly, he thinks already in 1871 of his own country in world terms, something that becomes a major theme nearly thirty years later in the last novel.

2 NyA XVI, 349.

3 Ibidem.

4 See "Kriegsgefangen", NyA XVI, 48.

experiences of the French are faithfully recorded, he is also conscientious in his reportage of nasty incidents, though he points out their exceptional character, e.g. the interrogation by a bad-mannered official in the 'Moulins' section of "Kriegsgefangen".[1]

The anecdotes in "Aus den Tagen der Okkupation" fall into three groups: historical anecdotes, anecdotes connected with the recent events of the war and occupation, i.e. stories about the armed forces, and personal anecdotes, which relate to Fontane's own experience during his travels in France at Easter 1871. Thus, stories from the immediate past and the present are mingled, so that a vivid picture of the France of 1870-1871 is presented. The author tries to put this in perspective by having regard for the more distant past. Such matters as the cultural outlook and the contemporary attitudes of the French are of particular interest to him, and he was already experienced as an onlooker from the outside through his years in England in the eighteen-fifties. Fontane draws on historical anecdotes in "Aus den Tagen der Okkupation" when the context appears to call for them. No doubt another writer would have ignored them, or some of them at any rate, had he been engaged on a similar subject. It was part and parcel of Fontane's make-up however and above all of his training through the compositon of "Wanderungen durch die Mark Brandenburg" to associate places visited with the historical events of which they were witness. Even where the present situation does not appear to call for it, Fontane does not resist the temptation to delve into the past of a place visited and to treat the reader to an atmospheric evocation. This happens, for example, in his digression from the description of the Battle of Amiens to give some historical background about the castle at Boves. Into this digression he fits an anecdote which also appears in "Vor dem Sturm". The story shows Henry IV of France refusing to disturb his unfaithful mistress, Gabrielle d'Estrées, and his rival lover. When brought to her boudoir where the rendezvouz was

1 NyA XVI, 65. Having given the exact words of the interview, Fontane continues: "Die Unterredung selbst habe ich hierher gesetzt, weil sie die einzige Insolenz ist, der ich während der ganzen Zeit meiner Gefangenschaft ausgesetzt gewesen bin" (ibid. 66).

taking place, he declined to enter, saying: "Cela la facherait trop."[1] The inclusion of this story here shows the many levels at which some of Fontane's stories simultaneously aim. Firstly, Henry IV is always associated with the quality of tolerance. Secondly, his humour, urbanity and refinement[2] are qualities which are demonstrated in the story and which Fontane himself particularly admired. He found these qualities in the French, and it seems likely that he is implicitly indicating these characteristics to his fellow-countrymen as being worthy of note. The anecdote may seem far removed from the harsh realities of the warring French and Germans of 1870, but technically speaking, it provides both the reader and the narrator respite from reportage on the battles.

The digression on Henry IV takes up less than two pages but it neatly ends the chapter on the first battle of Amiens and relieves the reader of the longueur of wading through two battle descriptions at one go. Fontane fills out the entertaining digression with observations about the subsequent life of Gabrielle d'Estrées, and even includes a further little digression about Francis I's views on the fickleness of women. Finally, this chapter is rounded off with a personal anecdote of an encounter with a count from Picardy, who tried to convince Fontane of the unaristocratic origin of Gabrielle d'Estrées. By moving from battle description to piquant tales from sixteenth-century France, then back to Fontane's personal experience of the present (in so far as it is connected with the past) and finally on again to the second battle description, Fontane provides a varied and interesting narrative. The reader's curiosity with regard to details of the military engagements is satisfied, and his own as well as the narrator's diligence is rewarded with refreshing anecdotes from past and present. The inclusion of Fontane's encounter with Count Chassepot from Picardy is a little masterpiece in its own right for it allows Fontane to move away from the sixteenth century back to the present in a way which makes the

1 NyA XVI, 274.

2 These qualities also inform the figure of the king in Heinrich Mann's "Henri Quatre" novel which had a message for the Germans in the 1930's.

sixteenth-century material relevant to Fontane's own journey through France, which is after all the basis of the book as a whole, as its sub-title, "Eine Osterreise durch Nordfrankreich und Elsaß-Lothringen 1871", indicates. The example of the Henry IV digression shows how neatly Fontane moves between the time levels of past and present in this work, and how he avoids, for example, through the use of little personal encounters like that with Count Chassepot, awkward transitions between history and the present situation.

However, the sifting of facts and anecdotes from the historical past in "Aus den Tagen der Okkupation" is not undertaken merely from the point of view of entertainment or of providing a well-knit narrative. There is a serious and, one might say, almost didactic purpose behind the appearance in this work of an historical figure like "le bon roi", Henri IV.

The reader might erroneously assume that stories of Henry IV and other historical figures are included in the narrative, simply because they were favourite pieces in the furniture of Fontane's mind. This is not however the case, and it is in examples like this that one can see the great care with which Fontane treats the many strands of his narrative. An important factor which becomes apparent from Fontane's whole attitude to the present situation of France is his consciousness of the great break between past and present. From his observations during the periods spent in France in the 1870-1871 upheaval, he believed that the French displayed a lack of historical consciousness and that this was connected with a certain lack of idealism. Several of his own encounters are narrated with the intention of illustrating this lack and the resulting materialism and nonchalance of the contemporary French. The fact that the French had almost forgotten their "bon roi", one of Fontane's favourite historical figures, is implicitly taken as an illustration of a serious abyss between the French and their own past.

Fontane sees this in the French approach to the teaching and learning of history: the French Revolution and the Second Empire have suppressed interest in more remote periods of French history. Here the contrast with his own country is at its most striking for Fontane, for he feels that every schoolboy is as familiar with the earlier names and events of Prussian history as with the later ones. Furthermore, he is aware of a lack of the sense of localization in the approach to the writing of history on the part of local historians in France, whereas in England and Germany the concrete objects and places which played their part in particular historical events are of importance to the historians themselves and thus become fixed in the minds of the people in connection with those events.[1] With the concreteness which characterizes Fontane's observations, however, implications like the foregoing are not made simply in the form of theoretical discussion, but are embedded in the narrative through his descriptions of concrete objects. Thus, the neglected condition of the statue of Henry IV in Saint Denis may become for Fontane a symbol of the general disregard for the nation's past which he feels is to be ascertained in contemporary France. Such disregard is not merely observed as an isolated phenomenon either, but is tied in by Fontane with the present political situation. The defeat of the French in the Franco-Prussian war is ultimately seen by him as being the result of the degeneration of the nation's moral fibre, so to speak, – of its lack of idealism and of the materialism which Fontane feels is to be observed everywhere in France. In the fourth section of "Aus den Tagen der Okkupation", the coachman's tone of voice in speaking of a rich banker or industrialist leads Fontane to make the following generalization on his observations about the French:"Das unbedingt Häßlichste, dem ich in Frankreich begegnet bin, ist diese Devotion vor dem Golde. Arme Kerle; sie haben keinen Gott und keinen Glauben mehr und knixen vor La France und – Rothschild.[2] But in his summary on the career and fate of Napoleon III in the final chapter, Fontane expresses the view that adoration of the Golden Calf is now a universal phenomenon.[3] Not only the poor condition of Henry IV's statue,

1 Cf. NyA XVI, 287. Fontane shows his own concern for exactness in the matter of historical localities in the passage about the precise spot on which Napoleon III and Bismarck conducted their talk at Donchery. See ibid. 397.

2 Ibid. 424.

3 Ibid. 511. Fontane had plenty of opportunity to observe materialism in Victorian England, and his revulsion, especially when materialism was allied

but also the neglect of the graves of the kings and queens of France and the destruction of the Vendôme column are symbols for Fontane of the degeneration of the country.[1]

When seen in this light further passages, which may seem at first glance to be mere historical digressions on the part of the writer of the "Wanderungen", turn out to be part of this indictment. Not for itself alone therefore does Fontane recount in the narration the story of Diane de Poitiers and her ostentatious monument to her dead husband with its hypocritical dedication. Fontane is not content with describing this insincerity; he goes further and includes a generalization which imputes mendaciousness to the French in general: "Die Franzosen waren immer groß nach dieser Seite hin."[2] This little sentence gives us the clue for the inclusion of the passage on Diane de Poitiers: it is not merely a case of another piquant story about a royal mistress, which contains, like the Garbielle d'Estrées anecdote, an element of entertainment value. Diane's story provides a link also between past and present:

> "Ich hab' es gesehen, aber ich glaub' es nicht", – nach diesem berühmten Satze scheinen sich Liebe, Ehe und Treue, samt allen dahin einschlagenden Fragen und Zweifeln, in "la belle France" in alten und neuen Tagen reguliert zu haben.[3]

The picture presented of Diane de Poitiers in the first of the chapters devoted to Rouen has as its counterpart in the second of these chapters the enthusiastic account of Joan of Arc's last days. As in the case of Henry IV, Fontane does not dwell on her because she is his

with hypocrisy, is frequently expressed in his correspondence. On this subject cf. C. Jolles: 'Th. Fontane und die Ära Manteuffel' in "Forschungen zur Brandenburgischen und Preußischen Geschichte" 49, 1939, p. 107-108.

1 The least convincing portion of Fontane's description of the French situation is that in which he tries to see in their approach to the learning of history (e.g. "Alles oberflächlich", ibid. 286 – after references to well-known anecdotes) the reason for the lack of 'pietas' which he observes in the French of 1870. This can lead to such prejudiced statements as "Verräterei macht in Frankreich immer populär" (ibidem).

3 NyA XVI, 294.

4 Ibidem.

favourite heroine. Various anecdotal details of her imprisonment and her recantation, then subsequent recantation of the recantation, as well as Bishop Cauchon's callous "Bon appetit!"[1] to his colleagues on the announcement of her condemnation are included here. This account lives through its contrasting of the purity and goodness of Joan with the callousness and even bestiality of the authorities and their representatives. However a further step in contrasts is taken by Fontane when he includes an anecdote from his personal experience while looking at the saint's statue in Rouen. Like that of Henry IV in Saint Denis, it is damaged: the arm and the pommel are missing. Fontane detects a mixture of patriotism and frivolity in the remark of a passing citizen: "Ihr Arm wird wieder wachsen. Gott hat immer Wunder an ihr getan." He himself sees this statue with its broken arm and damaged sword as a symbol of religious courage in France: the statue's condition being at once ludicrous and telling.[2]

The note of criticism of the degeneration in present-day France has already been sounded distinctly in "Aus den Tagen der Okkupation" in the final section on Amiens, which is devoted to Peter of Amiens and which brings to an end Section Three of the first volume of the work. Here Fontane takes the mediocrity of the statue's expression as the starting-point in external reality for his indictment of the lack of idealism in France. In contrast to the selflessness of the hermit he sees the lack in contemporary France of surrender to a great idea, while the ideals of the French Revolution are interpreted as freedom: the destruction of everything traditional, equality: the dragging down of everything elevated, and brotherhood: contempt for morality. France's surrender to materialism and all that is empty and deceptive in modern times, has brought about a sorry state of affairs, which must again be reversed by a new idealism.[3] "Das I d e a l e ist es, was not tut."[4]

It cannot be said that Fontane's forte in 1871 is such cultural criticism. The reader often has the feeling that he either says too

1 NyA XVI, 298.
2 Ibid. 300.
3 Ibid. 281-282.
4 Ibidem.

little, or as here, goes too far. Later, in a literary and symbolical approach to similar problems in his own country, as in "Frau Jenny Treibel" and "Der Stechlin", Fontane is much more successful and convincing. In the passages of criticism of France in "Aus den Tagen der Okkupation", Fontane gets the idea across with more artistic success when he let an episode or anecdote speak for itself (with perhaps a hint from himself of a more interpretative nature), than when he indulges in lengthier attempts to analyse the whole of the French outlook and the reasons for the present decline that he observes in France. This is not surprising in any case, given the concrete turn of Fontane's mind.[1] Theorizing was never his strong point.

Fontane's attitude to the French Revolution in so far as it is expressed in "Aus den Tagen der Okkupation" is summarized in his observations about the debased interpretation of the three revolutionary principles, which he sees as prevailing in the France of 1870. He regrets the fact that the Revolution has destroyed to a large extent the link between the French and their earlier past. The destruction of monuments, statues and graves undertaken by revolutionaries seems to him a visible sign of this break with the past, of the French alienation from their history. Sometimes in "Aus den Tagen der Okkupation" Fontane includes an anecdote from the Revolution in the interests of filling in local colour. This happens in his description of the visit to Liancourt Castle, when he includes some remarks about the career of Francois Alexandre Frédérique, Duke of La Rochefoucauld, who probably built the castle. The anecdote here concerns the Duke's famous reply to Louis XVI in 1789: "Pas un revolte, sire, une révolution".[2] This

1 Pierre-Paul Sagave sees Fontane's attitude in both "Kriegsgefangen" and "Aus den Tagen der Okkupation" as Hegelian in its emphasis on the state rather than on the individual. Sagave also points out the fact that Fontane argues as an amateur historian. (See P.-P. Sagave: 'Fontane et la France 1870-71' in IASL 1, 1976, p. 163) The value of Fontane's works on wartime France for us today lies not so much in the validity of his criticism of the state of the nation as in what it reveals to us of Fontane, both as a person and writer, in the 1870 period.

2 NyA XVI, 198.

anecdote is not recounted for its own sake, but because it concerns the founder of Liancourt, and Fontane as always is anxious to link a place with anything historical which can at all be connected with it, even as in this case, where the place in question is not actually the place alluded to in the anecdote. The stories about the French Revolution in "Aus den Tagen der Okkupation" almost invariably concern destruction. In the Strasbourg section Fontane deliberately indicates to the reader that his choice of anecdote is determined by his wish to pick on the more amusing aspects of some revolutionary incidents, such as the mounting of a large red tin hat on the Cathedral tower, instead of destroying it as a symbol of repression![1] It is not the more horrific aspects of the Terror which Fontane wants to depict here, but the lighter and therefore (the reader supplies for himself) the less well-known aspects of the Revolution's effects in this particular locality. Fontane's conservatism in 1870 (as opposed to his sharp social criticism of later years, particularly the eighteen-nineties) leads him to give the overall negative picture of the effects of the Revolution on development in France contained in "Aus den Tagen der Okkupation". This attitude probably found favour with the more conservative Prussian readers.

Most military anecdotes are concerned, not with actual engagements, but with remarkable, curious or funny incidents on the periphery of the fighting. Frequently, anecdotes to do with the military are set in the soldiers' free time, or before and after battle.[2] The personal and individual element which gives the anecdote its special flavour is of course lacking in large scale martial engagements and only certain aspects of these, often where there is a departure from the norm, are appropriate for anecdotal narration. It is not

1 "Der wahnwitzige Teterel machte den Vorschlag, den Turm abtragen zu lassen, 'da er das Egalitätsprinzip verletze'. Als es unterblieb, wurde ihm wenigstens die Genugtuung, daß der Münsterspitze eine kolossale rote Blechmütze aufgestülpt wurde." (NyA XVI, 487)

2 A favourite theme of military anecdotes is comments of leaders after battles e.g. the Napoleonic one narrated in "Meine Kinderjahre" in connection with Louis Fontane's 'Socratic method', where Napoleon says to Durot after the battle near Preußisch-Eylau that he had got to know the sixth European great power: "la boue" (NyA XIV, 124).

surprising therefore that anecdotes concerning the armed forces and military engagements form the smallest group in "Aus den Tagen der Okkupation". Only a few stories are directly concerned with military action. Each of them is concerned with a somewhat unusual, but ultimately very understandable human reaction to a battle situation. The story of the storming by the Prussians of the fortress of Saint Privat, for example, brings home the primitive and elemental aspect of pent-up aggression, when the Prussians take to attacking the French defenders with stones from the walls, rather than with the more sophisticated weapons at their disposal.[1]

During his description of the visit to Garenne, Fontane includes in a footnote the story related to him by an officer about the fierce cannonade of Garenne, which spared neither friend nor foe, so that both French and Prussians sought shelter behind the thickest tree trunks. Fontane remarks on the victory of the common instinct of self-preservation over national agression.[2] Such little anecdotes bring out general human characteristics which manifest themselves in extreme situations. This emphasizes the common ground between the hostile armies and reinforces Fontane's general aim of presenting to his reader the human face of these events, especially the humanity of the official 'enemy'. But such stories are rare, and Fontane's difficulty in collecting even ordinary facts about military engagements is perhaps best shown in his account of his attempts to elicit material about the famous battle at Armansvillers only a few days after the event. In this case, the soldiers whom he approaches have no interest in divulging information about a battle which captured the attention of the whole of Europe. Instead, the soldiers are full of a tale about a scuffle at billiards with some of the local citizens, and the narrator is obliged to take refuge in a resigned statement: "Immer nur das Neue und Nächste gilt".[3]

Some of the anecdotes in "Aus den Tagen der Okkupation" concerning the forces in occupation are designed to give comic relief. One important aspect of Prussian success in France was the

1 NyA XVI, 453.
2 Ibid. 368.
3 Ibid. 377.

bravery of the Bavarian troops, which becomes synonomous for the French with cruelty and fiercesomeness. In the "Sedan" section of the second volume of "Aus den Tagen der Okkupation" an anecdote about a Bavarian captain illustrates the Bavarians' humorous though perhaps exaggerated reaction to their new-found reputation. Of the many anecdotes circulating on this topic, Fontane relates just one.

> Ein kleiner Embonpointcapitaine mit Birnennase und dickem flachsgelbem Schnurrbart trat nie anders ins Quartier als unter Aufführung solcher Szene. Er ließ die Dame des Hauses rufen. Diese erschien in Schwarz. "Madame", so begann er, "recevez vous mes ordres pour demain matin. Huit heures café; pour déjeuner un enfant rôti." Nun Tränen und Geschrei. Der Kleine aber trat dann in infernaler Gemütlichkeit an die Dame heran, legte seine Hand auf ihre Schulter, und sagte "Ne pleurez pas, ce sont les traditions de ma famille."[1]

Such an anecdote is useful on several counts: it draws attention to an historical fact – the bravery of the Bavarians, or rather, the way in which this has been warped by old wives' tales; it also characterizes the humorous reaction of the Bavarians to a situation in which they are the losers in personal terms: since they cannot change their new reputation they turn it to good account by making fun of it.

As narrator Fontane sees the dubious element of this, given the understandable attitude of the French after the bloody battle of Bazeilles of 1 September 1870. This anecdote is placed in the text section entitled "Bazeilles", immediately preceding a description of Fontane's ride over the scene of the battle. The Bazeilles sub-section serves therefore to provide introductory local colour of an amusing nature. The anecdote proves that the proverb can be turned back to front: "Nicht immer, im Widerspruch mit dem Sprichwort, holt die Wahrheit die Lüge ein".[2] The amusing element in the anecdote is tinged with the horror of the French lady, remembering the local massacre of her countrymen (dresses in black), and now confronted

1 NyA XVI, 361. Giving the conversation in the original French reminds the reader of Fontane's descriptions of his father's favourite anecdotes with their element of French quotations. ("Meine Kinderjahre", Ch. 10, 13 & 16)
2 NyA XVI, 361.

with the Bavarian joker. A similar element of the mixture of horror and the incongruous is discernible in the straight narration at the end of the Bazeilles section. Here, as so often, Fontane sees in the physical objects around him a symbolical pointer to the times: a very high factory chimney, carrying the date of construction 1870 "eine echte Friedenskolonne"[1] now stands as a memorial to the Battle of Bazeilles. The subtle congruence of anecdote and narration lifts this little section of "Aus den Tagen der Okkupation" to a high level of poetic achievement, which is often reached by Fontane in this work whenever individual human fates or physical objects point to the loss of life in war.

As befits a work with a strong autobiographical slant, anecdotes from Fontane's personal experience in France form the largest of the groups of anecdotes in "Aus den Tagen der Okkupation". Such anecdotes may be connected with amusing incidents which befell the author on his travels, or they may give an insight into some aspect of French and German attitudes at the time. Often they provide the contemporary reader with the kind of inside view not given in official or newspaper accounts of the occupation. Sometimes also, the narrator can conveniently end his discussion of a subject with an anecdote, or use an anecdote to make the transition to another subject. It has already been noted that Fontane sometimes combines past and present through the interweaving of historical anecdotes with those from his personal experience, e.g. the citizen's remark about the broken arm on the statue of Joan of Arc, which brings to an end Fontane's excursus into the fifteenth-century past, and the story of his encounter with Count Chassepot which rounds off the tales about Gabrielle d'Estrées.

Sometimes, Fontane even illustrates an incident from his present experiences with an historical anecdote,[2] e.g. in commenting on his temperance in Epernay and Reims, which contrasts with his feeding on champagne and oysters in Dieppe. This situation is humorously

1 NyA XVI, 362.

2 This is a technique which Fontane later develops to its full potential in the fiction. The past is interwoven with present through the anecdotes whose weight of relevant meaning illuminates the present.

brought out with the statement that he is acting according to the principle of his 1848 compatriot who having passed the corner shop three times finally rewarded himself for his abstemiousness.[1] Similarly in his description of a visit to the bedroom occupied by William I of Prussia at Rézonville during the war, Fontane is reminded by an illustration of a French chef letting his cutlets burn, while consulting the cookbook, of an anecdote about Louis Napoleon burning mutton while studying Benedetti.[2] Fontane's rich store of anecdotes appears to have provided him with constant associations during his travels, and when they appear sufficiently relevant or interesting he includes them in his texts.

The question of religion in France interests him because he finds an ambivalence in French anti-clericalism. From his observations he believes that the French are cynical in their talk about religion and the clergy, although at the same time they show themselves to be not fully emancipated from their influence. Fontane therefore is quick to note external signs of this ambivalence, e.g. the way a clergyman is greeted with respect.[3] During a coach-ride his French companions enlighten him that the reason for a large attendance at a place of pilgrimage is that there is dancing in the evening there.[4] For Fontane the decline of religion in France fits in with the overall pattern of a debasement of ideals there. An amusing anecdote recalls Fontane's discomfiture during benediction in Strasbourg Cathedral. He dwells on the conflicting emotions of not wanting to bend the knee out of respect for his own faith and not wanting to stand up for fear of giving offence to the congregation. His summary here is typical of his talent for finding value in a paradoxical situation: "Alles was wahrhaft erhebt, heiligt auch".[5] This story gives an insight into Fontane's personal reactions. His capacity for telling a story in which he himself is shown up in an embarrassing or even

1 NyA XVI, 309.
2 Ibid. 443.
3 Ibid. 373. For Fontane even the anti-clericalism of the Paris Commune is an inverted form of admiration for the clergy.
4 Ibid. 429.
5 Ibid. 494.

ridiculous light is one of his most endearing features as a narrator.[1] His capacity for noting ironies is evident in many of the recorded incidents, e.g. the discovery that he and the other visitors had been standing on the container holding the remains of the French kings, while they were in the very act of reading their names from the marble plaque in Saint Denis Cathedral.[2] During a tour of the cathedral the guide, a young Prussian officer, remarks to the amusement of the German, but not of the French visitors present that the statue called "La fortitude de la France" has been put for the time being in the cellar.[3] An example of a larger-scale irony comes with Fontane's description of his encounter with an American in the tower of Strasbourg Cathedral.[4] This passage is a masterpiece of Fontane's art of narration. The naïveté of the American is accepted by Fontane as typical of the tendency of all Americans to unerringly veer from every subject to the theme of 'back home'.[5] He accepts this in the sense that he sees the whole direction of modern European culture as being in itself an Americanism with its speed, mobility and telecommunications. The contrast between the impressive cathedral which is the 'most powerful symbol of German art and German greatness',[6] and the simple confidence of the American's claim: "America, that's the world", (which Fontane does not dare contradict) is highly ironic.[7] Fontane describes the man in a slightly amused fashion: "Ich bin noch

1 This is also the case for example in the story about his mistaking an ill-educated local magistrate for a district medical doctor. Cf. NyA XVI,467.
2 NyA XVI, 246.
3 The rather arch quality of this story is counteracted by Fontane's description of his own extreme embarrassment at being asked by the guide to tell the three French ladies present to leave the party before the visit to the crypt with the remains of the kings of France. (NyA XVI, 245)
4 Heinz Grothe cites this as being typical of Fontane's anecdotes which possess "bemerkenswerte Pointierfreudigkeit, festumrissene Absicht und deutliche Konturen". (H.Grothe: "Anekdote", p. 63)
5 NyA XVI, 490. People from Leipzig and Berlin do too, writes Fontane in the relativizing manner which is so typical of him.
6 Ibid. 491.
7 Ibidem.

keinem Amerikaner begegnet, der nicht ein 'Editor' war, gewesen war oder zu sein hoffte",[1] but this does not detract from the fact that the man's utterance is treated with seriousness. This anecdote seems to call into question the whole situation which brought about the genesis of this book: the problems of the two European countries at war. This is done through the anecdote's focussing on the extreme confidence (however naïve) of the large continent's representative who has only five minutes to devote to the Franco-Prussian war and the "rising german (sic) nation". The story is a masterpiece of anecdotal narration, not simply in its own right, but in the context of Fontane's book on the German occupation of France. The writer's chance meeting with a native of a different and far-off country implies that the assumptions behind this example of European aggression are dubious, or at best irrelevant. Lack of knowledge of Europe's (specifically Germany's) cultural greatness gives the American 'editor' the freedom to confidently state America's importance in world terms.

With oblique irony, therefore, Fontane throws a question-mark even behind his own work on the Prussian-French conflict which is of such little importance to this representative of another continent. With tact, Fontane refrains from interpreting his own anecdote, leaving it as an artistic expression to speak for itself. Its position near the conclusion of "Aus den Tagen der Okkupation" hints at a wider perspective in which such wars as the recent one are made questionable. Thus the personal encounter, which incidentally gives the reader an insight into Fontane's social approach, becomes a comment on a whole cultural situation. The Strasbourg anecdote combines qualities of the best anecdotes: novelty, freshness, irony, wit, verve and 'Nachdenklichkeit',[2] that thought-provoking quality

1 NyA XVI, 491.

2 In a passage from the Hesekiel chapter of "Von Zwanzig bis Dreißig", Fontane seems to take this quality for granted in the case of the anecdote: " ... denn historischen Anekdoten habe ich nie widerstehen können, bin auch jetzt der Meinung, daß sie das Beste aller Historie sind. Was tu' ich mit den Betrachtungen? Die kommen von selbst, wenn die Kleinen und großen Geschichten, die heldischen und die mesquinen, zu mir gesprochen haben." (NyA XV, 252-253)

which makes the story linger in the mind. Its origin in a personal encounter gives it an autobiographical value over and above its function as a cultural comment.

More directly critical in the Strasbourg section of "Aus den Tagen der Okkupation" are Fontane's observations on the subject of the Alsace-Lorraine problem. He suggests that the German occupiers might not provide the most congenial type of administration. A personal encounter with a boastful "Jung-Roland"[1] illustrates this point, and concretely shows the difficulties ahead for the German administration in the new Reichsland.

Many of the personal anecdotes in "Aus den Tagen der Okkupation" owe their origin to Fontane's sense of isolation at Easter 1871 in his strange position as unofficial Prussian without hostility, as observer of a situation brought about for political and military reasons, as human being for whom human situations are of more interest and value than the so-called great events of history. It is this factor which lends poignancy to many of Fontane's personal encounters with the French as well as with his fellow-countrymen in occupied France. In small anecdotal touches he is able to reveal the plight of individuals whose lives have been ruined by the war, e.g. the story of Gottfried Heller bringing Fontane to view the mass of rubble which was until recently his home,[2] or the three little orphan girls in "La Maison Blanche" whose singing moves him.[3]

One feature of the employment of anecdote in "Aus den Tagen der Okkupation" identifies the work stylistically with the early Fontane. This is the fact that irrelevant stories are used in some cases to describe certain situations. The only link exists in an association in the mind of Fontane. In both "Kriegsgefangen" and "Aus den Tagen der Okkupation" the writer is naturally interested in the reaction of the French to him from the point of view of his nationality. Indeed,

1 NyA XVI, 483-484.

2 Ibid. 271. Fontane comments here on the phenomenon which illuminates his own reasons for employing the personal anecdote so frequently in order to describe contemporary affairs: only the story of an individual's fate brings home the reality behind statistics of death and destruction.

3 Ibid. 387.

the contrast in the encounters of French and Germans constitutes a large part of the characterization in both books. In "Aus den Tage der Okkupation" one anecdote brings out the clear differentiation made by the French during the war and the occupation between Prussian and German. Fontane's own reaction to this situation, he tells the reader, is to always introduce himself immediately as a Prussian in order to avoid mistakes and embarrassment. To illustrate this procedure, he narrates the anecdote about the wife of the "Kreuz-Zeitung" editor, Prussia's most conservative newspaper, who always introduced herself as the wife of the editor of the "Neue Preußische Zeitung", because she felt that the newspaper's official title administered the 'milder dose' first. Fontane presents the French whom he meets with the 'stronger dose' first, i.e. that he is a Prussian rather than a German. The situation is thus illustrated through the use of the "Kreuz-Zeitung" anecdote, but for the reader this tends perhaps to make the passage less, rather than more comprehensible. Phrases like "die mildere Dosis" from anecdotes like this one became household words with the Fontanes, and the writer probably finds it hard to resist the temptation of quoting them in his work.

Even less successful, in the sense that it is a less interesting story, is the anecdote which Fontane employs to illustrate his boredom during a five-hour wait at the Saint Quentin railway station. This boredom lends enchantment to even the normally uninteresting official notices in a copy of the "Kreuz-Zeitung" which he is able to borrow. To illustrate the relativity of one's judgements on such matters – at home these pages are always passed over as boring, abroad stuck at a railway station with nothing to read, everything in the paper is 'lovely' – Fontane tells the anecdote of Franz Kugler's son. Having been asked what story by Heinrich Smidt he would like for his birthday, he replied categorically: "Ganz egal; von Heinrich Smidten ist alles schön."[1] Again this appears to be a life-long favourite anecdote of Fontane, for he relates it twice in his correspondence with Paul Heyse and once again (where it is

1 NyA XVI, 404.

much more appropriate than in "Aus den Tagen der Okkupation") in the Heinrich Smidt chapter of "Von Zwanzig bis Dreißig".[1] This little story is essentially an o r a l anecdote, and may have been very successfully related in the Fontane-Kugler circle, but for the general public it is neither interesting nor amusing enough to illustrate something with which it has no intrinsic connection. The otherwise well-narrated chapter on Saint Quentin with its amusing account ot how Fontane came by the copy of the newspaper is rather spoiled by the introduction of this irrelevant anecdote. In many instances in the fictional works the same gap of relevance exists between the anecdote and the context, but it is part of Fontane's skill to make them relevant and appropriate.

It has been already seen that the anecdote about Henry IV and Gabrielle d'Estrées provides an interesting and – from the point of view of variety – necessary digression during the description of the Battle of Amiens. Besides having at least a link with the landscape in that area, Henry IV also plays a part in Fontane's overall interpretation of the French situation, and thus the introduction of an apparently unconnected anecdote is not as disturbing as the two examples given above.

A final example shows again a tendency to spoil an otherwise fine piece of narrative. The anecdote in question is recounted as an introduction to the main anecdote of the section, i.e. to the story of the Bavarian captain who required a roast child for his meal. This anecdote, as we have seen, fitted in admirably to its context, but the whole is somewhat jeopardized by Fontane's use of another unrelated anecdote. The link between the two is the mocking of female fears. Fontane states that he is giving an example of how "gesunde Naturen" react to the horrific role attributed to them by others.[2] The Berlin anecdote concerns the reaction of taxi-drivers to timid ladies who, frightened by an assault and robbery case of 1882, used to ask if the horse were a grey (like the one in the assault case). The more humorous drivers would reply: "Det is er

1 With factual variations each time. Cf. NyA XVI, 561.
2 NyA XVI, 361.

Madamken!"[1] This story is amusing in itself, but it is perhaps too far removed from the war-time background of France in 1870 to seem appropriate. Fontane, by adding that the incident may only have been supposed to have taken place, gives it more similarity with the present situation, i.e. the a l l e g e d fiercesomeness of the Bavarian soldiers. However it must be said in conclusion that on the whole the anecdotes in "Kriegsgefangen" and "Aus den Tagen der Okkupation" do not suffer from arbitrary inclusion. Those mentioned here are simply exceptions that prove the rule.

Of the three different types of anecdotes to be found in "Aus den Tagen der Okkupation", the military, the historical and the personal, the most interesting is undoubtedly the last. It was in the interests of collecting information and experience on the spot that Fontane undertook the Easter journey in the first place. As he remarked to Emilie in a letter of 4 April 1871: "Das Büchermachen a u s B ü c h e r n ist nicht meine Sache."[2] It is precisely the unbookish atmosphere in this work which represents its charm, no matter what objections the reader may raise on account of its unsatisfactory analysis of the reasons for the present troubles in France.[3] As in Fontane's "Wanderungen durch die Mark Brandenburg", his personal experience in each place, whether battlefield, village or famous cathedral, strikes the imaginative element in his nature, which ensures that the literary expression of that experience will be gripping, even if the incidents themselves are frequently trivial enough. Humour and a good deal of irony directed against himself are the main characteristics of Fontane's personal anecdotes in this work, which make it in this respect almost as fascinating as his official works of autobiography, "Meine Kinderjahre" and "Von Zwanzig bis Dreißig". Fontane's sense of concrete detail ensures that the reader often has a better and more precise impression of a situation which is related through the medium of

1 NyA XVI, 361.

2 "Theodor Fontanes Briefe an seine Familie". Edited by K. E. O. Fritsch, Berlin 1911, vol. 1, p. 216 (Fontane's emphasis)

3 Cf. also the strange statement in "Der Krieg gegen Frankreich" that the humiliation of France was a decree of destiny. (NyA XIX, 549)

anecdote than when he attempts to encapture it in direct discussion.

The personal anecdotes of his experiences in France are of course only to be found here, while the historical anecdotes employed can be found elsewhere. The interest of such historical anecdotes lies therefore not so much in themselves, but in the use Fontane makes of them: how he fits them in, what connections he makes between them and the present, to what extent they enliven his description of a visit to a particular locality, and the manner in which he incorporates them into an overall view of the situation in France. Particularly noteworthy is the ease with which Fontane moves between the different time levels of immediate present and remoter historical era.

By nature Fontane instinctively turned away from depicting phenomena generally regarded as important or great, and turned instead to aspects which might be considered of secondary importance. In the field of literature this meant the avoidance of depicting – from the inside as it were – depths of passion. In the historical field it means that he paid more attention to figures not in the forefront of the stage. Local history was thus a rich field for Fontane, in particular the enlivening of landscapes, the charm and beauty of which for him were made really interesting through historical associations. As regards the description of imposing and famous buildings the same aspect of Fontane's nature appears. The reader does not find such descriptions. Rather Fontane uses the presence of a famous building to record his personal experiences and impressions – thus gaining an indestructible quality which is far more rewarding to the reader than factual descriptions of buildings and places which are in any case accessible. Fontane's reserve in the face of the large Gothic cathedrals of France is more than compensated for by his choice of anecdotal narration of personal encounters in them.[1]

Fontane does not view the French as either aggressive or incompetent. Nor is he making demands on them à la Treitschke.

1 Cf. Conrad Wandrey's phrase about Fontane's "stete Reserve auch vor den großen Gegenständen, sei es nun Potsdam-Preußen oder die gotischen Kathedralen Frankreichs". (C. Wandrey: op. cit., p. 336)

Indeed, he warns his countrymen after the annexation of Alsace-Lorraine about the loyalty to France of this province.[1] In the wake of the war Fontane adopts the role of writer-mediator, though in a quite unassuming and characteristically unpresumptuous way. He can present to his own countrymen an antidote to all fanatical propaganda by showing a picture of the alleged enemy. The picture, which does not contain a trace of the concept of 'Erbfeindschaft', is painted with a mixture of factual personal experience and historical detail. The alleged enemy may have lost his ideals (Fontane's interpretation), but he remains in terms of social intercourse, even in the company of a representative of the victors, just, amiable and charming. We can be quite certain that Fontane's criticism of materialism in the France of the early eighteen-seventies did not stem from nationalism on his part. He had already been sickened by the materialism of Victorian England, the adoration of the Golden Calf, and he later attacked the same fault in his own country, e.g. in a humorous but none the less effective way in "Frau Jenny Treibel". Even in "Aus den Tagen der Okkupation" he mentions the ubiquitousness of materialism in the modern world. The presentation of a negative interpretation of the present state of France in terms of her lost values does not detract from the sympathy and delight with which Fontane portrays the country and its inhabitants. Themes which are important in these two autobiographical war books re-appear in Fontane's correspondence in a an even more open and direct manner, e.g. his criticism of the notion that Prussians or Germans have the best education system, or that its 'products' are better at the basic skills than those of other countries like France or England.[2]

1 See the Strasbourg section in "Aus den Tagen der Okkupation". Cf. Joachim Remak: "The Gentle Critic", p. 43.

2 See his letter to Emilie from Italy (10. 8. 1875): "Überhaupt will es mir nicht glücken, es im Auslande zu irgendeiner patriotischen Erhebung zu bringen ... Weder das 'ewige Gesiege' noch die fünf Milliarden haben unsere Situation gebessert. Es hieß unmittelbar nach dem Kriege, 'wir seien nun ein für allemal etabliert, der so lange vermißte Respekt sei da'. Aber ich merke nichts davon. Alles dreht sich nach wie vor um England und Frankreich ... Im Grunde genommen ist es recht so, denn das was wirkliche

Anecdotes, whether personal ones of Fontane's experience or about the experiences of the armed forces in France, are aimed at illustrating general points about human nature, characterizing the present military situation, or bringing out in an entertaining, amusing and sometimes tragicomical way the irony of the victor's position in a vanquished land. Fontane's openmindedness to other cultures never allows him to portray his country's 'official' enemy in an ignoble light – the individual encounters show the personal charm of the French. But those qualities which Fontane is dismayed to find in the French, such as materialism, lack of ideals, over-emphasis on individual freedom and a loss of the sense of history are also conscientiously recorded. It is these characteristics on which Fontane places the blame – rightly or wrongly – for the contemporary political and military low ebb in France.

2. "Meine Kinderjahre" (1894)

From the beginning of his work on his autobiography, Fontane was aware of the effect which love of anecdotes would have not merely on individual sections, but also on the overall composition of the work. In the introduction to "Meine Kinderjahre", he writes: "Als es mir feststand, mein Leben zu beschreiben, stand es mir auch fest, daß ich bei meiner Vorliebe für Anekdotisches und mehr noch für eine viel Raum in Anspruch nehmende Kleinmalerei mich auf einen bestimmten Abschnitt meines Lebens zu beschränken haben würde."[1] Fontane's lack of self-importance, his ability to regard himself with irony and his very highly developed self-knowledge as an artist would have prompted him to restrict the number of volumes of the proposed autobiography. Not for him was the prospect of filling, for example, five volumes as Felix Dahn was doing during

Superiorität schafft, fehlt uns trotz Schulen und Kasernen nach wie vor." (Erler: "Briefe" vol. 1, p. 426-427)

1 NyA XIV, 7.

the first half of the nineties.[1] Such comprehensiveness in a work dealing with himself and his own life would have seemed inappropriate to one such as Fontane, even in an era in which autobiographies and memoirs running to several volumes were common.[2]

In the autobiographical works Fontane partly reconstructs his own life. The lives of those around him, both of relatives, close friends and more distant acquaintances are also important. But beyond that, he is intent on reproducing the atmosphere of a period or of a way of life. In the case of "Meine Kinderjahre", this is the existence of a small boy in a little harbour town on the Baltic Sea during the first third of the nineteenth century. With this comes the plan of depicting the family of Huguenot stock with its own special traditions of which Fontane always remained very conscious. By simply drawing on memorable events and impressions of his childhood up to the age of twelve years, Fontane is able to provide "etwas Zeitbildliches"[3] as well as an insight into his own make-up. Here already the reader encounters perhaps the most striking element in Fontane's autobiographical work i.e. its lack of self-centredness. Although the self and observation of the self is the legitimate object of all autobiography, for Fontane it is not placed at the centre of the stage. Where the self is presented, it appears modestly and often with that self-persiflage which characterizes many of Fontane's

1 Felix Dahn: "Erinnerungen". Leipzig 1890-1895. Fontane's opinion of Dahn is pithily expressed in his diary in connection with a review by Dahn: "Dahn war immer ein Haselant und Phraseur" ("Tagebuch" 21. 2. 1881: NyA XXI, ii, 880). He describes Dahn's memoirs as 'ghastly' in a letter of 9. 11. 1892 to Friedlaender. ("Briefe an Friedlaender", p. 248) in spite of his pleasure at Dahn's laudatory description of a "Tunnel" session on Fontane's ballads. See Dahn: op. cit. vol. 2, p. 435-437.

2 Fontane himself enjoyed reading the memoirs of friends and acquaintances e.g. Fr. Spielhagen: "Finder und Erfinder". Leipzig 1890, Wilhelm Lübke: "Lebenserinnerungen". Berlin 1891, J. Rodenberg: "Bilder aus dem Berliner Leben". Berlin 1891[3], L. Pietsch: "Wie ich Schriftsteller wurde". Berlin 1892 and Karl Büchsel: "Erinnerungen aus dem Leben eines Landgeistlichen". Berlin 1865. In particular, he enjoyed the story-telling in such works: "daran erkennt man den eigentlichen Schriftsteller" (Briefe an Friedlaender", p. 288)

3 NyA XIV, 7.

allusions to himself in his correspondence. Thus the self-importance and the tendency to self-defence found in many autobiographies is completely lacking in his autobiography. This does not mean that Fontane was unaware of his own worth. Various statements in his letters over the years prove that, even where this was not recognized by others, Fontane himself had a realistic view of his own standing and achievement. Sometimes he erred on the side of self-deprecation with regard to his view of the lasting value of his works, but never on the side of self-praise.

"Von Zwanzig bis Dreißig" deals with Fontane's existence between the years 1840 and 1850, but only one-seventh of this work has his own life as its main centre of attention. Even that seventh brings in a great deal of material which does not directly concern him, such as his wife's background and childhood. The 'Zeitbild' element is extremely strong in "Von Zwanzig bis Dreißig" because of the picture given in it of the many writers and figures of the intelligentsia in Berlin with whom Fontane was in contact during these years. The anecdote plays a vital role in both "Meine Kinderjahre" and "Von Zwanzig bis Dreißig".

A sense of disappointment has been voiced by several critics about the fact that Fontane's autobiography of childhood pays apparently little attention to the revelation of his inner self. This is the line adopted by Roy Pascal in his work on autobiography.[1] However, a larger degree of flexibility has been shown in more recent work on the autobiography as a genre with regard to the concept of 'autobiography proper' or 'true autobiography', a criterion which is applied to Pascal's examination of various autobiographies. Recent commentators on autobiography refrain from setting up a canon by which to judge the permissible or the impermissible in the definition of what can be termed autobiography.[2] Elizabeth Bruss

1 See Roy Pascal: "Die Autobiographie. Gehalt und Gestalt". Stuttgart 1965, p. 116-117. The English original of this work: "Design and Truth in Autobiography" (Cambridge, Mass. 1960) does not contain the passage on Fontane.

2 See for example James Olney: 'Autobiography and the Cultural Moment: A Thematic, Historical and Bibliographical Introduction' and 'Some Versions

sets forth a small number of basic characteristics of the autobiography as a genre, but even in these refrains from stipulating "whether autobiography must concern the 'inner' or the 'outer' self or devote more time to the delineation of self than to others".[1] Clearly the flexibility of such an approach is more likely than the normative approach to lead to profitable research on the autobiographical writings of an author who, like Fontane, though attracted to the autobiographical genre, is in fact shy of directly discussing himself. Since the appearance of Pascal's criticism of "Meine Kinderjahre", a few commentators have concentrated more on the aspect of indirect autobiography in the story of Fontane's childhood.[2] They find that the attention given to other aspects actually contains an indirect self-portrait of Fontane himself. Given his predilection for indirect means of portrayal – a striking feature of his fiction, particularly of the novels he wrote in the eighteen-nineties, the decade which also saw the appearance of "Meine Kinderjahre" and "Von Zwanzig bis Dreißig" – it is not surprising that the works on his own life should also use the art of suggestion.

Throughout "Meine Kinderjahre" there is evidence of Fontane's awareness that the anecdotal mode enlivens the straight narrative. Even the biographical sketch of his father, Louis Henri Fontane, which constitutes a major part of the introduction, contains an

of Memory, Some Versions of Bios: The Ontology of Autobiography' p. 3-27 and p. 236-267 respectively of "Autobiography: Essays, Theoretical and Critical". Edited by John Olney. Princeton 1970, and John Olney: "Metaphors of Self: The Meaning of Autobiography". Princeton 1972.

1 E. Bruss: 'Eye for I: Making and Unmaking Autobiography in Film' in "Autobiography ..." as above, p. 299-320. See also by the same author: "Autobiographical Acts: The Changing Situation of a Literary Genre". Baltimore, London 1976, p. 14.

2 Cf. for example W. Müller-Seidel: 'Fontanes Autobiographik' in JbDSG 13, 1969, p. 397-418, H.-H. Reuter: "Fontane", Band 2, p. 757-773, and Günter Niggl: 'Fontanes "Meine Kinderjahre" und die Gattungstradition' in "Sprache und Bekenntnis: Sonderband des Literaturwissenschaftlichen Jahrbuches". Ed by. W. Frühwald and G. Niggl, 1971, p. 257-279.

important anecdotal element. The introductory sketch of Fontane's mother, Emilie Labry Fontane, is only half the length of that of his father, and this sketch is as lacking in anecdotal elements as the father's is characterized by them. This factor becomes a principle throughout the story of Fontane's childhood. The passages concerning Emilie Fontane contain an anecdotal element only so far as Emilie's reactions to her husband's actions are concerned. Fontane's brothers and sister, Jenny,[1] are not mentioned individually in the work. In the introductory sketch on the family biographical details about Fontane's father and grandfather, Louis and Pierre Barthélemy are outlined against the larger historical background (Wars of Liberation, the fall of Lombard, Battle of Jena) and the development of the family fortunes on the male side is enlivened with anecdotes of both Theodor's and Louis' deprivations with regard to clothing as schoolboys. This essentially trivial topic portrays the strained circumstances of the family in both generations, thus spanning an historical period of over a quarter of a century, from circa 1806 with the father's entry into the "Graues Kloster" school until Fontane's entry into the 'Gewerbeschule' in 1833. Father and son share a sense of humour regarding their past exposure to ridicule from schoolmates, and a personal rapport and similarity between them is indirectly indicated through this first pair of personal anecdotes, given in the form of a conversation between father and son. Not merely humour joins the two, but even the content of their stories and the friendly rivalry of their claim to having been the worst and most ridiculously dressed boys in their milk and orange-coloured outfits.[2]

The easy transitions between different generations – from Pierre Barthélemy to Louis to young Theodor – are accompanied by Fontane's capacity to glide gracefully between general historical references and personal recollections. The poor clothing anecdote is a lively way of humorously presenting a fact which must have been depressing for the family, i.e. the sorry state of their finances. This

1 His sister, Elise, was born (too late for the story in any case) in 1838.
2 NyA XIV, 10.

anecdote introduces the subject of schooling which leads Fontane easily to that subject which is of such great importance in the autobiography as well as in the development of the author himself, namely Louis' unconventional store of knowledge. The manner in which this knowledge is imparted to him seems to have awakened in the boy a natural feeling for narrative and a preference for the anecdotal approach to history. Fontane records two stories about his father's experiences as a soldier in the Wars of Liberation. The first anecdote serves to characterize the high national feeling of the 1812-1813 period. But Louis also uses the story to reject any claim to heroism on his part. The sober tones of this anecdote and its setting in Louis' narrative remind the reader of the common-sense approach to the problem of heroism voiced by Professor Schmidt in "Frau Jenny Treibel" and Dubslav and Lorenzen in "Der Stechlin". In the 1812 anecdote, a noblewoman gives a box on the ear to an apprentice in a Berlin fabric shop on hearing that he prefers his position behind the counter to being elsewhere, i.e. in combat.[1] This anecdote, which is included in order to back up Louis' claim that fear of ostracism and not heroism prompted him to enlist, holds the balance with his other war-time story that of the lateral shot at the Battle of Groß-Görschen on 2 May 1813. Although not heroic, he is not a coward caught by a bullet while retreating![2]

This initial portrait of Fontane's father contains almost all the elements of the more detailed presentation of his personality in the rest of the autobiography. Here already we find those characteristics of his father, which on reflection can be seen as characteristics inherited by the author: humour, self-persiflage, lack of pomposity, charm, ease in discourse, rapport with the listener. The faults included in this early sketch (such as Louis' occasional lapse of politeness in dealing with university-educated but less informed townspeople, or the reference to the fatal leisure his father enjoyed – an early indirect allusion to his passion for gambling) are not damning, and it is only with the portrait of Emilie Fontane that

1 NyA XIV, 12.
2 Ibid. 13.

the tension between the parents, which underlies all the scenes between them in the autobiography, is first mooted.[1]

The artistic nature of Fontane's mode of procedure with regard to the use of anecdote in "Meine Kinderjahre" is evident in the way he prepares and anticipates his subject-matter. He does not attack a subject and deal with it exhaustively on a single occasion. Frequently a subject is broached several chapters before he returns to deal with it in more detail, or with a different purpose in mind. This may be partly because the different strands of his narrative interweave into various areas of interest, but it is also due to the carefully planned method of the autobiographer. An example of this is the manner in which Fontane deals with his father's love of historical anecdotes, in particular those about Napoleon and his marshals. Louis' knowledge, especially in this area of history, far transcends that of better educated members of Swinemünde society. Fontane sees his own mode of conversation as an inheritance from his father, and even 'hears' his father when re-reading conversations from his own novels. It is clear therefore that the figure of Louis is of the greatest importance from the artistic point view. In Chapter 10 during a dinner party conversation, Louis makes the statement that he too would have offered his wife, like Doctor Bertrand, to Napoleon on Saint Helena, which leads in this chapter to the delightfully rendered scene of parental disagreement.[2] The Napoleonic theme reappears under the guise of the father's 'Socratic method'[3] of teaching the young Theodor history, which contrasts with the more sober methods employed by Doctor Lau and Doctor Philippi, described in Chapter 13. Chapter 16 provides the father's recapitulation forty years later (during Fontane's visit to him in 1867) of the anecdote of Marshal Ney's execution. This anecdote with its reflection of Ney's resignation to death and his lack of pomposity is admirably suited to

1 Notwithstanding the fact that Fontane generously vindicates his mother of blame for the unhappy relationship, the charm of the picture of Louis makes the reader wonder if Fontane did not secretly question the wisdom of her acerbic reactions to her husband's escapades, great and small.

2 NyA XIV, 94-98.

3 Ibid. 95 and 125.

the resignation of Fontane senior in the face of his own imminent death. Th chord struck by the conversation about Napoleon and Doctor Bertrand in Chapter 10 proves the superiority of Louis over his conversation partners and above all his lack of middle-class prudery in conversation. The same chord recurs in Chapter 13 with the education topic, and sounds for the last time in Chapter 16 as an artistically appropriate ending for the last meeting between father and son.[1] The major factors in the characterization of Louis Fontane can be seen, therefore, to have been associated with his interest in the Napoleonic period: superiority in social discourse, lack of fear of the risqué, incompatibility with his wife, exciting if eccentric educational approach, humour and resignation.

The employment of a further historical anecdote in Chapter 16, this time from the Thirty Years' War, allows Fontane to link the theme of death with another subject which was of vital importance in his father's fate, i.e. money. The story concerns the burning by the Swedes of a bailiff from Neuenhagen for the sake of money.[2] In the light of the fate of Fontane senior, there is a touch of humour in his general comment on the subject of money in this connection: "Man soll nicht einen Amtmann rösten, um es zu kriegen; aber wenn man was hat, dann soll man's festhalten."[3] Both father and son agree in the sequel to this anecdote that their taste would not allow them to sleep in the room in which this historical incident took place, although some people actually do. This sequel is a subtle reminder to the reader of a conversation between Louis and the young Theodor recorded in Chapter 11, in which both of them express their horror at the court official calmly smoking and working in the room which witnessed the gruesome murders committed for the sake of money by a local.[4] Fascination with murder and ghost stories

1 Fontane's father shows the appropriateness of Ney's last words, as caught in the anecdote, to the human condition: " 'Pourquoi tous ces titres? ... Michel Ney .. rien de plus ... et bientôt un peu de poudre.' Und dann fielen die Schüsse. Ja, 'bald bloß noch ein bißchen Staub.' Eigentlich paßt es auf jeden und zu jeder Stunde." (ibid. 160)

2 NyA XIV, 165. The story is also told in "Oderland" (NyA X, 87).

3 Ibidem.

4 Ibid. 104.

provides a further parallel between father and son. The money theme in the Thirty Years' War anecdote provides the cue for Louis to reinterpret his life's problems, mainly the problematical marriage, the miseries of which were often caused by his own gambling.

The motif of punishment, or of the parents' reaction to misdemeanour, recurs in Chapters 11, 14, 15 and 17. This factor alone characterizes the incompatibility of the parents in a small but significant way. Through anecdotal narration of the adventures of childhood and of his parent's reactions to them, Fontane is able to give both a picture of himself as a boy and a characterization of his parents as well as a partial explanation for their separation in later years. The reappearance of the same subject-matter under different guises ensures that the reader is not tired by a more systematic and exhaustive approach to the topic of punishment and the incompatibility of the parents. Here again Fontane's art is characterized by its subtle suggestions, and little stories and scenes from childhood give the background directly to the reader with the vivid dialogue of the characters, instead of pontificating statements and tedious psychological analyses on the part of the narrator.

Throughout "Meine Kinderjahre", Fontane as an artist is conscious of the dual purpose alluded to in the foreword, namely the presentation of his own boyhood and a picture of the times, the internal and the external world.[1] A study of the anecdote in "Meine Kinderjahre" helps to demonstrate how Fontane ensures smooth transitions between the general and the particular plane. In some cases the general atmosphere which he wishes to characterize is dealt with at the beginning of a chapter, while the narrative again focusses on the particular level (the boy himself or his parents) towards the conclusion.[2] This method ensures that those chapters

1 Günter Niggl has drawn attention to the fact that no autobiographer in Germany since Goethe either intended or realized such a close linking of the internal and the external world. See G. Niggl: op. cit., p. 266.

2 A letter of 26. 12. 1892, written before Fontane's corrections on "Meine Kinderjahre" began, shows both his confidence and his doubts about his approach which favoured the description of 'trivialities': " ... ich weiche

which emphasize the 'Zeitbild' element remain within the realm of autobiography and do not become digressions. Chapters 6, 7, 8 and 12 focus attention on the world outside the family confines and set a larger backdrop behind the small boy's story. In these chapters, the autobiographer gives special emphasis to the artistically indispensable Swinemünde atmosphere as well as the historical background of the years 1827-1832. In the chapter trilogy, "Die Stadt, ihre Bewohner und die Honoratioren", "Die Schönebergs und Scherenbergs" and "Die Krauses", Fontane wishes to interweave the immediate family's relationship with its milieu with the vivid picture of a small Baltic port and the account of the colourful prominenti of its society. The anecdotes which he chooses to characterize and enliven the narrative about the town are of the simplest nature possible. They are quietly humorous and are told in the nonchalant manner which he assumes for such trifles. Chapter 6 gives, apart from a description of the harbour section of Swinemünde, pen portraits of members of three families and six other 'Honoratioren'. A schematic outline of the chapter's contents shows how Fontane is at pains to continually move the plane of the narration back from the physical and social background to himself or his parents. Such an outline runs as follows: colourful portrait of port, sense impressions on Fontane, boy and man; two anecdotes on ships, (the Mentor and the Royal George); port description ending with the "Pavillon" where Fontane 'père' was in the habit of losing his money; reconstructed conversation between Louis and his sister-in-law on the honourableness of being a croupier.[1] The first section of Chapter 6 ends with this conversation. Already here Fontane's mode of procedure is clear: an imaginary

von dem Ueblichen ab und erzähle nur Kleinkram. Meine Überzeugung, daß das das Richtige sei, ist unerschüttert, aber daneben bleibt doch die Frage, ob ich's im Maß richtig getroffen und wenn richtig getroffen, ob das Publikum Lust hat, meinen Standpunkt gelten zu lassen." ("Briefe an Friedlaender", p. 205-206) Many of the anecdotes are indeed concerned with trivialities, but the overall effect of the work is not lessened thereby, and the public loved the book.

1 NyA XIV, 56.

walk through Swinemünde leaves the central 'Kirchenplatz' where the Fontanes lived as soon as possible in favour of the 'Bollwerk', "eine Uferstraße, wie sie nicht poetischer gedacht werden konnte".[1] The description of the poetic area of the town reminds the reader of Franziska's tales from her childhood in "Graf Petöfy".[2] Then the Mentor and the Royal George anecdotes interrupt and enliven with their unusual and dramatic element the descriptive flow of the port scene. In the two anecdotes, Fontane himself comes to the fore, firstly as the small boy who has a favourite ship, and secondly as an adult in England watching the recovery of a ship which had sunk in the eighteenth century.[3] The end of the imaginary walk down the harbour brings the narrator to the "Pavillon" which by an association of ideas can bring the narrative back to those gambling habits of Louis Henri already indicated in the references to money and marital problems in Chapters 1, 2 and 5.

Thus, the figures of father and son loom surprisingly large in an ostensible picture of the town of Swinemünde. The rest of Chapter 6 following this introductory section has as its base a similar pattern. The general Swinemünde element alternates constantly with references to the Fontanes. The schematic outline is as follows: international nature of population; practical jokes under influence of alcohol, (example: anecdote of tooth extraction); reference to worse tricks played by wealthy families in the country; anecdote of Fontane couple being left by noble couples to accompany each other to table at private dinner party ("Eh bien, Madame, Dieu le veut");[4] gambling anecdote about father; the Königks, fate of Königk's son, commented on as a paradox by Louis Henri; the

1 NyA XIV, 52.

2 See NyA II, 59 f. For a thought-provoking chapter on the importance of the poetic element in the Swinemünde background, see Reuter: 'Neuruppin und Swinemünde' in "Fontane", vol. 1, p. 87-110.

3 Fontane is unable to resist the evocation of a powerful memory and relates the anecdote of the recovery of the Royal George, witnessed by him in Portsmouth in 1858. As is his wont in the case of not strictly relevant anecdotal material, he puts it in a long footnote.

4 NyA XIV, 59.

clergyman Kastner, a son of Kastner becoming Professor in Kazan, Louis Fontane's inevitable reference ot the population of Kazan; Mayor Beda's Southern beauties, his Spanish wife and daughters, Fontane's visit to Beda's son in Scotland in 1858; the beauty of Swinemünde women – Louis' enthusiasm for the Thomas belles, which is shared by his son; anecdote about shipping director Bauer, whose lack of formal education is mirrored in his calling the three leading families, the "Triumphirate der Stadt";[1] Consul Thompson, famous for his punch and the merchant, Schultze, famous for lemonade and tenor voice. The narrator sees in him a reflection of himself at certain periods of his career: there is not much difference between singing and poetry.[2] This outline of Chapter 6 shows how frequently Fontane makes the link between either himself or his parents and the prominent citizens and families of Swinemünde. Similarly, the external description of the harbour is deliberately brought to a close with a focus on the problematic gambling habits of the father. This is not done in a lachrymose way, but with the quiet, though not unfeeling humour which characterizes even Fontane's treatment of the tension of his parents' marriage. The final 'Triumphirate' anecdote is an amusing example of small town politics: the prominent citizens feel threatened by Bauer's arrival and their relief in discovering that he is an autodidact is expressed in the glee with which they recall his blunder: "An dem unglücklichen 'ph' war seine Macht gescheitert".[3]

The middle chapter of this trilogy, Chapter 7, contains no anecdotes in its account of the Schöneberg and Scherenberg families. However, especially when taken in conjunction with the other two chapters, it provides the vital key to an interpretation of Fontane's artistic (as distinct from the merely informational) intention in this trilogy. The two focal points in Chapter 7 are the exciting nature of the shops in Swinemünde (example: the Schöneberg shops) and the artistic strain in the solid merchant family of the Scherenbergs. Only in the last paragraph does Fontane bother to bring the external

1 NyA XIV, 66.
2 Ibid. 67.
3 Ibid. 66.

line of the narrative back to his own family, with the mention of his mother's relationship with the Scherenbergs. The fact that he hardly ever entered their house is expressly mentioned. Why then does he go to the trouble of writing almost a whole chapter on the Scherenbergs, particularly when he has already written a none too successful book on the most famous literary member of the family, Christian Friedrich Scherenberg? The focal points of the chapter, seen in the context of Fontane's art of suggestion provide the answer: the exciting nature of the Schöneberg shops is forever allied in Fontane's mind with the artistic strain in his own make-up. He forbears throughout the childhood autobiography directly treating of himself as an artist. Yet he tells the reader in the foreword that the child is father to the man – this legitimizes writing about one's boyhood. Since he does not review the Fontane family for artistic ancestors, (a justifiable investigation, when one considers Pierre Barthélemy Fontane's position as drawing master in the royal household[1]) an indirect parallel must be found. The Scherenbergs are the parallel, and Fontane indirectly indicates this by mentioning conversations with Konsistorialrat Fournier, the "expert in this field",[2] namely the field of the Huguenot families in Prussia. The fact that the Scherenbergs married into 'French colony' families is seen as responsible for the unusual artistic strain evidenced through three generations of this merchant family. It is the combination of commerce and art that strikes Fontane in the Scherenbergs, and the reader supplies the question tacitly suggested, if merchants can do it, why not chemists?[3] The shops in Ruppin, Fontane's birth-place, had "etwas Kleines und Spießbürgerliches, das der

1 Even this item about Fontane's ancestry, of which most families would be proud, is ironized by the author through his reference to Schadow's remark in his diary (NyA XIV, 9) that Pierre Barthélemy's French was good!

2 NyA XIV, 71.

3 Hans-Heinrich Reuter calls the Scherenberg section "eine bezeichnende, insgeheim autobiographische Passage der 'Kinderjahre'. "(H.-H. Reuter: 'Entwicklung und Dialektik des Heimatreflexes im Werk Theodor Fontanes' in WB 1965, p. 66)

Phantasie nirgends Nahrung gab",[1] while those in Swinemünde have an evocative mixture of paraphernalia for sailors and tasteful objects for the home.

Chapter 8 on the Krauses family contains three anecdotes. Thr first is a personal one concerning Fontane's attempt in 1837 to visit old Privy Counsellor Krause in the Hotel de Portugal in Berlin.[2] The second concerns a conversation in which Frau Kommerzienrätin Krause surprises the theologian, Marheineke, with her knowledge (culled from "Meyers Konversationslexikon"!) of the Idealist philosophers.[3] The third anecdote returns to the Fontane home with an account of Louis Fontane's reaction to being fooled by his fellow townsmen into thinking that he had been admitted to the Freemasons in a ceremony marked by its hocus-poxus.[4] The intention of Chapter 8 is to provide the reader with a background of an aspect of Swinemünde life which is by association intimately connected with the artistic element brought up in Chapter 7. In matters of refinement, the Krauses set the tone in Swinemünde, as the Schönebergs did in stability and affluence and the Scherenbergs in talent and intellect. The descriptions in Chapter 8 give a detailed account of the Krause household with emphasis on those unusual features which made an impression on the young Fontane. Again here it is the lack of 'Spießbürgerlichkeit'[5] (symbolized by the Krauses' furniture in comparison to that of the Fontane household) which brings Fontane to deal with the Krauses in detail. In the matter of a general appreciation of the Swinemünde atmosphere he sees the possibility of only one interpretation, namely, that it was characterized by a most unusual lack of philistinism for such a small place.[6] Pettiness and narrow-mindedness were absent, in spite of the tendency to practical joking illustrated in Chapter 6 with the tooth extraction anecdote and in Chapter 7 with the 'Konversations-

1 NyA XIV, 69.
2 Ibid. 75.
3 Ibid. 79.
4 Ibid. 80.
5 Ibid. 77.
6 Ibid. 80.

lexikon' and Freemason anecdotes. The Freemason story has the advantage of bringing the narrative back to the external autobiographical base with the immediate family. It not only shows up a general facet of Swinemünde life, one which Fontane has been playing off in Chapter 8 against the refinement embodied in the head of the Krause family, but also is yet another in the long chain of stories and anecdotes which reflect Frau Fontane's sober disapproval of her husband's demeanour and his characteristic acceptance of defeat with good humour. Another indication of the importance Fontane attaches to the Swinemünde atmosphere is his closing remark in Chapter 8 that he experienced a similar superiority of tone later only in artistic and literary circles, but never as something which prevailed over a whole town.[1]

The portrait of Swinemünde in this chapter trilogy (its ugliness and beauty, it bankrupt and affluent, artistic, refined, roguish and respectable citizens, above all its international atmosphere) provides a broad base for the growing boy. It was a place with "Weltbeziehungen"[2] whose consuls fly their international flags on Hohenzollern holidays and in which a hypothetical captain could deck out his ship for a journey to Cape Horn in Schönebergs' shop.[3] If the reader considers that Fontane's purpose in painting the atmosphere of the Baltic town in the early part of the nineteenth century is merely "secondary",[4] or that Fontane relates it only sporadically to the story of his own life,[5] then the significance of this whole section of the childhood story is either lost, or at best seriously diminished. Besides the linking of the general and particular with reference to the town and himself in Chapters 6, 7 and 8, Fontane bridges an even greater gap in Chapter 12. Here political events across Europe are linked with the little boy through the account

1 This mention of artistic and literary circles is the most direct reference to the importance of the town for his literary development. See NyA XIV, 80.

2 "Der Stechlin", NyA VIII, 124.

3 See NyA XIV, 69.

4 Alan Robinson: 'Recollections in Tranquillity', p. 123.

5 Roy Pascal: "Die Autobiographie", p. 116: "Nur ab und zu versucht er, Ton und Farbe einer Situation, wie sie das Kind erlebte, wieder hervorzurufen".

of the avid interest he paid to newspaper accounts of the revolutions around 1830. True to form, this interest is depicted for its poetic appeal to the boy, and his excitement is caught in the references to the laterna magica images of political upheavals of the 1820's, his delight at fetching the daily newspapers from the "Kronprinzessin Elizabeth" and reading aloud accounts of the French take-over of Algeria, the July revolution, the Belgian fight for independence and the Polish revolution of November 1830.

Fontane's comparatively lengthy discussion at this point – mainly from his standpoint as an a d u l t – hinges around his ambivalent attitude towards revolution. It is not without significance that he stresses his feeling for order and for the aesthetic element. Chapter 12 is a tour de force in its combination of evocation of the past (the small boy and the revolutions), the present (a problematical perhaps 'immoral' attitude which ambivalently wants the strong side to win – from a sense of order – as much as it wants the cause of freedom to prevail) and an apparent excursus on the writing of military history. The presence of an officer called von Witzleben, who gave Fontane's war books sympathetic reviews in the 1860's and 1870's, is used as a cue for the apparent digression, which ends with the categorical statement that writing on wars is the same as writing ('ordinary') history and should be subject to a large extent to criticism from a literary, and not merely a military point of view.[1] This appears to have come a long way from the little boy collecting the newspapers at the quay in 1830. The unspoken connection here is of course, as in the case of the linking of the general and the particular in Chapters 6 to 8, the artistic one. The plea for the aesthetic appreciation of works on war history goes side by side in this chapter with the laterna magica pictures of political upheavals of the 1820's and the cannon shots playing 'ducks and drakes' on the Swinemünde harbour in 1831. Without once saying it outright, Fontane underlines again and again the importance of his early political impressions for him as an a r t i s t. This is the real significance of Chapter 12 so far as the autobiography

1 NyA XIV, 119.

is concerned: it does not merely provide an amusing account of a precocious youngster with prodigious reading talents and political finesse. Beyond that, the very way in which Chapter 12 is written provides the reader with the clue to why it was written, within the framework of Fontane's overall purpose. The poetic importance of these early reading experiences is indicated slightly more specifically in his recording of his joy at the fact that the Belgian revolt started during the performance of Auber's opera "La muette de Portici" on 25 August 1830 in Brussels. The riots started precisely at the point where a revolutionary song was being sung.[1]

Chapter 12 finishes on the level of external autobiography once more, with the account of the withdrawal of the cholera cordon, of Thompson's farewell supper for the officers and Louis Fontane's farewell speech. Events on the broad European front and the implicit look forward to the effect on Fontane as a creative artist of the early reading once more give way to the simpler account of incidents in the town and, inevitably, to a further example of Frau Fontane's disapproval of her husband's demeanour, this time the bone of contention being the pharmaceutical allusions in Louis' speech.

This review of Fontane's procedures in Chapters 6, 7, 8 and 12 has shown the author's ease in linking the general and the particular: the general being the picture promised in the foreword of a Baltic coast town in the early nineteenth century, as well as the historical backdrop of revolutions and wars in Europe, which, as Fontane points out, were plentiful precisely during the half-decade spent by the Fontane family in Swinemünde between 1827 and 1832. Both of these general elements are, however, included not as a mere backdrop, but are linked with the theme of the artistic influences on the young Fontane. The particular level is that of the boy himself, or also frequently of his father – both are so closely linked that what affects the one affects the other. The anecdote's place is in the enlivening of the narrative, the provision of concrete illustration of

1 " ... ich fand dies unbeschreiblich schön, vielleicht in der dunklen, für eine Poetennatur immerhin schmeichelhaften Vorstellung, daß hier ein Lied eine politische Tat geweckt oder gezeitigt habe." (NyA XIV, 114)

general statements made by Fontane as narrator and it also always serves to bring the narrative back to the line of the external autobiography.

The elements of the autobiography of boyhood could be summarized in the form of certain key-words from which a significant picture emerges. These key-words would be: cosmopolitan; historical; dramatic; refined; artistic; entertaining; charming; fascinating. Such elements provide pivotal points of the narrative, whether it deals with Theodor, Louis, Swinemünde, the townspeople or the revolutionary period. These epithets can be applied to Fontane as an adult and as a writer. Had he set out to demonstrate blatantly that these aspects of his background had a profound influence on him as an adult and as a writer, the effect would have been quite different. Such a direct approach would have necessitated detailed psychological analysis of himself, and would propably eventually tire the reader and prompt his disbelief. By showing this phenomenon indirectly in an artistic way and leaving the reader to draw his own conclusions, Fontane skirts both risks of appearing self-centred as a personality and flat as an artist.[1] He introduces the reader to the enchanted land of childhood,[2] but it is only an apparent landscape. In reality, it is a deliberate portrait of the artist.

It is mainly through the static nature of the past evoked that Fontane is able to impose artistic unity on the story. As has been pointed out, a great deal of the narrative concentrates on the Swinemünde element of Fontane's boyhood, thus giving the work almost total unity of place.[3] The fact also that the characters are not shown as developing, but as they w e r e, imposes a further unity. Time almost stands still[4] so far as the Swinemünde period is taken as a unit. Fontane takes care not to show himself as a boy at different stages of development. The intermezzo with Louis Fontane in 1867 is the only time-break of serious consequence. It includes the

1 Compare Felix Dahn's continual and tedious self-portrayal in his autobiography.
2 See Georges May: "L'autobiographie". Paris 1979, p. 107-108.
3 Approximately eighty per cent, according to Günter Niggl: op. cit., p. 267.
4 See ibidem.

author's appreciation – again in story form, not through psychological analysis – of the inexorable tragedy of his parents' relationship as well as the premonition of death. Such factors were both temporally and experientially beyond the scope of the small boy. The element of unity, which must have been one of Fontane's aims here, is also one the major factors which earns the work its defining subtitle, "Autobiographischer Roman". We have seen that the recurrence of certain motifs was aided by the employment of anecdotes under different sections of the autobiography, and that these recurrences in themselves added to the unity of the work. Without doubt "Meine Kinderjahre" as a narrative operates on a very selective basis, one which probably prompted Roy Pascal to say that Fontane's account of himself was "ein im Grunde zu sehr vereinfachtes, spannungsloses Bild der kindlichen Seele."[1] Perhaps the subtitle should receive more attention. It may be misleading to take too literally Fontane's humorous suggestion that it protects him against claims of factual error. For Fontane, just approaching the zenith of his achievement in fiction, the use of the word "novel" in the subtitle cannot merely have been a form of self-protection. It has been recognised in general critical literature on autobiography that the character of the autobiographical persona as well as those of the other personae in an autobiographical narrative are to a certain extent fictional. It is above all the selectivity with which Fontane approaches the story of his boyhood that marks "Meine Kinderjahre" as an artistic structure. He was not intent on including everything, for this is not possible. It is w h a t he picks (in particular the poetic element linking the general and the particular) and especially h o w he treats it which brings home to the reader the truly artistic endeavour of the novelist in his autobiography of boyhood. It is perhaps a matter of taste if one believes that this principle of selectivity finally produces only an 'over-simplified picture', or it may be that such a verdict is based on a disappointed search for information of the psychological, self-analytical kind. In such a search the literary, artistic element of Fontane's boyhood story does not receive due attention.

1 R. Pascal: "Die Autobiographie", p. 117.

3. "Von Zwanzig bis Dreißig" (1898)

In turning from the happy and comparatively easy task of artistically reliving his childhood for the composition of "Meine Kinderjahre", Fontane, when he began to write "Von Zwanzig bis Dreißig" in the winter of 1894 must have suffered that jolt which autobiographers experience in dealing with their adult place in society.[1] His modesty and self-effacement are apparent in "Von Zwanzig bis Dreißig" in the sections on his literary colleagues. This is also the case however in the outline given of his own career in the 1840's and in the sections on his private life. For Lilian Furst, this quality of self-effacement is the cause of the unsatisfactory nature of "Von Zwanzig bis Dreißig", although it was commendable in Fontane as a human being.[2] The sections on Fontane's literary friends[3] occupy the bulk of his autobiography, so that only approximately one-seventh of the work is reserved for Fontane's private life. A striking feature of Fontane's presentation of his friends and acquaintances in "Von Zwanzig bis Dreißig" is the marked lack of that semi-hagiographical note which mars some other contemporary works of a biographical and autobiographical nature.[4] The modesty which is characteristic of the autobiographical sections has its counterpart

1 Cf. Georg Misch: "Geschichte der Autobiographie", vol. 1 part 1, p. 589, (Bern 1949³) and vol. 4, part 2 (Frankfurt am Main 1969) p. 17. Also Bernd Neumann: op. cit., p. 60-82, Philippe Lejeune: "L'autobiographie en France". Paris 1971, p. 75-76, and Esther Salaman: "From Aksakov and De Quincey to Tolstoy and Proust". London 1973, p. 7.

2 Lilian R. Furst: 'The Autobiography of an Extrovert: Fontane's "Von Zwanzig bis Dreißig"' in GLL 12, 1958-59, p. 293.

3 In her study of Fontane's autobiography, Brenda Doust draws attention to the portrayal of the figures of Louis Schneider, Richard Lucae and George Hesekiel as well as to the portrayal of the atmosphere of the "Kreuz-Zeitung". See op. cit., p. 158-179.

4 In an explanatory passage, he seems to refer obliquely to the hagiographical approach by stating that his own treatment of his contemporaries, warts and all, is undertaken with the knowledge that his countrymen had for their heroes, not saints, but figures with obvious faults, such as Frederick the Second, Wrangel and Bismarck. (See NyA XV, 164-165)

in the biographical sections in a sense of realism and proportion.[1]

The personalities who played a part in this stage of Fontane's life and in the city of Berlin in the 1840's are brought before the reader's eyes through extensive use of the anecdote. Because of the numerousness of these characters, only a short space is allotted to each individual. The anecdote stands out as the principal method of character portrayal in "Von Zwanzig bis Dreißig". Because of the diversity of the component parts, the impression given by the second part of his autobiography is much less unified than that provided in the autobiography of boyhood. Instead of an evocation of the rather uniform (in any case Fontane's artistically u n i f i e d) childhood background, he was obliged to evoke different kinds of atmosphere: of Leipzig, of London, of life in the army, of the literary life in Berlin, of the Berlin revolution of 1848, and of his professional life as pharmaceutical chemist and temporary teacher. Of necessity, this backdrop contains a mass of threads which are not always closely related, and a story emerges that lacks the organic impression given by "Meine Kinderjahre". The anecdote is important in both parts of the autobiography for its function in revitalizing a personally experienced past. We saw that in "Meine Kinderjahre" it was used, not primarily for its information value or in order to characterize outsiders (non-members of the Fontane family) for their own sakes, but in order to assist in the artistic intention of providing indirect characterization of the author himself.

In "Von Zwanzig bis Dreißig" the anecdote is used to a large

1 In writing to Rodenberg of his anxiety that the Storm chapter of "Von Zwanzig bis Dreißig" might not have been acceptable, he discusses the principle of his procedure in general with regard to the treatment of others: "Mein Interesse für Menschendarstellung ist von der Wahrheit oder doch von dem, was mir als Wahrheit erscheint, ganz unzertrennlich; ich muß mich im Guten und Bösen, im Hübschen und Nichthübschen über ihn aussprechen können; wird mir das versagt, so hört das Vergnügen für m i c h auf. Ich gehe aber noch weiter und behaupte: auch für andre. Das Zeitalter des Schönrednerischen ist vorüber, und die rosafarbene Behandlung schädigt nur den , dem sie zuteil wird." ("Briefe an Rodenberg", p. 83-84. Fontane's emphasis) Anecdotes play an important role in the presentation of both sides of the personalities dealt with – "im Hübschen und Nichthübschen".

extent as a method of characterization of many individuals, some of whom have otherwise faded into obscurity, others who at any rate still have their place in literary history, but all of whom were a living part of the Berlin of the middle and latter part of the nineteenth century. For although the title "Von Zwanzig bis Dreißig" suggests only the years of that decade in Fontane's life, i.e. 1840-1850, the content of the work draws on a much larger section of time, and Fontane's knowledge of the people described is necessarily influenced by his experience of them right up until the eighteen-nineties, the period of composition.[1] The imposition of an external time-limit does however impart a certain unity to the book, and the majority of the anecdotes used in it stem from this decade. By concentration on depicting his friends and literary acquantinaces as personalities Fontane both gives himself more scope for the employment of anecdotes and saves his work from taking on the tone of a cosy literary history. Moreover, he was thereby spared the presentation of an evaluation of the literary works of his less talented colleagues. An impression of his personal evaluation of their work creeps only sporadically into "Von Zwanzig bis Dreißig". Fontane's explicit aim is to present his friends for what they were, and not for what they achieved. He is careful to note already in June 1895 in a letter to Julius Rodenberg, the later editor of the magazine version of the "Tunnel" chapter, that it was "mehr menschlich als literarisch gehalten".[2] His presentation of the various characters in the form of potted biographical sketches is itself conducive to the introduction of anecdote, and frequently a complete sketch depends for its structure on a string of anecdotes. The writer's intention in using the method of brief biographical sketches is elucidated in a further letter to Rodenberg: "Die kürzeren biographischen Skizzen verfolgen den

1 Cf. Lilian Furst: op. cit., p. 287. Hans-Heinrich Reuter also writes in this connection: "Lediglich die beiden Eckpfeiler der acht Bücher des Werkes – vom Eintritt in die Rosesche Apotheke bis zur Hochzeit und Auflösung des 'Literarischen Kabinetts" – suchen äußerlich einen zeitlichen Rahmen abzustechen, den der Erzähler allerorts ebenso nach ruckwärts wie nach vorn überschreitet, das Buch zu einem kritischen Lebensrückblick 'von zehn bis achtzig' ausweitend." (H.-H. Reuter: "Fontane", vol. 2, p. 758)

2 "Briefe an Julius Rodenberg", p. 76.

Zweck, die Buntheit der Gesellschaft zu zeigen, was doch, auf das Wesen des Tunnels hin angesehn, eine gewisse Bedeutung hat."[1] It is the same 'Mannigfaltigkeit',[2] apparently, as that which would have been predominant in the proposed last part of Fontane's autobiography, "Kritische Jahre – Kritiker-Jahre". In the fragment of this plan, he already apologizes to his prospective readers for jumping from one subject to another and thus forfeiting unity for the sake of variety.[3] Upwards of forty personalities from the newspaper, publishing and literary world of contemporary Berlin are brought into Fontane's account in "Von Zwanzig bis Dreißig". Some of these are dealt with within the space of a few pages, and the impression is inevitably created that too much is attempted in too little space. This impression is underlined by Fontane's method of separating off a sub-section for each member of the "Tunnel" club. On the other hand, the "Tunnel" section is extremely interesting in its own right, but it appears to throw the rest of the autobiography out of balance.

The role of the anecdote in the context of the portrayal of literary Berlin in "Von Zwanzig bis Dreißig" is straightforward. It is used to provide information, to characterize the people Fontane has chosen to mention, to preserve their manner of speaking and of looking at the world and to present the atmosphere of collegiality among them, e.g. the portrayal of the atmosphere on the "Kreuz-Zeitung". An advantage of the method is that it spares Fontane unnecessary psychological analysis of figures with whom he was associated. The anecdote is particularly effective in relieving the author of pontificating about his friends and acquaintances. The little stories are factual and dramatic and speak for themselves. They do not simply rely on the writer's authority as would a plain statement about some psychological aspect of his colleagues. Fontane does not have to pose as an authority on human nature while he has little characteristic stories to tell. This is particularly clear in the portraits of Louis Schneider and George Hesekiel. Schneider

1 "Briefe and Julius Rodenberg", p. 87.

2 "Kritische Jahre – Kritiker-Jahre" (NyA XV, 388)

3 Ibidem.

was not particularly well liked by Fontane, although he respected him and was grateful for his help. This is acknowledged in the portrait. The anecdotes on Schneider however give us an impression of his sharp tongue, his lack of a poetic talent (in spite of his importance in the writers' club), the lessons he has learned from life and an explanation of his political position. True to form, and in keeping with statements in the letters to Rodenberg, Fontane does not try to prettify the pictures of his contemporaries, but the anecdotes show the less pleasant aspects without malice. The portrait of Schulrat Methfessel, a Prussian bureaucrat "comme il faut", is entirely negative. He is characterized as being irritatingly conscious of giving everyone his title at each mention. Fontane comments also on Methfessel's unsociable habit of watching the time in company. This little subsection ends with a typically Fontane-like investigation: did Methfessel possess true 'Menschlichkeit'? The anecdote about his treatment as school inspector of a young girl for some indiscretions in her diary and of the school headmistress shows that his action was out of all proportion with the incident, and Fontane for once actually words a condemnation in the gentle terms that he, had he been in Methfessel's position, would have acted differently.[1] An interesting light is incidentally thrown on education in nineteenth-century Berlin by this little anecdote. Its main function, however, and that which Fontane no doubt had in mind, is the fair examination of Methfessel's character as expressed in this public action, and the anecdote is a reminder of Fontane's growing criticism of Prussianism in the eighteen-nineties.

Nastiness to inferiors must have been a quality which Fontane particularly abhorred, for it is frequently the source of an anecdote, as here in the one about Methfessel. Louis Schneider is also criticised for his retort to young poets seeking his approval of their literary

1 Cf. NyA XV, 231-232. The Methfessel portrayal brings to mind how Fontane managed to make even dull people interesting. This is the result of his keen eye for observation of human life: "Die langweiligen Menschen (sind) gerade so nett und unterhaltlich, wie die interessanten", as Ebba remarks in "Unwiederbringlich" (NyA V, 144).

efforts: "Ich pflege mir meinen kleinen Bedarf selbst zu machen."[1] Fontane adds an extra touch to the portrait by characterizing Schneider through the Lenau anecdote he had already used in "Graf Petöfy". Lenau's considerate and diffident treatment of a waitress who versified in her spare time, contrasts with Schneider's brusque and hurtful attitude towards aspiring poets. The refinement of feeling evidenced in the Lenau story is lacking in Schneider, and an ironical twist of the situation is his own lack of poetic ability. However, Fontane does justice to Schneider's good qualities in the rest of this portrait, and the theatre anecdote applied by Schneider to survival through trial and suffering ("um neun ist alles aus"[2]) is later preserved in "Der Stechlin", when Dubslav ruminates after trying visits to his sick bed: "um zwölf ist alles aus."[3] With this application of the theatre anecdote to everyday life, Fontane is able to end the section on Schneider on a grateful and pleasant note, in spite of other criticisms: "Ich bin ihm bis diese Stunde dankbar: Um neun ist alles aus."[4] In spite of their differences, he can write with sincerity about Schneider: "Was über den Menschen entscheidet, ist seine Gesinnung, Ehrlichkeit der Überzeugungen. Und d i e hatte Louis Schneider ... "[5]

1 NyA, XV, 244. In "Christian Friedrich Scherenberg", Fontane considers the officious treatment by Heinrich Smidt of his literary acquaintance but j u n i o r colleague at the War Ministry Library, Scherenberg, important enough to devote more than half a chapter to it. In both the Schneider and the Smidt anecdotes, it is the ill-treatment of w r i t e r s that catches Fontane's attention.

2 Ibid. 247.

3 NyA VIII, 303. Fontane's second last letter to his wife written two days before his death also uses the phrase " ... Nicht im Sinne einer Todessehnsucht, sondern nur in dem tiefen Verlangen nach Ruhe. Freilich spukt das andere darin vor, was auch wohl recht gut ist." H.-H. Reuter: "Theodor Fontane: Von Dreißig bis Achtzig", p. 494.

4 NyA XV, 247.

5 Ibid. 241.

One section of Fontane's reminiscences, Chapter 7 of "Von Zwanzig bis Dreißig", on George Hesekiel, deals more with Fontane himself than does any other subsection on the members of the "Tunnel" club. The reason for this change of emphasis is due to the need which Fontane must have felt to come to terms in his autobiographical writings with his collaboration in the 1860's with thc ultra-conservative "Kreuz-Zeitung". Hesekiel is dealt with by Fontane in two sections in Chapter 7. No more than half of the chapter bearing his name actually concerns Hesekiel himself. It is clear therefore that Fontane's central concern in the chapter is not really Hesekiel but the newspaper for which they both worked. In Hesekiel's case, working for it induced no crisis of conscience, as he was extremely conservative in political outlook.Fontane makes the point that this prevented Hesekiel's being fully accepted by the "Tunnel" group, which was on the whole 'nationalliberal'.[1]

The author's digression on the "Kreuz-Zeitung" is flanked on either side by his treatment of Hesekiel, so that this man's career and personality are the subject of the beginning and the end of the chapter. Several anecdotes characterize Hesekiel, bringing out his generosity, wit and self-persiflage. Like Lucae and Schneider, he had an excellent command of language and was a great narrator of anecdotes. Fontane directly refers in connection with Hesekiel's talents as a narrator of anecdotes to his own predilection for the historical anecdote. Hesekiel was "der Mann der historischen Anekdote".[2] However, it is personal anecdotes about Hesekiel which Fontane uses to portray this character, e.g. his

1 See NyA XV, 252. For doubts on this as a proper description of the political colouring of the "Tunnel" club, see the editorial commentary on the "Sitzungsprotokolle und Jahresberichte des Tunnels über der Spree" in Theodor Fontane: "Autobiographische Schriften." Edited by G. Erler, P. Goldmann and J. Krueger. Berlin, Weimar 1982, Band III, 2, p. 73.

2 NyA XV, 258.

humorous reaction to the bad humours of their "Kreuz-Zeitung" colleague, the popular writer, Hermann Gödsche,[1] or his roguish observation that nobody could gainsay him in argument with the support of the "Konversationslexikon", since he had written most of the articles himself.[2] The sincerity of Hesekiel's friendship for Fontane is attested in a little story about his reaction to the latter's observation that he found it difficult to approach people for financial loans. Hesekiel's answer to this: "Gott erhalte dir diese Ungeschicklichkeit"[3] contrasts in its seriousness and sincerity with the other Hesekiel anecdotes, which depend for their effect on his verbal brilliance. Fontane's relationship with Hesekiel was marked more by interest in him than by attraction to him as a person.[4] In the anecdotes here, the colleagues are already on familiar terms, but in reality their close friendship dates only from 1859. One must assume therefore that Fontane used later anecdotes to fill in the details of the pen-portrait, or else that he uses the familiar form of address in order to add to the immediacy of the scenes and catch more closely the atmosphere of collegiality among the journalists. The figure of Hesekiel serves as a narrative 'peg' on which Fontane hangs all kinds of 'garments', such as the life of the newspaper, a vindication of the conservatives, and a discussion of his own political stance. All the anecdotes included in the "Kreuz-Zeitung" digression are meant to show that the conservatives were not as stiff and stolid as might have been expected. Not surprisingly, therefore, the stories used demonstrate what kind of social life obtained on the newspaper, and questions of practical politics are ignored.

1 Hermann Gödsche used the pseudonym Sir John Retcliffe for his 'sensational novels. Since a little anecdote like this also gives the atmosphere among the colleagues on the newspaper, it is quoted here in full: "Es kam vor, daß Goedsche mit einem gewissen Feldherrnschritt auf der Redaktion erschien und hier ohne daß das Geringste vorgefallen war, ein ungeheueres Ergriffensein über einen rätselhaften und vielleicht gar nicht mal existierenden Hergang zur Schau stellte. Hesekiel sagte dann, um diesen falschen Rausch zu markieren, ruhig vor sich hin: 'Goedsche hat heute wieder seine Zahntinktur ausgetrunken'." (NyA XV, 260)

2 Cf. ibid. 253.

3 Ibid. 256.

4 Cf. ibid. 252.

A string of anecdotes constitutes the body of the portrayal of the leading conservatives whom Fontane and his colleagues met through their association with the "Kreuz-Zeitung". Each story reveals some aspect or small incident connected with these men, bringing out their wit, ease of manner, humanity and self-disparagement. One of the Senfft-Pilsachs declares, for example, in response to Fontane's unspoken attempt on their first meeting to guage the extent of his conservatism: "Ich denke über alles anders".[1] This anecdote reveals the intention behind all the anecdotes in this section of the newspaper. It is the human, charming side of such men which appeals to Fontane. He considers it worth preserving, especially because such factors are of importance in his own aesthetic attachment to the aristocracy. The following statement is attributed to one of the Gerlachs: "Ich würde es für klug und wünschenswert halten, wenn wir ehrenhafte Leute von der Presse ganz in ähnlicher Weise wie die Geistlichen an uns bänden, ich meine durch Heirat".[2] With such a story, Fontane wishes to show how little the conventional picture of the Junker has in common with the reality, or at least, as he put it in a typical modifying phrase, what brilliant exceptions were to be found among the cleverest and best of them.[3]

Official meetings with men from the 'Kultusministerium' provide the press-men with proof that many of these are approachable and charming, rather than stiff bureaucrats. Fontane hopes to expose this reality in part with his portrait of Privy Councillor Stiehl. Ferdinand Stiehl does not at all conform to the conventional notion of a civil servant, and is thus admirably suited as an introduction to Fontane's portrayal of a line of conservatives in this section of the Hesekiel chapter. While some of Fontane's letters mention Stiehl in a derogatory way,[4] here the man's humour and self-persiflage

1 NyA XV, 267.
2 Ibid. 261.
3 Ibid. 270.
4 He calls him a 'pompous lout' in a letter of 17. 3. 1872 to Mathilde von Rohr. Cf. NyA XV, 580. The portrait of Stiehl in "Von Zwanzig bis does not give an unversed reader an insight into the fact that he was symbolic of the narrowest kind of Prussian reactionary. The "Stiehlschen

are emphasized. The bulk of Fontane's section on the "Kreuz-Zeitung" is devoted to personalities which come under the heading of the "Cercle intime",[1] i.e. the private parties held in the home of Tuiscon Beutner, who was editor-in-chief of the paper from 1853 to 1872. Fontane's association with this ultra-Loyalist newspaper contrasts sharply with the critical attitude displayed openly in the letters and indirectly in the fiction of his later years. It is inevitable therefore that he should give some explanation during the writing of this section of "Von Zwanzig bis Dreißig" of this apparent paradox. In an extended footnote, he distinguishes between "politischen Anschauungen und menschlichen Sympathien".[2] From the human point of view, he is attracted to the Prussian Junker. He does not share their retrogressive politics but is attracted to those who hold these views. The anecdotes in the "Kreuz-Zeitung" passage deal, appropriately enough for the distinction made in this footnote, with various human qualities of leading Conservatives. Pen-portraits are given of men like Court Preacher Kögel, Arnold von Pilsach, 'Generalsuperintendent' Büchsel and one of the founders of the "Kreuz-Zeitung", Hermann Wagener. Whereas their names are not familiar to the general reader of today, these people were prominent in their day, and as such would have been of interest to contemporary readers. Although this section is almost an apologia for the Conservatives, it is not altogether flattering. Büchsel, e.g. is described as a mixture of Newfoundlander and a fox. The story

Regulative", his regulations for primary schools were notorious. The 'pompous lout' almost became a fictional character. In a fragment of a plan for a literary work, conceived possibly in 1878, "Die Geschichte der Frau v. M., spätere G. R. St.", Fontane jotted down the outlines of a story based on Stiehl's second marriage to Auguste von Massow, née von Canitz (1822-1904), in which Stiehl would have be characterised as a vain anecdote narrator in whom sensuality and Christianity make an unedifying mixture. See NyA XXIV, 211-213 and 836. Clearly, the fictional character based on Stiehl, had it been realised according to plan, would have been less complimentary to the man than the section on him in Fontane's autobiography.

1 NyA XV, 263.

2 Ibid.270.

which lends support to the portrait of Büchsel humorously indicates his cunning and directness. Büchsel's foxiness made him more interesting, Fontane points out, though not more admired.[1]

Fontane claims that the decade spent with the "Kreuz-Zeitung" was a period of contentment for him and names as the main reason for this the pleasantness of life on the newspaper and even more of its social life. The little anecdotes used to describe the Conservatives are intended to portray concretely the reasons why Fontane felt attracted towards the Conservatives. The attraction was on the human side, it was an aesthetic attraction, and this feature, paradoxical as it may seem, remained with Fontane even through the years of his growing disillusionment with the Prussian establishment. By nature Fontane welcomed all expressions of refinement, gentleness and good breeding. It is certainly significant that in this passage he deals only with the social intercourse connected with the newspaper. He is at pains to indicate the freedom of opinion which he encountered in these conservative circles. Two anecdotes support this general point. One is attributed to Professor Friedrich Julius Stahl, who was known for his Lutheran orthodoxy and arch-conservatism. Fontane is aware of the surprise which an anecdote like the following would cause to a reading public acquainted with Stahl's ultra-Loyalist image. He quotes with visible approval Stahl's observation at a meeting of the newspaper men: "Meine Herren, vergessen wir nicht, auch das konservativste Blatt ist immer noch mehr Blatt als konservativ".[2] An anecdote about Privy Councillor Heinrich Abeken and Bismarck is used to characterize the professor of art, Wilhelm Hensel. The story is borrowed by Fontane from Moritz Busch's book "Graf Bismarck und seine Leute"[3] and concerns the chancellor's reprimand to Abeken for getting distracted from his business by the approach of Prince Karl. Fontane falls here into the trap of using a n y anecdote, when he lack an appropriate one. To characterize Hensel with an anecdote about Abeken is unduly stretching the possibilities of the form. However, the

1 NyA XV, 258.
2 Ibid. 259.
3 Leipzig 1872.

Byzantinism shown by both Heinrich Abeken and Wilhelm Hensel illustrates the opinion Fontane wishes to voice that, in spite of appearances to the contrary, there is in fact more sycophancy in contemporary Prussia than even in the era of Frederick William I. The opinion expressed here is in agreement with Fontane's frequent harking back to the eras of Frederick William I and Frederick II with regard to the degree of 'freedom' enjoyed by the individual 'in spite of the crutched stick'.[1]

The anecdotes in the passage on the "Kreuz-Zeitung" fulfil Fontane's stated intention in using them, i.e. they bring out those human qualities which he found attractive in these conservative characters. This certainly proves the correctness of the statement in the extended footnote on his own political leanings, but that this is not an adequate portrayal of his own politics need hardly be underlined. Something of the paradoxical nature of his politics as shown in the "Kreuz-Zeitung" digression can be seen in his two statements about the treatment of the Conservatives in letters to Julius Rodenberg. On 10 February 1896 he writes that the account is "ganz von der heitren und beinah schmeichelhaften Seite" and adds: "Was durchaus der Wahrheit entspricht".[2] However, that this is not the whole truth is intimated in the more sober comment of 13 March 1896 that the conservatives do much better out of his account than they deserve.[3] This statement from the correspondence provides an antidote to Fontane's attempt in "Von Zwanzig bis Dreißig" to gloss over the full reality of the past.

An important aspect of Fontane's association with the conservative newspaper was the opportunity it afforded him to mix with aristocratic and conservative circles. This opportunity and the leisure afforded him working for the "Kreuz-Zeitung" to write the "Wanderungen" no doubt modified his view in looking back on this

1 Cf. NyA XV, 266. These two monarchs occur again and again in Fontane's works in connection with the positive values of 'good old Prussia'. Contemporary historiography agrees with Fontane's revaluation of Frederick William I, although it expresses itself in different terms.

2 "Briefe an Rodenberg", p. 80.

3 Ibid. p. 86.

decade, as both of these aspects were of vital importance to his development as a writer.[1] The anecdotes in the "Kreuz-Zeitung" digression are not sufficiently entertaining or important however to convince the reader that Fontane is not here putting forward a biassed account of this decade of his life. The ironical standpoint adopted for his treatment of his own revolutionary fervour in 1848 in the same work is a counterpart to the incomplete nature of his treatment of the decade of his collaboration on the "Kreuz-Zeitung". When Fontane gives free rein to the artistic description of a personal experience, his mixed attitude towards the "Kreuz-Zeitung" is much more apparent, e.g. in the amusing scene of his interview with Tuiscon Beutner. Here as so often in Fontane's works and correspondence, the juxtapositon of concrete objects demonstrates an irony which relieves the narrator of further comment. The Iron Cross embroidered on a cushion and the image of the Crucifixion seem to be the poles between which the conversation of Fontane and Beutner oscillates. Later one of Fontane's beloved culinary metaphors describes more caustically in a letter the use of religion to bolster the régime: the Sunday editions of the paper produce an"Adelssauce mit einem Bibelspruch als Champignon – aber ranzig".[2] His critical approach is more apparent in the mise en scène of the Beutner interview or in the culinary metaphor of the correspondence than in the uncomfortable rationalizations about the Conservatives in "Von Zwanzig bis Dreißig".

"Totus mundus exercet histrionem"

The intimacy and informality of the narrative account for much of the charm of Fontane's reminiscences. His overriding interest is catching through anecdotal means those typical features of the characters dealt with. Thus, even the smallest incident can be of

1 Cf. H. Nürnberger: "Der frühe Fontane". München 1967, p. 300.
2 "Briefe an seine Familie", vol. 2, p. 61.

value in the portrayal.[1] In the case of the more eccentric figures,[2] like Wollheim da Fonseca and Hermann Maron, emphasis is placed more on those external aspects which made them stand out e.g. the anecdote about Maron's outsize pipe hanging out onto the busy Berlin street,[3] or Wollheim da Fonseca's challenging 'Charité Rendant' Müller to a duel for deliberately lighting his cigar at Fonseca's "ewige Lampe".[4] Each of these stories seems trivial, and yet the human weaknesses of the people concerned are admirably caught with a precision hardly to be expected from the informality both of the events and of the manner in which Fontane reports them. In both cases, the fault which underlies the events is a certain self-conscious play-acting which Fontane discerns in his colleagues and acquaintances, and which is very frequently the reason for the narration of one of his anecdotes. Wollheim da Fonseca's particular form of self-conscious role is that of the ultra-Catholic. Thus the lamp anecdote, in which the intended duel turns – after a speech by Louis Schneider against duelling – into a drinking session, shows extra irony in its characterization of the papal knight. Maron's pipe attracting the attention of all the serving-girls on the street and the customers trying to enter the shop underneath indicates the joy which Maron took in being the centre of attention. A certain element of theatricality in Maron reappears several times in Fontane's account of him, and is especially apparent in the tale of Maron's gruesome end, his suicide at breakfast, due to financial troubles,

1 NyA XV, 209. Theodor Storm's son bit Wilhelm von Merckel "unseren kleinen Kammergerichtsrat, vor dem wir alle einen heillosen Respekt hatten", in the calf under the table during a dinner at Storm's house. This essentially trivial, though amusingly recounted, event has a place in the overall characterization of Storm as deviating rather deliberately from the norm, on grounds of his talent and his local patriotism. His contempt for Prussian meticulousness and discipline (cf. ibid. 208) is thus caught in this tiny incident of his not showing enough disapproval of his son's naughtiness.

2 The "Tunnel" had quite a number of these: Scherenberg, Schramm, Streber, Wollheim, Sankt Paul and Goldammer. (See ibid. 299)

3 See ibid. 31.

4 Ibid. 190-191.

having first put a bullet through his unsuspecting wife's head.

A further example of eccentricity among Fontane's literary acquaintances is provided by Theodor Storm's pronounced local patriotism, his 'Husumerei'[1] which Fontane found unattractive. The characteristic is shown very graphically in the observation that Storm would even insist that his own brew of tea was superior to all others! This pronounced brand of local patriotism as well as the element of exhibitionism (e.g. the scarf anecdote[2]), and the pose as 'Unschulds-erotiker'[3]: all of these factors add up to a picture of Storm to whom Fontane could not fully warm, in spite of his deep admiration for him. In this analysis in "Von Zwanzig bis Dreißig" of the differences betweeen himself and Storm, Fontane uses terms which are of basic importance for an understanding of both writers: "Er war für den Hüsumer Deich, ich war für die Londonbrücke; sein Ideal war die schleswigsche Heide mit den roten Erikabüscheln, mein Ideal was die Heide von Culloden mit den Gräbern der Camerons und Mac Intosh."[4] According to Fontane, this is basically what prevented a closer friendship between them. Storm's attitude towards Prussia was an off-shoot of his local patriotism. Fontane can agree on the one hand with Storm's criticism of his own country, but on the other hand he disagrees, since he finds that such criticism by members of other German states stems from precisely those faults for which they reproach Prussia: presumptuousness and a sense of superiority.[5] The anecdotes in the Storm section provide an extremely lively account of the two men's meetings, and they are more memorable

1 NyA XV, 200,

2 See NyA XV, 212-213.

3 An unusual note of sharpness creeps into Fontane's observations in this passage and seems to stem from his revulsion from this aspect of Storm's works. Part of a letter of 15. 6. 1883 to Emilie throws further light on his appraisal of the differences between Storm and himself in this regard: "Das ich aber den Stormschen 'Bibber' nicht habe, das ist mein Stolz und meine Freude: Storm ist ein kränkliches Männlein und ich bin gesund trotz meiner äußren Kränklichkeiten." "Briefe". Edited by Schreinert/Jolles, vol. 1, p.201.

4 NyA XV, 210.

5 Ibid. 200.

than the general observations which Fontane includes in the account in order to give balance to the portrait.

A general aspect of Fontane's criticism of the eighteen-thirties and forties underlies his criticism of Storm, and is a theme to which he returns several times in his works. It is not simply that Fontane sets out in the Storm chapter of "Von Zwanzig bis Dreißig" to show the poet's weaknesses or even to explain why he himself could not warm to him. The differences are greater than the personal element, and some of Fontane's observations show that he could really appreciate Storm, both personally and as a poet. But the 'Dichterallüren'[1] of Storm's younger days are put by Fontane into the context of the alleged superiority of writers over people who are not artistically talented. Fontane's opinion on this is very concrete and down-to-earth: for him the phenomenon lay in excessive self-esteem on the part of poets and their underestimation of ordinary folk. The phenomenon, where it lives on in the nineteenth century, reminds Fontane of Romanticism[2] with its use of irony as self-protection. Its biting edge was not at all to Fontane's taste, and in particular his criticism is levelled at those post-Romantic lesser spirits who adopted airs of irony and of genius. It is this critical background which explains Fontane's impatience with the Storm of the forties and fifties, as well as his pleasure in discovering a maturer Storm without these foibles in old age. This underlies the conciliatory note at the end of the Storm chapter.

One of the earlier groups dealt with by Fontane in his autobiography, "die Sieben Weisen des Hippelschen Kellers", is presumably dealt with in the interests of the 'Zeitbild'.[3] This group around the Young Hegelian, Juilius Faucher (1820-1878), with whom Fontane also associated during his first professional stay in

1 Cf. NyA XV, 213.

2 To make this connection in the Storm chapter he simply alludes to the poem by Eichendorff "Von Engeln und von Bengeln" (i.e. poets and philistines) which was published in 1824.

3 The author's footnote shows that he regards the "Seven" as one of the most interesting phenomena Berlin has ever seen, outside of Bismarck. See NyA XV, 41.

London, is characterized by a certain Bohemianism which did not disdain practical jokes (e.g. leading a correspondent of a South German newspaper astray with a false political rumour, or begging for money which the Seven Sages spent in the wine-tavern).[1] However, not the Bohemianism as such earns Fontane's criticism – it makes for interesting anecdotes and helps him to paint a vivid picture of the times – but rather the cruel edge of the Seven's irony as directed against others. It is for this reason that Fontane includes the Saß anecdote which will be examined below. Friedrich Saß was the object of the Seven's jokes on account of his extraordinary height. For Fontane, the Saß anecdote is an example of a milder version of this wit, which is still current in the eighteen-nineties. That the Seven's mania for pulling people's legs could also be directed against each other is at least recorded in a Schelmuffsky-type anecdote about Faucher's six-week absence during which he claimed to have experienced wonderful adventures, a tale considered most unlikely by his companions.

In the Scherenberg book, Fontane had already devoted a passage to criticism of the Titanism of Berlin literary circles of the eighteen-thirties and forties. This was characterized by boastfulness, arrogance and a tendency towards a "Tieckian irony which consisted in making one's conversation partner feel how stupid he was".[2] This naive arrogance in certain quarters in the earlier part of the century is illustrated (as in "Von Zwanzig bis Dreißig" by the Friedrich Saß anecdote and other stories) in the Scherenberg book by an anecdote about Bruno Bauer(1809-1882), who was a member of the Seven. He worked with the "Kreuz-Zeitung" and was thoroughly disliked by Fontane. During a dinner-table conversation with Georg Hesekiel, Bauer drew parallels between his own family and the Bonaparte brothers, likening himself to Jérôme Bonaparte.[3] Fontane relates

1 Cf. NyA XV, 36 and 39.
2 Cf. NyA XIV, 253.
3 Bruno Bauer – ironically enough in the light of Fontane's criticism of his presumption in this conversation – actually had more influence on world history than Jérôme, because of his critique of Christianity and his influence on Marx. Fontane must presume the reader's familiarity with the figure of

this anecdote to give an example of the naïve way in which many intellectuals assumed Titanic identities, which expressed itself in having themselves introduced as young Goethes, Napoleons and Caesar Borgias! In Fontane's view, such presumptuous foolishnesss has been swept away by political developments, and thus, the present – the late nineteenth century – is at least in this respect an improvement on and preferable to that arrogant past. The section on Julius Faucher in "Von Zwanzig bis Dreißig" echoes this sentiment: "Man weiß jetzt, daß ein Philister ersten Ranges ein großes Genie sein kann, ja, erst recht, während man sich ein solches, in den dreißiger und vierziger Jahren, ohne bestimmte moralische Defekte nicht gut vorstellen konnte. Jedes richtige Genie war auch zugleich ein Pump- und Bummelgenie. Von dieser Regel gab es nur wenig Ausnahmen."[1] Such criticisms which recur in his work show that Fontane is at pains in "Von Zwanzig bis Dreißig" to give the background of the times with regard to these literary circles and to link the anecdotes which characterize specific individuals with general phenomena affecting the age. Thus the Bohemianism of the "Seven Sages from Hippel's Wine-tavern" is not recorded simply in order to enliven the narrative of Fontane's literary acquaintances and to provide amusing anecdotes. These functions are also fulfilled by the section on the Seven, but it is fitted into the context of an overall criticism of an aspect of literary life which Fontane himself encountered but of which he could not approve.

A note on Fontane's anecdotes about writers

Anecdotes about the difficulties of writers, struggling or otherwise, are quite common in Fontane's works. In his book on Christian Friedrich Scherenberg, several anecdotes are recounted in order to underline his poverty, e.g. about his receiving a lark as a present

Bauer as a prominent Young Hegelian, but he does not deal with him at all as a theologian, philosopher or historian.

1 NyA XV, 34.

instead of payment for private lessons and his using black sealing-wax to cover cracks in his boots.[1] Such anecdotes are not very significant in themselves, but they do give the reader a more vivid picture of day-to-day events in the early life of Scherenberg before his association with the "Tunnel" club. One of the most interesting scenes in the Scherenberg book occurs in Chapter 15, where Fontane's disappointment and bitterness about a slight from Louis Schneider is recorded. The close of the chapter shows Fontane and Scherenberg united in sympathy over their sufferings as poets, while Scherenberg consoles Fontane with a reference to the poet's position in Schiller's poems "Teilung der Erde" and "Resignation".[2] The slight in question gives some autobiographical background to the passage in "Von Zwanzig bis Dreißig" on Schneider's meanness to writers. In the Scherenberg book, he records the fact that Schneider, as editor of "Der Soldatenfreund" sent him only four louis d'or instead of the expected eight, for eight patriotic poems. The omission in "Von Zwanzig bis Dreißig" of any reference to a personal slight from Schneider is interesting: it shows how much Fontane wished to keep his assessment objective. Since meanness to writers was a general feature of Schneider, and was not just restricted to this incident concerning the publishing of Fontane's poems, the account in "Von Zwanzig bis Dreißig" dispenses with the personal anecdote. This might have introduced a note of personal animosity, and the characteristic feature of Schneider's personality can be illustrated just as well with an anecdote about his treatment of young writers in general.

Critics have drawn attention to the similarity between Fontane's writings on his own life and the work on Scherenberg.[3] The various anecdotes in the Scherenberg book add to the picture given in "Von Zwanzig bis Dreißig" of a writer's existence in nineteenth-century Prussia. Had the Scherenberg monograph not already been written in the eighteen-eighties, it would have provided an excellent

1 Cf. Chapters 3 and 4 of "Christian Friedrich Scherenberg oder das literarische Berlin von 1840 bis 1860".

2 NyA XV, 298.

3 Cf. Charlotte Jolles: "Theodor Fontane", p. 105.

chapter in "Von Zwanzig bis Dreißig.[1] Originally planned as an essay (which would have been more appropriate), the work on Scherenberg soon took on book format. The new format demanded more attention to Scherenberg's works than the essay format would have, and this is precisely the aspect which Fontane was at pains to avoid.[2] He regarded Scherenberg with more interest as a 'Zeiterscheinung'[3] than as a writer. The manner of Scherenberg's acceptance at court and his post in the library of the Ministry for Defence throw light on the position of the writer vis-à-vis the authorities in the mid-nineteenth century.[4] In the anecdotes about slights on writers recorded by Fontane the reader can see a reflection of his reaction to treatment of himself. The struggles of the young writer are the subject of many passages in the correspondence with Wolfsohn and Lepel[5] and indeed, in all his correspondence the writer's problems in society are a theme. In the often-quoted letter of 30 November 1876 to Mathilde von Rohr, Fontane complains bitterly about the Kaiser's refusal to give him any financial support after the publication of "Der Krieg gegen Frankreich". The letter contains an anecdote about the reaction of the early Persian epic poet, Firdausi, to royal lack of recognition of his talent: "Firdusi, als er dem Schach Mahomet sein Helden-Epos brachte, erhielt 200,000 Silbermünzen zum Geschenk und schenkte, in bittrem

1 Fontane indicates that Scherenberg's eccentricities were most often the subject of conversation among the literati and others at the Merckels' dinner-parties, the man's personality and his ambivalent position – seine Hinundhergezerrtwerden von zwei sich befehdenden Parteien" – being "eine nie versagende Quelle der Erheiterung". (NyA XV, 299)

2 Fontane saw that a re-reading of Scherenberg's works would crumble his resolve to write the book about him. See his letter of 3. 8. 1889 to M. Lazarus ("Briefe". Ed. Pniower/Schlenther, Berlin 1910, vol. 2, p. 205.)

3 NyA XIV, 338.

4 Walter Müller-Seidel draws attention to the parallel between Fontane's political ambivalence and Scherenberg's position of "Hofpoeten zwischen Königtum und Sozialdemokratie" in 'Fontanes Autobiographik' in JDSG 13, 1969, p. 407.

5 Cf. Charlotte Jolles: 'Zu Fontanes literarischer Entwicklung' in JDSG 8, 1960, p. 401.

Unmuth, die ganze Summe einem Badeknecht zu Gasna, denn er hatte geglaubt 200,000 G o l dmünzen erwarten zu dürfen."[1] It is clear that a writer who struggled so long for recognition will be inclined to see in all instances of disregard to writers a reflection of his own fate.

In the unfinished essay "Die gesellschaftliche Stellung des Schriftstellers in Deutschland"[2] written during the eighteen-eighties, Fontane shows how seriously he was affected by the the low social status of writers, and how much he regretted that they enjoyed such little respect from the population in general. At a hypothetical dinner-party with a sprinkling of government officials and other prominent personalities, he posits that even such a successful and highly-acclaimed author as Paul Heyse (the later Nobel prizewinner) would never be placed beside the hostess. For Fontane, this social factor shows that even the most successful (i.e. not financially disadvantaged) writer would never be fully accepted as being in the first rank, socially speaking, in Prussia-Germany.[3] He sees this disregard for writers partly as a result of that aspect of Prussian society which he himself often criticised, namely, its exaggerated respect for all titles, distinctions and official positions. On the other hand, he also blames writers themselves for the miserable standing of the profession: a certain amount of role-playing had brought them into disrepute. Poverty in any case was no recommendation in

1 Schreinert/Jolles: "Briefe" vol. 3, p. 174. Fontane's version differs slightly from Heine's version of the same incident in the "Romanzero" poem "Der Dichter Firdusi", which Fontane loved. In Heine, the messengers of the Shah receive one third each of the poet's reward, the bathing attendant the final third.

2 NyA XXI/ii, 452-464.

3 Paul Heyse, the 1910 Nobel prizewinner, is a particularly good example for Fontane's argument. His success and esteem in society contrast with the experience of many better contemporary writers, but even this does not make him totally acceptable. See also Eva Becker: ' "Zeitungen sind doch das Beste": Bürgerliche Realisten und der Vorabdruck ihrer Werke in der periodischen Presse' in "Gestaltungsgeschichte und Gesellschaftsgeschichte. Festschrift für Fritz Martini". Edited by Helmut Kreuzer. Stuttgart 1969, p. 382-408.

society. The writer's position as critic of society inevitably, and through no fault of his own, made him suspect to the ordinary citizen. Two anecdotes in this essay illustrate how little was thought of writers in nineteenth-century Prussia. In the first, the son of the Romantic writer, Adalbert von Chamisso, is asked by the (highly respected) General Karl von Möllendorf if his father, of whom Möllendorf has never heard, had a r e a l profesion as well. The fact that this story of young Chamisso's entry into the second Garde-regiment includes such a prominent and respected military man as Möllendorf gives it extra point. The possibility of the story's being apocryphal is irrelevant to Fontane, since it aptly describes a phenomenon which is prevalent in Prussia and "could happen any day".[1] Fontane never objected to fictitious anecdotes, as long as they were representative.

The second anecdote in this essay concerns an incident which happened Fontane – ironically enough in the Ministry for Cults and Education – while waiting with a professor of theology in an ante-room to the Minister's office. The professor's indignant reply in the negative to the messenger's question as to whether both men "belonged together" was accompanied by a tone of voice which Fontane "would have liked to bring to court".[2] The personal tone into which this insult goads Fontane suggests how deeply concerned he was at this particular manifestation of a lack of refinement on the part of his countrymen. For the anecdote is merely a particular instance of a general phenomenon in Prussia. Two anecdotes in Fontane's works about writers who were well-regarded by their respective societies contrast with the more numerous anecdotes about disregard for authors. Significantly, the two writers in question do not hail from Prussia-Germany, Sir Walter Scott from Scotland and João de Deus from Portugal.[3] An incident from the life of Walter Scott, himself "ein unerreichter Anekdotenerzähler"[4] in Fontane's view, provides him with the

1 NyA XXI/ii, 458.
2 Ibidem.
3 For the Joao de Deus anecdote, see above p. 189-194.
4 NyA XXI/i, 413.

matter for both a poem and a prose anecdote contained in his essay on Scott of 1871. The basic tale is taken from the abridged two-volume edition of John Gibson Lockhart's biography of Scott. A comparison of both of Fontane's versions of the anecdote with the original shows the amount of poetic licence he took with the incident.

Walter Scott in Westminister-Abtei

Ganz London flaggt und jubelt und rennt:
"Heut wird er König, der Prinz-Regent!"
Schon wartet seiner die Klerisei
Vorm Altar der Westminster-Abtei,
Vorm Eingang aber, in Plaid und Kilt
Und im Helme, draus der Helmbusch quillt,
Über den Platz hin, zieht Spalier
Das Regiment S c h o t t i s c h e F ü s i l i e r!

Und wie gefegt der ganze Plan.
Wer aber die zwei, die da sich nahn?
Sie hoffen auf Zutritt, auf Gunst und Glück;
Umsonst. Kommandoruf: "Zurück!"

Und die Menge, sie lacht, und der eine wird bleich,
Aber der andre: "Dacht' es gleich;
Das alte Lied vom Schaden und Spott,
Lachen wir mit, S i r W a l t e r S c o t t!"

Und sieh, eh' noch der Name verklang,
In die Front ein blutjunger Fähnrich sprang,
Seinen Degen senkt salutierend er:
"Richt't euch; präsentiert das Gewehr!
Hoch König Georg und segn' ihn Gott,
Aber Platz, Füsiliers, für Sir Walter Scott!"

Der Weg ist offen, der Weg ist frei,
Sir Walter betritt die Westminster-Abtei.
Die Schotten flüstern: "Das war e r!"

Der Krönungszug kam weit hinterher.[1]

1 NyA XX, 158-159.

Lockhart's version (1837)

Missing his carriage, he had to return on foot from Westminster, after the banquet – that is to say between two and three in the morning – when he and a young gentleman his companion found themselves locked in the crowd, somewhere near Whitehall, and the bustle and tumult were such that his friend was afraid some accident might happen to the lame limb. A space for the dignitaries was kept clear by the Scots Greys. Sir Walter addressed a sergeant of this celebrated regiment, begging to be allowed to pass by him into the open ground in the middle of the street. The man answered shortly that his orders were strict – that the thing was impossible. While he was endeavouring to persuade the sergeant to relent, some new wave of turbulence approached from behind, and his young companion exclaimed in a loud voice: "Take care, Sir Walter Scott, take care!" The stalwart dragoon, on hearing the name, said : "What! Sir Walter Scott? He shall get through anyhow!" He then addressed the soldiers near him – "Make room, men, for Sir Walter Scott, our illustrious countryman!" The men answered: "Sir Walter Scott! – God bless him!" and he was within a moment within the guarded line of safety.[1]

Fontane's essay version (1871)

Vierzehn Jahre später stand sein Ruhm auf der Höhe. Es war am Krönungstage des Prinzregenten; Scott war in London und suchte einen Platz in Westminster-Abtei zu gewinnen; aber spalierbildene schottische Füsiliergarde schloß alle Zugänge ab. "Laßt uns gehen, S i r W a l t e r S c o t t", sagte endlich sein Begleiter mit lauter Stimme und suchte den Dichter, dem das lange Stehen seines Fußes halber schwer wurde, aus dem Gedränge zurückzuziehen. Aber bereits hatte der diensttuende Offizier den Namen des Angeredeten gehört. Er sprang vor: "Füsiliere, Platz für Sir Walter Scott!" und unter dem Hurra seiner Landsleute und dem immer erneuten Zurufe: "God bless you, Sir Walter" schritt der überraschte und tiefbewegte Dichter auf die Kirche zu.[2]

1 "Life of Sir Walter Scott" (Abridged). Edinburgh 1837-1838, p. 209-210. Cf. NyA XX, 741 and Gerald W. Spink's notice: 'Fontane's Poem: "Walter Scott in Westminster-Abtei" ' in MLR 28, 1933, p. 489-490.

2 "Walter Scott", NyA XXI/i, 418. In the context the dating of this event

Fontane's versions of the Scott anecdote takes a number of liberties, the most important being the timing of the incident. Both his poem and the essay version place the event as happening before the coronation. The irony of that situation is worked out rather dramatically in the poem with its final line: "Der Krönungszug kam weit hinterher" and in the Scotsmens' whispering to themselves about Walter Scott, not about George IV: "Das war e r!" A great difference of effect obtains between a story which makes the writer precede a king on his way to coronation and a version (Lockhart's) which shows him merely saved from street turbulence and allowed to walk in the space reserved for dignitaries, hours after the whole occasion is over. Fontane omits the lame Scott's unsuccessful attempt to free himself from the necessity of walking with the turbulent crowd by speaking to the fusilier sergeant. Thus the effect of the writer's being suddenly freed through no efforts of his own is created – a spontaneous mark of respect shown by the military for the poet! Fontane can therefore add the works "überrascht und tiefbewegt" to his version, with the added climax that the writer is moving t o w a r d s a great occasion and is not involved in the less dignified home journey in the early hours of the morning after the banquet.

It is not without significance that this anecdote occurs, without any reference to the writer's position as such or to the situation in Prussia-Germany, in an essay written relatively early in Fontane's career as a writer. The reader is inevitably reminded of the ironical note given to the Schillerian line in Fontane's poem "Es soll der Dichter mit dem König gehen".[1] In the Prussian-German situation described in "Die gesellschaftliche Stellung des Schriftsteller in Deutschland" the writer could not even go 'with' the king, not to speak of going 'before' him as is the implication in Fontane's version of the Scott anecdote.[2]

would be 1825, an incorrect dating as indicated in NyA XXI/i, 699. The possibility mooted by Kurt Schreinert (ibidem) that it might refer to an annual coronation commemoration ceremony is incorrect, since Lockhart plainly refers only to the coronation of George IV in 1821.

1 NyA XX, 404-405.

2 The financial position of the best writers in Germany when Fontane's Scott

The anecdotes on writers given as examples here, and the many which occur in "Von Zwanzig bis Dreißig" provide a picture of the writer's position vis-à-vis society and Fontane's reaction to this phenomenon. The situation had not changed very much by his death in 1898.[1] His reaction to the celebrations for his seventieth birthday in 1889 shows a mixture of irony and indifference. The belated distinction of a minor Hohenzollern decoration in 1889 and the 'Schillerpreis' of 1891 were rather paltry recognitions of his stature. He did not even claim a very prominent place in society for the writing profession. In "Die gesellschaftliche Stellung des Schriftstellers in Deutschland" he gives preference over writers to many other professions for a high place in the social scala, to people like technical inventors who have changed the world.[2] This is reminiscent of Lorenzen's heroic type, inventors and explorers. What Fontane did object to was the general preference in Germany for any mediocrity, who was "state approved"[3] and "seven

article appeared is a good indication of how they were honoured by society: sixteen thalers for a ream was Fontane's remuneration from the publisher, Hertz, around 1870. See Reinhard Wittmann: 'Das literarische Leben 1848-1880' in "Realismus und Gründerzeit: Manifeste und Dokumente zur deutschen Literatur 1848-1880". Edited by Max Bucher, Werner Hahl, Georg Jäger and Reinhard Wittmann. Stuttgart 1976, vol. 1, p. 208. Wittmann quotes Eduard Schmidt-Weißenfels: 'Die Literatur und der Buchhandel' in "Börsenblatt für den deutschen Buchhandel" 34/157, 1867, p. 1713, that a talented and well-known writer with a family would need twelve hundred thalers to live in reasonable comfort, while he would have to produce eight to twelve novels annually to reach this earning capacity!

1 Paul Meyer reports Fontane's expression of amusement and sadness in 1892 when his name was not even recognised by the official dealing with his testament. See P. Meyer: op. cit., p.96 and NyA XXIII/ii, 1027.

2 See NyA XXI/ii, 456.

3 This aspect of Prussianism which Fontane found particularly distasteful reappears in a second, shorter essay on the social status of the writer: "Die gesellschaftliche Stellung des Schriftstellers" (published in 1891), an essay which shows more distance from his subject than the longer unfinished essay of the 1880's "Die gesellschaftliche Stellung des Schriftstellers in Deutschland". The shorter essay contains a passage on this aspect of Prussianism which has many counterparts in Fontane's correspondence:

times examined", as he often put it, to anyone who earned his (usually meagre) bread with the pen. Although he does not make the connection in explicit terms, the predominance of anecdotes in his work about disregard for writers in Prussia-Germany suggests that this situation may be a factor underlying his constant questioning of the Germans' claim to a superior culture. The foreign provenance of both of the outstanding anecdotes which show writers being acclaimed by their countrymen may be an indirect comment on Fontane's part on the situation of the writer in his own country.

Comparison of anecdotes in "Von Zwanzig bis Dreißig" with their counterparts in other sources

A comparison of anecdotes found in other sources with their counterparts in "Von Zwanzig bis Dreißig" serves to show how Fontane modifies his material for use in his own autobiographical work. Since nearly all the anecdotes found in "Von Zwanzig bis Dreißig" come from conversations, often from Fontane's direct experience with his colleagues, or from their repertoire of stories about their lives, only a small number of the anecdotes in this part of Fontane's autobiography are available in another printed source.

Among the stories contained in Chapter Two of "Von Zwanzig bis Dreißig" which are intended to characterize the exploits of the "Seven Sages from Hippel's Wine-tavern", Fontane includes a story about the Republican journalist, Friedrich Saß, who on account of his extraordinary height, was the butt of the Seven's jokes. Fontane's

"Die Macht des amtlichen Ansehens immer groß bei uns, ist in einem beständigen Steigen geblieben, ohne daß die Behörden des Staats diese Ansehenssteigerung für sich gefordert hätten; es ist ihnen umgekehrt dies gesteigerte Ansehen freiwillig entgegengebracht worden. Die Anschauung, daß nur Examen, Zeugnis, Approbation, Amt, Titel, Orden, kurzum alles das, wohinter der Staat steht, Wert und Bedeutung geben, beherrscht die Gemüter mehr denn je, und die freien Genies, die 'Wilden', immer süspekt gewesen, sind es jetzt mehr denn je." (NyA XXI/i, 494) version of the anecdote about Friedrich Saß at Notre Dame in Paris paraphrases the version printed in the satirical-political magazine, "Kladderadatsch". He conscientiously notes that the anecdote appeared in the magazine at the beginning of the eighteen-fifties, i.e. after the break-up of the Seven.

The "Kladderadatsch" version (1850)

Kaum hatten wir (Louis Napoleon und "Der Gelehrte", pseudonym of the writer of the article) die höchste Spitze des Kirchturms erreicht und ich meine Nase zu einer Dachluke hinausgesteckt, als mir eine Zigarre entgegen gehalten und ich im reinsten Deutsch gefragt wurde: Haben Sie vielleicht etwas Feuer? "Saß! Lieber Saß! wie kommen Sie hier her?" rief ich. Denn denken Sie sich! Friedrich Saß, unser großer Flottensaß,[1] stand vor mir. Er war vorübergegangen, hatte mich an Fenster erblickt und war an Notre Dame herangetreten.[2]

Fontane's version (1898)

Der lange Saß war damals politischer Korrespondent in Paris, und das Blatt, ich glaube der Kladderadatsch, das sich mit ihm beschäftigte, zeigte zunächst, hoch aufragend, die beiden Türme von Notre Dame. Auf einem dieser Türme aber stand niemand Geringeres als Louis Napoleon selbst, unwirsch und halb verlegen, weil ihm die Zigarre ausgegangen war. Indessen Hülfe war nah. Der mit seinem Kopf gerade bis an die Balustrade reichende Saß kam rauchend vorüber und wurde denn auch von Louis Napoleon herangerufen und kameradschaftlich um Feuer angesprochen.[3]

Appropriately enough for the context of his own work, and in keeping with his practice in anecdotal narration elsewhere, Fontane drops the figure of the article writer, whose presence would take away from the immediacy of the amusing imaginary encounter. That the incident takes place between a Napoleon and the German political correspondent, Saß, rather than between two German journalists in Louis Napoleon's presence, as in the "Kladderadatsch"

1 A reference to Friedrich Saß' work: "Deutschlands Flotte". Berlin 1842, in which he took the view that Germany should found her own fleet.

2 "Kladderadatsch. Humoristisch-satirisches Wochenblatt", Berlin, 27. 1. 1850, p. 2.

3 NyA XV, 39-40.

version, increases the interest of the anecdote. While Louis Napoleon is not characterized at all within the scope of the "Kladderadatsch" Saß anecdote, in Fontane's version the tiny details of his annoyance and embarrassment are added, which heighten the dramatic nature of the incident. Similarly, Fontane's ending is more unusual in that the German journalist is called on in a friendly way by Louis Napoleon for a light. Louis Napoleon reappears in the "Kladderadatsch" version only after the incident has taken place, where the writer claims that the French ruler was "pikirt"[1] by it. "Der Gelehrte" takes this opportunity of withdrawing. In Fontane's version, Louis Napoleon's natural acceptance of Saß' enormous height provides the counterpart to the "Kladderadatsch" writer's amazement at Saß' presence in Paris, which is an element of the political satire.

Equally interesting is a comparison between one of Fontane's anecdotes concerning Court Reader Louis Schneider and Schneider's own version of the tale in his memoirs. Fontane is dealing in this passage of "Von Zwanzig bis Dreißig" with Schneider's readings at the Prussian court, readings which discredited Schneider politically among his "Tunnel" colleagues.[2] The anecdote concerns an alleged statement by Tsar Nicholas I about Schneider's loyalty to Prussia.

Schneider's version (1879)	Fontane's version (1898)
General von Rauch, damals schon Generaladjutant, stand von Sanssouci aus begreiflich in ununterbrochener Korrespondenz mit dem Kaiser und sagte mir einst – es war Ende 1848 oder Anfang 1849 – der Kaiser habe ihm, da alles in Preußen drunter und drüber gehe, geschrieben	Als im Sommer 49 Nikolaus nach Berlin kam, ließ er Schneider ins Palais rufen und äußerte sich über den traurigen Zustand, in den Preußen geraten sei. "Sehn Sie, Schneider, richtige Preußen gibt es überhaupt nur noch zwei: ich und Sie."[3]

1 "Kladderadatsch", ibidem.

2 While Fontane did not sympathize with Schneider's politics either, he did not let that hinder his appreciation of him. The anecdotes here are intended to show the personal relations between Nicholas and Schneider.

3 NyA XV, 241.

"Es gibt nur noch drei gute Preußen, das bin ich, Sie, lieber Rauch, und Schneider." Wir lächelten über die sonderbare Zusammenstellung.[1]

Even if Fontane's memory of Louis Schneider's oral version of this anecdote deceived him, a glance at the reminiscences of Schneider, already published in 1879, would have shown him the correct version of the incident. It is unlikely that Fontane composed his comparatively lengthy sketch on Schneider without referring to the man's own memoirs. In his version, Fontane introduces certain modifications against the original: the omission of the figure of von Rauch[2] and of the correspondence element, greater exactitude in fixing season and date, and a direct encounter between the important characters, namely the Tsar and Schneider, which did not occur in reality. These alterations mirror Fontane's approach to anecdote narration throughout his works: they always serve to tighten the structure of the story line and to emphasize the interesting and dramatic nature of the incident. As in the Saß anecdote the third party is left out, and to Fontane it is irrelevant if this is the party who relates the story (Saß) or is the actual interlocutor of the famous person (Rauch). This is not simply the case with Fontane's fictional works, where such alterations might be expected under the rubric of poetic licence, but also in the much more factual context of the memoirs. The truth may be altered (as long as the final product is not seriously misleading), and the alterations are always in the interests of producing a more pointed, dramatic, interesting or amusing anecdote. Having dropped Rauch in the Schneider anecdote, he also drops the letter factor, which makes the point of the story less immediate – the letter could have been

1 Louis Schneider: "Aus meinem Leben". 3 Bde., Berlin 1879, vol. 1, p. 394.

2 This is the case, for example, in the Barfus anecdote, where the original narrator, who also played a part in the anecdote, Christoph Graf Dohna, is dropped from the anecdote as related in "Frau Jenny Treibel". See above p. 58. In "Der Stechlin" Emil Frommel's anecdote loses in Fontane's version the third party, the servant, in order to make the encounter with Kaiser William I more immediate and dramatic. (See above p.170)

retained as one to Schneider, but Fontane prefers to make the story more vivid by creating a fictitious appointment between the Tsar and the actor. The Tsar's language in the sentence "Sehn Sie, Schneider, r i c h t i g e Preußen gibt es überhaupt nur noch zwei: ich und Sie" shows characteristics of the dialogue in Fontane's fiction and in the speech reported in his correspondence: elision of the fina 'e' in the verb ('sehn') and particular emphasis on one word ('r i c h t i g e') as well as the verbal confrontation of unlike objects or persons: "ich und Sie" (Tsar of all the Russias and Prussian actor,[1] who is disliked because of his Russian sympathies). The implicit exclusion of the Prussian royal family from this confederation of 'real Prussians' gives the anecdote its extra verve. The particularly Fontane-esque language elements bring the famous character closer to the reader and show him in a more human light than the more 'correct' language used by the Tsar in Schneider's original version. Thus, Tsar Nicholas shares the colloquial tendency which Fontane adopts for Tsar Alexander in the Kolter anecdote in "Unterm Birnbaum" and for Kaiser William I in the Frommel anecdote in "Der Stechlin".

To characterize a fault of Louis Schneider, Fontane tells the Lenau anecdote which he had already used in "Graf Petöfy" in the eighteen-eighties.[2] Schneider is characterized here "ex negativo" for the nobility of soul which he does n o t possess in contrast to the poet Lenau. At first sight, it may alienate the reader through its drawing on a figure completely outside the scope of "Von Zwanzig bis Dreißig". In contrast to the "Graf Petöfy" version, Fontane introduces the anecdote in the autobiography with the generalization: "Charakteristisch für einen Dichter wird es meist sein, wie er sich zu Mitdichtern, auch zu ganz kleinen und unbedeutenden, zu stellen weiß".[3] This is not simply an empty flourish, because we see the same indignation reflected in Fontane's book on Scherenberg at Heinrich Smidt's treatment of Scherenberg.

1 Hans-Heinrich Reuter describes Schneider as a "Reaktionär von reinstem Wasser" ("Fontane", vol. 1, p. 198).
2 See above p. 41-44.
3 NyA XV, 243.

Significantly, in the version in "Von Zwanzig bis Dreißig" there is no reference whatsoever to the quality of the poetic efforts of the waitress. In the original biography, the poems were said to be sentimental, while in "Graf Petöfy" they were described as 'not even mediocre'. This little difference brings out subtly Fontane's point in the autobiogrpahy that the noble-minded writer will treat colleagues with tact and gentleness, i r r e s p e c t i v e of the quality of their work, or of his opinion of them as artists. In the autobiography version of the story, Fontane again omits the reference, which had been one of the distinguishing points of the "Graf Petöfy" version, namely that Lenau had stayed away from the restaurant in order not to have himself served by a colleague. Instead he enters a new relationship with her and 'always' treats her "mit zartester Rücksicht"[1] because his nature will not allow him to act any differently. This change contrasts with Schneider's frequent meetings with young poets and his ungenerous treatment of them. The "Von Zwanzig bis Dreißig" version ends with the statement "von Gleichgültigkeit oder gar Überhebung keine Spur".[2] These last two differences as against the fictional version are intended to condemn Schneider all the more roundly for his arrogance. The Court Reader's meanness and pettiness with regard to paying the young poets, who were in the habit of showing him their efforts, are dealt with by Fontane in a further anecdotal touch. This story, while it helps to fill out the portrait of one individual, also gives some impression of the life of struggling writers in the Prussia of the eighteen-forties. Fontane accompanies the story with the generalization: "Damals kam es noch vor, daß blutarme junge Dichter ihre Dichtungen in einer kleinen Stadt auf eigene Kosten drucken ließen und nun, dies ihr Heftchen anbietend, bei ihren Mitdichtern um eine Wegzehrung[3]

1 NyA III, 44.
2 NyA XV, 243.
3 Fontane's use of the word 'Wegzehrung', borrowed from the language of the craftsman, suggests an association between writing and 'Handwerk', which indirectly tells us something about Fontane's view of his art. Furthermore, the anecdote about Lenau and the waitress which follows this passage is given more plausibility by the link with craftsmanship.

baten".[1] The language used by Fontane cleverly brings out the contrast: on the one hand, the young poets are 'blutarm', yet they sacrifice to have their poems printed, offer their 'Heftchen' to other writers; on the other hand, there is the favoured and successful Louis Schneider habitually offering them a small amount of money with the assurance that it has never been refused.[2] Instead of a passage d e s c r i b i n g Louis Schneider's meanness and insolence in dealing with these poor young writers, Fontane uses in his characterization the more dramatic and memorable method of contrasting two stories to make the point. The 'real' poet and noble-minded person, Nikolaus Lenau, thus becomes a contrast figure to Louis Schneider, although he is not of course a personage in Fontane's memoirs. The fact that Fontane used the Lenau anecdote once more in "Von Zwanzig bis Dreißig" although he had already used it in "Graf Petöfy" indicates the importance which he himself attached to the qualities of refinement and generosity (both of which are demonstrated by Lenau) as well as his appreciation of the tale as a good story.

In the majority of cases in "Von Zwanzig bis Dreißig" anecdotes from conversation, such as that about encounters between Louis Schneider and struggling young poets, are successfully transposed into the written word. Therefore the portraits of people like Richard Lucae, Louis Schneider and George Hesekiel are successfully reincarnated in Fontane's autobiography. That he was aware of the main difficulty inherent in his mode of presenting anecdotes from the everyday life of social intercourse is clear. The danger lay, even for the expert anecdote narrator, in the possibility that such stories appear either trivial or irrelevant in the written context. As a writer Fontane was conscious of the narrow dividing-line between those stories, which can easily cross from the realm of conversation into the realm of the written word, and those stories which cannot satisfactorily make that transition. In the case of Fontane's

1 NyA XV, 243.
2 Cf. ibid. 244. Louis Schneider's verbal skill, which is an important item in Fontane's portrait of him in "Von Zwanzig bis Dreißig", is also shown in this story, but in a way which clearly brings out its negative aspect.

treatment of his wife, Emilie, in "Von Zwanzig bis Dreißig", the shortcomings of his use of the oral anecdote become apparent. In an attempt to describe his wife's illogicality, he relates a story about his losing a coat, which two messengers are to try to recover. By the time the second messenger arrives without the coat, Emilie remarks: "So sind sie also alle beide weg".[1] This anecdote was probably the source of some amusement to the family and represented for them a characteristic feature of Emilie, but for the reader who only knows her while reading "Von Zwanzig bis Dreißig" through the author's presentation, the story is simply not important or interesting enough to produce a satisfactory portrait. It refers to only one of Emilie's characteristics, and such a limitation leaves the reader dissatisfied with the author's account. Beyond this, there is only the well-known tale of "Swinegel und sine Fru", which is used to describe the marriage relationship, as well as an obeisance in the direction of Emilie's thriftiness and untiring help with the copying of Fontane's works. The fact that Fontane had in mind other examples of his wife's illogicality is clear from the three variants in the manuscript, later removed before the printing.[2] All concern trivial household matters in snippets of conversation. The fact that Fontane was dissatisfied with all these examples is clear from his removal of them from the text, and his apology in the printed version for transferring the coat anecdote into the literary context signals his awareness of his lack of success in this passage. His apology includes the assertion that such 'little features' are best for describing a person. Granted, but the feature in question is much too trivial to stand for the whole person. Fontane's procedure of cutting out a treatment of the inner self went rather too far in the delineation of the relationship with Emilie. The passage on the marriage is rather too trivial and too harmless to satisfy the reader. No doubt a great deal of anecdotal material was available to Fontane for a treatment of his relationship with Emilie, but it would have necessitated a much closer portrayal of the relationship than is provided in "Von Zwanzig bis Dreißig".

1 NyA XV, 319.
2 See ibid. 612.

While the anecdote was admirably suited for the portrayal of outsiders like Schneider and Hesekiel, it would perhaps have been too revealing for a portrayal of the close relationship of husband and wife. Significantly, those portraits of much closer friends like Lepel and Merckel also use far less anecdotes than the portraits of people like Hesekiel, Lucae or Schneider. Again Fontane's apparent wish not to include too much revelatory material with regard to those closest to him seems to underly this lack of anecdotes. Furthermore, in the portraits of people who were not really close to him, Fontane was able to bring out much more strongly the 'Zeitbild' element.[1] For this, the anecdote is admirably suited.

To have included more material on his wife, he would have had to deal with the problematical element of their relationship. The frequent ill-humour of Emilie during the copying of his manuscripts, for example, is not mentioned at all in his acknowledgement of his debt to her for this in "Von Zwanzig bis Dreißig". Fontane settled for giving almost nothing, the bare minimum of information on this relationship in "Von Zwanzig bis Dreißig", and the reader is inclined to wonder if Emilie is included (and obviously the portrait give him difficulty) only because it would have seemed insulting to leave her out altogether. The result of his dilemma is the unsatisfactory partial portrait based on a few essentially trivial anecdotes.

From a review written relatively early in Fontane's career, it is possible to deduce some of the principles which underly his own efforts in the employment of anecdote and to understand why he included so many of them in his autobiography. The review gives an appreciation of Julius Rodenberg's book "Studienreisen in England: Bilder aus Vergangenheit und Gegenwart."[2] Fontane was admirably

1 Cf. Bernd Neumann: "Identität und Rollenzwang: Zur Theorie der Autobiographie". Berlin 1970, p. 62, on the link between the 'reality principle' and the writing of memoirs – the aim of memoirists may be the preservation of the past: "sie wollen Geschichte überliefern". In Fontane's case, this aim is not meant in the more grandiose sense of memoirists who themselves played a major role in the shaping of historical events. His intention is to preserve the marginal, which is not of itself important enough to survive without help.

2 Leipzig 1872.

suited as a reviewer of the work, due to his own comparatively broad knowledge of English life and to his development as a writer up to 1873. His confidence is expressed at the beginning of the following quotation which goes on to emphasize the harmony and balance of Rodenberg's use of, inter alia, the anecdote.

> Kulturbildliche und sittenschildernde Spezialarbeiten, die den mit englischer Geschichte f e s t e r, r e i c h e r, g l ü c k l i c h e r in seinem Besitze machen, – dahin möchten wir diese "Studienreisen in England" charakterisieren. Eine Fülle von Betrachtungen, Notizen, Anekdoten, die aber nicht buntverworren auf den Leser eindringen, sonder überall einen so wohlüberlegten, paßlichen Platz gefunden haben, daß sie fast mehr mehr zur C h a r a k t e r i s t i k einer bestimmt gegebenen Situation als zur bloßen Unterhaltung sich darbieten. Einem drüber waltenden k ü n s t l e r i s c h e n G e s e t z ist alles untergeordnet; nichts tritt wilkürlich auf; auch das Amüsanteste dient noch einem anderen Zweck als nur dem, amüsant sein zu wollen. Dabei ist Maß gehalten in der Auswahl; man empfindet wohltuend einen hinter dem Gegebenen sich verbergenden Reichtum, der nur fein genug ist, sich nicht auf jeder Seite geltend machen zu wollen.[1]

It is clear from this extract that already in the early eighteen-seventies Fontane was highly conscious of the necessity of avoiding arbitrariness in the use of the anecdote. However amusing little stories might be in their own right, they must like other aspects of narrative be subject to an overall artistic intention. They should serve to characterize particular situations. Further on in the review Fontane gives an example of Rodenberg's choice of anecdote in his coverage of London clubs and coffee-houses. The story is about two members of the Hellfire Club and concerns the riposte of the radical John Wilkes to the Marquis of Sandwich's taunting question as to whether he would die of venereal disease or on the scaffold: "Das wird ganz davon abhängen, ob ich mir die Mätresse oder die Grundsätze Euer Herrlichkeit aneigne."[2] Fontane goes to the trouble of

1 NyA XVIII/i, 557.

2 Ibid. 559. and J. Rodenberg: op. cit., p. 173. In fact, Rodenberg's book is not as lively and anecdotal as Fontane's positive review would suggest, although for its time and readership it probably fulfilled its purpose very well.

quoting this anecdote in order to bring home to the reader the kind of political anecdote which adds life to Rodenberg's narrative. By contrast, it illustrates his own generalization about a specific lack of coverage in Germany of writing on the German way of life. The necessity of such documentation is a problem to which Fontane alludes several times in his work, and he includes in his demand for such 'Tagesliteratur' the recording of such apparent trifles as witty toasts, anecdotes and puns.[1]

In Fontane's statement towards the end of this review: "Aber nur das Aufgeschriebene lebt fort"[2] there is an echo of his often-stated opinion of the necessity of recording small and apparently secondary items, whether it be little stories about members of the families of the March Brandenburg, or less-known historical events, or reports of personal experience, or finally anecdotes about well-known personalities which however are in danger of disappearing forever. The same sense of urgency in Fontane's almost didactic tone towards the end of this review reappears in his emphasis in "Kritische Jahre – Kritiker-Jahre" on the need to collect anecdotes about the actor, Theodor Döring, before it is too late.[3] The same need is recorded in "Von Zwanzig bis Dreißig" with regard to anecdotes about Court Preacher Büchsel.[4] Fontane's aim therefore in the context of the autobiographical works can ben seen as saving

1 NyA XVVIII/i, 560.

2 NyA XVIII, 561. This opinion is also voiced in "Aus den Tagen der Okkupation" in connection with the books of Max von Schlägel and Oskar von Marschall on their period as prisoners of war in Bitsch during the Franco-Prussian war: "Auch darin hat Bitsch Glück gehabt. Nicht jede unbedeutende Feste genießt des Vorzuges, während ihrer Belagerung zwei Schriftsteller in ihren Pavillons und Kasematten zu beherbergen, frische, lebendige Erzähler, die nun zu Spezialhistoriographen eines an und für sich geringfügigen, historisch-verschwindenden Gegenstandes werden. Aber eben durch die Darstellung, die der Gegenstand findet, wird er über sich selbst erhoben und hört auf, ein Verschwindender zu sein. Denn nicht auf die Tat kommt es an, sondern auf das Wort, das sie festhält und überliefert. Das Wort allein macht lebendig; was stumm ist, und wär' es das Größte, ist tot." (NyA XVI, 474)

3 NyA XV, 404.

4 See ibid. 269.

from emphemerality aspects of everyday life – in "Von Zwanzig bis Dreißig" it is mainly the life of literary Berlin in the mid-nineteenth century. Anecdotes here supply information, assist characterization, preserve aspects of little-known people or little-known aspects about well-known people. In particular where Fontane renders an account of the anecdotes of other characters, their mode of speech is preserved (apart from some added Fontane-esque touches!) and the reader may thus enjoy the wit of these characters, as well as appreciating the author's skill in condensing and giving a literary cloak to essentially oral anecdotes.

It is in the context of the ideas found in the review of Julius Rodenberg's book "Studienreisen in England" that one can see a justification for the treatment of little-known characters in the literary clubs of Berlin – that is, a justification over and above the perfectly legitimate one of recording or registering Fontane's own encounters and relationships with these literary men. Most of them, even those in the "Tunnel" club, the best of all the groups, are now hardly more than names.[1] It is precisely because of this factor, which Fontane realized partly in advance of the event, that men like Wollheim da Fonseca and Hermann Maron are included in his reminiscences. His memoirs cannot provide a 'Zeitbild', as they are obviously intended to do, unless such people are included. Fontane was aware that such men added to the variety of literary Berlin and that once their literary efforts lapsed into oblivion their personalities would also be forgotten. Not, however, if they are recorded by some more eminent person whose work will live on, although Fontane is too unassuming to even hint at this. Because Paul Heyse and Theodor Storm received such wide acclaim during their lifetime, Fontane does not find it necessary to deal with them at undue length in his own reminiscences, whereas oddities like Goldammer and Wollheim da Fonseca, whose literary efforts were of no value, were important to him precisely because they help to

1 In the opinion of Lilian R. Furst: 'Autobiography of an Extrovert', p. 287, "their exploits, eccentricities and family affairs are certainly not of the slightest interest".

illustrate the diversity which he saw as characteristic of the "Tunnel" group.

This feature of preferring to preserve that which has less likelihood of otherwise surviving is mirrored in Fontane's work in the field of history. For him, not the events of great moment which change the course of history are of the utmost importance, but rather items of a secondary nature. These less known or little-known aspects help to give an intimate picture or to bring a human being close to the reader. The anecdote's emphasis on a single action in which the human being reveals his nature for a brief moment makes it a form which is particularly suited to characterize eccentrics.[1] This congruence between the reality of the situation (i.e. that there were many eccentrics in the "Tunnel") and Fontane's natural propensity to the anecdotal form makes for a happy relationship between his material and his procedure in the "Tunnel" section.

The study of the anecdote in Fontane's autobiographical writings shows the varied functions to which the author applies it. In those autobiographically inclined works from the Franco-Prussian war period, anecdotes showed in a concrete and convincing way to the victorious Germans that the French were also human beings. Indeed, Fontane underlines again and again in anecdotal narration the amiability of the French in almost all instances of his dealings with them. Anecdotes enliven the descriptive passages of the books on France and make those chapters in which battles are described more palatable to the non-military reader. Furthermore, we saw that Fontane interweaves little stories from the past with anecdotes of his personal encounters and experiences in such a way that his personal outlook on the reasons for the French defeat becomes clear. His stories are meant to reveal that the French have lost respect for their past, but in particular for ideals and 'higher' values. In this view the state, the law, and the church were institutions which the ordinary Frenchman viewed with suspicion, and to the conservative Fontane of the early eighteen-seventies this cynicism allied to crass materialism was responsible for the downfall of the French nation

1 Cf. "Reallexikon der deutschen Literaturgeschichte". Berlin 1958 vol. 1, p. 65.

which had just expressed itself in its military defeat. The mingling of past and present in this pattern of interpretation is a remarkable feature of the use of anecdote in "Aus den Tagen der Okkupation". Sometimes, Fontane uses a tiny anecdotal detail to bring the narrative onto a more evocative or poetic level. The value for the present-day reader of these works does not lie in their examination of the reasons for the French defeat in the Franco-Prussian war. Fontane was not an historian and above all was not aware in 1870 of the machinations of Bismarck. His works on France have their value for us as records of his outlook, of his poetic transformation of experience, and of course as plain facts which add to the external line of his autobiography.

The examination of Fontane's boyhood autobiography showed that here the anecdote is used for far less factual reasons than might be expected. It does without doubt provide the reader with information which is autobiographical in that it concerns the actual past of Fontane and therefore gives us a picture of his most intimate surroundings in childhood. Besides that, a picture of the times emerges in which the small Baltic port in nineteenth-century Germany again comes to life. The most interesting feature here is how Fontane interweaves the two planes, the particular level of his boyhood story with the general background of the town, and indeed of the historical era. In doing so, he clearly, though indirectly, shows the profound significance which this background had upon himself as a developing artist. The portrait of his father in particular, which is anecdotally rendered, shows evidence of being a self-portrait, and anecdotes, both Louis Fontane's stories and those told by his son about him, play a major role in this indirect autobiographical confession. Conversations and scenes have anecdotal motifs. In summary, it can be said that the anecdote as used in "Meine Kinderjahre" shows a level of artistry and poetic finesse which is only to be expected from Fontane in the decade which saw from his pen such brilliant and lasting works as "Effi Briest", "Frau Jenny Treibel" and "Der Stechlin". The subtitle of "Meine Kinderjahre" was seen, from the point of view of Fontane's deliberate and careful selection and presentation of his material, to be fully justified and not merely useful as a tag to protect the author from criticism.

"Von Zwanzig bis Dreißig" proved to be rather more problematical than the boyhood autobiography, because of the rift between the more personal side of its story (which dispensed largely with anecdote) and the record of personalities from the literary world of Berlin. A whole spectrum of Berlin society becomes the actual subject of the largest section of the book, while Fontane's accounts of himself and in particular details of his most intimate relationships with wife and family, are deliberately avoided. It was difficult therefore to speak of the anecdote in the book as a whole, even if the sections on other literary characters showed a plethora of anecdotes. Although Fontane simply plays the witness for a great deal of the narrative, it was possible to point out an element of that mode of indirect autobiography, which was already such a significant aspect of "Meine Kinderjahre". In particular, this concerns the problem of the struggling author, but even more important is the anecdotal approach to the account of the "Kreuz-Zeitung" which attempts, albeit unsatisfactorily, to explain Fontane's position vis-à-vis conservatism. Comparisons of his versions of anecdotes with other writers' versions of the same stories gave further information on his manipulation of fact in the intersts of good story-telling and the care with which he treats minutiae in order to vary a story and make it appropriate to its context.

It is certainly possible to say, on grounds of a study of the anecdote, that Fontane's aim in producing an account of literary Berlin, which did justice to its variety, was realized. Fontane likes to appear to be on the sideline in his reports and character sketches of his companions and acquaintances of Berlin literary life. Yet throughout the character sketches and little incidents, general observations occur which bear testimony to his view of life, to his experiences in connection with human relationships, his abhorrence of the artificial and the affected, and his knowledge of the art of writing. The pen-portraits of Berlin life and characters are executed with a fine humour and irony, and with a painstaking regard for truth. The right choice of material and productive appropriation of it by means of his own language and style are two important factors governing Fontane's use of anecdote in "Von Zwanzig bis Dreißig". As he writes in a discussion of Heinrich Smidt's work, every historical incident which one sets out to describe must be taken from some source, so that the nucleus of the matter lies in the right choice and in the transposition of the material into one's own language.[1] Friedrich Spielhagen's dictum "Finden, nicht erfinden"[2] contains a truth which for Fontane is most worthy of observance, and means almost everything in the art of narration".[3] The fact that he makes these observations in connection with a minor writer, is immaterial, for often his best insights are indeed revealed indirectly through discussion of someone else, not himself. This principle runs through both volumes of the autobiography.

The final volume of Fontane's autobiography, "Kritische-Jahre – Kritiker-Jahre", would if executed not only have given a picture of Fontane's life as theatre-critic for the "Vossische Zeitung" (the years 1870 until 1889) but would have also stretched back into the eighteen-fifties and sixties, thus taking the reader back to where "Von Zwanzig bis Dreißig" left off.[4] The fragments of this proposed work show that, particularly in the sections concerning his work as theatre-critic, it would like "Meine Kinderjahre" and "Von Zwanzig bis Dreißig" have contained an anecdotal element.[5] The greater cosmopolitanism of the Berlin[6] of Fontane's later years would probably have lent greater breadth to these planned reminiscences.

1 NyA XV, 224-225.

2 Expressed in his essay "Finder, of Erfinder?" (1871) and later incorporated in the larger work "Beiträge zur Theorie und Technik des Romans". Leipzig 1883, p. 1-34.

3 NyA XV, 225.

4 See Aufbau, Abteilung III, vol. III/2, p. 145.

5 Several anecdotes are already contained in the section of "Kritische-Jahre – Kritiker-Jahre" dealing with Berlin actors between 1870 and 1890, especially the actor Theodor Döring (1803-1878). The last paragraph on Döring shows how important Fontane considered the collection of such anecdotes: "Man hat Wrangel-Anekdoten gesammelt, die mir immer wie ein Schatz vorgekommen sind, nicht unserer Literatur, aber unseres eigenartigen preußisch-militärischen Lebens und somit richtige wundervolle documents humains. Es würde sich verlohnen, auch Döring-Anekdoten zu sammeln. Aber es müßte bald sein. Über ein kleines, und es ist zu spät." (NyA XV, 404)

6 Cf. the heading planned for a chapter or section: "Berlin wird Weltstadt" (ibid. 398)

Conclusion

The anecdote is a characteristic feature of Fontane's prose and constitutes a major distinguishing element of his style. Throughout his career, it formed an integral part of his prose, whether in the travel books, the fictional work, or the biographical and autobiographical material. An anecdotal element can also be discerned in some of his letters, essays[1] and short tales.[2] His work since the eighteen-sixties had given him a mastery in the telling of anecdotes long before his career as a novelist officially began with the publication of "Vor dem Sturm" in 1878. As far as the anecdote is concerned, his task as a fiction writer was rather more difficult than was the case with similar material in "Wanderungen durch die Mark Brandenburg". In the latter, the anecdote plays a major role in bringing before the reader hundreds of historical characters, ranging from the well-known to the almost forgotten. In this way, Fontane peopled the landscape of the March Brandenburg for his contemporaries and performed a valuable service in preserving worthwhile material, much of which might have otherwise been lost to a wide readership. In the fictional context, however, the anecdote's function is not to provide interest, preserve the past, instruct or entertain, although it may sometimes fulfil some of these functions in an incidental manner. The apprenticeship of the "Wanderungen" ensured that he could feel confident with regard to approaching anecdotal material, but the more difficult aspects of his task in the fiction related to settling into place within a whole artistic structure essentially alien material. While it is relatively easy for a writer to have his characters characterize themselves through the stories they

1 On the anecdotal element in Fontane's essays and journalism see Charlotte Jolles: 'Theodor Fontane als Essayist und Journalist' in JIG 7, 1975 Heft 2 p. 98-119, especially p. 114. For an example from the essay on Walter Scott, see above p. 282-285.

2 See the stories "Im Coupé" and "Eine Frau in meinen Jahren", written in the eighteen-eighties.

tell, or even the ones to which they listen, and to make the anecdote perform other technical functions, the employment of anecdote becomes much more problematic for the writer who wishes to unify various strands of his works through having an inner relatedness between large themes and a whole complex of little inserted stories.

Fontane's review of Julius Rodenberg's book on England shows that very early in his career he had already given thought to the problem of subjecting the anecdote to the overall artistic law in the interests of achieving a well-constructed whole. The ideas in this review obviously reflect his thinking during the actual composition of "Vor dem Sturm" which has a pronounced anecdotal element. The danger that anecdotes might simply be included by writers for their value as entertainment or amusement was therefore already apparent to Fontane at least as early as 1873. In 1878 Fontane reviewed Felix Eberty's book "Berlin vor fünfzig Jahren",[1] calling it "ein wahres 'Schatzkästlein' von Anekdoten aus der damaligen Zeit".[2] This time Fontane identifies a problem which was to concern himself greatly later in the production of "Von Zwanzig bis Dreißig", namely, the difficulty experienced by writers who in their works have tried to transfer anecdotes form their natural oral form into the written word. This he sees as being mainly a question of tone: "Ein bißchen zu breit, so ist die Langeweile da, ein bißchen zu hochtrabend im Ausdruck, und das Komische schlägt ins Alberne um."[3] Expansiveness is a feature which cannot be complained of with regard to Fontane's own anecdotes. This aspect became clear in the study of his version side by side with the same story told by another writer. The extent of Fontane's artistic finesse is particularly striking

1 Berlin 1878.

2 NyA XVIII/i, 639.

3 Ibid. 640. Just before the conclusion of his review on Eberty's book, Fontane quotes one of the anecdotes from it – an amusing one which brings out the gift of repartee shown by Eberty's grandmother or great-grandmother even on her deathbed (See ibidem). The difficulty of transferring a verbal anecdote about such a situation into the written word is obvious – and its success is an excellent example to illustrate Fontane's general point in the argument here.

in such comparisons. Invariably his version was simpler, more restrained, much less verbose and briefer than the original version. Where dialogue was included, the language was altered by Fontane to make it more colloquial and natural. Details which lent the story greater precision or political relevance were sometimes added, and in other cases made more apparent. The economy of Fontane's anecdotes is remarkable. In order to reach that economy all extraneous details are omitted, and often characters are dropped altogether in order to make a story more immediately comprehensible, or to make the point more striking and relevant. The fact that Fontane takes liberties with such matters shows that the overriding concern for him was the artistic one. Factual details could be altered in the interests of a better story. Similarly, he accepted even inauthentic anecdotes, as long as they were characteristic. The representative nature of an historical anecdote was more important than its genuineness.

When using very well-known anecdotes, such as those about Frederick II, Fontane preferred to present them in an elliptical way e.g. in calendar illustrations in "Schach von Wuthenow", in the barest references in "Vor dem Sturm" and "Frau Jenny Treibel" and "Der Stechlin". Such elliptical reference shows that Fontane is using well-known material in order to make a more general point. He was not providing information about a figure as familiar as Frederick, but using characters' knowledge of Frederick's life and relying on readers' knowledge of the same in order to show up some aspect of the period presented in the novel: pre-1806 in "Schach von Wuthenow", 1812/1813 in "Vor dem Sturm", and more broadly in maturer novels, "Frau Jenny Treibel" and "Der Stechlin" to hint at larger considerations.

The common denominator of many of Fontane's most memorable anecdotes is their stress on the quality of humanity. In the anecdotes he used about them Henry IV, Lenau, Rodenstein, Christian IV of Denmark, Barfus, João de Deus and William I show different aspects of a true humanity. The nuances vary from the honest and natural (Henry IV, Rodenstein and Christian IV) the charitable, which includes refinement of feeling, through self-abnegation, respect for and understanding of others (Lenau, Barfus,

João de Deus and William I) to the truly heroic (Greely). A striking feature of some of the anecdotes examined is the oblique criticism contained in them. In our analysis of "Vor dem Sturm" we saw that Sängebusch changes from the rather sentimental loyalist of the source story and other versions to almost a 'frondeur', whose real loyalty was to Prussia. Two reflections on the anecdote about Frederick William IV's sausage suggest dissatisfaction with the political situation: Czako's embarrassed reaction to the story because he is modern and Dubslav's musings that the monarch's present is really almost bribery and that 'Fronde' may sometimes be appropriate for the nobility. An apparently laudatory anecdote about Bismarck in fact casts doubt on the capacity of the Prussian nobility to hold any longer its role as a leading force in society, an interpretation which concurs with Lorenzen's analysis of Prussian society. Lorenzen uses the story about João de Deus to point up his theory that modern society must change its philosophy of egotism to one of caritas and sacrifice for the good of all. Frommel's positive story about William I becomes, when Dubslav has finished his reflections on it, a subtle sidesweep at William II. The Greely anecdote is used to plead for flexibility and indirectly warn against a blinkered upholding of an immutable code.

Of Fontane's autobiographical writings, the work in which his treatment of the material comes closest to that in the fiction is undoubtedly "Meine Kinderjahre". Here the anecdote functions both as a purveyor of factual material for the purposes of conjuring up biographical and autobiographical portraits and to suggest by hidden allusion the outlines of a portrait of the artist. Both "Meine Kinderjahre" and "Von Zwanzig bis Dreißig" share the author's intention of portraying a picture of the times. The fact that Fontane saw this as an important aspect is clear from observations within the works themselves and also from his review of Rodenberg's and Eberty's books. The principle behind his statement "Ich behandle das Kleine mit derselben Liebe wie das Große"[1] is that which informs his picture of a writer's life, both his own and

1 In a letter to Emilie of 8. 8. 1883. "Briefe". Ed. Schreinert/Jolles, vol. 1 p. 237.

and that of many others in nineteenth-century Prussia. Through the medium of anecdote, his literary acquaintances come to life. Often their very speech forms are preserved in Fontane's anecdotes. Even the most successful of them in his day, Paul Heyse, is today little more than a name to most readers. But in Fontane's reminiscences these writers live on for a larger public. General attitudes on the part of writers and aspects of the 'Zeitgeist' are illustrated in "Von Zwanzig bis Dreißig" through the use of anecdotes. Peoples' faults are frequently the source of an anecdote, but in treating them Fontane is never malicious. The experience of other writers can also be seen partly as a parallel to his own case, and thus some biographical material is also obliquely autobiographical. The hagiographical strain in contemporary biographical and autobiographical works does not feature in Fontane's treatment.

In "Aus den Tagen der Okkupation" anecdotes from the past and present interweave to provide an overall interpretation of the contemporary malaise in France. As in all of Fontane's works, the anecdote is a major factor here in the enlivening of the narrative by providing relief from description and observation. A human face is given to the larger events of history. The stories of individuals and accounts of personal experiences bring to the reader (Fontane's contemporaries and the following generations) a vivid presentation of the France of 1870 which can be enjoyed irrespective of the reader's attitude to the writer's interpretation of the reasons for the downfall of France. The advantages enjoyed by Fontane in reporting on France were not least due to his personal sympathy for the French character and his personal lack of chauvinistic pleasure at the military defeat of the French.

The anecdote is very concrete, and as such appealed to Fontane's frame of mind. His forte was not theorizing, and he cannot be called a philosophical writer. He saw himself not as a producer of great imaginative works, but as a writer who preferred to re-form material from real life into literary works, in the way suggested by Friedrich Spielhagen's critical motto: "Finden, nicht erfinden". A great many of Fontane's fictional works are based on stories told to him by acquaintances, or incidents from the newspapers. Such an outline of an individual's fate could strike his imagination and set off the complex process of artistic creation. Clearly, the anecdote appeals to such a talent. It exists independently of the author, yet can be shaped and altered to suit his wish. Much of the artistry in Fontane's use of little anecdotes within his larger fictional works is concerned with making an appropriate home for the little independent form. Because he was such a master of the art of conversation, the transitions from his own conversational text to the actual anecdote taken from another source are performed with consummate ease. According as Fontane matured as a creative writer, the conversational element in his fiction increases in importance, and plays a vital role in his work as the main vehicle through which the characters and themes are revealed. The fact that the plot element is of such little importance, notably in "Der Stechlin", and that conversation is of such importance by contrast, gives great scope to the novelist for the use of anecdote.

The diverse functions of the anecdote in Fontane's work may be briefly summarized. In all contexts the anecdote adds an element of entertainment. It often includes a touch of humour, sometimes of irony. The narrative is enlivened through the use of anecdote. Abstract generalizations and theorizing can be made concrete and tangible through the telling of an illustrative anecdote to prove the writer's point. In the fictional and biographical contexts the anecdote often characterizes the person who relates it or is the subject of the story. In the fiction not only the anecdote narrator but also the listener may be revealed in the telling. The teller's situation can be consciously externalized through the anecdote. The expression of emotion can therefore be spared. This means that Fontane consciously employs the anecdote in order to avoid sentimentality and to achieve distance. The change or development of characters may be indicated through their use of an anecdote which would have been inappropriate for them at an earlier stage. Through the anecdote Fontane may lend importance to minor figures.[1]

1 Among the examples of minor figures who relate anecdotes are the following: Frau Hulen, Klemm, Stappenbeck, Bamme, Sander, Prince Louis Ferdinand, Bülow, Schleppegrell, Distelkamp, Koseleger, Frommel. Heide

Where there is an important element of retardation, the anecdote may function as a pointer towards some significant factor of plot or character. The anecdote is useful for exposition and it occurs for this reason quite frequently in the earlier parts of Fontane's works. On the other hand, it can have an important function towards the end of fictional works in offering the reader a pointer towards an interpretation. The anecdote may provide a parallel to the main plot. The present may have a reflection in the historical past which is drawn on for the purposes of clarification of the present. Historical anecdotes may provide useful guidelines for the elements of plot and characterization, as well as aid in the provision of local colour. This is especially useful in cases where the background is likely to be less well-known to Fontane's readers. An interpretation of a whole historical era can be hinted at through the use of a complex of little inserted stories within a fictional work. A class or group of people may show its values through its choice of or reaction to certain anecdotes. The era which is historical for the present-day reader but which was contemporary for Fontane is subjected to close scrutiny in his works, and this era is constantly being described and evaluated through parallels and contrasts which are provided by anecdotes. These are not stories from contemporary life only, but also stories from the past. Thus, this historical past plays an extremely important role in the evaluation of the present, not just the characters' evaluation of the present, but that of the author himself. Thus, the Prussia which Fontane held so dear and criticized so much in his later years, is constantly being illuminated and evaluated with the help of stories from the past and in particular

Buscher claims in her thesis that Fontane's minor characters gain importance during the course of his work (see H. Buscher: "Die Funktion der Nebenfiguren in Fontanes Romanen mit besonderer Berücksichtigung von "Vor dem Sturm" and "Der Stechlin". Diss., Bonn 1969, p. 236) in that they perform functions which might earlier have been allotted to more important characters. However, already in "Schach von Wuthenow" important 'messages' were carried through the medium of anecdotes told by minor characters. Minor characters like Distelkamp and Frommel seem to have been included by Fontane precisely in order that they may relate one anecdote.

from far-off places. A list of the places of origin of the anecdotes used in Fontane's fiction shows the breadth of his interests: America, Brasil, China, Denmark, England, France, Germany, Italy, Portugal Russia, Siam, and Spain.[1] Thus real world-wide associations in the sense symbolized in "Der Stechlin" are created through the anecdotes in Fontane's works as a whole. These stories interweave with those of Prussian origin and the historical periods of their origin stretch from the fifteenth century to the contemporary period, the late nineteenth century. Fontane's propensity for relating the seemingly unrelated, for making associations between phenomena which are not actually connected, is well served by the anecdote. The exotic and the far-off, whether in time or place, come together with the near at hand and the ordinary, and with this congruence Fontane is able to make allusions and suggest parallels in a most artistic way. Because the anecdote is first and foremost a story, no matter what use the author puts it to for the purposes of allusion and interpretation, it avoids the risk inherent in essentially political works like "Schach von Wuthenow" or "Der Stechlin" that conversation which is either overtly political or can be read as being implicitly so, becomes boring or tendentious. The anecdote is particularly helpful therefore in keeping conversation on a level of entertainment which is appropriate for the fictional characters. Because the ramifications of the inserted stories are often far wider than is suspected by the characters, one may speak of a highly conscious degree of 'stage-management' on the author's part. As in life, the anecdotes that people tell reveal something of their own make-up, but beyond that in the enclosed world of the fictional work, these stories have associations which reach far beyond the ken of the characters, and are used by the author for many different technical reasons, as well as to help provide an interpretation of the world that he is protraying. It is clear that a consistent tying-in of anecdote and underlying themes was an area of perfection in narration towards which Fontane was striving from the beginning of his career as a novelist.

1 In spite of Fontane's interest in the Dark Continent, Africa is not represented by an anecdote in his fiction or autobiography.

Not surprisingly, the level of the success achieved varies from work to work. It is not a case of linear development in Fontane's art of perfecting the use of the anecdote. It is to be expected that the earliest works of fiction, "Vor dem Sturm" and "L'Adultera" should show some weaknesses on the part of the inexperienced novelist. Such weaknesses include the use of anecdotes in en bloc characterization, unrealistic devices such as the reference of characters to sources for their stories, and overuse of anecdotes over a short space. Already in the early eighteen-eighties, in "Schach von Wuthenow" a much greater degree of unity is achieved with regard to the anecdotes employed in the fictional framework. Here the characters still tend to use anecdotes for the purpose of winning arguments, but Fontane's use of conversation has already improved considerably as against "Vor dem Sturm", and thus on the whole, the anecdotes in "Schach von Wuthenow" appear better integrated into the fictional work. "Graf Petöfy" (1884) manifests a certain unevenness in its employment of anecdote, while Fontane's publication of the following year "Unterm Birnbaum" shows a very high degree of sophistication in this regard. Here the anecdotes combine to aid prefiguration and characterization, as well as to give a picture of the decade of 1830-40, as they had done sucessfully, but perhaps without quite the same degree of sophistication, for the period 1812-13 in "Vor dem Sturm" and 1806-07 in "Schach von Wuthenow". "Cecile" (1887) employs anecdotes very succesfully on the level of plot, theme and characterization, and anecdotes inserted make partial revelations appropriate to the detective-type story. In "Unwiederbringlich" of the early eighteen-nineties, the anecdotes function successfully on the level of technique with regard to theme, prefiguration, characterization and the creation of the Nordic atmosphere, but do not manage to marry the public and the private spheres as in "Vor dem Sturm", "Schach von Wuthenow" and "Unterm Birnbaum". With "Frau Jenny Treibel" and "Effi Briest" in the nineties, Fontane's art of the anecdote maintains a high level of achievement, in respect of theme, plot, characterization, and the suggestion of emotion, but avoidance of sentimentality. Fontane's art of the anecdote in "Der Stechlin" leaves aside considerations of plot and characterization and concentrates on a socio-political presentation of contemporary Germany. The anecdotes alone could have earned Max Rychner's praise of "Der Stechlin" as one of the wisest games ever played with the German language.[1] When Fontane gives the anecdote a new position as a story within a story within the framework of larger literary genres, he lets it become a focal point from which numerous associations emanate that connect it with other aspects of the work in which it stands. The past becomes integrated into and meaningful in the present, and the reader is spurred to further thought and active participation.

Fontane was convinced that the typical was boring, if blatantly presented as such. The greatness of his fictional works lies perhaps ultimately in their successful merging of the individual and the typical. His characters are presented as individuals, yet the reader, like Fontane himself, sees that the characters are also types and that they portray typical problems. His personal propensity to a mixture of the individual and the typical is no doubt the reason for his attraction to the anecdote, which itself thrives on such a mixture.

In all Fontane's writings the anecdote is an expression of his disapproval of negative aspects of his day: self-importance, rhetorical claptrap and studied ceremoniousness. His belief in and employment of anecdote contrasts sharply with the monumental pomposity of the Wilhelmine Era with its love of grandiose ostentation and its cult of an allegedly heroic past. In Fontane's art, anecdotes are a mosaic from the past, preserved not as fossilized artefacts, but re-arranged in a new pattern and invested with new meanings.

1 Max Rychner: 'Fontanes Stechlin' in NSR Neue Folge 16, 1948-49, p. 168.

List of Abbreviations

AG	Acta Germanica
Aufbau	Aufbau-Ausgabe der Werke Fontanes
DU	Der Deutschunterricht (Stuttgart)
DVjs	Deutsche Vierteljahresschrift für Literaturwissenschaft und Geistesgeschichte
EG	Etudes Germaniques
Euph.	Euphorion
FBl	Fontane-Blätter
FMLS	Forum for Modern Language Studies
GLL	German Life and Letters
GQ	German Quarterly
GR	Germanic Review
GRM	Germanisch-Romanische Monatsschrift
IASL	Internationales Archiv für Sozialgeschichte der Literatur
JDSG	Jahrbuch der Deutschen Schiller-Gesellschaft
JFDH	Jahrbuch des Freien Deutschen Hochstifts
JIG	Jahrbuch für Internationale Germanistik
LfL	Literatur für Leser: Zeitschrift für Interpretationspraxis und geschichtliche Texterkenntnis
Mh	Monatshefte (Wisconsin)
MLR	Modern Language Review
NR	Neue Rundschau
NSR	Neue Schweizer Rundschau
NyA	Nymphenburger Ausgabe der Werke Fontanes
Seminar	Seminar. A Journal of Germanic Studies
TB	Talmud Babli
ZsfdB	Zeitschrift für deutsche Bildung
WB	Weimarer Beiträge
WW	Wirkendes Wort
ZsfdB	Zeitschrift für deutsche Bildung
ZsfdPh	Zeitschrift für deutsche Philologie
ZsfRuG	Zeitschrift für Religions- und Geistesgeschichte
ZsVGB	Zeitschrift des Vereins für die Geschichte Berlins

Bibliography

I. Fontane's Works and Correspondence

"Sämtliche Werke". München 1959 ff. Hrsg von Edgar Groß, Kurt Schreinert, Rainer Bachmann, Charlotte Jolles, Jutta Neuendorff-Fürstenau, Peter Bramböck (Nymphenburger Ausgabe).

"Romane und Erzählungen in Acht Bänden". Berlin und Weimar 1969. Hrsg. von Peter Goldammer, Gotthard Erler, Anita Golz und Jürgen Jahn. Berlin und Weimar 1969 (Aufbau-Ausgabe: Abteilung I).

"Wanderungen durch die Mark Brandenburg". Hrsg. von Gotthard Erler und Rudolf Mingau. Berlin und Weimar 1976 ff (Ausbau-Ausgabe: Abteilung II).

"Autobiographische Schriften". 3 Bände. Hrsg von Gotthard Erler, Peter Goldammer und Joachim Krueger. Berlin und Weimar 1982 (Aufbau-Ausgabe: Abteilung III).

"Briefe Theodor Fontanes. Zweite Sammlung". Hrsg. von Otto Pniower und Paul Schlenther. 2 Bände. Berlin 1910.

"Briefe an Georg Friedlaender". Hrsg. von Kurt Schreinert. Heidelberg 1954.

"Theodor Fontanes Briefe an seine Familie". Hrsg. von Karl Emil Otto Fritsch. Berlin 1904.

"Von Dreißig bis Achtzig. Sein Leben in seinen Briefen". Hrsg. von Hans-Heinrich Reuter. Leipzig 1959.

"Fontanes Briefe in zwei Bänden". Hrsg. von Gotthard Erler. Berlin und Weimar 1968.

"Briefe". 4 Bände. Hrsg . von Kurt Schreinert. Zu Ende geführt und mit einem Nachwort versehen von Charlotte Jolles. Berlin 1968 ff.

"Briefe an Julius Rodenberg. Eine Dokumentation". Hrsg. von Hans-Heinrich Reuter. Berlin und Weimar 1969.

II. Other Sources and Critical Literature.

Ackermann, Friedrich: 'Das Komische in der Anekdote'. in DU 18, 1966, S. 10-25.

Anderson, Paul Irving: "Meine Kinderjahre": die Brücke zwischen Leben und Kunst. Eine Analyse der Fontaneschen Mehrdeutigkeit als Versteck-Sprachspiel im Sinne Wittgensteins'. In "Fontane aus heutiger Sicht". Hrsg. von Hugo Aust. München 1980, S. 143-182.

Attwood, Kenneth: "Fontane und das Preußentum". Berlin 1970.

Aust, Hugo: "Theodor Fontane: 'Verklärung'. Eine Untersuchung zum Ideengehalt seiner Werke". Bonn 1974.

'Die Bedeutung der Substitute für die Interpretation. Zu Fontanes "Unterm Birnbaum".' In DU 29, 1977, S. 44-51.

"Literatur des Realismus". Stuttgart 1977.

"Fontane aus heutiger Sicht". München 1980.

Avery, George C.: 'The Chinese Wall: Fontane's Psychograph of "Effi Briest".' In "View and Reviews of German Literature. Festschrift for Adolf Klarmann". München 1974, p. 18-38.

Bance, Alan: "Theodor Fontane. The Major Novels". Cambridge 1982.

Barfus-Falkenberg, Franz Wilhelm von: "H.A. Graf von Barfus. Königl. Preuß. Generalfeldmarschall. Ein Beitrag zur Kriegsgeschichte unter den Kurfürsten Friedrich Wilhelm und Friedrich III von Brandenburg". Berlin 1854.

Bausinger, Hermann: "Formen der 'Volkspoesie'. " Berlin 1968.

Becker, Eva D.: ' "Zeitungen sind doch das Beste" Bürgerliche Realisten und der Vorabdruck ihrer Werke in der periodischen Presse.' In "Gestaltungsgeschichte und Gesellschaftsgeschichte. Festschrift für Fritz Martini". Hrsg. von Helmut Kreuzer. Stuttgart 1969, S. 382-408.

Behl, C.F.W.: 'Über das Anekdotische.' In "Die Literatur" 38, 1936-37, S. 8-11.

Bertram, Ernst: 'Anekdote'. In Ernst Bertram: "Nietzsche: Versuch einer Mythologie". Berlin 1929. Nachdruck Bonn1965. Mit einem Nachwort von Hartmut Buchner. S. 249-259.

Beyer, H: 'Anekdote'. In "Reallexikon der deutschen Literaturgeschichte". Hrsg. von Paul Merker und Wolfgang Stammler. Berlin 1925-26, Band 1, S. 44-45.

Blessin, Stefan: ' "Unwiederbringlich" – ein historisch-politischer Roman? Bemerkungen zu Fontanes Symbolkunst.' In DVjs 48, 1974, S. 28-49.

Böckmann, Paul: 'Der Zeitroman Fontanes'. In DU 11, 1959, S. 59-81.

'Theodor Storm und Fontane. Ein Beitrag zur Funktion der Erinnerung in Storms Erzählkunst.' In "Schriften der Theodor-Storm-Gesellschaft" 17, 1968, S. 85-92.

Bose, Günter/Brinkmann, Erich: "Circus: Geschichte und Ästhetik einer niederen Kunst". Berlin 1978.

Boßhart, Adelheid: "Theodor Fontanes historische Romane". Diss. Zürich 1956. Winterthur 1957.
Brinkmann, Richard: "Theodor Fontane: Die Verbindlichkeit des Unverbindlichen". München 1967. 2. Aufl. 1977.
"Theodor Fontane: Der Dichter über sein Werk". Hrsg. von Richard Brinkmann in Zusammenarbeit mit Waltraud Wiethölter. 2 Bände. München 1977[2].
Bramsted, Ernst K.: "Aristocracy and the Middle Classes in Germany. Social Types in German Literature 1830-1900". Chicago and London 1964. (Reprint of 1937 edition).
Brüggemann, Diethelm: 'Fontanes Allegorien'. In NR 82, 1971, p. 290-310; p. 486-505.
Bruford, Walter Horace: ' "Frau Jenny Treibel" (1892)'. In W. H. Bruford: "The German Tradition in Self-Cultivation. 'Bildung' from Humboldt to Thomas Mann". Cambridge 1975, p. 120-205.
Bruss, Elizabeth: 'Eye for I: Making and Unmaking Autobiography in Film'. In John Olney (ed.): "Autobiography: Essays, Theoretical and Critical". Princeton 1970, p. 299-320.
"Autobiographical Acts: The Changing Situation of a Literary Genre". Baltimore and London 1976.
Bucher, Max/Wittmann, Reinhard (Hrsg.): "Realismus und Gründerzeit: Manifeste und Dokumente zur deutschen Literatur 1848-1880". 2 Bände. Stuttgart 1975-1976.
Büchsel, Karl: "Erinnerungen aus dem Leben eines Landgeistlichen". Berlin 1865.
Bülow, Heinrich Dietrich von: "Der Feldzug von 1805 militärisch und politisch behandelt" (Anonym) 2 Bände. Leipzig 1806.
Busch, Moritz: "Graf Bismarck und seine Leute". Leipzig 1872.
Buscher, Heide: "Die Funktion der Nebenfiguren in Fontanes Romanen unter besonderer Berücksichtigung von "Vor dem Sturm" und "Der Stechlin". Diss. Bonn 1969.
Chevanne-Wautot, Reine: "La répresentation de l'actualité politique dans "Le Stechlin" de Fontane". Diss. Paris 1970.
Clausewitz, Carl von: "Nachrichten über Preußen in seiner großen Katastrophe". Berlin 1838. Nachdruck Berlin 1888.
Dahn, Felix: "Erinnerungen". 5 Bände. Leipzig 1890-1895.
Dalitzsch, Max: 'Studien zur Geschichte der deutschen Anekdote". Diss. Freiburg im Breisgau 1922.
"Das Große Deutsche Anekdotenlexikon" Erfurt 1843-44. Unveränderter fotomechanischer Nachdruck, München-Pullach 1969.
Demetz, Peter: "Formen des Realismus. Theodor Fontane: Kritische Untersuchungen". Frankfurt am Main 1964.
"Kitsch, Belletristik, Kunst: Theodor Fontane". Berlin 1970.

Devine, Marianne: 'Erzähldistanz in Fontanes "Effi Briest". In "Formen realistischer Erzählkunst". Edited by Jörg Thunecke in conjunction with Eda Sagarra. Nottingham 1979, p. 544-549.
Denkler, Horst (Hrsg.): "Romane und Erzählungen des Bürgerlichen Realismus. Neue Interpretationen". Stuttgart 1980.
Diedenhofen, Karl: "Theodor Fontane und Thomas Mann. Eine vergleichende Untersuchung als Beitrag zu den Problemen der Ironie und des intellektuellen Elements in der Literatur". Diss. Bonn 1951.
Diogenes Laertius: "Lives of Eminent Philosophers". With an English translation by Robert Drew Hicks. 2 vols.London, New York 1925.
Disraeli, Isaac: 'A Dissertation on Anecdotes". London 1793. Reprint New York 1972.
Doderer, Karl: "Die Kurzgeschichte in Deutschland". Wiesbaden 1953. Nachdruck Darmstadt 1969.
Dohna, Christoph Graf zu: "Die Denkwürdigkeiten des Burggrafen und Grafen Christoph zu Dohna (1665-1733)". Eingeleitet, erläutert und deutsch herausgegeben von Rudolf Grieser. Göttingen 1974.
Doust, Brenda: "An Examination of Theodor Fontane's Autobiographical Writings". M. Phil. Thesis, King's College London 1970.
Dreyfuß, Alfred: 'Fontane und der Seiltänzer'. In FBl 19, Heft 3 1974, S. 220-222.
Eilert, Heide: ' " ... und mehr noch fast, wer liebt". Theodor Fontanes Roman "Unwiederbringlich" und die viktorianische Sexualmoral'. In ZsfdPh, 101, 1982, S. 527-545.
Eisele, Ulf: 'Realismus-Problematik. Überlegungen zur Forschungssituation'. In DVjs 51, 1977, S. 148-174.
Erler, Gotthard: "Zur Entstehungs- und Wirkungsgeschichte Fontanescher Romane. Aus den Kommentaren zur achtbändigen Ausgabe der Romane und Erzählungen, die zum 150. Geburtstag des Dichters im Aufbau-Verlag Berlin und Weimar erscheint". FBl. Sonderheft 2, 1969.
Ernst, Joachim: 'Gesetz und Schuld im Werk Fontanes'. In ZsfRuG 3,1953 S. 220-229.
Ester, Hans: "Der selbstverständliche Geistliche: Untersuchungen zu Gestaltung und Funktion des Geistlichen im Erzählwerk Theodor Fontanes". Leiden 1975.
Eten, Günter K.: "Wilhelm Schäfer: Stil und Weltbild seiner Anekdoten". Diss. Marburg 1938.
Ettlinger, Josef: "Theodor Fontane: Ein Essai". Berlin 1904.
Ferrara, Mario: "Sprachliche Verdichtung in Fontanes Roman 'Der Stechlin'." Diss. Wien 1969.
Fielding, Henry: "The History of Tom Jones". London 1909.
Frei, Norbert: "Theodor Fontane: Die Frau als Paradigma des Humanen". Königstein/Taunus 1980.

Freund, Winfried/Freund-Spork, Walburga .: "Weltgeschichte aus der Froschperspektive – Ein Versuch über die Anekdote in Theorie und Praxis'. In Lfl 1979, S. 116-127.
Friedemann, Käte: "Die Rolle des Erzählers in der Epik". Leipzig 1910.
Friedenthal, Richard: 'Vom Nutzen und Wert der Anekdote'. In "Sprache und Politik. Festgabe für Dolf Sternberger". Hrsg. von Carl-Joachim Friedrich und Benno Reifenberg. Heidelberg 1968, S. 62-67.
Friedrich, Gerhard: 'Die Schuldfrage in Fontanes "Cécile". In JDSG 14, 1970, S. 520-545.
Frommel, Emil: "Gesammelte Schriften". Band 10. Berlin 1898.
Fürstenau, Jutta: "Theodor Fontane und die märkische Heimat". Berlin 1941.
Furst, Lilian R.: 'The Autobiography of an Extrovert: Fontane's "Von Zwanzig bis Dreißig" '. In GLL 12, 1958-59, p. 287-294.
Gärtner, Karlheinz: "Theodor Fontane: Literatur als Provokation". Bonn 1978.
George, Cavan: "Erinnerungen eines Preußen aus der napoleonischen Zeit". Grimma 1840.
George, Edward Frank: 'The Symbol of the Lake and Related Themes in Fontane's "Der Stechlin".' In FMLS 9, 1973, p. 143-152.
Gilbert, Mary: "Das Gespräch in Fontanes Gesellschaftsromanen". Leipzig 1930.
Glaser, Horst: 'Theodor Fontane: "Effi Briest"(1894). Im Hinblick auf Emma Bovary und andere'. In "Romane und Erzählungen des Bürgerlichen Realismus. Neue Interpretationen". Hrsg. von Horst Denkler. Stuttgart 1980, S. 362-377.
Gleichen-Rußwurm, Alexander von: "Weltgeschichte in Anekdoten". Berlin 1929.
Greely, Adolphus Washington: "Three Years of Arctic Service: An Account of the Lady Franklin Bay Expedition of 1881-84". New York 1886. German translation by Reinhold Teuscher: "Drei Jahre hoch im Norden". Leipzig 1887.
"Reminiscences of Adventure and Service". New York, London 1927.
Grenzmann, Wilhelm: 'Anekdote'. In "Reallexikon der deutschen Literaturgeschichte". Hrsg. von Werner Kohlschmidt und Wolfgang Mohr. Berlin 1958^2, S. 63-66.
Greter, Heinz Eugen: "Fontanes Poetik". Bern, Frankfurt am Main 1973.
Grieve, Heide: "Aspects of Fontane's Narrative Technique. The development of his novel in the context of German and European prose fiction". Ph.D. Thesis., Norwich 1975.
Grothe, Heinz: "Das neue Narrenschiff". Stuttgart 1968.
"Anekdote". Stuttgart 1971.
Günther, Vinzent: "Das Symbol im erzählerischen Werk Fontanes". Bonn 1967.
Gusdorf, Georges: 'Conditions et limites de l'autobiographie'. In "Formen der Selbstdarstellung. Festgabe für Fritz Neubert". Hrsg. von Günter

Reichenkron und Erich Haase. Berlin 1956, S. 105-109 und S. 111-121.
Hahl, Werner: "Reflexion und Erzählung. Ein Problem der Romantheorie von der Spätaufklärung bis zum programmatischen Realismus". Stuttgart, Berlin, Köln, Mainz 1971.
Hahn, Anselm: "Theodor Fontanes 'Wanderungen durch die Mark Brandenburg' und ihre Bedeutung für das Romanwerk des Dichters". Diss. Breslau 1935.
Hajek, Siegfried: 'Anekdoten in Theodor Fontanes Roman "Vor dem Sturm" '. In "Jahrbuch der Raabe-Gesellschaft" 1979, S. 79-93.
Hardy, Barbara: "Tellers and Listeners". London 1974.
Harms, Kathy: "Formale Aspekte im Romanwerk Theodor Fontanes". Ph.D. Thesis, Northwestern University 1973.
Hauschild, Brigitte: "Geselligkeitsformen und Erzählstruktur. Die Darstellung von Geselligkeit und Naturbegegnung bei Gottfried Keller und Theodor Fontane". Frankfurt am Main, Bern 1981.
Hayes, Charles Nelson: "Symbol and Correlative in Theodor Fontane's Fiction". Ph.D. Thesis, Brown University 1967.
Heimann, Moritz: 'Autobiographisches von Theodor Fontane'. In Moritz Heimann: "Die Wahrheit liegt nicht in der Mitte". Mit einem Nachwort von Wilhelm Lehmann. Frankfurt am Main 1966, S. 175-189.
Hein, Jürgen (Hrsg.): "Deutsche Anekdoten". Stuttgart 1976.
"Die Anekdote'. In "Formen der Literatur". Hrsg. von Otto Knörrich. Stuttgart 1981, S. 14-20.
'Die literarische Anekdote, ihre Entwicklung und ihre Stellung in der Literatur'. In "Universitas" 37, 1982, S. 637-642.
Hesekiel, George: "Neues Berlinisches Historienbuch". Berlin 1851.
"Graf d'Anethan d'Entragues". Berlin 1856.
Heuser, Magdalene: 'Fontanes "Cécile". Zum Problem des ausgesparten Anfangs'. In ZsfdPh 92, 1973, S. 36-59.
Hillebrand, Bruno: 'Theodor Fontane: Der skizzierte Raum'. In Bruno Hillebrand: "Mensch und Raum im Roman. Studien zu Keller, Stifter, Fontane". München 1971, S. 229-283.
Höfele, Karl-Heinrich: 'Theodor Fontanes Kritik am Bismarckreich'. In "Geschichte in Wissenschaft und Unterricht" 14, 1963, S. 337-342.
Hoffmann, Rudolf: 'Die Anekdote in ihrer national-politischen Bedeutung'. In ZsfdB 10, 1934, S. 424-432.
Iggers, George C.: "The German Conception of History. The National Tradition of Historical Thought from Herder to the Present". Connecticut 1968.
Jäckel, Günter: 'Fontane und der deutsch-französische Krieg 1870/71'. In FBl Heft 2, 1970, S. 92-115.
Jennsen, Christian: 'Die deutsche Novelle und Anekdote von Kleist bis Wilhelm Schäfer'. In "Hochschule und Ausland" 14, 1936, S. 625-631.
Jørgensen, Sven-Aage: 'Nachwort' zu Theodor Fontane: "Unwiederbringlich". Stuttgart 1971, S. 287-309.

Jolles, André: "Einfache Formen". Tübingen 1930.
Jolles, Charlotte: 'Theodor Fontane und die Ära Manteuffel. Ein Jahrzehnt im Dienst der Preußischen Regierung'. In "Forschungen zur Brandenburgischen und Preußischen Geschichte" 49, 1937, S. 57-114; 50, 1938, S. 60-85.
"Theodor Fontane and England. A Critical Study in Anglo-German relations in the Nineteenth Century". Master of Arts Thesis, University of London 1947.
'Zu Fontanes literarischer Entwicklung' In JDSG 8, 1960, S. 400-424.
' "Und an der Themse wächst man sich anders aus als am Stechlin". Zum Englandmotiv in Fontanes Erzählwerk'. In FBl 1, Heft 5, 1967, S. 173-191.
'Theodor Fontane als Essayist und Journalist'. In "Jahrbuch für Internationale Germanistik" 7, 1975, S. 98-119.
"Theodor Fontane". Stuttgart 1976[2].
Kaltenborn, Rudolf Wilhelm von: "Briefe eines alten preußischen Offiziers". Band 1, Hohenzollern 1790.
Kolbe, Jürgen: "Goethes 'Wahlverwandtschaften' und der Roman des 19. Jahrhunderts". Stuttgart 1968.
Kupisch, Karl: 'Der Deutsche zwischen 1850 und 1865'. In ZsfRuG 18, 1966, S. 108-142.
Lübbe, Hermann: 'Fontane und die Gesellschaft'. In "Literatur und Gesellschaft vom 19. ins 20. Jahrhundert. Festgabe für Benno von Wiese". Hrsg. von Hans Joachim Schrimpf. Bonn 1963, S. 229-273.
Lukács, Georg: 'Der alte Fontane'. In Georg Lukacs: "Deutsche Realisten des 19. Jahrhunderts". Berlin 1952, S. 262-307.
Mann, Thomas: 'Der alte Fontane'. In "Gesammelte Werke". Band 9. Frankfurt am Main 1960, S. 9-34.
'Noch einmal der alte Fontane'. In ibid. S. 816-822.
Martini, Fritz: "Deutsche Literatur im Zeitalter des bürgerlichen Realismus 1848-1898". Stuttgart 1974[3].
Marwitz, Friedrich August Ludwig von der: "Aus dem Nachlasse Friedrich August Ludwig von der Marwitz". 2 Bände. Berlin 1852.
Massenbach, Christian von: "Historische Denkwürdigkeiten zur Geschichte des Verfalls des preußischen Staates seit dem Jahre 1794". Amsterdam 1809.
May, Georges: "L'Autobiographie". Paris 1979.
Mayer, Karl: "Lenau. Eine Biographie". Stuttgart 1853.
Mende, Dirk: 'Frauenleben, Bemerkungen zu Fontanes "L'Adultera" nebst Exkursen zu "Cécile" und "Effi Briest" '. In "Fontane aus heutiger Sicht". Hrsg. von Hugo Aust. München 1980, S. 183-213.
Meyer, Herman: 'Theodor Fontanes "L'Adultera" und "Der Stechlin" '. In Herman Meyer: "Das Zitat in der Erzählkunst. Zur Geschichte und Poetik des europäischen Romans". Stuttgart 1961, S. 155-185.
Meyer, Paul: "Erinnerungen an Theodor Fontane 1819-1898". Berlin 1936.

Mill, Hugh R.: "The Siege of the South Pole". London 1905.
Mirsky, Jeannette: "To the Arctic: The Story of Northern Exploration from Earliest Times to the Present". New York 1948. Reprint with a new introduction. Chicago 1970.
Misch, Georg: "Geschichte der Autobiogrpahie". Band I, 1. Bern 1949 und Band IV, 2. Hrsg. von Berndt Neumann. Frankfurt am Main 1969.
Mittenzwei, Ingrid: 'Theorie und Roman bei Fontane'. In "Deutsche Romantheorien". Hrsg. von Reinhold Grimm. Frankfurt am Main 1968, S. 233-250.
"Die Sprache als Thema. Untersuchungen zu Fontanes Gesellschaftsromanen". Bad Homburg v.d. H., Berlin, Zurich 1970.
Mommsen, Katharina: "Gesellschaftskritik bei Fontane und Thomas Mann". Heidelberg 1973.
Monecke, Wolfgang: 'Der historische Roman und Theodor Fontane'. In "Festgabe für Ulrich Pretzel". Berlin 1963, S. 278-288.
Müller, Klaus-Detlev (Hrsg.): "Bürgerlicher Realismus. Grundlagen und Interpretationen". Königstein/Ts. 1981.
"Morgenblatt für gebildete Leser", Jahrgang 56, Nr. 29 (16. 7. 1862), S. 693 f. ('Der Emaillierungsproceß der Madame Rachel').
Müller-Seidel, Walter: 'Fontane und Bismarck'. In "Nationalismus in Germanistik und Dichtung. Dokumentation des Germanistentages in München vom 17. -22. Oktober 1966". Hrsg. von Benno von Wiese und Rudolf Heuß. Berlin 1967, S. 170-201.
"Fontanes Autobiographik'. In JDSG 13, 1969, S. 397-418.
"Theodor Fontane. Soziale Romankunst in Deutschland". Stuttgart 1975.
'Fontane und Polen. Eine Betrachtung zur deutschen Literatur im Zeitalter Bismarcks'. In "Formen realistischer Erzählkunst. Festschrift für Charlotte Jolles". Edited by Jörg Thunecke in conjunction with Eda Sagarra. Nottingham 1979, S. 433-447.
Neumann, Bernd: "Identität und Rollenzwang: Zur Theorie der Autobiographie". Frankfurt am Main 1970.
Neumann, Gerhard: "Ideenparadiese: Untersuchungen zur Aphoristik von Lichtenberg, Novalis, Friedrich Schlegel und Goethe". München 1976.
Neureuter, Hans Peter: 'Zur Theorie der Anekdote'. In JbFDH 1973, S. 458-480.
Nicolai, Friedrich: "Anekdoten und Karakterzüge aus dem Leben Friedrichs des Großen". Berlin 1787[3].
Niggl, Günter: 'Fontanes "Meine Kinderjahre" und die Gattungstradition'. In "Sprache und Bekenntnis. Sonderband des Literaturwissenschaftlichen Jahrbuches 1971". Hrsg. von Wolfgang Frühwald und Günter Niggl. S. 257-279.
Nostitz, Karl von: "Aus Karl von Nostitz Leben und Briefwechsel". Dresden 1848.

Nürnberger, Helmuth: "Der frühe Fontane. Politik – Poesie – Geschichte. 1840-1860". Hamburg 1967.
Oelschläger, Hans: "Theodor Fontane. Sein Weg zum Berliner Gesellschaftsroman". Diss. Marburg 1954.
Ohl, Hubert: "Bild und Wirklichkeit: Studien zur Romankunst Raabes und Fontanes". Heidelberg 1968.
Olney, John: "Metaphors of Self: The Meaning of Autobiography". Princeton 1972.
'Autobiography and the Cultural Moment: A Thematic, Historical and Bibliographical Introduction'. In John Olney (ed.): "Autobiography: Essays, Theoretical and Critical". Princeton 1970, p. 3-27.
'Some Versions of Memory/Some Versions of Bios: The Ontology of Autobiography'. In John Olney (ed.): ibid. p.236-267.
Pascal, Roy: "Design and Truth in Autobiography". Cambridge, Massachusetts 1960. Revised edition in German: "Die Autobiographie. Gehalt und Gestalt". Stuttgart 1965.
Paulsen, Wolfgang: 'Theodor Fontane. The Philosemitic Antisemite'. In Publications of the Leo Baeck Institute Year Book, 26, 1981, p.303-322.
'Zum Stand der heutigen Fontane-Forschung'. In JDSG 25, 1981, S. 474-508.
Peschken, Bernd/Krohn, Claus-Dieter (Hrsg,): "Der Liberale Roman und der preußische Verfassungskonflikt". Stuttgart 1976.
Petersen, Julius: 'Fontanes Altersroman'. In Euph. 29, 1928, S. 1-74.
Petsch, Robert: 'Von der Kunst der Anekdotenerzählung'. In "Schünemanns Monatshelte" 2, 1928, S. 1055-1061.
Pietsch, Ludwig: "Wie ich Schriftsteller wurde". Berlin 1892.
Pongs, Herman: 'Die Anedkote als Kunstform zwischen Kalendergeschichte und Kurzgeschichte'. In DU 9, 1957, S. 5-20.
Powell, Theodore: "The Long Rescue". London 1961.
Preisedanz, Wolfgang: "Humor als dichterische Einbildungskraft. Studien zur Erzählkunst des poetischen Realismus". München 1963.
"Theodor Fontane". Hrsg. von W. Preisendanz, Darmstadt 1973.
Rainer, Ulrike: 'Effi Briest und das Motiv des Chinesen'. In ZsfdPh. 101, 1982, p. 545-561.
Reinhardt, Hartmut: 'Die Wahrheit des Sentimentalen' Bemerkungen zu zwei Romanschlüssen bei Theodor Fontane: "Frau Jenny Treibel" und "Effi Briest" '. In WW 29, 1979, S. 318-326.
Remak, Henry H. H.: 'Kritische Gedanken anläßlich einer Fontane-Biographie'. In Mh 65, 1973, S. 27-38.
'Politik und Gesellschaft als Kunst: Güldenklees Toast in Fontanes "Effi Briest" '. In "Formen realistischer Erzählkunst. Festschrift for Charlotte Jolles". Ed. by Jörg Thunecke in conjunction with Eda Sagarra. Nottingham 1979, S. 550-562.

Remak, Joachim: "The Gentle Critic. Theodor Fontane and German Politics 1848-1898". Syracuse, New York 1964.

Reuter, Hans-Heinrich: 'Entwicklung und Dialektik des Heimatreflexes im Werk Theodor Fontanes'. In WB 1965, S. 55-74.

'Entwurf eines kritischen Überblicks über den Stand und die Perspektiven der gegenwärtigen Fontane-Forschung anläßlich des Theodor-Fontane-Symposiums in Potsdam'. In WB 12, 1966, S. 674-699.

'Grundpositionen der "historischen" Autobiographie Theodor Fontanes' in "Theodor Fontane in unserer Zeit". Potsdam 1966, S. 14-36.

"Fontane". 2 Bände. Berlin 1968.

'Fontanes Realismus'. In "Fontanes Realismus. Wissenschaftliche Konferenz zum 150. Geburtstag Theodor Fontanes in Potsdam". Hrsg. von Hans-Erich Teitge und Joachim Schobeß. Berlin 1972, S. 25-64.

'Die Englishe Lehre. Zur Bedeutung und Funktion Englands für Fontanes Schaffen'. In "Formen realistischer Erzählkunst. Festschrift for Charlotte Jolles". Ed. by J. Thunecke. Nottingham 1979. S. 282-299.

Rhyn, Hans: "Die Balladendichtung Theodor Fontanes". Bern 1914. Nachdruck Nendeln/Lichtenstein 1970.

Richter, Karl: "Resignation. Eine Studie zum Werk Theodor Fontanes". München 1966.

Riechel, Donald C.: 'Fontane und Goethe'. In "Formen Realistischer Erzählkunst. Festschrift for Charlotte Jolles". Ed. J. Thunecke. Nottingham 1979, p. 417-427.

Ritscher, Helga: "Die Entwicklung der politischen Anschauungen Theodor Fontanes". Diss. Göttingen 1951.

Robinson, Alan: 'Recollections in Tranquillity: An examination of Fontane's "autobiographical novel" '. In "Erfahrung und Überlieferung. Festschrift for C. P. Magill". Ed. by Hinrich Siefken and Alan Robinson. Cardiff 1974, p. 113-125.

"Theodor Fontane. An Introduction to the Man and his Works". Cardiff 1976.

Rodenberg, Julius (i.e. Levy, Julius) "Studienreisen in England: Bilder aus Vergangenheit und Gegenwart". Leipzig 1872.

"Bilder aus dem Berliner Leben". Berlin 1891^3.

Rohner, Ludwig: "Theorie der Kurzgeschichte". Frankfurt am Main 1973.

Rosenfeld, Hans–Friedrich: "Zur Entstehung Fontanescher Romane". Groningen/Den Haag 1926.

Rothe-Buddenberg, Margaret: "Spuk im Dachboden. Der Dachboden in der deutschen Prosaliteratur als Negation der gesellschaftlichen Realität". Bonn 1972.

Ruttmann, Irene: 'Nachwort' zu Theodor Fontane: "Unterm Birnbaum". Stuttgart 1971, S. 129-136.

Rychner, Max: 'Fontanes Stechlin'. In NSR, NF 16, 1948, S. 168-178. Auch in: Max Rychner: "Welt im Wort. Literarische Aufsätze". Zürich 1949, S. 266-285.

Sagarra, Eda: "A Social History of Germany 1648-1914". London 1977.
' "Eingepökeltes Rindfleisch oder Spargel und junges Gemüse" – the Christian Social Background to "Der Stechlin" '. In "Formen realistischer Erzählkunst. Festschrift for Charlotte Jolles". Edited by J. Thunecke in conjunction with E. Sagarra. Nottingham 1979, p. 577-586

Sagave, Pierre-Paul: "Theodor Fontane: Schach von Wuthenow. Text und Dokumentation". Frankfurt am Main, Berlin 1966.
'Schach von Wuthenow als politischer Roman'. In "Fontanes Realismus". Hrsg. von H.-E. Teitge und J. Schobeß. Berlin 1972, S. 87-94.
'Theodor Fontane et la France 1870/71'. In IASL 1, 1976, p. 160-177.

Salaman, Esther: "From Aksakov to De Quincey to Tolstoy and Proust". London 1973.

Saltarino, Signor (i.e. Otto, Hermann W.): "Das Artistentum und seine Geschichte". Leipzig 1910.

Schrader, Ingeborg: "Das Geschichtsbild Fontanes und seine Bedeutung für die Maßstäbe der Zeitkritik in den Romanen". Limburg 1950.

Schurz, Anton X.: "Lenaus Leben". Stuttgart, Augsburg 1855.

Schuster, Peter-Klaus: "Effi Briest. Ein Leben nach christlichen Bildern. Tübingen 1978.

Schwarz, Peter-Paul: ' "Tragische Analysis" und Schicksalsvorausdeutungen in Fontanes Roman "Effi Briest" '. In Sprachkunst 7, 1976, S. 247-260.

Seiffert, Hans Werner: 'Zu Fontanes "Effi Briest" '. In "Theodor Fontanes Werk in unserer Zeit". Potsdam 1966, S. 81-94.

Sheehan, James John: "The Career of Lujo Brentano. A Study of Liberalism and Social Reform in Imperial Germany. Chicago 1966.

Shears, Lambert Armour: "The Influence of Walter Scott on the Novels of Theodor Fontane. New York 1922.

Sieper, Clara: "Der historische Roman und die historische Novelle bei Raabe und Fontane". Berlin 1930.

Sommer, Dietrich: 'Prädestination und soziale Determination in Fontanes Romanen'. In "Theodor Fontanes Werk in unserer Zeit". Potsdam 1966, S. 37-52.
'Das Polenbild Fontanes als Element nationaler Selbstverständigung und -kritik'. In WW 16, Heft 11, S. 173-190.
'Probleme der Typisierung im Spätwerk Theodor Fontanes'. In "Fontanes Realismus" Hrsg. von Hans-Erich Teitge und Joachim Schobeß. Berlin 1972, S. 105-120.

Spielhagen, Friedrich: "Beiträge zur Theorie und Technik des Romans". Leipzig 1883.
"Finder und Erfinder. Erinnerungen aus meinem Leben". Leipzig 1890.

Spink, Gerard W.: 'Fontane's Poem "Walter Scott in Westminster-Abtei" '. In MLR 28, 1933, p. 489-491.

Spremberg, Hugo: 'Fontanes "Unterm Birnbaum' Nach mündlicher Überlieferung und handschriftlichen Aufzeichnungen'. In "Brandenburgische

Zeitschrift für Heimatkunde und Heimatpfleg"e 6, 1928, S. 26-27.
Stamm, Israel: 'Goethe – Nietzsche – Fontane'. In GR 13, 1938, S. 252-258.
Stern, Joseph Peter: 'Theodor Fontane. The Realism of Assessment'. In J.P. Stern: "Idylls and Realities. Studies in Nineteenth-Century German Literature". London 1971, p. 163-178.
Stierle, Karlheinz: 'Geschichte als Exemplum – Exemplum als Geschichte. Zur Pragmatik und Poetik narrativer Texte'. In "Geschichte – Ereignis und Erzählung". Hrsg. von Reinhard Kosellek und Wolf-Dieter Stempel. München 1973, S. 347-375.
Strauß, Gerda: "Die Anekdoten F. C. Weiskopfs". Diss. Leipzig 1965.
Strech, Heiko: "Theodor Fontane: Die Synthese von Alt und Neu. 'Der Stechlin' als Summe des Gesamtwerks". Berlin 1970.
Subiotto, Frances: 'The Function of Letters in Fontanes "Unwiederbringlich" '. In MLR 65, 1970, p. 306-318.
Thanner, Josef: "Die Stilistik Theodor Fontanes. Untersuchungen zur Erhellung des Begriffs 'Realismus' in der Literatur". Den Haag, Paris 1967.
Thomas, Lionel T. C.: 'Fontane's "Unterm Birnbaum" '. In GLL 23, 1970, p. 193-205.
Turk, Horst: 'Realismus in Fontanes Gesellschaftsromanen'. In "Jahrbuch der der Wittheit zu Bremen" 9, 1965, S. 407-456.
Ueding, Cornelie: 'Utopie auf Umwegen: Zwei Szenen in Fontanes Roman "Cecile" '. In "Literatur ist Utopie". Hrsg. von Gerd Ueding. Frankfurt am Main 1978, S. 220-253.
Vaget, Hans Rudolf: 'Schach von Wuthenow: "Psychographie" und "Spiegelung" im 14. Kapitel von Fontanes "Schach von Wuthenow" '. In Mh 61, 1969, S. 1-14.
Vondung, Klaus (Hrsg.): "Das wilhelminische Bildungsbürgertum. Zur Socialgeschichte seiner Ideen". Göttingen 1976.
Wagner, Walter: "Die Technik der Vorausdeutung in Fontanes 'Vor dem Sturm' und ihre Bedeutung im Zusammenhang des Werkes". Marburg 1966.
Wandrey, Conrad: "Theodor Fontane". München 1919.
Weber, Dietrich: ' "Effi Briest" – "Auch wie ein Schicksal". Über den Andeutungsstil bei Fontane'. In JFDH 1966, S. 457-474.
Wedereit, Gerhard: 'Leitmotivische Wiederholung: Beobachtungen zu Technik und Ethos in Fontanes "Frau Jenny Treibel" '. In AG 7, 1972, S. 117-125.
Wehler, Hans-Ulrich: "Bismarck und der Imperialismus". München 1976[4]. "Das deutsche Kaiserreich 1871-1918. Göttingen 1975[2].
Wichmann, Hermann: "Frohes und Ernstes aus meinem Leben. Berlin 1898.
Widhammer, Helmut: "Die Literaturtheorie des deutschen Realismus". Stuttgart 1977.
Wiese, Benno von: 'Theodor Fontane: "Schach von Wuthenow" '. In Benno von Wiese: "Die Deutsche Novelle von Goethe bis Kafka". Düsseldorf 1962, Band 2, S. 236-260.

Wigger, Hedwig: Joao de Deus'. In Das "Magazin für Literatur des In- und Auslandes", Jahrgang 65, Nr. 9 (29. 2. 1896), S. 297-298.

Wittmann, Reinhard: 'Das literarische Leben 1848-1880'. In "Realismus und Gründerzeit. Manifeste und Dokumente zur deutschen Literatur 1848-1880". Hrsg. von Max Bucher, Werner Hahl, Reinhard Wittmann. Stuttgart1975, Band 2, S. 151-257.

Wölfel, Kurt:' "Man ist nicht bloß ein einzelner Mensch". Zum Figurenentwurf in Fontanes Gesellschaftsromanen'. In ZfdPh 82, 1963, S. 152-171.

Wruck, Peter: 'Zum Zeitgeschichtsverständnis in Theodor Fontanes Roman "Vor dem Sturm". In FBl 1, 1965, S. 1-9.

"Preußentum und Nationalschicksal bei Theodor Fontane". Diss. Berlin 1967.